M000104735

The Passion of the Servant

The Passion of the Servant

A Journey to the Cross

Don N. Howell, Jr.

RESOURCE *Publications* · Eugene, Oregon

THE PASSION OF THE SERVANT
A Journey to the Cross

Copyright © 2009 Don N. Howell, Jr. All rights reserved. Except for brief quotations in critical publications or reviews, no part of this book may be reproduced in any manner without prior written permission from the publisher. Write: Permissions, Wipf and Stock, 199 W. 8th Ave., Suite 3, Eugene, OR 97401.

Resource Publications
A division of Wipf and Stock Publishers
199 West 8th Avenue, Suite 3
Eugene, Oregon 97401

www.wipfandstock.com

ISBN 13: 978-1-60608-207-2

Manufactured in the U.S.A.

Contents

Contents

Introduction

Testimony of the Four Gospels

The New Testament opens with four Gospel accounts that introduce the reader to Jesus Christ. These Gospels are *Passion narratives with extended introductions*. From the very beginning the redemptive drama moves toward the cross. The final week of Jesus' life, Passion Week, takes up nearly 40% of the entire narrative. The four Gospels provide four different perspectives on the life of Jesus.

Matthew portrays Jesus as the one who brings to completion the long preparatory record of the Old Testament. The first verse of the New Testament establishes the connection: "The book of the genealogy of Jesus Christ, the son of David, the son of Abraham." Jesus' life and death are the fulfillment of the drama of salvation history that begins with Abraham, the father of the nation Israel (Gen 12:1–3), and continues with David, her paradigmatic monarch (2 Sam 7:11–16). Jesus is the climax of prophetic hope.

Mark's Gospel, drawn from Peter's sermons to the church in Rome, identifies Jesus as the Son of God who comes to carry out the redemptive mission. This fast-paced account traces the steps of the obedient Son-Servant who moves forward, without haste or distraction, to accomplish the will of his Father "to give his life as a ransom for many" (Mark 10:45).

Luke is the longest of the Gospel accounts, one that filled an entire thirty-two foot papyrus scroll. He addresses the work to one Theophilus, probably a new believer preparing for Christian baptism. In this preface to his two-volume work, Luke-Acts (Luke 1:1–4), the author clarifies his method of production:

(i) Other second generation Christians had already begun to produce piecemeal accounts of the life of Christ which Luke deemed inadequate to meet Theophilus' need. (ii) The materials that Luke used were eyewitness traditions passed down, both oral and written. (iii) He engaged in careful historical investigation with sound criteria to sift the reliable accounts from the spurious. (iv) The outcome was an orderly account, though not necessarily a rigidly chronological one. His stated purpose is to undergird Theophilus' assurance in the truthfulness of the traditions about Jesus that he has been taught.

Finally, the apostle *John* produced a more reflective Gospel, one that brings out the deeper qualities of this Person who comes to carry out the will of his Father. One commentator compares John's Gospel to a pool in which a child can wade and an ocean in which an elephant can swim. Couched in some of the simplest Greek of the New Testament are some of the most profound mysteries of the Christian faith. Jesus is both God and man; eternal, preexistent and glorious, yet weak, vulnerable and mortal. The one who is the divine Word from the Father (John 1:1–3) sits down by a well in Samaria, thirsty and exhausted from the journey (4:6-7). The one who claims to have existed before Abraham (8:58) and willingly accepts the acclamation "my Lord and my God" from the lips of Thomas (20:28), is the one who weeps at the tomb of his friend Lazarus (11:34–35) and who commits the care of his mother to his beloved disciple as his life ebbs away on the cross (19:27). The mystery of the incarnation is for John the incomparable expression of the love of the Father who sends his only begotten Son into the world (3:16), and the love of the Son who lays down his life for his friends (15:13).

This is the fourfold account of Jesus Christ, King and covenant keeper (Matthew), obedient Son-servant (Mark), the perfect Man among men (Luke), and the eternal Son of God (John), the only person ever born whose central purpose in living is to die. The Gospels are *Passion narratives with extended introductions.*

Long-Awaited Advent of the Servant-King

WORD OF THE FATHER

(John 1:1–13)

A PERSON COMMUNICATES ONE'S thoughts to others by means of the spoken or written word. John identifies Jesus as the vehicle through which God, the invisible creator and sustainer of life, discloses himself to the human race. As the "Word of the Father, now in flesh appearing," Jesus reveals who God is and what he is like. His disclosure is reliable and authoritative because he himself shares the divine nature. Jesus is both fully divine and yet "with God," that is, distinguished from him. From this perspective, shared by all of the New Testament authors, the church fathers of the second and third centuries constructed the doctrine of the Trinity: God is one and yet three, one undivided eternal essence and yet comprised of three distinct persons, Father, Son, and Spirit.

This prologue (1:1–18) introduces a number of the leading themes of John's Gospel: light and darkness, life, belief, testimony, the world, truth, glory and grace. The Word was with God from all eternity and shared in his work of creation. All animate and inanimate beings owe their existence to the Creator. John moves from creation to incarnation in verse 4, attributing to Jesus not only the gift of animated existence, but also spiritual life which comes from his illuminating work in the hearts of those who believe. As the "light of the world" (John 8:12; 9:5), the Word dispels the blinding darkness of the heart caused by sin. The darkness is unable to thwart the penetrating influence of the light.

But this is no mere appeal to abstract ideas removed from the concrete experiences of people. Jesus' saving work draws near by planting itself in history. His coming is announced by a desert prophet, John the Baptizer, whose thunderous promises and warnings break 400 years of prophetic silence. John's role is critical but subsidiary: he comes "as a witness, to bear witness" (1:7), a beautifully redundant expression for one whose unwavering commitment is to point people toward the true light who alone possesses the power to illumine, cleanse and restore people to a relationship with the Creator. A witness is one who has abandoned neutrality, steps out of the way, and now speaks as an earnest endorser of another. The Baptizer's sole mission is to lead others to faith in Jesus.

Yet this historical invasion of the space-time world by the Word is not welcomed by all. The "world" is John's expression for the domain of human existence which has lost its way, alienated from the Father, and blinded to its own spiritual condition. As Jesus enters this world, one which he himself made, there are contrasting responses. Shockingly, the ethnic people into whom he is born, the Jews, apart from a tiny band of followers, fails to recognize him as their Messiah. This is one of the severest of theological scandals which all of the New Testament writers, in one way or another, will have to address. But alongside the line of rejection is the line of reception. There are the ones who receive him, that is, believe in him and thereby experience a new birth, one that springs not from sexual procreation but from the divine initiative and activity. This new birth gives its recipients the exclusive right to be called the children of God, privileged members of a new family with God as their Father and fellow receivers as their brothers.

⇨ Are you like John, a faithful and true witness pointing people to Jesus Christ? Are you serving as his eager endorser, in word and deed, to those around you?

WORD OF THE FATHER, NOW IN FLESH APPEARING

(John 1:14–18)

Historical evidence indicates the Apostle John spent the final decades of his life in Ephesus and wrote his Gospel to help the growing churches in that area of western Asia Minor bring people to faith in Jesus as God's Son (John 20:31). The Greek and Roman gods were either too near or too remote. The ancient Greek pantheon of capricious deities that mingled with humans and shared all of their flaws had, by the first century of the Christian era, been largely discredited. More sophisticated worshippers embraced the ideas of Plato and Aristotle that God resides in the higher domain of spiritual realities, wholly separate from and untouched by the defilement of the physical world. John expounds a God who is holy love: the eternal Word, separate from a creation that owes its existence to him, becomes flesh, and makes his dwelling among those he comes to redeem. In this instance "flesh" denotes finiteness, transience, vulnerability, and weakness. Apart from sin, Jesus takes upon himself all of the properties of humanness.

As an eyewitness of Jesus' earthly life for the better part of three years, John strains for the vocabulary that can describe the incomparable Man. He draws on some of the richest Greek terms available and pours into them Hebrew meanings.

1. *Glorious* (1:14): God's Shekinah glory that filled the tabernacle/temple in Old Testament times now takes up residence in Jesus. "Glory" means manifested majesty, or the essential character of someone disclosed for all to see. God communicates what he is like through his incarnate Word.

2. *Preeminent* (1:15): John (the Baptist, not the Apostle, who never refers to himself by name in his Gospel) witnessed to the superiority of One who, though arriving subsequently on the historical scene, existed before him from all eternity.

3. *Gracious* (1:16): The readers of the fourth Gospel endorse John's appraisal ("we have all received") of Jesus as the giver of grace—a continuous, uninterrupted, inexhaustible and satisfying measure of God's unmerited favor. Here is a God who, unmoved by any external pressures, forgives sinners and qualifies them to be his children because he delights to do so.

4. *Truthful* (1:14, 17): Twice John combines the qualities "grace and truth" as a composite attribute of the Word. This is a Hebrew literary device known as a hendiadys, which employs two words for one complex meaning: "gracious truthfulness" or "truthful graciousness." Jesus embodies these two characteristics in perfect balance. In extending grace to people, he never compromises his integrity; his unbending standards do not hinder his offer of grace to those in need. The Mosaic law with its strict and detailed commands made its violators feel the full force of God's deserved judgment hanging over them; the gracious truthfulness of the new covenant in Christ brings rescue from that judgment for those who believe.

5. *Divine* (1:18): The Word is God's one and only Son, uncreated but be-gotten from all eternity. He dwells in God's "bosom," that is, shares his essential nature. Therefore he alone is qualified to provide an authentic disclosure of what God is like. Later Jesus will say, "Whoever has seen me has seen the Father" (John 14:9). Turn your eyes upon Jesus and you will see even more—the glory and grace of the invisible God.

⇨ Review our simple definitions of glory, grace and truth. Is your life be-ing characterized more and more by these same qualities as you reflect on the life of Christ?

DAVID'S ROYAL SON

(Matthew 1:1–17; Luke 3:23b–38)

The Old Testament prophets anticipate the coming of a Messiah in the line of David, a Ruler-Redeemer commissioned to restore Israel to her appointed destiny of mediating God's grace to the Gentile world (Ps 89; 132; Isa 9:6–7; 11:1–5; Jer 33:14–26). These prophecies draw on the Lord's covenant with David to establish one of his offspring on the throne of his kingdom forever (2 Sam 7:12, 13, 16). The New Testament opens by introducing Jesus Messiah as the son of Abraham and David. He is the fulfiller of the covenant promises given to these preeminent individuals in the earlier stages of redemption his-tory. Matthew and Luke detail the family history of Jesus in order to establish his credentials as the Son of David.

Matthew's is a *descending* genealogy, one that runs downward from ancestor to descendant. From Abraham to Joseph, husband of Mary, there are forty-one names in three sections: (i) Abraham to David; (ii) Solomon to Jeconiah; (iii) after the Babylonian exile, Shealtiel to Jesus.

Abraham
David (Bathsheba)
Solomon
Jeconiah
Shealtiel
Jacob
Joseph

Matthew views Jesus as the one who brings to completion all of the hopes of the nation of Israel expressed in the Lord's promises to Abraham and David. It is remarkable that he includes five women in the genealogy, three of which are Gentiles: Tamar, Rahab, Ruth, Uriah's wife, and finally Mary, "of whom Jesus was born." God's grace has carefully superintended the forward movement of the redemption story.

Luke's is an *ascending* genealogy, one that runs upward from descendant to ancestor. There are seventy-seven names, including the names of Jesus at the beginning and of God at the end. From Abraham to David the list is identical to Matthew's, but then branches to David's son Nathan not Solomon.

Adam, son of God

Abraham

David

Nathan (2 Sam 5:14)

Neri

Shealtiel

Heli

Luke's concern is to validate Jesus' relationship not only with the line of redemptive promise in Israel (Matt), but with the entire human race, Jew and Gentile, which springs from the first man, Adam. Luke's genealogy, unlike Matthew's, occurs not at the beginning of that Gospel but after the birth narratives and the account of John the Baptist's preaching of repentance. Here is the credentialing of one who comes to bring God's salvation to all who acknowledge their need of forgiveness.

Both genealogies, then, mean to establish the Davidic lineage of Jesus Messiah. Matthew records the line of Joseph, husband of Mary, through whom comes Jesus' legal claim to the throne of David. Luke focuses on the humanity of Jesus and the universality of God's saving mercies. His pedigree is traced back to Adam; his physical lineage from Mary, whose father is Heli, is also a Davidic one.

⇨ Read the prophetic texts provided in the first sentence above in order to review why it was so important for Matthew and Luke to establish the Davidic lineage of Jesus. Reflect on the way God superintended his "progress of redemption" going back to Abraham and even to Adam. What is unique about Jesus' birth that makes two genealogies necessary?

A MIGHTY ANGEL VISITS AN OBSCURE PRIEST

(Luke 1:5–25)

Luke's account of the birth of the Savior begins with a humble priest and his barren wife situated in the hill country of Judea, probably Hebron. Zechariah, whose Hebrew name means "the Lord remembers," and his wife Elizabeth were devout keepers of the law of Israel whose opportunity for a child was rapidly disappearing with each passing day. The aging priest was chosen by lot, a common method of selection by drawing stones from the fold of a garment, to represent his division to serve in the Jerusalem temple. Because Abijah's was one of twenty-four priestly divisions with 300 priests per division, this was a rare, perhaps once in a lifetime, chance for Zechariah to serve on this central stage. One of his duties was to supply and burn fresh incense on the incense altar in the holy place to accompany the morning and evening sacrifices offered at the altar of burnt offering in the courtyard (Exod 30:7–8). Worshippers were gathered in the outer courts of Israel praying for the Lord's mercies for themselves, their families, and their nation.

At the time of the evening sacrifice, 3:00 in the afternoon (Acts 3:1), Zechariah was overcome with fear as the mighty angel Gabriel appeared at the right side of the altar. Centuries earlier, at the same time, this bearer of prophetic revelation, had communicated to Daniel an outline of God's redemptive program (Dan 9:21). The sight of the angel awakened in the pious Zechariah fears of divine judgment lest he had inadvertently failed to carry out his duties according to their minutely detailed prescriptions. But Gabriel's message was one of comfort not rebuke. Rather than fear, Zechariah is to rejoice for Elizabeth will bear a son. Here was the divine response to the importunate prayers of the couple. The boy's name, John, "the Lord is gracious," would daily remind his parents of a faithful, prayer-answering God.

This would, however, be no ordinary child. First, he will bring them great joy when God exalts John to a place of prominence. Second, he will be set apart as a lifelong Nazirite, abstaining from fermented drink, to symbolize his consecration as a prophet of God (Num 6:1–4); his Spirit-filled character will support a prophetic ministry of unusual power. Third, his lifestyle and preaching, in the pattern of Elijah's, will be to prepare the people of Israel for the coming of the Messiah by calling them to return to their covenantal obligations. The disintegration of family relationships that resulted from substituting external rituals for heart loyalty will be healed; the foolishness of rebellion will be exchanged for the wisdom of obedience.

Zechariah can only respond with incredulity. He focuses on the human extremity—how often have his prayers been disappointed over the years—rather than on the divine opportunity. The sign of authentication to the skeptical priest is to be his inability to speak until the time the promise is fulfilled. When Zechariah emerges from the temple to greet the assembled worshippers, he is unable to pronounce the Aaronic benediction (Num 6:24–26).

The happy sequel to the completion of his duties in the temple is a safe return home, a wife who becomes pregnant, and the waiting for a son whose proclamation will awaken the prophetic voice and bring renewed hope to a nation. Elizabeth stands in a long line of barren women—Sarah, Rebekah, Rachel, Hannah—touched by God to bear sons of destiny in the progress of redemption.

⇨ How do the prayers of God's people fit into the sovereign outworking of his saving purposes? What do we learn here about the intersection of divine sovereignty and human activity? How should this encourage us in our prayer life?

THE ANNUNCIATION

(Luke 1:26–38)

Gabriel is once again dispatched from heaven to announce the Lord's favor upon a woman, this time a virgin in a rural village pledged to be married. Jewish betrothal occurred often shortly after puberty, thus Mary was barely in her teens. This preparatory period lasted up to one year, was legally binding, and could only be severed through divorce or death. Sexual relations were forbidden until after the formal wedding procession in which the groom escorted the bride to his home; infidelity during the betrothal period was considered adultery, a capital crime under Jewish law.

Mary, like Zacharias before, is terrified when greeted by the angel. The troubled girl has been chosen as an instrument of grace and is promised the divine presence. She will bear a son whose name will be Jesus, "the Lord saves." The son of Mary will also be the Holy Son of God who will claim David's throne and rule over the house of Jacob forever. Mary would have recalled from the synagogue services the Old Testament readings which spoke of a restored nation under a new Davidic ruler, a messianic Son over an eternal kingdom (2 Sam 7:12, 13, 16; Ps 89:20–29; Isa 9:6–7).

Mary protests that she has had no intimate relations with any man: "How will this be, since I am a virgin?" She clearly sensed that the conception was imminent and would occur before the completion of her betrothal to Joseph and the consummation of their marriage. While Zechariah was rebuked and judged for a query of unbelief, Mary's logical supplication is met with a gentle but mysterious explanation. Her conception will be a supernatural one: the Holy Spirit will plant the child in her womb, permanently uniting in the Son full humanity with undiminished deity. Mary is informed of her relative Elizabeth's miraculous pregnancy to strengthen her assurance in the God who can do the impossible.

Why did the Savior enter the world through a virgin birth, or more accurately, a virginal conception, which both Luke and Matthew validate in their historical record (Matt 1:18, 23; Luke 1:26, 27, 34)? God could have united his Son to humanity through an act of direct creation as he did in the case of the first man, Adam. The narrative never fully explains the necessity, but the language of Gabriel's answer to Mary suggests some answers. First, the virginal conception through the Holy Spirit's agency underscores the uniqueness of Jesus: he is both the Holy Son of God and son of Mary who assumes all of the properties of human nature except for the defilement of original sin (Rom 8:3; Phil 2:7). Second, this is the sovereign intervention of God in history, an act of majestic power bringing into the world one like no other, qualified to redeem all people through his coming death and resurrection; only the sinless and eternal God-man would be able to reconcile sinful people to the Holy Father. Third, grace pervades the scene. Divine favor descends to a humble girl in an obscure setting through an unprecedented conception of an incomparable baby.

Mary's response is not, as in the case of Zechariah, forced silence but voiced submission. How little Mary really understood at the outset is shown in her subsequent struggles to grasp her son's mission (John 2:1–5; Mark 3:21, 31–32). There is no mention of any qualms over how this unplanned pregnancy would be relayed to Joseph. Assuming the posture of a servant, she joyfully acquiesces in the purposes of a God whose goodness and power she has come to trust.

⇨ Construct a simple definition of a "servant" (Luke 1:38) based on Mary's response to the announcement that she has received from the angel of the Lord.

MARY'S MAGNIFICAT

(Luke 1:39–56)

When informed by Gabriel of Elizabeth's pregnancy, Mary quickly set out for the three to five day journey south to visit her beloved relative, perhaps an aunt or older cousin. Mary remained with Elizabeth for three months, until the time of the birth of her son. Mary's initial greeting moved the baby to leap in his mother's womb. Elizabeth's Spirit-filled pronouncement of blessing included the remarkable acknowledgment that Mary would be "the mother of my Lord." Elizabeth's child will prepare the way for the mission of Mary's son when they reach adulthood.

Mary's song of joy begins by magnifying "God my Savior" for making this lowly handmaiden from Nazareth the instrument of unending blessing for the coming generations. The theocentric hymn, one of four in the birth narrative of Luke's Gospel (followed by Zechariah [1:68–79], the angelic host [2:14] and Simeon [2:29–32]), extols the God who is orchestrating these momentous events—his holiness, mercy, grace, power, providential care and trustworthiness. Mary especially celebrates the Lord's overthrow of normal human values and power structures. The Lord humbles the proud, the mighty and the rich, but exalts the lowly and the weak. Israel had long been oppressed by the surrounding Gentile nations. The golden age of David and Solomon was a distant memory. Shortly after Solomon's death, the united kingdom broke apart; Assyrians swept the northern tribes away in 722 BC to be followed nearly 140 years later by the Babylonians' destruction of Jerusalem and its temple. For the next five centuries, apart from a brief period of freedom under the Maccabeans, Israel was a pawn in the power politics of the Near East. Persians, Greeks, Egyptians, and Syrians successively ruled over the Jews and now the Romans had reduced Judea to a backwater province of their mighty empire. The Roman governor, his soldiers quartered in the Fortress Antonia, kept a suspicious eye on the worshipping throngs in the temple courts below. The high priest, no longer from the biblical line of Zadok, presided over a ruling council far more committed to material profit than in preserving the nation's spiritual heritage; the temple courts were a merchandizing center more than a place of prayer. And far away from the corridors of power came an angel to two humble families, one in the tiny village of Nazareth in Galilee and one in the hill country of Judea. God is at work through two mothers and their children in a way contrary to natural expectations. He delights to bring about surprising reversals of fortune.

Mary's rehearsal of God's control of history comes in a series of seven declarations, with main verbs all in the past tense: He performed mighty deeds, scattered the proud, brought down rulers, exalted the humble, filled the hungry, sent the rich away empty, and helped his servant Israel (1:51–54a). The verbs point retrospectively to God's preservation of his people through the threats of these past centuries, but also presage a secure future under his continuing care. The keynote of "mercy" extended to unending generations frames these declarations (1:50, 54b–55). Luke's unfolding narrative will make it clear, moreover, that God's salvation through Mary's son is offered to all who believe and repent, apart from gender, age, social status, economic class, or ethnicity. Israel, the seed of Abraham, becomes anyone and everyone who embraces the son of Mary, the Son of God.

⇨ Spend a few moments rehearsing, like Mary, God's faithfulness in your own life experiences, particularly during times of testing. Frame a series of praises in the past tense and then remind yourself that God's mercies govern and unite past, present and future.

JOHN'S BIRTH AND ZECHARIAH'S BENEDICTUS
(Luke 1:57–80)

A son is born to Elizabeth and Zechariah in detailed fulfillment of the angel's earlier promise to the aging priest (Luke 1:13–14). Their friends and relatives recognize and rejoice together in the Lord's mercies shown to the aging couple. As commanded by the angel, the parents confirm that his name is to be John, "the Lord is gracious," a surprise to those who expected this long-desired firstborn son to be his father's namesake. His naming occurs on the eighth day when the boy is circumcised according to Jewish custom (Lev 12:3). The restoration of Zechariah's faculty of speech and the unusual naming makes everyone wonder, "What then will this child be?" Gabriel has already provided the answer to that question (Luke 1:15–17). His parents will nurture their son toward his God-intended destiny.

Zechariah's song of praise is also a Spirit-inspired prophesy. He remembers the covenantal promises to David and to Abraham which promise a future of hope and peace for God's people. Deliverance from foreign oppression and the establishment of Israel under God's rule in security and righteousness recalls such Old Testament promises as Isaiah 9:6–7 and Jeremiah 23:3–8.

But then the priest-prophet turns his attention to the climactic promise of the new covenant prophesied by Jeremiah (31:34b), the forgiveness of sins. John's role is to be the forerunner who prepares the way for the coming of the Lord (Isa 40:3; Mal 3:1), the prophet of the Most High who announces the arrival of the Son of the Most High (Luke 1:32, 76). This one who follows John will bring more than national deliverance from the oppression of foreign rulers. He will bring the knowledge of salvation through the forgiveness of sins. His very name Jesus, "the Lord saves" (Luke 1:31; Matt 1:21), addresses this deepest of human dilemmas, the spiritual darkness, death and alienation that have enfolded the lost race of the first Adam. Salvation in the New Testament is deliverance from both the penalty—eternal separation from God—and the power—inescapable and dominating control—of sin. Jesus, as heralded by John, comes not as national liberator but as heart cleanser and soul restorer.

Zechariah's poem echoes the common biblical metaphor of light dispelling darkness by its penetrating power. Balak prophesied that "a star shall come out of Jacob" (Num 24:17). Isaiah anticipates the dawning of "a great light" that will shine upon a people walking in darkness under the shadow of death (Isa 9:2). One day the light of the Lord himself will shine upon the peoples of the earth so that there will no longer be need of the brightness of the sun or the reflected radiance of the moon (Isa 60:1–2, 19–20). Malachi speaks of "the sun of righteousness" which "shall rise with healing in its wings" (Mal 4:2). Now Zechariah's son steps forth in the prophetic tradition, as its last and greatest representative, to announce the coming of the "rising sun" (NIV) which comes from heaven to dispel darkness and remove estrangement through his gift of salvation through the forgiveness of sins. His death and resurrection, only dimly hinted at in the opening chapters of these Passion narratives, will come into clearer focus as the revelation progresses.

Years of preparation now follow as the boy grows to manhood in the desert of Judea, strengthened in his spirit for the task ahead. Thirty years later "the word of God" will reverberate once again after four quiet centuries, as John seeks to rouse Israel from her spiritual slumber.

⇨ In what ways does sin cloud the mind and darken the path of a person? Reflect upon Luke 1:77–79 and note the variety of ways that salvation addresses the entirety of our human makeup.

JOSEPH'S TESTING AND OBEDIENCE
(Matthew 1:18–25)

The revelation of a son had come earlier to Mary who spent the next three months visiting her relative Elizabeth. Now, beginning to show signs of pregnancy, she returned to Nazareth. Matthew, in full agreement with Luke, states that the child was "from the Holy Spirit." Joseph's faith in Mary is tested to the breaking point. He concludes, as any thinking person would, that she has been unfaithful. His love for Mary precludes exposing her openly as an adulteress, which under Jewish law was a capital crime (Deut 22:23–24). In the first century under Roman rule, a husband could quietly end the relationship with a certificate of divorcement.

As he struggles over the dilemma, a prophetic word comes from the angel of the Lord, most likely Gabriel. This child has been conceived by the Holy Spirit and will bear the sins of his people, captured in the name Jesus. Joseph is called to believe the unbelievable, a virgin-born son who will become the long-awaited Redeemer. Steady resolve replaces paralyzing fear in the heart of this righteous man who passes the test by taking Mary to be his lawful wife. In all of Scripture only Abraham, when asked to sacrifice Isaac as a burnt offering (Gen 22:2), was subjected to an equally severe test of faith. Abraham's son, spared by a ram provided by the Lord (22:13–14), anticipates Joseph's greater son who will become the perfect sacrifice for sin.

Matthew sees the details of the birth narrative fulfilling direct prophecies from the Old Testament. This is the first of forty-seven Old Testament quotations that Matthew applies to the life and death of Jesus. The Spirit-caused conception of Jesus in the womb of a virgin fulfills Isaiah 7:14: "Behold, the virgin shall conceive and bear a son, and shall call his name Immanuel," the Hebrew name meaning "God is with us." The forgiveness of sins provided by Jesus' death will reconcile people to God as their loving Father. Isaiah's famous prophecy was given originally in a context of political turmoil in Israel seven centuries before the birth of Christ. Ahaz, king of Judah, was under threat from the adjacent kingdoms to the north, Ephraim (or Israel) and Aram (or Syria), who wished to coerce Judah to join a coalition against the threatening superpower to the east, Assyria. Ahaz even considered entering into a counter-alliance with the cruel Assyrians against his own kinsmen, the northern tribes. Isaiah urged Ahaz to trust in the Lord for Judah's security rather than in military alliances. A "sign" was offered to bolster Ahab's weak faith: the son whose name, Immanuel, would confirm the Lord's protection.

Isaiah saw history through bifocal lenses and his Spirit-inspired prophecy enfolds both near and distant events. Initially the prophecy is fulfilled by the son born to Isaiah and his wife, Maher-Shalal-Hash-Baz (Isa 8:1–4), whose name signifies the ravaging effects of the Assyrian armies as they sweep away Aram and Ephraim: "quick to the plunder, swift to the spoil." Isaiah's son is called Immanuel twice as the immediate sign to Ahaz (Isa 8:8, 10). But the ultimate signification of God's nearness is the birth of the son to Mary, whose intervention will remove the far greater ravages of sin and death. Isaiah's son points, by way of contrast, to Mary's son.

Joseph's noble response to the angel's word is quiet submission. He remains the faithful protector of his betrothed spouse and patiently waits for the birth of Immanuel. The language implies that Joseph and Mary had normal sexual relations after the birth of her son. The child is named Jesus on the eighth day, the day of his circumcision.

⇨ How does God appeal to our faith, like Joseph's, in trying circumstances? How can we, like Joseph, learn the lesson of calm obedience when severely tested?

BIRTH OF JESUS

(Luke 2:1–7)

The preparatory events that culminate with the birth of Jesus center on a humble couple, Joseph and Mary, in the small village of Nazareth tucked away in the rolling hills of southern Galilee. To the south Nazareth held a good view of the valley of Jezreel, the ancient battleground where near eastern armies squared off. This plain cut across northern Israel from east to west and provided Jewish pilgrims traveling south to Jerusalem, who wished to avoid Samaria, a direct route to the Jordan River valley. To the distant north on a clear day one could see the snow-peaked summit of Mt. Hermon. Nazareth was overshadowed by Sepphoris, just five miles to the north, the impressive former capital of Galilee built by Herod Antipas who ruled Galilee, 4 BC—AD 39. Sepphoris is never mentioned in the Gospel accounts and Tiberias, the current capital of Galilee and headquarters of Antipas, is mentioned only in passing. God's gracious activity favors ordinary people in obscure settings away from the corridors of political influence.

Luke sets the events of redemption history in the framework of secular history. Caesar Augustus ruled over the Roman world (27 BC—

AD 14), of which Judea was the southern part of the imperial province of Syria. Quirinius was the governor of Syria, appointed directly by the emperor to maintain order in this particularly unruly territory due to the presence of its independence-minded Jewish subjects. Augustus issued a decree for the whole empire to be registered for a census, necessary for taxation assessments. Censuses were generally carried out every fourteen years (extant records refer to one in AD 6) and this one occurred late in the reign of Herod the Great, around 5 BC. In Judea Jews went to their ancestral towns to be registered, or to towns where they owned property.

Since both Joseph and Mary were of Davidic lineage, they made the three to four day trip south to Bethlehem, the hometown of David (1 Sam 17:12; 20:6). Their seventy-five mile trip brought them down through the hills south of Nazareth into the plain of Esdraelon, across the Jezreel valley eastward to Scythopolis where they turned south along the Jordan valley as far as Jericho. From Jericho to Jerusalem they followed the ridge of the Wadi Qilt, a precipitous 3,500 foot climb over seventeen miles. Bethlehem was six miles southwest of Jerusalem, just off the north-south road connecting the holy city to Hebron and the Negev. In that small village in extremely humble circumstances Mary's firstborn son entered the world. The Son of God and Savior, destined to be both suffering Servant and triumphant King, strides into human history at the divinely intended moment, "when the fullness of time had come . . . born of woman, born under the law" (Gal 4:4). The context that surrounds Jesus' birth is one of unadorned simplicity. Joseph and Mary planned to stay in the home of a friend or relative, but because of the overcrowding due to the census registration there was "no place in the home/guestroom" for them to stay (the traditional rendering "inn" is possible but less likely in view of the NT usage of the Greek term *kataluma* [Mark 14:14; Luke 22:11]). Thus the holy family was forced to lodge in the lower level of the home near to where the animals were kept, or as tradition asserts, in a cave. Mary wrapped the baby warmly in long strips of cloth and laid him in a manger, a wooden or stone vessel normally used as a feeding trough for domestic animals.

⇨ Read 2 Corinthians 8:9: What does the humble setting of Jesus' birth tell us about the character of God?

ANGELIC CHORUS AND THE SHEPHERDS' VISIT

(Luke 2:8-20)

In the fields near Bethlehem shepherds were tending to their flocks out-doors at night. This supports but does not demand a season when the climate is temperate. The sheep were probably being raised for sacrifice in the Jerusalem temple. Shepherds were part of a vocation despised by religious Jews because of the frequent contact with dead animals. The resulting ritual defilement kept shepherds from frequenting temple or even synagogue wor-ship unless they performed the elaborate purification rituals (Lev 11:39–40). Like Zechariah, Mary and Joseph before, the shepherds are terrified by an angelic visitation and likewise commanded not to fear. The angel announces the birth of one who will bring great joy to "all the people." The "good news" is the free offer of forgiveness to sinners who believe and repent, irrespective of ethnic or cultural heritage, religious affiliation, socio-economic class, age or gender. The baby of Bethlehem is identified as Savior and Lord: trust in his redemptive death and obedience to his authoritative commands form a complementary response to his full-orbed Person.

An innumerable chorus of angelic voices rings out from heaven cel-ebrating the birth of the special child. The massive volume drowns out any earthly choirs celebrating the Roman Emperor's birthday. The anthem is brief but profound: "Glory to God in the highest, and on earth peace among those with whom he is pleased" (2:14). This child will manifest the hidden essence of God's character, namely, that God is holy love; God's love will be dem-onstrated and his holiness satisfied in his Son's work of reconciliation. The result is that peace will replace enmity in the God-man relationship. Behind the Greek word rendered "peace" stands its Hebrew equivalent, *shalom*. When a Jewish person greets another with the term *shalom* it represents a wish of well-being for one's entire person, spiritually, socially and psychologically. New Testament peace is restored fellowship with God (Rom 5:1), harmony with others through the removal of all relational barriers (Eph 2:14–18), and inner peace which replaces anxiety (Phil 4:6–7). When the Christian believer sings "It is well with my soul," he or she is celebrating the comprehensive gift of peace which can only come from the "Prince of Peace" (Isa 9:6).

The shepherds resolved to go to Bethlehem and see the child whose birth has summoned heavenly acclamation. Checking each of the homes in the small town, they located the holy family with the child resting in a manger wrapped in strips of cloth. The shepherds believed the angel's

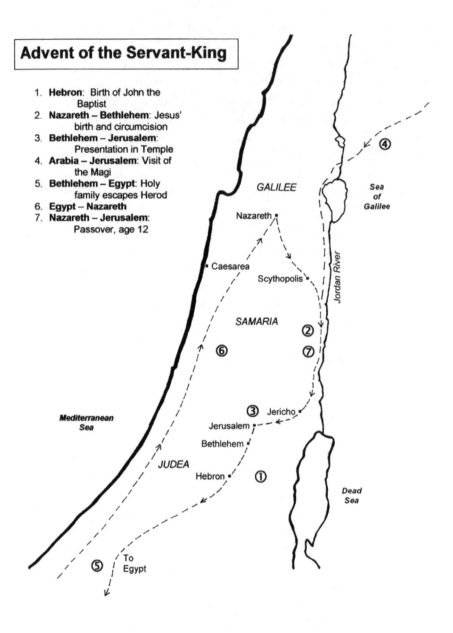

Advent of the Servant-King

1. **Hebron**: Birth of John the Baptist
2. **Nazareth – Bethlehem**: Jesus' birth and circumcision
3. **Bethlehem – Jerusalem**: Presentation in Temple
4. **Arabia – Jerusalem**: Visit of the Magi
5. **Bethlehem – Egypt**: Holy family escapes Herod
6. **Egypt – Nazareth**
7. **Nazareth – Jerusalem**: Passover, age 12

report which is confirmed in their visit to the amazement of all. Luke records that Mary "treasured up all these things, pondering them in her heart," an indication that her eyewitness report stands behind these birth narratives. Mary's reflective nature will in the course of her son's ministry guide her from confusion to grief to a settled trust (John 2:3–5; 19:25–27; Acts 1:14). The shepherds returned to their fields praising God for all they had heard and now seen.

God's chosen vessels of revelation now include a priest of lower rank with his barren wife from the hill country of Judea, a betrothed couple in a small village in Galilee, and ritually unclean sheep-herders in the fields around Bethlehem. The circle of privilege will soon widen to two devout worshippers in the Jerusalem temple and high-ranking visitors from Arabia.

⇨ To any person and every person with a contrite heart comes the promise of divine grace: "But this is the one to whom I will look: he who is humble and contrite in spirit and trembles at my word" (Isa 66:2). Reflect, like Mary, upon the Lord's goodness to you and turn that reflection into expressions of praise in imitation of the angels and shepherds.

PURIFICATION AND PROPHECY IN THE TEMPLE
(Luke 2:21–38)

Joseph and Mary were devout Jews who faithfully observed their ancestral traditions. They had their son circumcised on the eighth day (Lev 12:3) and named him Jesus, as the angel had earlier instructed them both (Luke 1:31; Matt 1:21). The Mosaic law stipulated that a woman was ceremonially unclean until the fortieth day after giving birth, in general until the normal menstrual cycle returned (Lev 12:1–7). Purification offerings were required according to a person's financial standing. In this case the offering of two doves or two young pigeons indicated the holy family was poor (Lev 12:8). The law also stipulated that the firstborn son belonged to the Lord and could be bought back by the payment of five shekels of silver which exempted him from temple service (Exod 13:2, 12–13; Num 18:15–16). Jesus, the one whose very name signified a mission to redeem others was, in the Old Testament sense, himself redeemed. The entire episode in the temple underscores his full identification with those he came to save.

An aged devout worshipper named Simeon enters the temple court at this providential moment and perceives the child to be the realization of a prophetic word that he would see the Lord's Christ before his death. His eulogy as he holds the child is a hymn of self-surrender and joyful resignation to the outworking of the divine purposes. Simeon has been yearning for "the consolation of Israel," the time when Messiah would bring comfort to his people in exile (Isa 40:1–2). In conjunction with the theme of Israel's redemption, which pervades the birth narratives (Luke 1:54–55, 68; 2:38; Matt 2:2, 6), Simeon's Spirit-inspired horizon expands to the light of revelation that will encompass the Gentile world. He draws on the panorama of Israel's greatest prophet, Isaiah, who sets the coming consolation of Israel (Isa 49:13; 51:3; 52:9; 66:13) in the framework of a worldwide proclamation of God's redemptive mercies to those outside of Israel (Isa 42:6; 49:6). The narrow stream of salvation history that began with Abraham and the family and nation that springs from him is now flooding its banks to water the Gentile world.

Simeon then speaks a prophecy to Mary, a sobering sequel to the pleasant tones of his prayer of dismissal. This child will become by divine appointment the great divider of humanity, the arbiter of human destiny, the discloser of human hearts. The "fall and rising" (2:34) refers to the judgment or blessing that will come to people in accordance with their response to his authoritative claims. His person and proclamation will create division even among family members (Luke 12:49–53), usher some in and throw others out of the kingdom (Luke 13:28–30), and become a stone either of solid security or of crushing defeat (Luke 20:17–18). Mary's own soul, in fact, will be pierced by sorrow (2:35). This is the first prediction of the Son's death in Luke's Gospel. On this most joyous season of her life, the birth, naming and then dedication of her firstborn child in the temple, comes a harbinger of grief when Mary will stand before the cross and watch her son's life ebb away (John 19:25).

A final blessing comes from an elderly prophetess, one Anna (Hebrew: Hannah) who joins the group in the court of women. Her many years of continuous worship in the temple, where repetitious sacrifices without power to atone for human sin were offered, climax with a prophecy of "redemption" (2:38). Emancipation from sin's slavery through the payment of a ransom would come through the perfect sacrifice, one that would pierce Mary's heart but provide consolation, redemption and revelatory light not only to Israel, but to the Gentile world as well.

⇨ Read through the Old Testament texts cited above in order to appreciate Augustine's dictum: "The Old Testament is the New Testament concealed; the New Testament is the Old Testament revealed."

WORSHIPPERS FROM THE EAST

(Matthew 2:1–12)

The Gentile theme continues as Magi from the east arrive in Jerusalem to inquire about "he who has been born king of the Jews." These men were esteemed astrologers-astronomers, likely from Babylonia where astrology was a long-established vocation. They mixed science with superstition, legitimate study of the movements of stars and planets combined with animistic predictions of such movements upon human and terrestrial affairs. It has been plausibly suggested that these were seekers after the true God whose attraction to monotheism might be traced to Daniel who served for nearly seventy years in the governments of Babylon and Medo-Persia. The magi may have been exposed to the Old Testament and its prophecies of a coming King in the line of David through the diaspora synagogues in towns along the Tigris-Euphrates rivers. That the purpose of their visit is to worship confirms their spiritual outlook. The star that has led them this far is a special instrument of supernatural guidance; its appearance in the east, steady movement to Jerusalem, and fixation over Bethlehem defies its association with any known astronomical phenomena such as comets, novas, or planetary alignments.

They must have brought quite an entourage, for all of Jerusalem, including the ruler of Palestine, Herod the Great (37–4 BC), was disturbed by their arrival. Tradition has assumed three wise men, drawn from the three gifts that they offer, but the text does not specify their number. Herod quickly summons an informal gathering of leading members of the Sanhedrin, the Jewish ruling council, and inquires if their tradition indicates the birthplace of the Messiah. Bethlehem was apparently recognized in official circles as the prophesied birthplace of Messiah, based on Micah 5:2. This text celebrates the special status conferred on this small Judean town, of meager reputation in Micah's day, due to the birth of the restored Davidic ruler who will righteously shepherd his people, Israel. Herod feigns a desire to join in their worship with his command to the magi to report to him the child's location once they find it. The religious leaders are implicitly censured for possessing biblical knowledge devoid of personal response; they know the details, but only Herod's interest is sparked.

Led by the star to the special child, the wise men are filled with joy, the characteristic response of those chosen to witness the redemptive drama (Luke 1:14, 44, 47, 58; 2:10). The holy family is now situated in a house, indicating this visit took place several weeks or even months after Jesus' birth. The concrete expression of their worship is three gifts: (i) gold, a symbol of royalty; (ii) frankincense or pure incense, an aromatic substance which is a biblical image for prayer and surrender of one's life to God; and (iii) myrrh, a resinous gum used in perfume and embalming (John 19:39), signifying death and mortality. The 3rd century church father, Origen, captures the significance: the Magi offered "gold as to a king, myrrh as to one who was mortal, and incense as to God." The worship of the magi recalls Old Testament passages such as Psalm 72:10–19 and Isaiah 60:1–9 where representatives from all nations stream to Jerusalem to offer gifts to the King of all the earth. Warned in a dream of Herod's evil intentions, the Babylonian visitors return to their country by a route that stays away from Jerusalem.

⇨ Does your worship spring from joy, lead to reverential bowing, and translate to concrete offerings as did that of the magi? Or, like the religious leaders, are you impressive in your biblical knowledge but lacking heart response to the person of Jesus? In the words of a contemporary song, "Give up on your pondering, fall down on your knees."

FULFILLMENT OF OLD TESTAMENT PROPHECIES

(Matthew 2:13–23)

Joseph is warned in a dream to flee to Egypt away from Herod's paranoia, which is now intensified by the secret departure of the magi. Following the angel's instructions, the holy family moves to Egypt to remain until Herod's death, slightly less than one year away. There was a large Jewish community in Egypt, particularly its largest city, Alexandria. Matthew sees this as the fulfillment of Hosea 11:1: "Out of Egypt I called my son." Hosea recalls God's gracious election of Israel as his adopted son, the redemption of the nation at the exodus event, and the present threat posed by seductive Canaanite culture. The divine author poured into these words deeper meaning beyond even the prophet's understanding. The history of Israel, then, prefigures the details of the earthly life of the Son of God: Jesus is born, threatened by Herod, taken to Egypt for protection, and then called back to Galilee.

Herod is enraged at the failure of the magi to report to him and he now takes action. His fear of the child, identified by his foreign guests as one destined to become "king of the Jews" (Matt 2:2), is translated into a decree that all male children two years old and under must be killed. Jesus is cast as a new Moses, whose infancy was likewise threatened by a cruel decree (Exod 1:22) and who, like his forebear, is on a mission of deliverance. The destruction of the babies of Bethlehem continues a long series of murderous acts attributed to Herod, which included his first wife, three sons, mother-in-law, brother-in-law, uncle and many others. Matthew views the lamentation of the mothers of Bethlehem as the fulfillment of Jeremiah 31:15. This text is a symbolic, poetic lamentation of Rachel (wife of Jacob and grandmother of Ephraim and Manasseh, the two most powerful tribes of the northern kingdom) for her "children" as they are being led to exile after Babylon's destruction of the kingdom of Judah in 586 BC. Jeremiah was predicting that what had overtaken the northern tribes nearly a century and a half before because of idolatry was now to be Judah's fate. Again, the deeper sense of the language connects the experience of Israel with the details of Jesus' life, in this case the wailing of the mothers of Bethlehem over the loss of their baby boys.

The angel makes a further appearance to Joseph in a dream and signals that it is safe to return to Israel because Herod is dead. But a further admonition directs him away from the unstable son-successor, Archelaus, who ruled as ethnarch over Judea and Samaria (4 BC—AD 6), and back to the safer environs of Nazareth. The return of the holy family to their former home is still another fulfillment, not of a single prophetic text but of a prophetic theme ("what was spoken by the prophets" [pl.]): "He shall be called a Nazarene." This obscure town tucked away in the hills of southern Galilee apparently possessed an unsavory reputation, judged by Nathaniel's initial response to Jesus' credentialing: "Can anything good come out of Nazareth?" (John 1:46). Far from discrediting Jesus, his origins in an obscure setting far removed from the austere religious environment of Jerusalem and its jealous custodians, qualify him to fulfill the many prophetic texts that portray the Messiah as one who is despised, rejected and marginalized (Ps 22:1, 6–8, 13–18; 69:7–8, 19–21; Isa 49:7; ch 53; Dan 9:26).

Jesus thus fulfills the Old Testament in the sense that he "fills to the full" the intended meaning of the divine author which is only partially satisfied in the historical setting of the human prophets who first addressed their own generation with these words.

⇨ Read 1 Peter 1:10–12: What do we learn in this passage about the limits and nature of OT prophecy? How does Jesus become the key to unlocking the meaning of the OT?

ON A MISSION FROM THE FATHER

(Luke 2:39–52)

Only one vignette of Jesus is recorded in the canonical Gospels between his infancy and emergence into public ministry around age thirty (Luke 3:23). At age twelve, when a child is transitioning into adulthood, Jesus accompanies his family in a caravan from Nazareth to Jerusalem for the annual Passover observance. This was the first of three major pilgrimage feasts (Pentecost and Tabernacles were the others), and the one that marked the start of Israel's religious calendar in the month of Nisan (March/April). The Passover on the fourteenth day of the month was followed by the Feast of Unleavened Bread (days 15–21). Devout Jews like Joseph and Mary celebrated the birth of their nation when the Lord through Moses delivered his people from bondage in Egypt. The Passover meal of roasted lamb, unleavened bread and bitter herbs recalled the slain lamb whose blood protected their firstborn sons from the destroying angel, the haste of their departure, and the harsh years of slavery (Exod 12:1–11).

After the eight-day festival the family caravan traveled toward home one day's distance, probably as far as Jericho, when his parents realized Jesus was missing. Retracing their steps, they eventually found him in the temple court engaged in dialogue with some teachers of the law. The onlookers were amazed at the young man. How could a Galilean village boy from humble stock and without formal training have acquired such insight and oratorical skills? Mary is exasperated and reproves her son for causing her and "your father" such anxiety over his safety. Jesus' reply seems on the surface to be one of blatant insensitivity to his parents' legitimate concern, but is best interpreted as a question of surprise rather than reproof: "Did you not know that I must be in my Father's house?" (2:49). These are the first recorded words of Jesus and reveal that even in adolescence he possessed not only supernatural insight into the meaning of the Hebrew Scriptures, but also a sense of filial consciousness and divine mission. He is preoccupied with the

Father's purpose for him, one which transcends all earthly ties. The Passover setting is crucial. At a time when Jewish pilgrims celebrated redemption from slavery through the blood of the lamb, Jesus refers to the Father's mission that he "must" fulfill. During this interchange in the court of Israel, was he summoning the theologians' attention to Old Testament passages that spoke of a suffering Servant whose death would culminate all of the sacrifices of bulls and rams that were being offered morning and evening at the bronze altar of burnt offering in the court of the priests? At the close of his Gospel, Luke records Jesus' exposition of Scripture in these very terms (Luke 24:27, 44). Here is the only person ever born whose express purpose in living is to die, a role which he embraces from the outset.

Jesus returned to Nazareth as the obedient son of Joseph and Mary. The 'silent years' from ages twelve to thirty are of little interest to the Gospel writers. Luke alone marks this period as one of maturation in four areas: wisdom, stature, favor with God, and favor with man. In the mystery of the incarnation the God-man, whose perfect deity is undiminished by his full humanity, grows intellectually, physically, spiritually and socially (2:40, 52).

⇨ Jesus embodies the qualities of authentic humanity as God intended. Does your life reflect the balanced and holistic four-fold pattern of maturation evidenced by our Example—deepening intellect infused with moral principles, physical vitality, growing intimacy with the Father, and expanding relational skill?

ADUMBRATIONS OF THE CROSS

Before moving on, it is important to trace one of the main threads woven throughout the fabric of the birth narratives. Over the infant, child and boy Jesus hovers the shadow of the cross. Webster defines the term "adumbration" as a sketch, vague foreshadowing, or obscure anticipation. The records of Matthew and Luke are replete with adumbrations of the cross. They are clear to the student who probes beneath the surface of the text for its deeper theological implications.

1. He is given the name Jesus, which means "the Lord saves," because he is a Savior who comes to provide his people the forgiveness of sins (Matt 1:21; Luke 2:11, 21).

2. The humble circumstances of Jesus' birth point to a Servant-King who comes to identify with ordinary people in lowly circumstances—wrapped in strips of cloth, he rests in a manger because there is no other lodging place in the overcrowded town of Bethlehem (Luke 2:7).

3. Simeon prophesies that Mary's own heart will be pierced with grief over the son whose ministry will divide families, determine destinies and reveal hearts (Luke 2:34–35).

4. The magi from the east offer three gifts to the child who is born King of the Jews, one of which is the spice of myrrh that signifies mortality and which will be used to embalm his crucified body (Matt 2:11; John 19:39).

5. As a native son of the obscure town of Nazareth, a "Nazarene," he fulfills the many Old Testament prophecies that speak of Messiah as a despised and rejected man far removed from the prestige normally associated with a royal visitation (Matt 2:23).

6. At the age of twelve Jesus has full consciousness of his special mission, eagerly engaged, literally, "in the affairs of my Father," in the temple courts at the conclusion of Passover season (Luke 2:49). His final meal some twenty years later will be a Passover supper against which he will interpret his impending death. One former Pharisee, like those whom he engages in the temple, will in due time rise to proclaim his significance: "Christ, our Passover lamb, has been sacrificed" (1 Cor 5:7).

As Jesus' ministry moves forward, the adumbrations will give way to more direct hints and finally to unmistakable predictions of the coming Passion. But from the genesis of the story everything is heading toward that final event where he cries out, "It is finished" (John 19:30).

2

Public Introduction of the Servant

Testimony, Temptation, Attestation

A DESERT PROPHET SOUNDS THE ALARM

(Matthew 3:1–6; Mark 1:1–6; Luke 3:1–6)

GOD'S VOICE SHATTERS FOUR hundred years of prophetic silence—which itself followed 1600 years of prophetic revelation from Abraham to Malachi—as it resounds through a strange figure in the barren wasteland of southern Judea. As with the prophets Jeremiah (1:2) and Malachi (1:1), "the word of God came to John the son of Zechariah in the wilderness" (Luke 3:2). Luke, the chronicler of sacred events, sets his record in the context of secular history. The ministry of the Baptist takes place in the time of five political leaders: the Roman emperor Tiberius Caesar (AD 14–37); the Roman procurator of Judea—now an imperial province of the second rank governed by direct appointees of Caesar—Pontius Pilate (AD 26–36); the tetrarch of Galilee, Herod Antipas (4 BC—AD 39); the tetrarch of Iturea and Trachonitis (NE of Sea of Galilee), Philip II (4 BC—AD 34), half-brother of Antipas; and Lysanias, tetrarch of Abilene (NW). Annas, the high priest from AD 6–15, had been deposed and replaced by his son-in-law, Caiaphas, but was still recognized as the rightful high priest by many Jews.

John's rough clothing—a camel's hair garment and leather belt—and his austere diet—locusts and wild honey—recall the stern ministries of the Old Testament prophets, especially Elijah (2 Kgs 1:8). His appearance is a visual protest against the self-indulgence of the religious authorities. John comes as the final and greatest prophet, privileged like a royal courier to announce the impending arrival of the Messiah. He is the messenger whose office is to stimulate heart-readiness before the Redeemer and Judge (Mal 3:1) and the forerunner who comes to prepare the way for the King who proffers salvation to all mankind (Isa 40:3–5).

His message is uncomplicated and penetrating: "Repent, for the kingdom of heaven is at hand" (Matt 3:2). Repentance, the reorientation of one's will and governing values, a radical transfer of allegiance from self to God, is the essential condition for entrance into the kingdom. The dawning of God's transforming reign, to be initially realized over the hearts of those who respond but eventually overtaking the universe, is both the impetus for repentance as well as its saving effect. This is a direct preview of the message that Jesus begins to proclaim in Galilee after his introduction by John (Matt 4:17). Repentance is the converse side of faith, two sides of the same coin; together they denote respectively turning away from sin and turning toward God. John, and Jesus after him, targets the reconstruction of the interior life not its external scaffolding. The demand—repentance—and the gift—God's saving rule—are proclaimed without respect to a person's social standing, ethnic heritage or religious achievements. Those who converge upon the Jordan to hear the prophet include Sadducees, Pharisees, Roman soldiers, Galilean fishermen and tax collectors.

The outward sign of repentance is public baptism in the waters of the Jordan. The historical precedent was probably proselyte baptism. Gentiles were required to undertake a self-immersion in water in order to become full-fledged members of the covenant community of Israel. For males, circumcision was required, a painful surgical operation for an adult. For all there was the vow to obey the dictates of the law, including abstention from unclean meats like pork. Because of the restriction and embarrassment created by such conditions, few Gentiles became full proselytes. The striking feature of John's baptism is that he demands it of all his listeners, Jews and non-Jews alike. All are placed on the same level, as sinners who need forgiveness.

⇨ What are the implications in John's message for Christian witness in the multicultural world of the twenty-first century? Do we evidence the kingdom perspective of John?

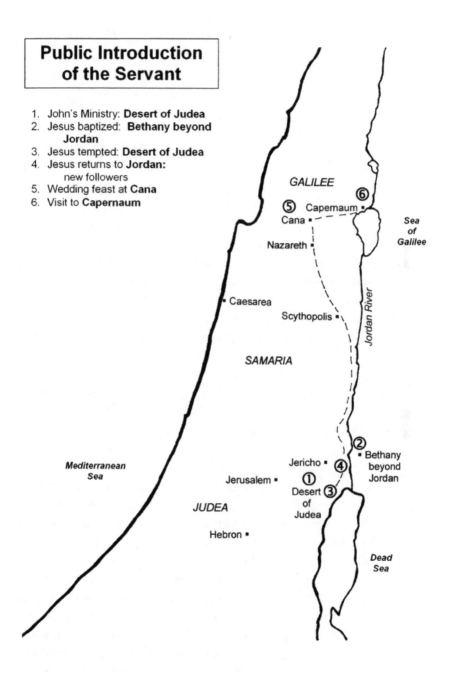

Public Introduction of the Servant

1. John's Ministry: **Desert of Judea**
2. Jesus baptized: **Bethany beyond Jordan**
3. Jesus tempted: **Desert of Judea**
4. Jesus returns to **Jordan:** new followers
5. Wedding feast at **Cana**
6. Visit to **Capernaum**

GALILEE

⑤ Capernaum •
Cana •

Sea of Galilee

Nazareth •

• Caesarea

Jordan River

Scythopolis •

SAMARIA

Mediterranean Sea

Jericho • ④

Jerusalem •

Desert ③
of
Judea

② • Bethany beyond Jordan

①

JUDEA

Hebron •

Dead Sea

THE INCOMPARABLY SUPERIOR ONE

(Matthew 3:7–12; Mark 1:7–8; Luke 3:7–18)

John promises salvation to those who repent, but judgment for those who refuse to surrender all forms of self-justification. Among his Jewish listeners are those taking refuge in their national identity. Being the physical sons of Abraham exempts them, so they reason, from the coming wrath of God to be poured out on their Gentile oppressors. John cuts the ground from under all appeals to national or cultural identity as the basis for security. Both the satiated members of the temple establishment (Sadducees) and the self-congratulatory teachers of the law (Pharisees) are among John's audience. The prophecy of Malachi, fulfilled by John, predicts a day when the Lord will come with a refiner's fire to purge the Levites who serve at the temple in an unworthy manner and all who act unjustly toward their neighbors (Mal 3:2–5). John's bold confrontation compares such people to deadly vipers, to fruitless trees uprooted by an ax, to chaff that will be separated from the wheat and burned.

John will not leave his listeners in the abstract with vague notions of faith and repentance. The evidence of their turning away from sin toward the Lord is a transformed character that produces good deeds. A person must replace hoarding of one's possessions with sacrificial giving to those in need. Tax collectors must renounce their common practice of exacting more than the government requires. Soldiers are to desist from extorting money from others by intimidation and false witness, being content with their wages. Repentance is proven by a changed life, by a radical reversal of priorities from self-aggrandizement to self-giving.

How does such heart transformation take place? John is not substituting one form of legalism for another. Rather he points his listeners toward one whose sandals he is unworthy to stoop down to untie and to carry. He comes as a witness to endorse another, as a servant under the authority of an incomparably superior one. While he administers a preparatory baptism in the element of water, this one comes to baptize "with the Holy Spirit and with fire." The Old Testament prophets speak of a day when the Holy Spirit will be poured out in order to empower people to live according to God's holy will (Isa 44:3–5; Ezek 36:25–27; 39:29; Joel 2:28–32). But there is also a day of reckoning when fire will consume the wicked (Isa 26:11; 66:15–16, 24). John shares the dual prophetic perspective of redemption and judgment that will ensue with the coming of the Messiah. But, as it will become clear in the teaching of Jesus, the inbreaking of God's kingdom comes at two decisive moments, inaugurally through the redemptive sacrifice of the suffering Servant and consummatively at the return of the conquering King. John fails to fully grasp the two distinct advents of Messiah and so speaks of a singular baptism "with the Holy Spirit and with fire." As he peers into the future, he sees the near and distant events like mountain peaks without full visibility of the valleys that separate them.

Baptism with or in the Spirit is referred to seven times in the New Testament, all but one of which rely upon John's initial saying (Matt 3:11; Mark 1:8; Luke 3:16; John 1:33; Acts 1:5; 11:16). The Acts references point out that John's prophecy finds fulfillment at the day of Pentecost when the risen Lord baptized the early believers with the element, in this case the person, of the Holy Spirit. This is the initial formation of the new covenant community, the church. Paul individualizes this doctrine as the act whereby Jesus (or God the Father) baptizes the believer at the moment of conversion into full membership in the body of Christ (1 Cor 12:13).

⇨ Does your profession of repentance translate into a radical change of conduct, one characterized by generosity, honesty and contentment?

JOHN'S BAPTISM OF JESUS

(Matthew 3:13–17; Mark 1:9–11; Luke 3:21–23a)

After the 'silent years' in Nazareth, Jesus emerges in the Jordan valley intent on being baptized in the waters of the Jordan by John. This is the initial act of his public ministry at around the age of thirty. John is preaching repentance and baptizing sinners in the waters of the Jordan near a village to the east called Bethany, just north of the Dead Sea (John 1:28). This event takes place in approximately *late Spring, AD 26.*

Since the act of baptism signified repentance from sin, John naturally responds to Jesus with reluctance: "I need to be baptized by you, and do you come to me?" John has just introduced this person whose superiority and two-fold baptism with the Spirit and fire sets him apart from the line of sinners in which he is standing. Jesus gently insists that baptism is fitting for him in order "to fulfill all righteousness" (Matt 3:15). Righteousness, one of the central motifs of Scripture, refers to being properly aligned with a standard and thus can be rendered rectitude, uprightness or propriety. Jesus speaks of being in congruity with the standard of God's character both relationally and morally, that is, being properly related to him and doing that which is in accord with his will. To fulfill all righteousness thus means to conform to God's holy character and to obey the entirety of his moral demands. Jesus is referring to the mission that the Father has assigned him. He comes not on a military offensive to establish the nationalistic aspirations of his countrymen, but on a redemptive mission which requires full identification with sinners. Though without sin, his baptism is an act of solidarity with sinners who are in need of forgiveness, which he will provide through his death and resurrection. He is fully conscious of his role as Isaiah's suffering Servant (Isa 52:13—53:12) from the outset of his ministry.

In the first of his four servant songs Isaiah portrays the Servant as fully equipped for his task by the empowerment of the Spirit (Isa 42:1). In rising from immersion in the waters of the Jordan, heaven opens and the Spirit descends and rests on Jesus like a dove, the symbol of peace (Gen 8:10). God the Father then breaks the centuries of prophetic silence directly with an audible authentication of Jesus' identity: "This is my beloved Son, with whom I am well pleased." God quotes his own word, a combination of Isaiah 42:1 which refers to his chosen Servant in whom he delights and Psalm 2:7 where he directly addresses the coming ruler in the line of David as "my Son." Together Jesus is identified as the Davidic King who will one day subdue the nations under his authority (Ps 2:8–12) and at the same time the Servant who will bring release to the captives of sin (Isa 42:2–7). He will accomplish his dual role as Servant-King, baptizer with the Spirit and baptizer with fire, according to the divine timetable and in the power of the Holy Spirit.

The baptism of Jesus, accompanied as it is by the Father's clarification of his identity and by the Spirit's empowerment of his work, underscores the perfect harmony of the three persons of the Trinity in the redemptive program. The entire act is properly interpreted as the formal commissioning to his public ministry. It adds nothing to Jesus' divine character, for he has already been introduced as Immanuel, "God with us" (Matt 1:23). The God-man is now set on the course of his life's work, assigned by the Father, to die as a substitute for those with whom he fully identifies in his baptism.

⇨ Read Philippians 2:5–8: What was the mindset of the preexistent Son as he contemplated the need of mankind? How are we called to imitate him, particularly in our relationships with one another?

TEMPTATION IN THE DESERT: JESUS AND ISRAEL

(Matthew 4:1–11; Mark 1:12–13)

Following his authentication as God's Son-Servant at baptism, Jesus is led by the Spirit to face the devil in the wilderness of Judea. In this clash there is an intersection of divine and satanic purposes. From God's side, the temptations are a test designed to fully credential the Son to represent sinners who have fallen prey to the allurements of the evil one. By passing the test, Jesus is vocationally qualified to stand in their place as a substitutionary sacrifice and to empathize with them as their High Priest (Heb 2:10, 17–18; 4:15–16; 5:8–10). From Satan's side, the temptations are enticements to sin, which are never attributable to God (Jas 1:13).

Matthew sets the temptations of Jesus against the background of Israel's failures to trust the Lord during their wilderness journeys. The prelude is forty days and forty nights of fasting. The allusion is to the forty years God tested Israel in the desert (Deut 8:2–3). This extended period makes the temptations severe but not unbearable (1 Cor 10:13). Jesus relies on the Spirit, who drove him into this conflict, and on the word of God ("it is written") to overcome the enemy.

1. *Stones to bread*: Satan challenges Jesus to prove his Sonship by turning some stones into bread to satisfy his hunger. This recalls the grumbling of the Israelites for food shortly after their miraculous departure from Egypt. Rather than trust the Lord's provision, which he will abundantly make in the form of manna, they long to return to their former place of bondage with its culinary delights (Exod 16:1–3). Jesus reminds the tempter from Deuteronomy 8:3 that spiritual priorities take precedence over physical ones.

- The question is, will Jesus miraculously satisfy his deep physical hunger or depend on God for physical sustenance while maintaining the priority of reliance on God's revealed will?

2. *Pinnacle of the temple*: The devil brings Jesus to the pinnacle of the imposing Herodian temple, over 150 feet in elevation, and beckons him to prove his Sonship by casting himself down. Satan is well-versed in the Bible and quotes Psalm 91:11–12 as a promise of angelic intervention to prevent Jesus from being harmed. But these verses are a pledge of protection from disasters that threaten faithful believers, not an excuse for presumption amidst dangers that are self-induced. Jesus

quotes Deuteronomy 6:16 which commanded the Israelites not to test the Lord as they did at Massah ("testing") when they demanded Moses produce water to satisfy their thirst. Rather than wait on God's supply, they brazenly questioned whether the Lord was even among them and would not abandon them to die in the desert (Exod 17:1–7).

- The question is, will Jesus presume to force God's hand and prove his Sonship by miraculous signs or follow God's veiled way of self-revelation?

3. *High mountain*: The devil takes Jesus to a high mountain where he can survey the splendor of powerful nations that encompass the earth. Satan promises to deliver this earthly power to Jesus if he will bow down and worship him. Jesus is being tempted to act like Israel which followed up her grumblings for food and water with open idolatry. While Moses remained on the mountain, the covenant nation made, bowed down and sacrificed to an idol cast in the shape of a calf (Exod 32:1–8). Jesus banishes the blasphemer from his presence with the prescription of Deuteronomy 6:13 that man's first duty is to serve the Lord God alone.

- The question is, will Jesus join a satanic alliance to secure political dominance over the nations or worship God alone and await his timing for enthronement?

⇨ Satan always offers short term gratification with disastrous long term consequences. How can we learn, like Jesus, to sacrifice momentary pleasures for lasting rewards?

TEMPTATION IN THE DESERT: JESUS AND ADAM

(Luke 4:1–13)

Luke places the temptations of Jesus against the context of Satan's tempting of Adam and Eve in the Garden of Eden (Gen 3:1–6). This accounts for his reversal of Matthew's ordering of the second and third temptations. This fits Luke's purpose in setting forth Jesus as the perfect Man, whose genealogy is traced back to the first man, Adam (Luke 3:38).

1. *Stones to bread*: Here Satan appeals to man's physical needs and desires, whether for a full stomach, sexual satisfaction, relational intimacy, emotional fulfillment or intellectual stimulation. Such human aspira-

tions are good gifts of God when enjoyed in their proper place, but when they displace God's rightful claim to one's primary allegiance they become destructive idols. Adam and Eve were provided abundant fruit from the trees in the Garden of Eden, but were clearly prohibited from eating from the tree of the knowledge of good and evil. Eve saw that the forbidden fruit was "good for food" and she began to doubt God's goodness. Jesus made the Word of God, not his need for bread, his governing priority.

2. *High mountain*: The devil then called attention to the nations of the world, especially Rome, that governed their subjects with raw political power and ruthless military might. As the "ruler of this world" (John 12:31; 16:11) under whose deceitful influence the world lives (1 John 5:19), Satan offers a share in his reign to those who play according to his rules. Eve saw that the fruit was "a delight to the eyes," even as earthly kingdoms must have impressed Jesus as he surveyed their splendor. But the God who made the world and will one day reclaim it demands exclusive worship, Jesus counters. He will not cede his glory to another (Isa 42:8).

3. *Pinnacle of the temple*: In tempting Jesus to cast himself down from the temple, Satan is inviting arrogant presumption in which a person tries to force God's hand. The desire for autonomy and independence from God's authority, making oneself the master of the universe, is at the heart of Satan's machinations in the Garden of Eden. God is a control freak who only wants to limit your potential, he whispers to Eve. She allows the devil's steady insinuations to weaken her confidence in the Lord, imagining the fruit is "to be desired to make one wise." Jesus reminds us that the one who trusts God need not put him to any test.

On a deeper level, the temptations of Jesus address the kind of role he is to assume in his forthcoming ministry. What kind of Messiah is he to be? Will he act as a social worker that addresses material needs but fails to touch the heart with God's love? Will he assume the role of a political revolutionary that uproots the social order but fails to refashion the character of its leaders with God's justice? Will he amaze and impress his audience as a wonder worker but fail to inform the mind with God's truth? The adumbrations of the cross, which we traced earlier, and the authentication of his identity as Son and Servant at his baptism form the backdrop to these temptations. Jesus is being enticed to assert one essential part of his character—Sonship, with all of its attendant powers—while avoiding the other—Servanthood, with its call to voluntary restrain the independent use of these prerogatives. To seize the crown without the cross, to abandon the Father's mission for him, this is the strategic agenda of the enemy. Jesus' triumph becomes our salvation.

⇨ The Apostle John organizes human sin into three categories: the lust of the flesh, the lust of the eyes, and the pride of life (1 John 2:16). Christian leaders who fall into sin invariably fail in the related areas of sex, money and power. Memorize Psalm 119:11, David's prescription for victory over sin.

THE LAMB OF GOD

(John 1:19–34)

John the Baptist is frustrated by the repeated attempts of his interrogators to probe his identity. He is not the Messiah, he has already told them (Matt 3:11), nor the literally resurrected Elijah ushering in the final judgment (Mal 4:5), nor the prophet like Moses who will speak a final word from God (Deut 18:15). No, no, no, he reiterates, he is only a voice preparing the way for another. Then, as Jesus approaches, he makes a startling confession: "Behold, the Lamb of God, who takes away the sin of the world" (1:29). Along with the anointing of Jesus by Mary of Bethany for the day of his burial (John 12:7), this is the clearest recognition by any person during his earthly ministry that Jesus has come to die.

The lamb, a docile and submissive animal, is at the center of the sacrificial imagery of the Old Testament. As Abraham led Isaac toward Moriah, he assured the boy that God would provide a lamb for a burnt offering, though it was a ram caught in a thicket that was sacrificed instead of his son (Gen 22:8, 13). It was the blood of the Passover lamb, sprinkled on the top and both sides of the doorframe, that protected Israel from the destroying angel (Exod 12:21–23). Two lambs were offered each day, one in the morning and one at twilight, as burnt offerings pleasing to the Lord who dwells among his people (Exod 29:38–45). Lambs were specified as guilt offerings under special circumstances, such as removing ceremonial defilement from those with infectious skin diseases (Lev 14:10–22), or from one who unexpectedly became unclean during the period of a Nazirite vow (Num 6:12). Most significant is Isaiah's description of the suffering Servant who, like a silent lamb led to its slaughter, bears the iniquity of the Lord's wayward sheep (Isa 53:6–7).

John seems to recognize that Jesus comes as the perfect offering toward which all of the ancient sacrifices of Israel's sacerdotal system pointed. The offerings of lambs, bulls, and goats were provisional means of atoning for Israel's sin, but had no efficacy to cleanse the heart and restore sinners to a right relationship with a holy God (Heb 9:13–14; 10:1–10). Here is the lamb of God who "takes away the sin of the world." The definitive removal of sin through a sinless substitute is at the heart of the New Testament gospel. "Sin" is in the singular not plural in John's confession. It is the totality of sin and collective guilt of the entire world that is taken away through Christ's death on the cross. As a lamb without blemish, he bears upon himself the penalty of death so that sinners may exchange their sin for his righteousness (1 Pet 1:19–20; 2:24).

John testifies that the Father revealed to him that the Incomparable One (1:27, 30), the Lamb of God (1:29), would be recognized by his permanent investiture with the Holy Spirit (1:33). This one who would first come as a sacrificial lamb would then create a new people through his work of Spirit-baptism. The order of John's confession anticipates the unfolding pattern of New Testament theology: Calvary is the prelude to Pentecost. The crucified Nazarene becomes the exalted Lord who mediates his presence through the Holy Spirit to his new covenant people. No wonder John is impatient at his stubborn questioners. They are missing the substance for the shadow, failing to see the sun because they are blinded by its reflection. As superior one, sacrifice and Spirit-baptizer, Jesus is none other than the Son of God (1:34).

⇨ How can we, as Christian witnesses, be more effective in pointing people away from ourselves to Jesus Christ? Like John we need wisdom and tact in telling people what they need to hear, not what they want to discuss.

THE LINE OF WITNESS

(John 1:35–51)

From John the Baptist's testimony emerges the first group of Jesus' disciples. These five men had seeking hearts for they came south from Galilee to hear the desert preacher's call to repentance. Their search was rewarded, for they had an encounter with the Messiah himself. This meeting with Jesus in the Jordan valley is the prelude to the later call of the four fishermen at the Sea of Galilee more than one year later. After initial exposure and the germination of faith, comes a period of reflection that leads to the decision to abandon all and follow the Lord.

The chain of witness moves along family lines. Andrew introduces his brother Peter to Jesus. John the apostle, the unnamed disciple, will eventually bring his brother James into the fold. Philip, who is called by Jesus directly, finds his brother Nathaniel and announces that Jesus is the Messiah foretold by Moses and the prophets. In each case there is the enthusiasm at their discovery as well as loving concern to introduce their brothers to Jesus. John the Baptist is the initial witness, willing to detach his disciples from himself and move their loyalty to another.

Though these five men reach an early conviction of Jesus' messianic status, they still entertain popular notions of a socio-political role for Messiah. They will struggle to understand the servant model that Jesus embodies. Their reeducation will be a torturous pattern of growth and regression over the next three years. Simon, who in this early setting is given his nickname, Peter (or Aramaic, Cephas), will not act like the "rock" that his new name signifies. But this volatile, impetuous spokesman for the other disciples will in time be a foundation stone that opens the door of the gospel to the Gentiles.

Jesus probes their motives: "What are you seeking?" Are they in pursuit of the kingdom of God through repentance, or, like the crowds, anxious to gain health and wealth? Are they seriously intent in following John's lead and learning for themselves who he is, or, like the religious leaders, eager only to debate and refute the evidence before them. Their request for an extended interview with Jesus proves the seriousness of their search. Nathaniel is the hardest sell. He is skeptical that Messiah could come from the obscure town of Nazareth. Rather than seek to logically refute his brother's objections, Philip simply invites him to "come and see," and Jesus does the rest. Nathaniel's sensitive conscience at the unsavory reputation of Nazareth elicits from Jesus a high complement: "Behold, an Israelite indeed, in whom there is no deceit" (1:47). Nathaniel is no Jacob. He is a straightforward man, free from manipulation and scheming. The supernatural knowledge that Jesus reveals of his private meditations under a fig tree convinces Nathaniel that his brother's testimony is indeed true.

The array of descriptive titles applied to Jesus in this first chapter of the fourth Gospel is impressive: the divine Word, the light, only begotten from the Father, the incomparable one, Lord, Lamb of God, Son of God, Messiah, King of Israel and Son of Man. All of the titles but the last are ascribed to Jesus by the author of the fourth Gospel, by John the Baptist, or by these early disciples. But the final one, Son of Man, will become Jesus' favorite self-designation. Jesus recalls Jacob's dream of a ladder that connected earth to heaven with the angels of God ascending and descending on it (Gen 28:12). Jesus applies this figure to himself as the Son of Man. He is the bridge between heaven and earth, one in unbroken communion with the Father who mediates the blessings of an opened heaven to those who believe.

⇨ Write down the names of your siblings, relatives or close friends that need an introduction to Jesus. Ask God for boldness to invite them to "come and see."

WATER BECOMES WINE: THE FIRST "SIGN"

(John 2:1–12)

Jesus and the first group of disciples were invited to a wedding in Cana, a village eight miles north of Nazareth in the hills of southern Galilee. The couple must have been close friends of his family since his mother Mary was there. In a Jewish wedding ceremony the groom led a procession to the bride's home who then, accompanied by her bridesmaids, processed to the home of the groom where the celebratory feast took place. When Mary realizes that the wine is running out, she appeals to her son to do something about it. She wants to relieve the potential embarrassment of the groom's family which is responsible for providing abundant hospitality for the guests. What she expects Jesus to come up with as a solution is left unclear.

Jesus gently reproves his mother, similar to his response at age twelve in the temple when he redirected her attention to his Father's affairs (Luke 2:49): "Woman, what does this have to do with me? My hour has not yet come" (2:4). Though he will in this case comply with her request, Jesus reminds his mother that he is on a divine mission with a set timetable and cannot be pulled off course by miraculously intervening in every human exigency that arises. The "hour," a fixed expression in the fourth Gospel, is the determined time for Jesus to act in an open disclosure of his messianic identity (7:6, 8, 30; 8:20), which is climactically realized in his submission to death on a cross (12:23, 27; 13:1; 16:32; 17:1). Mary must not interfere with either the timing—three years of public ministry precede the Passion—

or the method—humiliation before exaltation—of the full revelation of his authority as Messiah.

Mary remains undeterred by Jesus' reply, instructing the servants to carry out whatever her son requires. Nearby were six large water jars made of stone, each with a capacity of twenty to thirty gallons. The water was normally used for ritual purification in accordance with the detailed prescriptions for the washing of hands and utensils before the banquet (Mark 7:1-4). To honor his mother and to alleviate the present situation, Jesus commands the servants to fill the vessels with water to the brim, then to draw out some water and take it to the master of ceremonies. Between the filling (v. 7) and the drawing out (v. 8) the water is miraculously transformed into wine. Vessels used for ceremonial purification, symbolic of the old order, now contain wine, a symbol of the new covenant. New wine and fresh wineskins become the Lord's metaphor for the celebratory blessings of the new covenant which will require fresh forms to express their dynamic power (Matt 9:17). Wine becomes the symbol of the precious blood of Christ shed on the cross, the basis of the new covenant, and one of the two elements of its memorial feast (Matt 26:28-29).

The miraculous transformation is confirmed by the recognition of the wine's superior quality by the master of the banquet. He shares his surprise with the bridegroom at the reversal of custom, for in most cases such good wine would be served earlier not later; lesser quality wine would not offend after the guests' senses had been dulled a bit through drinking. This is the first of seven "signs" in John's Gospel, in this case a miracle of quality, where Jesus reveals his glory, his manifested majesty. "Sign" is John's distinctive term for a mighty work, an external proof, which authenticates the truthfulness of Jesus' claim to be the Son of God. The effect of the miracle upon the disciples is to strengthen their faith, but we are left to guess how it impacted, if at all, the servants who drew the water, the other guests, Mary, or the wedding party.

After the wedding in Cana, Jesus traveled to Capernaum with his family and disciples for a short visit (2:12). On the northwest shore of the Sea of Galilee, Capernaum will become the home base of Jesus' ministry following his return to Galilee. Had Jesus' mother and brothers (Joseph is not mentioned again) moved from Nazareth to Capernaum? Or was he, perhaps, surveying this major town on the route from Syria to Egypt through northern Galilee as a strategic center for his Galilean ministry? The "brothers" of

Jesus refer to the natural children of Joseph and Mary after Jesus was born; they did not believe in him during his earthly ministry (John 7:1–5).

⇨   Why are miracles not necessarily effective in moving people to a substantive faith in Jesus (John 2:23–25)? What is to be the basis of our confidence in his person?

3

Early Judean Ministry

Savior of the World

THE LAMB BECOMES A RAGING LION

(John 2:13–17)

T HE *EARLY JUDEAN* MINISTRY, approximately *Spring–Fall, AD 27* (nine
months), is recorded only in John's Gospel. Jesus headed to Jerusalem for
the first Passover of his public ministry (2:13). The entire eight-day festival,
Passover then Unleavened Bread, was a commemoration of Israel's redemption from slavery in Egypt. But as Jesus entered the outer court, the place
where seeking Gentiles could approach the holy Redeemer of Israel, it had
been turned into a commercial enterprise. First, shops had been set up for
selling animals needed for sacrifice. Any prayerful meditations of genuine
worshippers were drowned out by the clanging of coins and the movement of
sheep, cattle and birds across the courtyard. Instead of possessing the right to
pray in peace, the people found themselves in a noisy bazaar. Second, money
changers had set up tables to exchange the foreign coins of Jewish pilgrims
for the local currency required for purchasing the sacrifices. Apparently they
were making a handsome profit, in league with the animal peddlers, from the
exorbitant exchange rates being charged in the transactions.

Jesus was incensed. Fashioning a whip out of cord, he drove the animals
and their hawkers out of the temple, and then proceeded to overturn the
tables of the moneychangers. His success was aided by the supportive presence of pilgrims who likewise protested such flagrant profit-making at their
expense. This cleansing of the temple was Jesus' first decisive act of confrontation with the Jerusalem authorities. The Synoptic Gospels record a second
cleansing three years later on Monday of Passion Week (Mark 11:15–18

and parallels). Clearly the initial cleansing did not put an end to this deeply rooted and lucrative merchandising activity. Rather, it persisted and Jesus was forced to confront it again. The second cleansing sealed Jesus' destiny as one irreversibly opposed to the policies of the entrenched powers.

Behind Jesus' anger was a holy zeal for "my Father's house." Jesus' unique Sonship (he calls God "my Father" twenty-seven times in the fourth Gospel) demanded that he defend the holiness of God. The presence of such business ventures in the very place set aside as God's dwelling place among his people was a prostitution of worship. The sacred had become the profane. As they watched their Master erupt with indignation, his disciples recalled Psalm 69:9: "Zeal for your house will consume me." Psalm 69 is the plea of the righteous monarch, David, laboring under vicious attacks from enemies because of his faithfulness to the covenant. The New Testament authors see the cry of this godly sufferer as foreshadowing the sufferings of Christ. Jesus' motivations are in solidarity with the Psalmist in defending the exclusive claims of God upon his people's allegiance.

⇨ Do we see similar religious merchandising taking place in the twenty-first century? When is it appropriate and, in fact, compelling for believers to express holy anger? Is there a danger today for the church to forget its primary purpose—to disciple the nations—and become caught up with other competing agendas?

THE TEMPLE OF HIS BODY

(John 2:18–22)

After the attempt, with temporary success, to remove the emporium from the temple court, the religious leaders demand proof by way of a miraculous "sign" that Jesus possesses the authority to question their policies and, even more, to call God his Father. They were right to recognize that the true Messiah would prove his credentials through attesting signs (Isa 35:5–6). Later when John the Baptist is having doubts, Jesus points to his abundant miracles of healing as proof of his claims (Matt 11:4–5). But in this case he offers an enigmatic reply: "Destroy this temple, and in three days I will raise it up" (2:19). The Jews misunderstood the cryptic saying. Since their conflict with Jesus is taking place in the court of the Gentiles, they can be forgiven for interpreting this as a reference to the literal temple structure. Does he dare claim to be able to rebuild in the space of three short days the magnificent temple, should the Romans tear it down (always a threat), which Herod and his successors have been working on for forty-six years (19 BC—AD 27)? Three years later at his trial before the Sanhedrin, witnesses would remind the jury of this outrageous claim (Matt 26:61). He was mocked from the cross by onlookers who threw this empty boast back in his face (Matt 27:40).

But the author provides the interpretive insight to Jesus' intended meaning. He was speaking of the temple of his body which, after being torn apart, would be raised from the dead in three days. His bodily resurrection is to be the ultimate "sign" of his authority as Messiah. As one former Pharisee will later attest, he "was declared to be the Son of God in power according to the Spirit of holiness by his resurrection from the dead, Jesus Christ our Lord" (Rom 1:4). His sacrificial death, vindicated by the Father's raising him up on the third day, becomes the basis for a new relationship with God, no longer mediated through animal sacrifices in a physical temple. The cleansing of the temple is far more than a courageous attempt to rectify the old system; rather, it signifies that a new order of worship is to be enacted upon a perfect sacrifice and a glorious rebuilt temple, the risen life of Jesus Christ.

Jesus' saying intimates the fuller temple theology of the Epistles. Paul calls the new covenant community the temple in which the Spirit of God dwells and thus must be kept free from internal divisions and external compromises (1 Cor 3:16–17; 2 Cor 6:16). The body of the individual believer is the temple of the Spirit and must be managed in a way that honors God (1 Cor 6:19). Christ is the cornerstone of this building, the church, which rises to become a holy temple in which God takes up residence by his Spirit (Eph 2:20–22). In the new heaven and the new earth there will be no literal temple structure, for the Lord God Almighty and the Lamb are the temple (Rev 21:22). At each stage in the unfolding progress of redemption God mediates his presence more directly. During the old covenant era, his glory fills the holy of holies, shielded from the people by a thick curtain. During the inaugural stage of the new covenant, between the first and second comings of Christ, the Spirit of God makes the hearts of believers, both individually and corporately, his settled residence. Finally, in the renewed universe people experience unbroken intimacy with the Father, liberated "to glorify God and to enjoy him forever" (Westminster Shorter Catechism).

John the author admits that he and the other disciples failed to grasp the meaning of the temple saying until after Jesus rose from the dead. Then, by the illumination of the Spirit (John 14:26), they will recall this holy prediction and their faith will be strengthened.

⇨ Are there sins that cloud your intimate fellowship with God? Ask for his help to remove all obstacles so that the Spirit can live within you without disturbance.

NICODEMUS AND THE NEW BIRTH

(John 3:1–15)

While in Jerusalem Jesus was approached at night by a Pharisee named Nicodemus. He may have chosen to come at night out of fear of being seen. Later, however, Nicodemus protests the harsh measures being recommended against Jesus by other members of the Jewish ruling council, the Sanhedrin, of which he was a member (John 7:50–51). After the crucifixion Nicodemus, along with Joseph of Arimathea, another moderating member of the council, boldly steps forward to secure a proper burial for Jesus. It is more likely, then, that Nicodemus was not lacking courage and chose the evening hours because they would afford a better chance for extended conversation. Nicodemus is impressed by what he has seen and heard of Jesus. His initial words about Jesus being a teacher from God appear to be a genuine compliment rather than a flattering setup.

Jesus moves quickly to a topic of great interest to any Pharisee, the kingdom of God. But he says nothing about the nationalistic aspirations of Israel, freedom from the Romans, an earthly rule of Messiah from Jerusalem, or the uprooting of the social order—all central to the prevalent first century Jewish understanding of the kingdom. To enter the kingdom, Jesus reiterates, one must be born again. To enter the kingdom is to come under the dynamic reign of God over one's entire personality and to receive the gift of eternal life (3:15–16). Nicodemus can only think of a second physical birth, which is impossible. But Jesus means a radical spiritual rebirth, one originating in the life-giving work of the Holy Spirit. To be born "of water and the Spirit" (3:5) signifies the cleansing and regenerating work of the Spirit in the heart of one who believes in Jesus as God's Son. Nicodemus is still living and thinking on the plane of natural, transitory human existence, that is, the flesh. Jesus speaks of a sovereign work of the Spirit in the heart of a person that is mysterious and beyond human comprehension. Like the wind that blows, one can see its effects without knowing exactly where it comes from or where it is going. So the new birth visibly transforms its recipients while defying precise analysis.

Nicodemus remains baffled: "How can these things be?" Jesus issues a gentle reproof to one who is Israel's "teacher" and yet fails to comprehend the essential nature of the kingdom of God. Then his rebuke becomes stern. Nicodemus and the Pharisees cannot grasp his doctrine of the new birth because their reasoning operates only on the level of the material world. In fact, their failure to understand even "earthly things," such as the raising of the temple of his body (John 2:18–21), disqualifies them from receiving the "heavenly things" of his doctrine of the new birth.

Jesus claims to possess exclusive insight into spiritual truth because he, and he alone, came from heaven. His heavenly origin makes him uniquely qualified to reveal to people the things of God. But his incarnation does more than establish his credentials as revealer of God; it also qualifies him to become the Redeemer of those whose nature he assumes. As the Son of Man—first a suffering Servant, then a ruling King—he will be "lifted up" (3:14). This is a cryptic reference to his death on the cross. Jesus compares this coming event to a moment in Israel's history (Num 21:4–9). For grumbling against God and Moses the people were bitten by venomous snakes. In response to the peoples' confession, God directed Moses to make a bronze image of a snake and to lift it up on a pole. Those who had been bitten looked up to the replica and lived. So those who cast their glance upward in faith to the crucified Lord will receive eternal life.

⇨   What are the tangible effects of the new birth, like the sound of wind or the rustling of leaves in a tree?

SUPERFICIAL AND GENUINE BELIEF

(John 2:23–25; 3:16–21)

Faith can be a decisive surrender of oneself to and reliance upon God's Son. Yet not every act of 'believing' constitutes saving faith. The many in Jerusalem who believed in Jesus did so because they observed his miracles (2:23), but this was far short of a profound commitment of life and destiny, the complement of repentance. Jesus knew that the heart of a person was more than capable of emotional attachments which would not last, whether with his miracles, oratory, or personal dynamism. Later many "disciples" who had followed him during the early Judean and Galilean phases of his ministry stumbled at his uncompromising demands and turned back (John 6:66). So Jesus put little stock in the miracle-rooted belief of these

44

early professors. He looked for tangible signs of the new birth, not passing enthusiasm for the spectacular.

The most well known and often cited promise in Scripture is John 3:16. This begins the author's fuller explanation of salvation, which is the equivalent of entering the kingdom, experiencing the new birth, and receiving the gift of eternal life. The entire New Testament gospel is contained in a nutshell in this one verse. The gospel is the "good news" of God's saving activity in restoring sinners to a right relationship with himself, forgiving their sins and making them his children. First, the initiative in salvation is the self-sacrificing and unconditional love of God. His superlative gift to the world is the Son, both sending him into the world and delivering him to death. The cross is the measure of his love. Second, the object of salvation is the inhabited world of humanity. The free offer goes out to "whoever," unrelated to ethnicity, socio-economic status, gender or age. All people are potentially redeemable and are given a real opportunity to be saved. Third, the locus of salvation is the Son of God, the eternal second person of the Triune Godhead, fully God and fully man, whose death and resurrection provides the basis of salvation. Fourth, the means of salvation is faith in God's Son. One must believe from the heart, turning away from sin and placing one's full confidence in the person and work of Jesus Christ. While faith alone saves, James reminds us that the faith that saves is never alone. It is proven effectual by a changed life from which emanate good works (Jas 2:14–26). The great reformer, Martin Luther, used the Latin expression *fides apprehensiva* to describe saving faith—a faith that apprehends, lays hold of, embraces Jesus Christ, trusting in him as Savior and binding oneself to him as Lord. Fifth, the reward of salvation is the gift of eternal life. There will be no condemnation at the final judgment. Communion with the Father now and continuing joy in his presence for eternity is the free gift to those who believe.

Nevertheless the "good news" also has its reverse side. This message divides humanity into two parts, those who are willing to be subjected to the searching light of God's holiness and those who recede into the darkness because they fear exposure. God's intent is to save not to condemn, but for those who refuse the proffer of salvation there is judgment, eternal separation from the Father. Christ comes to judge the world, one writer comments, as little as the sun comes to cast its shadow, but just as the shadow is the natural consequence of the earth's movements so God's holiness demands that he judge those who violate his character. Though the initial ground of condemnation is original and actual sin, the stubborn refusal to trust in the Son seals a person's destiny and becomes the final cause of condemnation.

⇨ Have you placed your faith in the crucified and risen Jesus Christ, God's sole means of providing salvation? Is your faith evidenced by a changed life? Spend a few minutes thanking the Father for how very, very much he loves you.

A SERVANT-LEADER PAR EXCELLENCE

(John 3:22–36)

After the events surrounding the Passover (AD 27), Jesus moved to the Judean countryside, probably near Jericho in the Jordan valley. Many came to hear him while his disciples carried on a ministry of baptizing, confirming the continuity of Jesus' ministry with that of John the Baptist. Farther north at Aenon near Salim, south of Scythopolis, where there were abundant springs, John continued performing his preparatory baptism. Some of John's disciples expressed concern that Jesus was attracting far greater numbers than their Rabbi. John's influence was clearly diminishing, while Jesus' popularity was on the rise.

From John comes the noble response of a true servant-leader. Even when his own disciples exerted pressure to protect his circle of influence, John never forgot who he was and what his mission was all about—to point people toward Christ. John was neither inflated by the initial massive response to his ministry, nor disheartened by being eclipsed by Jesus. John is secure because of his profound confidence in the providential hand of God in his life. He is the forerunner who has been sent to prepare the way for Messiah. Therefore, the growing stature of Jesus is an authentication of the fruitfulness of his ministry, not its failure. For John, fulfillment comes in facilitating the success of another.

John draws on the illustration of the Jewish wedding with its three central characters, the groom, the bride, and the friend of the groom (the "best man"). The friend of the groom seeks to maximize the joy of the groom on his special day by keeping him on center stage. He performs an important but always subsidiary role so that the groom and bride can take satisfaction in each other. The friend's joy is found in hearing the happy tones of the groom's voice in expressing his vow of lifelong commitment to the bride. In this analogy Jesus is the groom, the community of disciples who enter the kingdom through faith and repentance is the bride, and John is the friend of the groom. John's attitude to Jesus' growing popularity is unbridled joy, not the fear and jealousy expressed by his disciples. In a famed summary statement John places himself and Jesus in their proper relationship to one another: "He must increase, but I must decrease" (3:30). The "must" in the two parallel clauses denotes divine purpose: the forerunner gradually fades into the distance once Messiah arrives to carry out the redemptive mission of his Father on center stage under a full spotlight.

The author of the fourth Gospel adds his own reflection on the theological significance of the Baptist's testimony to Jesus Christ (3:31–35; cf. 3:16–21). John is a natural, earthly man raised up by God for a special purpose; Jesus is the incarnate Son from heaven and thus preeminent. His heavenly origin ensures the faithfulness of his testimony. Tragically, most people choose religious conjecture over revealed truth. However, just as a seal on a document guarantees its authenticity, so the person who accepts Jesus' testimony certifies that God, who has given his Spirit to the Son without measure (John 1:32–34; 3:34), is himself truthful. There is nothing lost in the transmission from Father to Son because of the Spirit's work, guiding and empowering Jesus' sanctified humanity. One can be supremely confident that Jesus speaks God's very words. The perfect communion of Father and Son makes the promise of eternal life and the warning of divine wrath a message of grave importance. God is holy love, sacrificing his own Son to redeem people whose sins deserve his settled hostility. Destiny is defined by one's response.

⇨ From a Christian Hymnal locate the hymn, "May Jesus Christ Be Praised." Make the refrain of that hymn your prayer for the day.

A SAMARITAN WOMAN MEETS THE JEWISH MESSIAH
(John 4:1–26)

The most direct route from Judea to Galilee took pilgrims along the patriarchal ridge route to Shechem, then north and west through Samaria. The Samaritans had their own version of the five books of Moses, the Samaritan Pentateuch, and had built a rival temple on Mt. Gerizim which lay in ruins since its destruction by the Maccabean ruler, John Hyrcanus, in 128 BC. The Jews considered the Samaritans to be a schismatic sect with a syncretistic form of worship. In order to avoid ritual defilement, strict Jews would avoid Samaria and take the longer route through the Jordan valley.

Divine compulsion not geographical necessity, then, brought Jesus straight into the Samaritan heartland as he made his way to Galilee. Exhausted and thirsty from the trip north, Jesus sat down by a well at noontime when a Samaritan woman approached to draw water. He was in the village of Sychar near Shechem, which lay on the eastern edge of the valley that forms the pass between Mt. Gerizim and Mt. Ebal. How does Jesus go about pointing her to himself?

1. *Jesus engages the woman in conversation, avoiding unnecessary hindrances and challenging her to think more deeply* (4:7–10). Having no jar to draw water from the well, he simply asks her to provide him a drink. It is she, not he, who mentions the gender and culture barriers that normally would preclude such a conversation from even taking place. He transfers her attention from physical water, which quenches one's thirst temporarily, to living water which only he can provide. He wants her to begin thinking about who he is and why he has come.

2. *Jesus overcomes her initial discomfort by tapping into her latent spiritual longings* (4:11–15). The woman is uncomfortable, perhaps a bit offended, that this stranger seems to be making a claim that would place him above the renowned patriarch Jacob who built this very well and watered his flocks. She seeks refuge in her connection with the past; Jesus probes her present condition. He perceives that beneath her defensive moves are yearnings for spiritual reality. He offers her the free gift of eternal life, likened to living water "welling up" and permanently satisfying her heart's thirst for peace and forgiveness. Later Jesus uses the imagery of streams of living water flowing forth for the new covenant gift of the indwelling Spirit (John 7:38–39).

The woman has a hard time making the transition from the material to the spiritual plane. To her, this offer seems to be a way of relieving her of the tiresome task of carting water from the well to her home each day. If he is offering her a more convenient or more prosperous life, then she is all ears.

3. *Jesus confronts her spiritual condition, forcing her to come face to face with her sinful alienation from God* (4:16–19). The prerequisite for entrance to God's transforming rule, his kingdom, is repentance. Jesus

now bears down with a confrontational exposure of her moral history. When she initially denies that she is married, he stuns her with the knowledge of her five previous husbands, as well as her present partner to whom she is not married. Christ's witnesses cannot replicate their Lord's supernatural knowledge of a person's hidden past and present conditions, but can point people to the God who searches the heart and before whom "all are naked and exposed" (Heb 4:13). The woman now perceives she is standing in the presence of no ordinary man. Her confession that he is a prophet is the dawning of spiritual understanding.

4. *Jesus addresses her arguments without compromising the truth* (4:20–24). Now the woman retreats into her religious traditions, distancing herself from the Jewish rabbi: "Our fathers worshipped on this mountain (Gerizim), but you (Jews) say . . . in Jerusalem." Her method is to steer the conversation away from her immoral behavior by introducing theological controversy. But Jesus will not let her escape and forthrightly states, "Salvation is from the Jews." He reminds her that the true stream of salvation history is a Jewish one and she must come to God on his terms, through a Jewish Messiah. Truth must displace error for genuine conversion to take place.

Even so, a new order of worship is about to dawn in which geography and tradition will be replaced with direct access and supracultural privilege. True worshippers will come to the Father "in spirit and truth." Three features are central to worship under the new covenant. First, believers will enjoy personal communion with God as their Father at any time and in any place (1 John 1:3). Second, the Holy Spirit will now take up residence in the human spirit, energizing the child of God to approach their Heavenly Father with confidence (John 14:16–17; Rom 8:15–16). Third, God's revealed truth in the gospel of the death and resurrection of Jesus Christ is the centerpiece of worship. Believers offer to God their bodies as living sacrifices because of the redeeming mercies poured out upon them in Christ's sacrifice (Rom 12:1–2).

5. *Jesus calls her to a decision regarding his identity* (4:25–26). The Samaritan woman knows of a Messiah who will come in the end time and reveal the mysteries of God. She seems to disassociate this figure from Jesus, but this final evasive move only provides Jesus the opportunity for full disclosure: "I who speak to you am He." Now she must decide whether to continue to hunker down in her defensive trenches or surrender to

the authority of one who has disclosed her sin and offered her a new start. This is the moment of decision.

⇨ Review the five lessons above and ask how these might be applied in your particular context to make you a more effective witness for Jesus.

SAMARITANS CONFESS THE SAVIOR OF THE WORLD

(John 4:27–42)

The disciples arrive as the woman is departing. Jesus has a message for them as well, but it seems to go right over their heads. His conversation with a Samaritan, and a woman at that, shocks them into silence. Jesus' daily bread, he says, is to accomplish the will of his Father, a work that will reach completion in his death on the cross (John 4:34; 17:4; 19:30). The agricultural metaphor of sowing and reaping is the kingdom task of bringing the word of God to people, calling them to a verdict, and teaching those who believe to become fellow disciples.

Paradoxically, the first harvester is the Samaritan woman, not the confused disciples who can only think of literal bread. She returns to her village and invites her neighbors to consider if this one who "told me all that I ever did" could be the Messiah? No longer receding from the light, she is now glad to be exposed and made clean. Her sowing leads to reaping as many Samaritan villagers, moved by her testimony, spend two days with Jesus and proceed to a heartfelt confession: "We know that this is indeed the Savior of the world" (4:42). Despised shepherds, Babylonian magi, Galilean fishermen, Samaritan villagers—all are invited to receive eternal life from the Savior of the world. The Father seeks all who will worship him "in spirit and truth."

⇨ How important is it to understand the cultural setting of those to whom you are witnessing? How does Jesus show sensitivity without compromise?

DEEPENING SHADOW OF THE CROSS

The four Gospel accounts are *"Passion narratives with extended introductions."* Once again it is instructive to stop and recall how the shadow of the cross is deepening over the life of Jesus.

1. John the Baptist was understandably reluctant when Jesus came to the Jordan to receive baptism from him. This was a preparatory rite signifying repentance. But Jesus was determined "to fulfill all righteousness," that is, to carry out the Father's righteous will (Matt 3:15). His baptism is an act of identification with sinners whose redemption he will secure through his vicarious death.

2. When he rose from immersion in the waters of the Jordan, a voice from heaven declared: "This is my beloved Son, with whom I am well pleased" (Matt 3:17). The Father's composite quotation of Isaiah 42:1 and Psalm 2:7 identified Jesus as the chosen Servant who brings release to the captives of sin and the Son of God who will rule over the nations.

3. His authentication as Son-Servant at the baptism forms the backdrop to the three temptations in the wilderness. Jesus is being tempted to assert his Sonship while denying the humiliation intrinsic to his role as suffering Servant. Jesus refuses to seize the crown without the cross.

4. John the Baptist points his audience away from himself to "the Lamb of God, who takes away the sin of the world" (John 1:29). Through his death on the cross, the perfect offering toward which the Old Testament sacrificial system pointed, Christ takes upon himself the totality of sin and the collective guilt of the entire world.

5. Into his favorite self-designation, Son of Man, Jesus incorporates his full-orbed identity—the one who first comes to die (Servant) but one day returns to reign (King). He is the bridge between God and man, the one who brings the blessings of heaven to earth (John 1:51).

6. At the wedding in Cana, Jesus had to remind his mother that he was on a divine mission with a set timetable—his "hour" (John 2:4). She must not interfere with either the timing—three years of self-revelation before the Passion—or the method—humiliation before exaltation—of the Father's plan for him.

7. When Jesus promised to raise the temple in three days after its destruction, the Jews interpreted it as an outrageous boast regarding the massive Herodian temple complex. But he was speaking of the resurrection of his body, which would be the Father's vindication of his Son's effectual death for his people (John 2:19). A new order of worship, no longer mediated through animal sacrifices in a physical temple, was dawning.

8. Just as the people who had been bitten by snakes could look up to the bronze replica lifted up on a pole and be healed (Num 21:4–9), so those who believe in the Son of Man who is "lifted up" will receive eternal life (John 3:14–15). This is a cryptic expression in the fourth Gospel for Jesus' death on a cross (John 8:28; 12:32, 34).

9. Jesus told his disciples that his food is to finish the work assigned to him by the Father (John 4:34). The night before his death he prays that God will be glorified as he completes that work (John 17:4–5). Just before he yields his spirit to God in the final moments on the cross he cries, "It is finished" (John 19:30). How much the Samaritan villagers understood of his mission is unclear, but they embraced him as more than the Jewish Messiah. Here was one who invited them to worship the Father "in spirit and truth." Jesus saw them not as ritually defiled schismatics, but as people ripe to be harvested for God's kingdom. This one must truly be the Savior of the world (John 4:42).

4

Early Galilean Ministry

Dawning of the Kingdom

PROCLAIMING THE KINGDOM IN GALILEE

(Matthew 4:12, 17; Mark 1:14–15; Luke 3:19–20; 4:14–15; John 4:1–4)

THE PHARISEES WERE ACUTELY aware of the numbers of people flocking to Jesus in the Jordan valley and felt threatened. Many of his ideas contradicted their interpretation of the law and so their initial reservations turned to open hostility. This occasioned Jesus' withdrawal to Galilee. The Synoptic writers note that at this time John the Baptist was imprisoned by Herod Antipas, tetrarch of Galilee, for his stinging rebuke of Antipas for taking Herodias as his wife. Antipas had divorced his wife and married Herodias. She was his own niece and, at the time, wife of his half-brother Philip I. Ironically, in moving north Jesus was now in the territory under the jurisdiction of Antipas.

Luke stresses the Spirit-directed course of Jesus' life. After the Spirit descends on him at his baptism (Luke 3:22), Jesus is led by the Spirit to be tempted in the wilderness (4:1) and now inaugurates his Galilean ministry "in the power of the Spirit" (4:14). The *Early Galilean* phase is normally viewed as extending from his move to Galilee until the formal selection of the twelve apostles and the Sermon on the Mount, a period of approximately nine months *(Winter-Fall AD 28)*. This period is marked by Jesus' growing popularity, which reaches it peak with the Sermon on the Mount (Matt 4:23–25; 7:28—8:1). A series of controversies surrounding the proper observance of the Sabbath move the teachers of the law from initial anxiety to clear opposition (Mark 2:6, 16, 18). The three divergent lines of response to Jesus—rejection (Pharisees), ambivalence (crowds), acceptance (apostles)—begin to emerge at this time.

Jesus launches his ministry in Galilee with the proclamation: "The time is fulfilled, and the kingdom of God is at hand; repent and believe in the gospel" (Mark 1:15). The eschatological season anticipated by the Old Testament prophets has arrived. The precondition for entering God's kingdom is faith and repentance. As his ministry unfolds, it will become clear that the kingdom Jesus introduces is in some sense present (Matt 12:28–29; Luke 17:20–21) and yet awaits a future consummation (Matt 6:10; Luke 19:11). In its present dimension the kingdom is expressed in God's authoritative rule over the life of the individual person who receives Jesus Messiah. The future dimension will involve the uprooting and recreation of the present social order as the whole world, human and subhuman, is placed under God's lordship. The kingdom proclamation of Jesus is aimed not at establishing a theocratic state for a renewed ethnic Israel, but advancing the lordship of God over the lives of those who enter by repentance and faith the new Israel, which transcends ethnicity, gender and age distinctions. It will be a painstaking process of re-education for the disciples to grasp the transcultural character of the kingdom and to embrace the vision of kingdom harvest through sacrifice, kingdom righteousness through freedom, and kingdom greatness through servanthood.

As "the kingdom of the heavens/God" is the theme of Jesus' preaching, we offer the following *definition*, one which incorporates the expansive set of qualities that emerge from the numerous biblical texts: *"The kingdom of God is the present transforming rule of God over the entire personality of believing and repentant individuals, creating a community over which he reigns, and one day resulting in a redeemed universe that joyfully submits to his sovereign lordship."*

⇨ Read carefully through the definition of "kingdom." Note how it attempts to capture the following areas of emphasis in Jesus' teaching: a theocentric (God-centered) world view; heart transformation; present-future polarity; individual-corporate complement.

A ROYAL OFFICIAL'S DESPERATE PLEA

(John 4:43–54)

After his brief stay with the Samaritan villagers, Jesus moves north to Galilee. Though he arrives to an initial warm reception from the Galileans, the enthusiasm will not last. In Galilee Jesus will experience first hand the well known proverb, "A prophet has no honor in his own hometown." Welcomed but not honored is the paradoxical response from people attracted to him more for the benefits that he distributes than the kingdom that he offers (4:43–45).

His first recorded stop is Cana, the village eight miles north of Nazareth, where a few months before he had turned water into wine. This is the only glimpse that John's Gospel provides of the early phase of Jesus' Galilean ministry. While there a royal official of Herod Antipas stationed in Capernaum came to seek healing for his gravely ill son. It took the official nearly two days to make his way from Capernaum southwest along the plain of Genneserat, through the Valley of the Doves, and down through the hills of lower Galilee to Cana. For an aristocratic member of Antipas' royal court, probably a Gentile, to seek help from a marginalized Jew without formal credentialing reveals his desperation. Any amount of social shame is worth it if this reputed healer can save his beloved child. But Jesus at first seems to ignore the plea and issues a rebuke to the crowd, gathering with hopes of seeing something spectacular: "Unless you see signs and wonders you will not believe" (4:48). Jesus is skeptical about miracle-directed attraction which, when the crisis is over, has no staying power (John 2:23–25). While Jesus responds with compassion to people in need, his healing ministry is clearly more pastoral than strategic. Only when the amazement of the miracle stimulates deeper reflection on his person and claims does it serve the kingdom.

The desperate man is undeterred. This is no time to discuss theology. He begs Jesus to come to Capernaum before it is too late. The official reckoned that Jesus' actual presence, even his physical touch, would be necessary for healing. Then comes the powerful word: "Go; your son will live." Even though there was no tangible evidence of the miracle actually having taken place and the method of healing from a distance was contrary to all expectations, the official "believed" the word of Jesus and headed home with confidence in his son's restoration. Here is a faith that cast itself on the naked word of Jesus apart from external proof. As he made his way back to Capernaum, he was met by some servants with news that the boy had fully recovered from his sickness. He still wanted to be sure so he inquired as to the exact time of the recovery. Yesterday at 1:00 p.m. the fever subsided, they said, the very hour that Jesus announced the healing. The actual miracle, upon its verification, moved his initial faith to settled trust and brought his entire household into the kingdom. Another seeker from Capernaum, a Roman centurion whose gravely ill servant will be healed by Jesus' powerful word from a distance (Matt 8:5–13), will draw on the royal official's testimony and place his faith in Jesus. This was the second supernatural attestation of his person that Jesus performed in Galilee, both in the village of Cana, far from the corridors of power and influence (4:54).

⇨ What personal distress has brought you to a sense of desperation before God, where he and he alone can provide the solution? Imitate the Capernaum official and boldly ask for God's intervention. Do not waver, but trust and wait patiently for the answer.

TOUGH SERMON TO THE HOMETOWN FOLK

(Luke 4:16–30)

Traveling through the towns and teaching in the synagogues of Galilee, Jesus came to Nazareth. As he entered the familiar synagogue on the Sabbath, the eyes of all were fastened upon the hometown boy whose reputation as a preacher and healer preceded him (Luke 4:14–15, 23). The order of a first century synagogue service included:

(i)   The attendant's reading the Shema from Deuteronomy 6:4;

(ii) Opening prayer concluded by the congregational "Amen;"

(iii) Reading of a passage from the Pentateuch, then a passage from the Prophets;

(iv) Sermon or "word of exhortation" (Acts 13:15);

(v)   Benediction and the congregational "Amen."

(vi) The congregation stood when the Scriptures were read. The Hebrew text was followed by the Aramaic paraphrase, known as the Targum, since Hebrew was not widely understood by the laity. The teacher and the congregation sat during the sermon.

Jesus was the guest speaker and unrolled the Hebrew scroll to Isaiah 61. After reading the better part of two verses, he rolled up the scroll, gave it to the attendant and sat down. With the congregation on the edge of their seats, he began with the startling words: "Today this Scripture has been fulfilled in your hearing." In its historical context, Isaiah, anointed by the Spirit, prophesied the release of his fellow Judahites from captivity in Babylon. His language echoed the provisions in the year of Jubilee when debts were cancelled, indentured servants were freed, and land was returned to its original owners (Lev 25:10, 13). The literal bondage of slavery was a graphic picture of the binding domination of sin over human beings, impoverished, broken, darkened and held captive under its hegemony. Jesus boldly asserts that he is the one of whom Isaiah spoke in the first person singular. His kingdom is the season of the Lord's favor toward those who believe and repent. He cuts off the quotation before Isaiah's next words, "and the day of vengeance of our God" (Isa 61:2b) because this is the inaugural moment of the kingdom's in-breaking. Judgment will come in a future consummative moment upon those who refuse the offer.

At first, Luke says, "all spoke well of him" (4:22), pleased at the gracious tones of redemption he so eloquently expounded, but in a few moments the praise turned to murderous anger (4:28). What caused such a radical reversal? In moving from exposition to application, Jesus struck a raw nerve at two points. First, he rebuked their superficial attraction to him, which demanded that he duplicate here his mighty healing of the boy in Capernaum. Second, he expressed God's concern for non-Jews. He reminded them from their Old Testament that though there were many Israelite widows in Elijah's day, the prophet was sent to preserve the life of a poor Phoenician widow and her son (1 Kgs 17:8–24); and though there were many Jewish lepers in Elisha's day, he cleansed the Syrian general, Naaman, of his leprosy (2 Kgs 5:1–14). Enthusiasm for miracles and ethno-centrism characterized the core values of his listeners. But Jesus' kingdom is about holiness over happiness, heart transformation over material prosperity. God's gift of salvation is for the repentant, irrespective of one's ethnic lineage or religious resume. Jesus left Nazareth for Capernaum, providentially protected from the mob which would have crowned their Sabbath worship by murdering their favorite son.

⇨ Read Psalm 139:23–24 and pray, like David, for God to search your heart. Ask the Spirit to expose and to remove every "grievous way" such as a self-directed approach to God that seeks his goodies more than his glory.

A CALL TO CATCH MORE THAN FISH
(Matthew 4:13–22; Mark 1:16–20)

Capernaum was a major town on the northwest shore of the Sea of Galilee. It had a tax office (Matt 9:9), an office for Antipas' royal official (John 4:46), a garrison of Roman soldiers (Matt 8:9), and a synagogue (Luke 7:5). What now became Jesus' "own city" (Matt 9:1) was situated along a major trade route from Damascus to Egypt called the *via maris*, or "way of the sea," which ran through Caesarea on the Mediterranean coast. Thus Gentile business-men passed through this northern area of Galilee, which was very near the Gentile confederation of ten cities called the Decapolis. Matthew records Jesus' move to Capernaum as the fulfillment of Isaiah 9:1–2: whereas the tribal areas of Naptali and Zebulun were the first to suffer at the hands of Assyria and Babylon when they invaded Israel from the north, now the light of redemption is dawning through a greater son of David (Isa 9:6–7). God extends his grace to an oppressed, ridiculed, Gentile-ridden portion of Israel far away from the religious center of Jerusalem.

The ancient rabbis marveled at this most picturesque portion of the holy land: "Jehovah has created seven seas, but the Sea of Galilee is his delight." Like a Scottish loch surrounded by steep hills on the east and west, this lake, fourteen miles long and nine miles wide, provided livelihood to many fishermen who used nets to catch carp, tilapia and other varieties of fish. Three of the initial disciples of Jesus—brothers Andrew and Simon Peter and their business partner John—who spent the better part of a week with him in the Jordan valley (John 1:35–51) had returned to their homes and vocation. Over the past year these men had time to reflect on that encoun-ter and now their earlier confessions solidified into a lifelong commitment. Andrew and Peter were casting their circular fishing net on the surface of the water when Jesus arrived. His audible command was unmistakable: "Follow me, and I will make you fishers of men." First, the call was personal, to trust and obey him as their Master, to make Jesus Messiah the new gravitational center of their lives. Second, the call was costly, to leave career, family, pos-sessions, familiarity and comforts and to embark into an unknown future. They had a lot to consider. Along with the sons of Zebedee, their fishing cooperative was proving lucrative, judged by the equipment and hired work-ers they had acquired. To honor one's parents was the fifth commandment of the Decalogue and included caring for them in their old age. A couple of years later, when the initial enthusiasm has long worn off in the rough and tumble of kingdom ministry, Peter will remind Jesus of the great sacri-fice that he and the others had made to follow him (Matt 19:27). And Jesus will remind Peter that no one can outgive God and that all sacrifices will be abundantly rewarded (Matt 19:29). Third, the call was purposive. Jesus promises them a vocation that will yield a product far more significant than

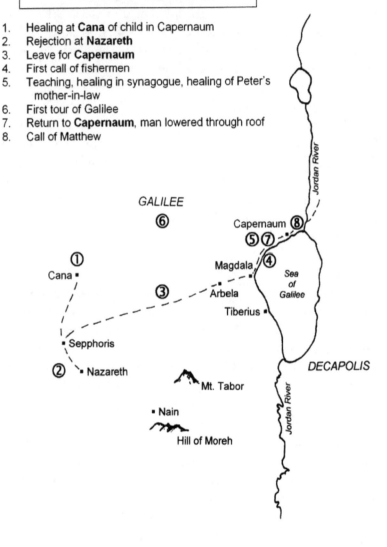

Early Galilean Ministry I: To Call of Matthew

1. Healing at **Cana** of child in Capernaum
2. Rejection at **Nazareth**
3. Leave for **Capernaum**
4. First call of fishermen
5. Teaching, healing in synagogue, healing of Peter's mother-in-law
6. First tour of Galilee
7. Return to **Capernaum**, man lowered through roof
8. Call of Matthew

a large haul of carp. He takes the responsibility to train them for their new vocation to fish for people.

Going a little farther along the shore, Jesus issues the same call to the two sons of Zebedee, James and John. They were in the boat with their father preparing their dragnets for deeper water fishing. As with Andrew and Peter, there was no hesitation. All four men immediately left their vocation and families to follow Jesus. The germination of faith in the Jordan valley led to a period of reflection, which grew into the radical decision to leave the past behind and trust their future to one they believed in their hearts was the Messiah and indeed the very Son of God.

⇨   Is your life as a disciple of Jesus, like these four, characterized by personal allegiance to him, by willingness to sacrifice those things which mean the most to you, and by a commitment to let him train you to be a discipler of others?

MIRACULOUS CATCH OF FISH

(Luke 5:1–11)

Luke's account of the call of Peter (Andrew not mentioned) and the sons of Zebedee probably took place the same day as the more abbreviated record of the call of the four fishermen in Matthew and Mark. The setting is once again the serene shore of the Sea of Galilee, here identified with the fertile agricultural plain that extends along its western flank, Gennesaret. Jesus entered Peter's boat, rowed it a short distance from shore, sat down, and began to teach the gathering crowd. The shoreline formed a natural amphitheatre so his voice could easily project to a large group.

Peter initially protested when the Lord commanded him and his partners to head for deeper water and lower the dragnets for a catch. These experienced fishermen had toiled all night and caught nothing. Still, he had the common sense to obey one who had shown supernatural insight on more than one occasion (John 1:48; 4:29). When they lowered the nets, the large catch of fish not only tore the nets but also began to sink both boats into which the haul was frantically loaded. Jesus had earlier reproved the disciples who could see the literal unripened wheat fields of Samaria and its schismatic inhabitants, but failed to perceive the rich harvest of souls ready to be reaped (John 4:35–38). Now with an acted parable more suited to their context, the lavish supply of fish overwhelmed their resources and pointed to the great catch of people to be brought under God's rule, if they would follow their Master's call and take advantage of his reciprocal commitment to make them fishers of men.

Peter was shaken loose from his prejudices. Forced to look deeper than the impending financial crisis—the loss of an unprecedented catch, ripping nets and sinking boats—, Peter fell to his knees and cried out: "Depart from me, for I am a sinful man, O Lord." Here was the dawning of spiritual insight, for "the fear of the Lord is the beginning of wisdom, and knowledge of the Holy One is insight" (Prov 9:10). Like Job, who abhorred himself when he came face to face with the Lord (Job 42:6), and like Isaiah, who lamented his ruin and unclean lips when he saw the King, the Lord Almighty (Isa 6:5), so Peter begins his journey of faith with a profound recognition of his own sinful heart and his unworthiness to stand in the presence of Majesty. In all the vicissitudes of the coming days, this conviction will never leave Peter. Contrition is the prelude of his decision to follow Jesus.

Jesus first calmed Peter's fears (Ps 34:4). He then assured Peter, representing John and James and the others that would be added, that the great haul of fish, which was preserved, was only a symbol for their higher calling of bringing people under God's saving rule. Jesus would use two metaphors for the comprehensive task which he was assigning these leaders in training, one at the beginning and one at the end of his ministry: Peter will fish for people (Matt 4:19; Luke 5:10) and he will feed God's flock (John 21:15–17). There are both evangelistic and pastoral roles in this great kingdom enterprise, which Peter will fulfill respectively through his proclamation of the gospel in Judea and Samaria and his instruction of the churches in Bithynia and Rome. For now, though, Peter and the other disciples are projects under construction. They are embarking on an adventure full of opportunities and fraught with perils.

⇨ A profound sense of unworthiness has been the shared experience of many of God's choicest servants—Augustine, Luther, Jonathan Edwards, Spurgeon, Hudson Taylor, Wang Ming Dao. Are you awed, like Peter, in the presence of your holy God?

CONFRONTED BY THE POWERS OF DARKNESS

(Mark 1:21–28; Luke 4:31–37)

Jesus was the guest preacher for the Sabbath service in the Capernaum synagogue. His manner of teaching amazed his listeners. Unlike the trained speakers they were used to, he did not quote other rabbis or appeal to the tradition of the elders to support his interpretations. He did not attempt, like the Pharisees, to micromanage their lives with a myriad of precise details to fit every situation in life. Jesus spoke with the zeal of the Old Testament prophets, demanding spiritual and moral response. He probed the hidden springs of peoples' hearts and laid them bare before a holy God. Most shocking of all, he spoke in the first person singular with the "authority" (Mark 1:22, 27) of a king demanding his subjects' attention. It is his self-awareness as the Son of God (Mark 1:1, 11), commissioned and authorized to proclaim the in-breaking of God's kingdom, with its demand for faith and repentance, which set him apart from the scribes.

In the middle of his exposition, Jesus was interrupted by the scream of a man who was inhabited by a demon. Sometimes called "unclean spirits" or "evil spirits," the demons are fallen angels who rebelled against God, were banished from heaven, are incorrigibly evil, and serve under the direction of the chief adversary of God, Satan (Matt 25:41; 2 Pet 2:4; Jude 6). There is an explosion of demonic activity during the earthly ministry of Jesus, as the kingdom of light begins to roll back the long unchallenged frontiers of darkness. The demon appears compelled by Jesus' royal authority to confess that this is the Holy One of God, the sovereign Lord who will one day mete out the destruction of Satan's counterfeit kingdom. Angels celebrated the Savior's birth with an anthem of praise (Luke 2:13–14); demons are driven to acknowledge his lordship; in the entire universe only human beings encounter Jesus and come away with doubts. While the demon is capable of speaking truth, it is a sinister attempt to stir up controversy, for the messianic title, "Holy One of God," conjured up in the minds of the first century Jewish audience a socio-political liberator who comes to release Israel from her Roman oppressors. The title carried nationalistic tones far removed from the mission of the Servant.

Jesus issues an authoritative command for the demon to shut up and depart. None of the ancient means of exorcism—unpleasant roots forced up the person's nose, invoking the name of a higher power, citation of magical formulas—are employed. There is no cajoling or coaxing, no interviewing

THE PASSION OF THE SERVANT

for information, no torturous struggle to force the demon to leave, as in some contemporary paradigms of spiritual warfare. The demon immediately complied and with violent convulsions and one final shriek departed. These associated phenomena indicate that there was total domination of the possessed individual's personality and that the demon preferred habitation over a wandering property-less state. The demon's intent, however, is to bring pressure from adoring crowds to detour Jesus from his mission as Servant and sacrifice. As his fame spreads throughout Galilee, such pressure will increase.

Jesus will face sustained conflict with demons who challenge at every turn, openly or behind the scenes, his extension of God's saving rule. It is always the nature of evil to be self-destructive. Satan will continue to deploy his forces against Jesus, manipulating the crowds, inciting the religious leaders, inspiring Judas, and, at times, deceiving even his disciples (Matt 16:23) to bring about the very event, Jesus' death, which will seal his own doom (John 12:31).

⇨ C. S. Lewis writes that Christians should be neither materialists nor magicians, neither underestimating the reality of Satan nor seeing demons behind every bush. What can we learn from this incident when we encounter what seems to be demonic activity?

PHYSICAL HEALING IN THE SERVANT'S ATONEMENT
(Matt 8:14–17; Mark 1:29–34; Luke 4:38–41)

Jesus moves from the synagogue to the house of Peter and Andrew hoping for some Sabbath rest after the unexpected intensity of the morning service. When he is informed that Peter's mother-in-law is suffering from a high fever, Jesus heals her with his touch and authoritative word. Each of the Synoptic writers focuses on a particular aspect of the healing: he touched her hand (Matt); he grasped her hand and helped her up (Mark); he rebuked the fever (Luke). Together the accounts capture Jesus' sensitivity, determination and authority. Her strength was immediately restored, confirmed by her waiting upon Peter's guests in the finest tradition of oriental hospitality. Peter had made the heart-wrenching decision to leave his home and career and to follow Jesus. Now the Lord honors his servant's obedience by caring for Peter's family. His grace will meet his servant's sacrifice at every point.

64

After sunset on the Sabbath, when normal activities resumed, many sick and demonized people gathered at the door of Peter's home requesting access to the famous healer. Jesus responded with compassion, laying hands on the sick and banishing demons with his powerful word. Matthew records the healings as the fulfillment of Isaiah 53:4: "He took our illnesses and bore our diseases." The fourth servant song of Isaiah (52:13—53:12) graphically describes the redemptive mission of the suffering Servant. The primary thrust of the Servant's work is to atone for his people's transgressions, iniquities and consequent guilt (53:5, 6, 8, 10, 11, 12). However, the wider effects of sin, in this case physical disease and psychological distress, are also alleviated in the Servant's atoning work (53:3-5). Matthew's holistic understanding of salvation—the restoration of heart, mind and body—emerges from his interpretation of the Servant's sacrifice in Isaiah's prophecy. To the question, then, is there physical healing in the vicarious death of Jesus, the answer must be a resounding affirmative.

Does this mean, however, as some maintain, that physical healing can be expected, or even demanded, in the present age? To this question we must answer firmly in the negative. First, the kingdom of God comes in two decisive moments, inaugurated through the death and resurrection of the suffering Servant and consummated at the return of the conquering King. Supernatural healing of all varieties signal the dawning of the messianic age (Isa 29:18; 32:3-4; 35:5-6), but the complete removal of the devastating physical, psychological and spiritual effects of sin await the new heaven and new earth (Rev 21:4; 22:1-5). One's theology of healing must reckon with the already-not yet character of God's rule during the period between the two advents of Christ. Second, Jesus prefers secrecy and withdrawal to open disclosure and public attention. He silences demonic testimony because he knows the intent is to stir up misguided notions of a Messiah who comes to work wonders or to pursue political agendas. Jesus knows that miracles have the capacity to detract from kingdom priorities. Third, while faith is often the bridge that brings the divine power to bear on the human extremity, it is not always the case. There is no mention here of the faith of Peter's mother-in-law. Sometimes Jesus performs a miracle to stimulate faith which is not present (Mark 4:35-41). Fourth, Jesus healed selectively, not universally. Just as God did in the days of Elijah and Elisha (Luke 4:25-27), Jesus chose to extend his power to certain individuals even when many others remained untouched (John 5:1-5).

⇨ Pray for a friend or loved one who has a physical malady and needs the special touch of the Healer. Be confident in God's power to heal now and trust his good purposes to be worked out even if the healing is delayed (until the resurrection of the body).

ENGAGEMENT AND WITHDRAWAL

(Matthew 4:23–25; Mark 1:35–39; Luke 4:42–44)

Growing numbers of people were coming to Jesus to be healed of their diseases or to be relieved of demonic oppression (Mark 1:28, 33). Jesus withdrew to be alone with the Father, refusing to allow the tyranny of the urgent to usurp what was of greater priority, preaching the good news of the kingdom to the unreached villages of Galilee. Jesus renewed his energies and recalibrated his priorities by rising early and going to a solitary place, most likely his beloved hills north of Lake Galilee, to spend time in prayer. Engagement and withdrawal was Jesus' pattern of ministry. Frenetic periods of evangelistic activity were punctuated by periods of prayer, study of the Scripture, and contemplation. Whether the pressure came from crowds impassioned by some of his most dramatic miracles (Mark 1:45; 2:12–13; 3:7–12; 5:20–21), the Pharisees enraged that he had healed a man on the Sabbath (Mark 3:6), his earthly family demanding his attention (Matt 12:46—13:1), or, as in this case, the disciples puzzled over his apparent disinterest in the expanding numbers, Jesus preferred quiet retreats where popular demands could dissolve into the Father's good plan. One can imagine Jesus responding to Peter's frustration—"Everyone is looking for you" (Mark 1:37)—with the words, "I know, that is why I had to get away." In prayer the hurried life became the mission-focused life.

Now he embarked with his four disciples on a preaching tour of the 240 towns and villages of Galilee, the first of three such itinerations (Luke 8:1; 9:6). The divine commission thrust him out to preach the kingdom (Mark 1:38; Luke 4:43). His authoritative preaching, authenticated by attendant miracles, accosted the whole personality with the demand for repentance. Jesus' demand was for voluntary submission to the lordship of God now, though the perfected kingdom would come in a glorious realm of God's unchallenged supremacy in the future. Matthew summarizes the threefold pattern of the first tour of Galilee: teaching in the synagogues; preaching to groups in the open air; healing diseases and exorcising demons. Jesus' fame has now spread to nearly every corner of Palestine and its adjacent territories: Syria to the north, Galilee, the Decapolis to the east and northeast, Jerusalem and Judea to the south, and Perea or Transjordan to the southeast. This forms the backdrop to the growing hostility of the religious leaders concerned not only about Jesus' influence over their Jewish subjects, but also for associating with Gentiles from areas considered ritually unclean and idolatrous.

Though his deliverance ministry touched a wide variety of afflictions— the demonized, paralytics, epileptics, those with painful maladies—all three Synoptics underscore that his central task is preaching, while the crowds' agenda is healing. The healings and exorcisms were in any case selective in range and provisional in duration. He responds with compassion to those who come to him, but does not launch a programmatic ministry of mass healing. Further, any healings that took place did not eliminate mortality or banish ongoing demonic activity from the land; at most they prolonged lives and provided present relief from debilitating conditions. We know from human experience that even the most faithful and prayerful of God's people can be attended by the most incapacitating of diseases in this life. Jesus' popularity, which will peak in this early phase of the Galilean ministry, will not last. Only those whose hearts are transformed by God's dynamic rule through faith and repentance will stay the course.

⇨ Are you faithfully investing quality time with God in prayer each day? Find that solitary place free from distraction where you can reenergize your spiritual batteries and refocus on the things that matter.

UNCONTAINABLE JOY OF A RESTORED OUTCAST

(Matthew 8:2–4; Mark 1:40–45; Luke 5:12–16)

A remarkable healing took place in one of the towns during the first tour of Galilee. A man tortured by the scourge of leprosy fell at Jesus' feet and begged for cleansing. No longer would he hide in quiet desperation. He acknowledged Jesus' ability to heal him while leaving the outcome to God's sovereign disposition: "Lord, if you will, you can make me clean." This was not a demand for a miracle but a humble plea for relief.

The terms used in the Bible, sometimes translated "leprosy," are generic for skin infections of various kinds. Detailed procedures are set forth in Leviticus 13–14 for regulating these skin diseases, which symptoms included sores, rashes, white spots, swelling, baldness, and boils. The priests were responsible for examination, quarantine, and pronouncement of the person ritually clean or unclean (Ch 13). There was an elaborate eight day procedure that was required for restoring a person to ceremonial purity after the skin disease was healed (Ch 14). While some of the cases of 'leprosy' in the Bible may have been skin diseases of shorter duration or where quarantine was not required (Num 12:1–5 [Miriam]; 2 Kgs 5:1–14 [Naaman]; Luke 17:11–19 [ten lepers]), others appear to be actual cases of clinical leprosy or Hansen's disease (2 Kgs 7:3–10 [Samaria lepers]; 2 Chr 26:19–21 [Uzziah]). The way his plea is framed ("if you will"), as if from someone who has often been disappointed and is now resigned to a cruel providence, his posture of prostration, and his uncontainable enthusiasm after the cure, may well indicate this man suffered, like the four lepers of Samaria or King Uzziah, of clinical leprosy. This horrific malady caused one's sensory nerve endings to be damaged so that the victim could no longer feel pain from heat or injury, thus leading to further destruction of hands, feet and limbs. Large spongy tumors formed on the face and body creating a repugnant deformity of one's features. Extended periods of severe pain and high fever were recurrent. Leprosy could last for decades with little relief. First century medicine, of course, did not yet recognize the nature of bacterial infections and often caused more harm than help (Mark 5:26). Along with the physical agony, the leper was banished from normal society due to the revolting appearance, ritual uncleanness, and the fear of the disease spreading. It could also signify the judgment of God for egregious sins, as in the case of Miriam and King Uzziah. All of this accounts for the personal degradation, social ostracism and spiritual alienation felt by lepers.

Moved by compassion, Jesus touched the man and pronounced him clean. Here was care for and identification with an untouchable. The healing was instantaneous. Then came the solemn charge. The former leper was to refrain from speaking about it and to obey the Levitical prescriptions for restoring his ceremonial purity "for a proof to them." Evidence to authenticate his authority as Messiah would be brought to priests in the Jerusalem temple so they could make a measured assessment according to Jewish law. Clearly Jesus is not attempting to conceal his identity, but to prevent the shallow enthusiasm of hordes of miracle seekers from drowning out his authoritative demand for kingdom-directed repentance. The man, however, blatantly disregarded his orders and published his good fortune far and wide. One should not judge too harshly the uncontainable joy of a man who has been rescued from such a blighted condition. Still, the messianic secret became an open one and Jesus was forced to withdraw from the crowds demanding his attention to a solitary place where he could pray.

⇨ All three Synoptic writers record that Jesus "touched" the leper. Why is this significant and what does it teach us about responding to the social outcasts of our world?

ON A COLLISION COURSE OVER A DIVINE CLAIM
(Matthew 9:1–2; Mark 2:1–5; Luke 5:17–20)

Jesus returned to Capernaum after his first tour of Galilee. The outcome was his growing reputation as a powerful preacher and healer of the sick. It is not surprising that the height of his popularity coincided with the first open confrontation with the Pharisees. Large numbers of people from Galilee, and as far south as Jerusalem, streamed to his residence, probably Peter's home. Among the visitors were Pharisees and teachers of the law (Luke 5:17, 21). The Pharisees upheld both the written law of Moses and the oral traditions which attempted to apply the ancient law to contemporary contexts. The scribes, the majority of whom were Pharisees, were trained biblical scholars and teachers. Jesus had much in common with these widely respected theologians. Like them, he affirmed the sovereignty of God, the reality of angels and demons, the moral accountability of people, the future resurrection of the dead, and final judgment. Some Jewish leaders even felt affinity with Jesus' teaching, like the Pharisee Nicodemus and his fellow member of the Sanhedrin, Joseph of Arimathea (John 3:2; 7:50–51; 19:38).

But there were crucial differences. The Pharisees and scribes taught a synergistic understanding of salvation, where faith and works, or grace and merit, combined to form the basis of a person's acquittal or condemnation at the final judgment. Jesus criticized their elevation of oral tradition to the level of Holy Scripture, effectively supplanting the power of the latter (Mark 7:9–13). He denounced their hypocritical legalism with a series of seven woes in some of the strongest language of his ministry (Matt 23). Clearly Jesus and the religious leaders were on a collision course.

Unable to enter the house because of the packed crowd, four men carrying a paralytic friend on a mat were determined to make their way to Jesus. They climbed to the roof by an external staircase and began to dig through the tiles made of brushwood or tree branches overlaid with mud and straw. Jesus recognized in their creativity and persistence an act of faith. Did this affirmation of faith include the paralyzed man, who otherwise remained wholly passive until his healing? The eyes of all present were surely cast upward as the branches and mud began to fall, a large hole opened up, and the paralyzed man was lowered to the feet of Jesus by ropes attached to the four corners of the mat. Then Jesus spoke tenderly, yet directly, to the paralytic: "Take heart, my son; your sins are forgiven" (Matt 9:2). The words seem out of place, an offer not suited to the need or occasion. But Jesus always sought out the heart of the matter, with a laser-like concentration on his mission. His very name signified that he has come to save his people from their sins (Matt 1:21; Luke 2:11). He is the Savior of the world (John 3:17; 4:42), the Lamb of God who takes away the sins of the world (John 1:29). The forgiveness of sins is the climactic promise of the new covenant which, by his death, he will ratify (Jer 31:34; Matt 26:28). The priest Zechariah celebrates the fulfillment of this promise (Luke 1:77) and his son prepares for it through his "baptism of repentance for the forgiveness of sins" (Luke 3:3). By issuing pardon for sin Jesus defines true healing as more than the restoration of physical wholeness. It is the removal of the barrier between man and God caused by man's disobedience of God's holy will. While the gift of forgiveness is far from the minds of the paralytic and his friends, Jesus offers far more than they could ask or imagine.

⇨ People often come to God to help them through immediate crises— physical illness, depression, financial setbacks, divorce. How can we address these felt needs, while pointing people to their greater need, forgiveness of sin and reconciliation with God?

AUTHORITY TO HEAL AND TO FORGIVE

(Matthew 9:3–8; Mark 2:6–12; Luke 5:21–26)

Jesus' initial words to the paralytic—"your sins are forgiven"—were designed to precipitate a conflict. Jesus was the master of holy provocation. The Pharisees immediately detect the force of his assertion and accuse him of blasphemy, for who can forgive sins but God? They accurately recognize that Jesus is staking a claim to a divine prerogative. In Jewish thought forgiveness of sins was a future declarative act of God at the final judgment. But Jesus offers forgiveness to this individual as a present gift, the projection of the future, as it were, back into history. This is the most exalted of claims and one that the Pharisees found deeply offensive. The defining issue that separates

Jesus from the religious leaders, then, the one which will seal his death, is not Sabbath-keeping, hand-washing, fasting, or association with Gentiles, but his unequivocal claim to be the Son of God (Mark 14:61–64). He leaves no middle ground, no room to maneuver. A person cannot maintain neutrality toward one who claims to possess the authority to forgive sins. Jesus forces his listeners to bow before him as Lord, revile him as a blasphemer, or dismiss him as a lunatic. His pronouncements are too direct and his claims too majestic to fit into the mouth of a benign ethical teacher or philosopher.

Murmurings among the legal scholars broke out immediately. Jesus, knowing their thoughts, launched a preemptive strike in the form of a rhetorical question. "Which is easier, to say, 'Your sins are forgiven,' or to say, 'Rise and walk'?" The expected answer is that obviously anyone can claim the authority to forgive sins, for that is an internal, spiritual transaction between a person and God. But a command to walk in this case demands a powerful miraculous healing of a helpless paralytic. The one command is merely verbal, the other demands that the speaker deliver or be unmasked before all as a fraud. In actuality, though, the declaration of forgiveness carries with it the claim of possessing a right reserved for God alone. The Pharisees grasped the implications when they asked, "Who can forgive sins but God alone?" The answer is no one can. There is thus irony in Jesus' words. His logic is that to forgive sin is the greater prerogative than to heal the sick; the listeners' logic is that to command healing is a more difficult pronouncement than to announce one's sins are forgiven. So Jesus adjusts his next action to fit their logic, but binds the miracle to its deeper meaning. Commanding the man to get up, take up his mat and return home, there is complete healing of the paralysis and restoration of the man's strength. He rose, took up his mat and went on his way praising God to the amazement of all. The healing was not just a display of power but an act to authenticate Jesus as the "Son of Man" exclusively endowed with the divine authority to forgive sins committed by people on earth. The more difficult prerogative (but lesser declaration)—to forgive sin—is authenticated by the power to heal the crippled man (the lesser prerogative but more difficult declaration).

As the narrative moves forward, it is clear the religious leaders are hardening in their opposition to one who has in recent days exorcised a demon, healed a fever, cleansed a leper, restored a paralytic and staked a claim to be the Son of Man with power to forgive sins. In the case of the crowd, shock and awe does not necessarily produce faith. In the case of the legal scholars, no amount of external proof has the power to undermine their theological presuppositions. They refuse to reexamine Jesus' claims even in the face of irrefutable evidence.

⇨ What are the implications from this incident, both positive and negative, for how we should assess modern deliverance ministries that emphasize external displays of power? Note two or three criteria which would distinguish the authentic from the spurious.

TAX COLLECTORS AND SINNERS

(Matthew 9:9–13; Mark 2:13–17; Luke 5:27–32)

Walking along the northern shore of the Sea of Galilee after a session of teaching, Jesus added a fifth member to his diverse team of core disciples. Levi, also called Matthew, was the tolls and customs tax official with a booth situated on the heavily traveled road that connected Damascus to the Mediterranean coastal highway south to Egypt. Tax collectors received commissions on the taxable products that passed through their territories. Their unquestioned power to assess the value of goods invited the opportunity for self-enrichment. Matthew's strategically placed office provided him a handsome income, judged by his ability to throw a lavish banquet for his friends (Luke 5:29). Because they were civil servants of their Roman overlords, tax collectors were despised by devout Jews and placed in the same class with brothel-keepers, even robbers. Tax collectors were not allowed to serve as judges or even witnesses in a civil trial. They were regarded as ceremonially unclean and often excommunicated from the synagogue.

Matthew was attending to his duties when Jesus passed his way. Any previous meeting between these two is unknown. Jesus' choice of a tax collector would certainly confirm the Pharisees in their initial assessment that Jesus was an impostor. What kind of Messiah would act like this? The first four disciples, practicing Jews, were almost certainly shocked. But Jesus' command to follow him, not a new set of legalistic prescriptions, was met by Matthew's willing abandonment of a lucrative career, present security and future prospects.

Matthew immediately cast his kingdom net into familiar waters and invited his fellow tax collectors, and other friends regarded from the Pharisaical point of view as "sinners," to his home to dine with Jesus. The pejorative label "sinner" was attached by religious Jews to any person outside the boundaries of acceptable behavior. It might be a person with a faulty moral record (Luke

7:37) or one who failed to follow God's will (John 9:31), but in this context signifies laxity toward the ceremonial rules surrounding table fellowship, a matter of grave importance to this strict sect. Jesus sat down at the feast and without hesitation enjoyed eating with those considered untouchables. The disciples were at a loss to answer the complaints of the Pharisees over their Lord's loose associations. Using the analogy of the physician whose concern is for the sick and not the healthy, Jesus defended his actions. The "sick" are the "sinners" who recognize their depravity and seek inner cleansing from the one who has claimed authority to forgive sins (Mark 2:10–11). Jesus' mission targeted sinners who enter God's liberating reign by means of repentance (Luke 5:32). Self-congratulatory "righteous ones" would find this gospel of the kingdom offensive. The Pharisees rightly understood that Jesus' offer of forgiveness to those who believe and repent, wholly unrelated to food laws, hand washing, and Sabbath observance, was a mortal threat to their very way of life.

In the presence of holiness Peter had fallen to his knees and cried out, "Depart from me, for I am a sinful man" (Luke 5:8). This is the sort of person, like those now reclining around the table, to whom Jesus could draw near. The label that became attached to him, "a friend of tax collectors and sinners" (Matt 11:19), was to Jesus a badge of honor. The four kosher disciples must now learn to enjoy the company of a former civil servant of Rome, whose heart like theirs had been transformed by his encounter with Jesus.

⇨ In your culture what types of people tend to be shunned or looked down on by 'polite and respectable' society? What needs to be done in the church to make such feel loved and welcomed, even as Jesus welcomed "sinners" into his presence?

THE WEDDING, THE NEW GARMENT AND THE NEW WINE
(Matthew 9:14–17; Mark 2:18–22; Luke 5:33–39)

The disciples of John the Baptist were puzzled that Jesus and his disciples did not practice regular fasting. Others who observed the practice of fasting by both John's disciples and the Pharisees also asked why Jesus' disciples "go on eating and drinking" (Luke 5:33 [NIV]). Fasting was associated with penitence or mourning. Although the Mosaic law only required fasting on the Day of Atonement (Lev 16:29), the Pharisees went further and fasted voluntarily on Mondays and Thursdays (Luke 18:12). John encouraged fasting as an expression of repentance in anticipation of the coming kingdom. Though their motives and outlook were very different, the Pharisees and John had this in common that they represented the old order. John was the final prophet who signaled the imminent end of the old with the coming of Messiah. The Pharisees were moral crusaders, attempting to rescue the old order from those who had corrupted it (Sadducees), as well as jealous guardians, seeking to enforce the old dispensation upon those who were advocating its replacement with the new (Jesus' disciples).

Jesus used three illustrations to explain what set his disciples apart from the others.

1. *Bridegroom*: In a Jewish wedding the bridegroom, attended by his friends, went after sunset to the home of the bride's family to fetch his beloved. She, with her bridesmaids, proceeded to the groom's home where the wedding feast was held. The next day the marriage was consummated. Then followed as much as seven days of festivity during which fasting and actions associated with mourning were proscribed.

   Jesus pressed home this familiar context to his inquirers. The presence of the bridegroom bestows joy. The guests at the wedding feast celebrate with eating and drinking. Only when the bridegroom is "taken away" from them—a veiled allusion to the Passion—will mourning be expressed by fasting. It is appropriate for John's disciples to fast because John's ministry is a call to repentance in advance of the King's arrival. But Jesus, the bridegroom, is now present with his betrothed people, a cause for joyous celebration.

2. *New Garment*: A patch from a new garment cannot be used to repair a tear in an old garment. Not only will the new garment be ruined, the tear in the old garment will get worse. Further, the new patch, not yet shrunk through washing, will not match the old fabric. In every way the old is incompatible with the new.

   Jesus' parable contrasts the character of the law with that of the kingdom. The preparatory stage of salvation history (law) has run its course and is giving way to the stage of fulfillment (inaugurated kingdom).

3. *New Wineskins*: If new wine is poured into brittle, worn out wineskins, already stretched to their limit by the old fermented wine, the skins will burst and the wine will be spilled. New wine must be put into new wineskins, if its contents are to be preserved and enjoyed, for example, at a wedding feast.

The parable means that new truth is to be accompanied by new forms for expressing that truth. Luke adds that one's acquired taste for old fermented wine makes the new wine taste awful (5:39). So the tenacious defenders of the old era, the Pharisees, find Jesus' revolutionary offer of the kingdom distasteful.

⇨ Read Jeremiah 31:31–34. In what ways is the new covenant, prophesied by Jeremiah, "not like" the old covenant enacted at Sinai? What are its fresh features? How can these three extended metaphors be applied to contemporary Christian attitudes and behavior?

5

Lord of the Sabbath

A PARALYZED BODY AND MIND

(John 5:1–14)

JESUS WENT UP TO Jerusalem to celebrate a "feast of the Jews" (5:1), most likely Tabernacles in *late September, AD 28*. Now a series of controversies surrounding Jesus' attitude toward their Sabbath traditions will turn the already hostile Pharisees and scribes (John 4:1; Luke 5:21) into his implacable enemies. North of the temple complex, near the Sheep Gate where sheep were sold for sacrifice, was the pool of Bethesda, actually twin pools with a colonnade on each of the four sides and a fifth in the area between the pools.

A large variety of disabled people lay alongside the pool, drawn to the supposed healing power of the spring-fed waters. An ancient tradition, later added to the biblical text, attributed healings to the angel of the Lord who from time to time would stir up the waters. The first person to reach the rippling waters would be restored. Out of the many, Jesus selected one man, an invalid of thirty eight years, to show his compassion and power. He first probed his inner condition: "Do you want to be healed?" From the man's answer it is clear that his hope for a cure has long passed. Not only is his body irreversibly damaged, but the monotonous years of sitting and watching, praying and hoping, all to no effect has left him with a paralyzed will. He blames his condition, whether honestly or not, on the ability of others to get to the stirring waters first because he lacks assistance. Not only is this a selective healing, Jesus chooses to restore a man who seems devoid of faith altogether.

Jesus' triple command—"Get up, take up your bed, and walk"—brings instantaneous healing and the restored man obeys. But before the Jewish

76

teachers can get there to interrogate the beggar who has been a fixture at the pool and is now walking around, Jesus disappears into the large crowds celebrating the feast. Remarkably, when the authorities do arrive they are coldly indifferent to the restored ability of the lame man to walk and show little interest in verifying a miracle which the Old Testament specifies as a messianic sign (Isa 35:6). Their sole concern is that the healing took place on the Sabbath. Augustine comments: "They sought darkness from the Sabbath more than light from the miracle." Once again Jesus has chosen a propitious moment to trigger a principled clash with the religious leaders.

The Pharisees had developed over several centuries an expansive network of rules that clarified in minute detail forbidden and acceptable activities on the Sabbath day. Later recorded in two tractates of the Mishnah, Shabbath (Sabbath) and Erubin (Limitations), thirty-nine classes of ordinary agricultural and domestic work, totaling 1,521 activities, are proscribed. In the present case, the healed man's carrying of his pallet technically violated the rule against "taking out aught from one domain to another." In a series of conflicts Jesus will peel off the encrusted layers of human tradition and recapture the original divine intention for observing the holy day. But before that, in this first encounter, he will make a series of elevated declarations that set him apart as the authoritative interpreter of the Sabbath command.

Some time later Jesus found the healed man in the temple court, this time not to beg but assuredly with a thanksgiving offering for his new ability to walk. He issued a warning: "Sin no more, that nothing worse may happen to you" (5:14). Jesus repeatedly disavowed linking specific sins to particular afflictions (John 9:1–3). Rather, the admonition seeks to turn the man's attention from his physical wellness to his spiritual deprivation. Unless he repents and surrenders to the lordship of God, a far worse fate will befall him than paralysis, namely, eternal judgment.

⇨ In what ways do we see the same phenomenon today where man-made rules obscure and obstruct the pure teaching of God's Word?

GIVER OF LIFE AND ARBITER OF DESTINY
(John 5:15–30)

The healed man openly identified Jesus as his healer which led to increased persecution from the religious leaders who considered Jesus a Sabbath-breaker. Jesus defended his conduct by expounding his exclusive relationship to God the Father. This is one of the most profound and elevated statements of the deity of Jesus found in the four Gospels. In his opening statement, "My Father is working until now, and I am working," Jesus places himself on a par with God (5:17). Jesus' healing of the paralytic is in tandem with the work of the Father who continues his unceasing redemptive activity even on the Sabbath day. His accusers grasp the implications of his words and now move from the charge of Sabbath-breaking to the charge of blasphemy (5:18; cf. Luke 5:21; John 8:58–59; 10:33). In a bold set of axioms, Jesus establishes his authority as rightful interpreter of the Sabbath in his oneness with God the Father in both nature and action.

1. *The Son acts in perfect concert with the Father* (5:19–20, 30).

   The incarnate Son acts in total dependence on his perfect knowledge of the Father's will. Their communion in love creates the unity of action of these two persons. Even "greater works" than sign-miracles of quality (John 2:11), distance (John 4:54), and time (John 5:9) will show this unity, a reference to the cross, the supreme work where Father and Son are glorified (John 12:27–28; 13:31–32). In all he does Jesus seeks to please the Father who sent him to complete the redemptive task. The initial paragraph begins and ends with this *inclusio* of the Son's unity with the Father (5:19, 30).

2. *The Son shares with the Father the prerogative of bestowing eternal life now and raising the dead in the future* (5:21, 25–26).

   The entire present-future continuum ("an hour is coming, and is now here") of life-giving power that belongs exclusively to God is shared equally by Father and Son. Both are sovereign in their elective purposes. These two persons are co-possessors and co-sources of eternal life now and resurrection life in the future.

3. *The judgment of people has been entrusted by the Father to the Son of Man* (5:22, 27).

   Just as the Father has committed without reservation all things pertaining to the redemptive mission into the capable hands of his Son (John 3:35), so the judgment of mankind has been entrusted to the Son. This fulfills Daniel's prophecy where the Ancient of Days, seated in his courtroom with the books of final human accountability opened before him, bestows authority, glory and sovereign power to the Son of

Man who then receives the worship of the nations and the scepter of an everlasting kingdom (Dan 7:9–14). His appointment as final judge of the living and the dead is the Father's highest seal of his Son's equality with him (Matt 25:31; Acts 10:42; 17:31).

4. *Father and Son are co-recipients of the honor accorded only to God* (5:23).

   As there is no rivalry in the Godhead, the Father delights in mankind's ascribing honor to the Son. In the same way, the Son delights in bringing glory to his Father (John 13:31–32; Phil 2:10–11). To honor one is to honor the other.

5. *The Son of God is the arbiter of human destiny* (5:24, 28–29).

   By believing Jesus' message that the Father sent him to be the Savior, a person is transferred from condemnation before God to eternal life with God. It is the Son's unmistakable voice that will call all human beings from their graves to the final accounting.

⇨ Remember these truths as you approach God the Father in prayer with audacious boldness through the name of his beloved Son in whom he delights.

INCREDIBLE CLAIMS VERIFIED BY CREDIBLE WITNESSES

(John 5:31–47)

Jesus' claim to share the divine prerogatives of life-giving, resurrection and judgment are backed by multiple testimonies. A witness is a committed advocate who stands unequivocally on the side of another to endorse their character and promote their interests. Five witnesses are cited to establish the credibility of his self-testimony.

1. *The Father's testimony is decisive and is the court of final appeal* (5:31–32, 37–38).

   Jesus accommodates his defense to the legal principle of Deuteronomy 19:15b: "Only on the evidence of two witnesses or of three witnesses shall a charge be established." Though Jesus' self-testimony is truthful because it is in full accord with the Father's testimony about him (John 8:14–18), it possesses no legal validity in the Jewish context

(8:13). Rather, it is the Father's witness that supports Jesus' self-claims. At the inaugural event of his public ministry, the Father summoned Israel to pay careful attention to the beloved Son of his good pleasure (Matt 3:17). However, the nation's leaders stand in solidarity with their forefathers who proved over the long course of history to be insensitive to the voice, appearance and written word of Yahweh. The triple reference here—his voice, his form, his word—recalls the Lord's terrifying descent on Mt. Sinai to give his people the law (Exod 19:16–25). The Old Testament is a record of covenant violation and now the pattern of disobedience continues with rejection of the promised Redeemer.

2. *John the Baptist was a burning lamp that provided light for a brief time* (5:33–35).

   John testified to the preeminent One who will baptize with the Spirit and with fire, the Lamb of God who takes away the sins of the world, the Son of God, the bridegroom and Messiah (John 1:29–34; 3:27–30). The Jerusalem leaders sent a delegation to the Jordan to inquire of John and, though initially aroused by his preaching, were unmoved by his call to repentance and rejected his witness to Jesus. They receded from the exposure of the light (John 3:19–21).

3. *The works of Jesus testify to his commission from the Father* (5:36).

   While his miraculous "signs" disclose his messianic authority, it is the accomplishment of the Father's singular "work" (John 4:34), chief among his "works" (pl.), that both defines and validates his divine commission. The journey that culminates at Golgotha is the redemptive task whose fulfillment is his very sustenance (John 17:4; 19:30). The plural "signs" reveal his supernatural power; the singular "work" embodies his sacrificial obedience.

4. *The Holy Scriptures testify of the coming of the Servant-King* (5:39–44)

   Though the Pharisees and scribes diligently search Scripture, their knowledge does not translate into insight. They build a law-based righteousness around a misunderstanding of texts such as Leviticus 18:5 ("You shall therefore keep my statutes and my rules; if a person does them, he shall live by them."), but fail to see that their righteous acts are as a "filthy rags" (Isa 64:6 [NIV]) and that their only refuge is the vicarious sacrifice of the suffering Servant (Isa 52:13—53:12). If they would remove their nomistic lenses, they would discover in the holy writings abundant testimony to Jesus (Luke 24:27, 44). Yet the more they study, the more they refuse to learn.

5. *Moses witnesses of Jesus and will stand as the accuser of those who reject him* (5:45–47).

Since the Torah prescribed their way of life, the Jewish scholars took pride in being disciples of the great law-giver (John 9:28–29). But Moses gave ample testimony to the coming Messiah in his five books (Gen 49:10; Exod 12:21; Lev 16:22; Num 24:17; Deut 18:15).

⇨ The Lord honors one who "trembles at my word" (Isa 66:2, 5). As you read God's Word, be careful not to replicate those who studied assiduously, but failed to hear his voice.

LORD OF THE SABBATH

(Matthew 12:1–8; Mark 2:23–28; Luke 6:1–5)

The hungry disciples began to pluck the heads of grain and to eat them as they passed through the fields in northern Galilee. Luke adds that they rubbed the grain in their hands to extract the kernels (6:1). This probably occurred in late Spring when barley and then wheat are harvested. The action itself was permitted in the Jewish law (Deut 23:25). However, the Pharisees quickly protested because the act was committed on the Sabbath. They interpreted the plucking as "reaping," and probably the rubbing as "threshing," two of the thirty-nine classes of work forbidden in rabbinical tradition (m. Shabbath 7:2). Yet even the rabbis lamented the burden created by centuries of scribal accretion: "The rules about the Sabbath, Festal offerings, and Sacrilege are as mountains hanging by a hair, for Scripture is scanty and the rules are many" (m. Hagigah 1:8).

Jesus turned to the Old Testament narrative to remind the Pharisees that when David and his men came to the village of Nob, the high priest Ahimelech fed the men with the consecrated bread which had just been replaced on the Sabbath by fresh loaves (1 Sam 21:1–6). Though this was a technical infringement of the law, since the priests had exclusive right to eat the "bread of the Presence" (Exod 25:30; Lev 24:9), concern for the physical needs of the famished refugees superseded the letter of the law. Further, Jesus argued, the priests themselves formally violate the Sabbath command against work by performing their cultic duties in the temple on the holy day (Matt

12:5). The Mosaic legislation required the priests to offer certain sacrifices on the Sabbath in addition to the daily offerings (Num 28:9–10). There are, then, biblical qualifications of the strict Sabbath command (Exod 20:8–11), which take into account the context and motivation of one's actions, factors which the Pharisees failed to consider in their narrow proof-texting censure of the disciples.

But the Pharisees saw it differently. To their way of thinking Jesus was a libertarian who underestimated the weakness of human nature and whose precedents would create a slippery slope to the reduced morality of the encroaching Gentile world. They assumed the role of holy defenders of God's law against this subversive Galilean rabbi whose disciples were reflecting his own contempt for the fourth commandment. Jesus looked deeper and sought to recover the original intent of the Sabbath ordinance: "The Sabbath was made for man, not man for the Sabbath" (Mark 2:27). In other words, the original divine purposes for the Sabbath, in imitation of God's creation rest of satisfaction, were renewal for man's body and nurture of man's soul in undistracted worship of God (Gen 2:2–3). Just as mercy prevails over animal sacrifice (Hos 6:6), so in the divine economy human need takes priority over technical compliance. This is why healing a paralytic or feeding hungry people was not only permissible, but in fact compelling action for one to undertake on the Sabbath, because it enhanced life and restored hope for desperate human beings. Hosea's principle of mercy over sacrifice (6:6), heart over tradition, was one that Jesus would often cite in debates with legalists (Matt 9:13).

Jesus ultimately appealed, however, to his own authority as Lord of the Sabbath to support his interpretation (Mark 2:28). His definitive appeal unmasks the central issue at stake between him and his detractors: not only have they lost sight of the deeper intent of the law, they have also failed to recognize the One who alone possesses the authority to unlock its meaning.

⇨ What is your attitude to the biblical principle of the Sabbath? Is it a binding obligation that restricts your freedom or a liberating opportunity for rest and worship?

SABBATH FOR MAN, NOT MAN FOR THE SABBATH

(Matthew 12:9–14; Mark 3:1–6; Luke 6:6–11)

The setting of a third conflict over the Sabbath was the Capernaum synagogue where Jesus and his disciples had come to worship. There was present in the service a man with a shriveled hand. The Pharisees initiated the controversy by asking Jesus if it was lawful to heal on the Sabbath. All three Synoptic authors disclose that the question was not an honest inquiry, but an attempt to bait Jesus into acting in such a way that they could produce evidence that he was a Sabbath breaker. Jesus turned their question back on them, but framed it as a moral rather than a legal choice: "Is it lawful on the Sabbath to do good or to do harm, to save life or to kill?" The Pharisees remained silent, but if forced to answer they would have argued that the healing could wait until the next day. In their tradition aid could be offered on the Sabbath only if it involved an immediate threat to life: "Whenever there is doubt whether life is in danger, this overrides the Sabbath" (m. Yoma 8.6). Healing of a crippled man could wait; a more urgent concern was the discrediting of their opponent.

Jesus was angered by such callousness of heart. He rebuked them for caring more for a sheep, which they would rescue on the Sabbath if it fell into a pit, than for a fellow human being in distress (Matt 12:11–12). He was not only angered but also "deeply distressed" (Mark 3:5a [NIV]). His anger was tempered with godly sorrow that his opponents seemed to have lost their capacity to feel the sufferings of others. Judgmental zeal that demanded compliance to a set of external standards had produced a heartless insensitivity toward human need of terrifying proportions.

Jesus commanded the man to stretch out his hand. Upon his obedience, the hand was completely restored to its normal function. Jesus did more than rescue one individual from a debilitating handicap. As Lord of the Sabbath, he freed the Sabbath from the shackles of binding legalism and restored it to its pristine biblical purpose. The Sabbath was designed by the Creator to be a day of rest, worship, renewal, joy and praise. The Sabbath was created to enhance and liberate, not to bind and constrict, the physical, emotional and spiritual dimensions of a person's life. In all three Sabbath controversies, Jesus acts in accord with the foundational principle: "The Sabbath was made for man, not man for the Sabbath" (Mark 2:27). Giving a hopeless paralytic the ability to walk, hungry disciples a meal of grain, and a crippled man a restored hand were worthy endeavors on a day designed to enhance man's praise of a gracious God.

The Pharisees responded not with joyful amazement, but with murderous fury. This conservative religious party that despised Roman rule with all of its corrupting influences formed a strange alliance with the Herodians, a political party in alliance with the secular authorities. In this case, adversaries became friends drawn in fraternity against a common enemy whose death they plotted (Mark 3:6). Ultimately the face off between Jesus and the legal scholars was about more than the concrete disputes of recent days—table fellowship with Gentiles, hand washing, fasting and the Sabbath. The heart of the conflict is Jesus' self-testimony. He claims to be the forgiver of sins (Mark 2:10), the Son of God equal to the Father (John 5:17–18), the Lord of the Sabbath (Mark 2:28). Violation of behavioral regulations could be punished by exclusion from the synagogue; assertion of divine titles and prerogatives was blasphemy and deserved capital punishment.

⇨ As you worship on the Christian Sabbath, the Lord's Day (Rev 1:10), contemplate what good deed you can do for another that will cause them to thank and praise God. Then translate your worship into service.

THE SERVANT OF GOD'S DELIGHT

(Matthew 12:15–21; Mark 3:7–12)

With a murder plot developing, another harbinger of the coming Passion, Jesus withdraws to the lake for a true Sabbath rest. But people troubled by demons and afflicted with diseases always find a way to locate him. Mark records the extent of those who gathered around him by the Sea of Galilee—from all areas of Palestine, as well as Idumea (S), Perea (E), Tyre and Sidon (NW). With compassion he heals and exorcises while commanding those who are restored to strict secrecy. His timetable will not be thrown off course by plotting Pharisees or by adoring crowds.

As the initial phase of the Galilean ministry draws to a close, Matthew, in characteristic fashion, finds in the healing ministry of Jesus the fulfillment of Isaiah 42:1–4. Part of the opening address, combined with a phrase from Psalm 2:7, was quoted by God the Father at Jesus' baptism: "This is my beloved Son, with whom I am well pleased" (Matt 3:17). He introduces the two phases of the mission of the Servant-Son. Jesus is the Servant who comes to die a redemptive death (Isa 42:1). Having completed the work of redemption,

Jesus takes his seat at the right hand of the Father where he is invested with royal authority as King and Lord (Ps 2:7). Isaiah's four servant songs (42:1–7; 49:1–7; 50:4–11; 52:13—53:12), which begin here, picture with increasing clarity the graphic details of the Servant's Passion.

1. *Isaiah 42:1–7*: Yahweh introduces his chosen servant as the Spirit-endowed emissary who tenderly stoops to free those locked in the dungeon of spiritual darkness. The universal scope of the servant's mission captures the prophet's imagination: justice for the nations (42:1), hope for the islands (42:4), light for the Gentiles (42:6). In spite of intense opposition, the servant does not cry out or quarrel, but trusts in God. He is gentle in heart to impart the kingdom to his disciples. He is not harsh toward the weak who are like bruised reeds or smoldering wicks, but makes known his salvation to child-like hearts (Matt 11:27–29). The justice he brings is the present gift of righteousness to the repentant who hope in his name.

2. *Isaiah 49:1–7*: The second song describes a servant who is at once "Israel" (49:3), and yet who testifies of his dependence on God's strength as he undertakes his appointed task to restore Israel (49:4–5) and to bring salvation to the ends of the earth (49:6). In other words, the suffering servant acts like the ideal Israel, fulfilling the promise of salvation to the nations that the empirical nation could not and would not mediate. The servant's weakness (v. 4a), dependency (v. 5) and rejection (v. 7) anticipate the fuller exposition of his suffering in the fourth song.

3. *Isaiah 50:4–11*: The third song develops further the themes of the earlier descriptions of the servant: his suffering (50:6), determination to complete his appointed role (50:7), final vindication (50:8–9), and word of salvation for those who dwell in spiritual darkness (50:10).

4. *Isaiah 52:13—53:12*: The fourth song paints the sufferings of the servant in its truest colors, deeper and darker than the muted shades of the earlier depictions. He suffers appalling humiliation and is vindicated by God (52:13–15). In a careful progression the song laments the servant's lowly demeanor and career of sorrows (53:1–3), expounds his death as a penal substitute for transgressors (53:4–6), marvels at his silence before his accusers (53:7–9), and celebrates the justification of many (53:10–12). The one whose highest pleasure is to fulfill the divine will for his life (53:10c) is the servant of God's delight (42:1).

Early Galilean Ministry II:
To Sermon on the Mount

1. To **Jerusalem** for Feast of Tabernacles
2. Return to **Galilee**: grain fields and synagogues
3. Withdrawal to *Sea of Galilee*
4. Calling of apostles and the Sermon on the Mount

GALILEE

④

Capernaum

②

Magdala

Cana •

Sea of Galilee

③

Tiberius •

• Sepphoris

• Nazareth

Mt. Tabor

①

• Nain

Jordan River

Hill of Moreh

①

SAMARIA

To Jerusalem ↓

Jordan River

⇨ Rehearse the central themes of the four servant songs of Isaiah and recall how the Gospels are *"Passion narratives with extended introductions."*

6

Sermon on the Mount

Charter of Kingdom Citizenship

TWELVE PILLARS OF THE NEW ISRAEL

(Mark 3:13–19; Luke 6:12–16)

URING THE *EARLY GALILEAN* period of ministry Jesus' fame with the
wider population grew and reached its peak when the crowds gathered to hear his Sermon on the Mount (Mark 3:7–12; Matt 7:28—8:1). The
Sabbath controversies, however, caused the initial misgivings of the Pharisees
to deepen into active opposition (John 5:18; Mark 3:6). As a result, Jesus began to concentrate his energies more and more away from the ambivalent
multitudes to the training of his committed disciples. The kingdom community began with the call of the four fishermen, then became five with the
addition of the tax collector, Levi. Now the time has come to fill out the company of the committed. A night of prayer preceded this momentous decision
(Luke 6:12). He formally commissioned twelve men to be his "apostles," that
is "ones sent forth" to proclaim the dynamic rule he was inaugurating (Luke
6:13). He chose "twelve" because the apostles are the foundation-pillars of
the new messianic community, replacing the twelve patriarchs of the tribes
of Israel. Here is the beginning of the eschatological people of God, the new
Israel, the church that Jesus will build (Matt 16:18; 18:17).

The appointment had a threefold purpose: (i) to be with him, that is,
for fellowship and instruction; (ii) to preach the dawning of the kingdom in
Jesus Messiah; (iii) to cast out demons which authenticated the authoritative
proclamation (Mark 3:14–15). Thus their appointment was to be with him to
listen and to learn, to call people to submission to God's rule, and to engage
in spiritual warfare against the counterfeit kingdom of Satan. Jesus rests his

legacy with a tiny group of individuals who as his "sent ones" will proclaim the kingdom to the nations, and enlist others as laborers in the harvest (Matt 9:37–38). Jesus' words and works recorded in the canonical Gospels reveal a leadership-training program designed to equip those who would in turn equip others. Surveying the whole, one can identify *three central lessons* that Jesus imparted with repetitive intentionality to equip the disciples as kingdom stewards.

1. *Kingdom harvest through sacrifice*: As a vision caster, Jesus gave his disciples the perspective of an advancing kingdom that, though small in its beginnings, will yield a great harvest among the nations. The harvest will be reaped through fearless proclamation in the midst of persecution. Jesus trained leaders who could endure suffering because they expected lasting fruit to come from their labors and because they believed that beyond their sacrifices awaited a glorious kingdom.

2. *Kingdom righteousness through freedom*: The righteousness of God's rule was a different kind of righteousness than that taught by the Pharisees (Matt 5:20). Jesus aimed at interior reconstruction rather than conformity to a set of external standards. Heart transformation could take place only by first removing the binding shackles of tradition and restoring one's direct interface with the penetrating vitality of Holy Scripture. As the heart and mind were invaded by God's Word a real, not contrived, righteousness could spring forth.

3. *Kingdom greatness through servanthood*: Elevation in the kingdom of God would be like no other model of leadership the disciples had ever encountered. Here was a kingdom where hearts governed by child-like dependence would rule, and where the ladder of success is achieved not by ascending but by descending its rungs. They must imitate the Son of Man who came not to be served but to serve.

⇨ The motto of the training school of Jesus is: "To know him and to make him known." Are you learning the three core lessons of sacrifice, inner holiness, and servanthood?

UNLIKELY CHOICES FOR A LEGACY

(Mark 3:13–19; Luke 6:12–16)

There are four lists of the twelve apostles in the New Testament:

Matt 10:2–4	*Mark 3:16–19*	*Luke 6:14–16*	*Acts 1:13b*
Simon, Peter	Simon, Peter	Simon, Peter	Peter
Andrew, brother	James, of Zebedee	Andrew, brother	John
James, of Zebedee	John, brother	James	James
John, brother	Andrew	John	Andrew
Philip	Philip	Philip	Philip
Bartholomew	Bartholomew	Bartholomew	Thomas
Thomas	Matthew	Matthew	Bartholomew
Matthew	Thomas	Thomas	Matthew
James, of Alphaeus	James, of Alphaeus	James, of Alphaeus	James, of Alphaeus
Thaddaeus	Thaddaeus	Simon the Zealot	Simon the Zealot
Simon the Cananaen	Simon the Cananaen	Judas, of James	Judas, of James
Judas Iscariot	Judas Iscariot	Judas Iscariot	(Matthias)

From the lists we note the following special points:

1. Simon Peter, who will become the "rock" of the church (Matt 16:18), is always listed first. He assumes the role of spokesman for the group, the *primus inter pares*, first among equals.

2. James and John, sons of Zebedee, are always listed together. Along with Peter, they comprise a special group of three within the twelve (Mark 5:37; 9:2; 14:33). Judged by their ambitious actions and fiery reactions (Mark 9:38; 10:35–40; Luke 9:54), the ascription "sons of thunder" was appropriate.

3. Judas Iscariot, the betrayer, is last in every list. He was also chosen in answer to prayer (Luke 6:12). Thus the betrayal of Jesus was an evil action for which Judas was responsible, but one ordained by God to fulfill salvation history (Mark 14:21).

4. Philip/Bartholomew and Thomas/Matthew are mentioned together in the Synoptic lists. They may comprise two more sets of brothers (Thomas is called Didymus [John 11:16], meaning "twin"), in addition to Peter/

Andrew and James/John. Alternatively, James of Alphaeus is brother to Matthew (Mark 2:14: Levi, of Alphaeus). Apparently Thaddaeus is the same as Judas, of James. Bartholomew may be another name for Nathaniel (John 1:45).

In summary, Jesus deliberately set the apostles in a relational setting with all of its potential for tension, conflict and personal growth. This was a most unusual collection of individuals. The one labeled the group's "rock" would emerge as a talkative reactionary. Two explosive brothers would be pushed forward by an ambitious mother and incite the jealousy of the others. Simon possessed a record as an anti-Roman zealot, while Matthew was a former civil servant of Rome. All were Galileans, except Judas Iscariot. There were possibly as many as four sets of brothers, providing ample occasion for sibling rivalries. James and John were first cousins of Jesus. From a human perspective, the chosen twelve seem unlikely material to form a unified company. Here are the people in whom Jesus invested his life and upon whom he rested his legacy.

⇨ Are you, like Jesus, investing in faithful men and women who can become equippers of others (2 Tim 2:2)? How much does prayer factor in your choice of people to invest in?

THE GREATEST SERMON EVER PREACHED
(Matthew 5:1–2; Luke 6:17–19)

Jesus proclaimed the dawning of the kingdom of heaven in a context charged with religious and political ideologies. The Pharisees were the dominant religious party and had forged a faith-works synergism, one that stressed God's gracious election of Israel, as well as rigorous obedience to the Mosaic law. The biblical teachings were supplemented by oral traditions that had grown over the four centuries since Malachi to massive proportions and, in practical effect, had achieved canonical status. The ordinary people of the land, especially in Galilee, were less strict in their adherence to rabbinical traditions, but fervent in their expectation of a Messiah who would free Israel from her Gentile oppressors and cleanse the temple from its corrupt priesthood. Thus the atmosphere was swirling with legalism, ethnocentrism, and socio-political activism. Into this arena Jesus declared the rule of God that would accost the entire personality of an individual and a community. He begins to equip his disciples by first giving priority to the heart as the governing force behind all authentic kingdom activity. Heart transformation would occur not by fencing in sinful human tendencies with extrabiblical norms, but by removing the binding yoke of tradition and laying bare the soul to the penetrating force of the unencumbered Word of God. Righteousness would grow from within through new covenantal freedom, defined not as the right to do as one pleases, but the Spirit-energized ability to reflect the very character of God. This is the message of the Sermon on the Mount, the charter of life under God's rule.

After the formal appointment of the twelve apostles to kingdom ministry, Jesus now turns his attention to reeducating them in the transformational values of kingdom citizenship. The *Sermon on the Mount* is primarily directed to the disciples (Matt 5:2; Luke 6:20), though by the end of the two or three day period of teaching large crowds have gathered in the hills north of Lake Galilee to listen in (Luke 6:17–19; Matt 7:28—8:1). The address must be interpreted in light of Jesus' kingdom theology (Matt 4:17, 23): the already-not yet rule of God that bears its force on the deepest recesses of the human heart. Out of this transforming dialectic springs a life of moral excellence and sacrificial service. Jesus' radical demands seek to reshape the entire personality. Its standards reflect the very perfection of God himself (Matt 5:48) and thus can only be perfectly fulfilled when the kingdom reaches its fullness. The sermon assaults all those who have submitted to God's reign with the cold fact that they are lawbreakers whose wretchedness can only be healed by divine grace. Nevertheless, triumphant kingdom living becomes the definite, albeit provisional, experience of all whose broken and contrite spirits "hunger and thirst for righteousness" (5:6), a righteousness not measured by external criteria but one that is aligned with the character of a holy God (5:20).

The Sermon on the Mount is but one-half of Jesus' full-orbed exposition of kingdom or new covenant living. Its necessary complement is the *Upper Room Discourse* given the night before his death (John 13:31—16:33). The earlier sermon establishes the standard of moral and spiritual virtue toward which kingdom citizens aspire; the latter discourse discloses the resource through whom righteousness can be, at least provisionally, attained—the Paraclete or Holy Spirit who now takes up settled residence in the heart of the believer (John 14:17). Just as two wings are necessary for the eagle to soar to majestic heights, so the kingdom citizen needs both the Spirit and the defining charter to live life successfully under God's rule.

⇨ Ask God for a mind to perceive and a heart to receive the wonderful truths of the Sermon on the Mount as you embark on its careful study.

TRUE HAPPINESS

(Matthew 5:3–12)

The sermon begins with a portrait of the "blessed" person. The eight beatitudes (from the opening refrain *Beati* in the Latin Vulgate) exhibit a threefold structure. First is the pronouncement "Blessed," meaning fortunate or happy because this kind of person is favored by God. Second, there is a descriptive qualifier. Each of these qualities focuses on the heart, the controlling center of the personality. The truly blessed person is one whose interior life aligns with the character of God. Third, there is the supportive conjunction ("for") followed by a benefit or reward. In the reward clause the present tense verbs in the first and final beatitudes form an *inclusio* around the future tense verbs of the middle six beatitudes. The rewards, then, are bestowed as gifts of the present-future kingdom. Each promise confirms rather than provides the reason for the blessedness. The language is declarative, but implicitly exhortational. These are the character attributes Jesus would have his disciples pursue.

The eight qualities are now listed with a descriptive definition supported by related texts:

1. *Poor in spirit*: a contrite person who has been crushed of self-reliance and who, recognizing their spiritual bankruptcy, places their complete trust in God's all-sufficient grace (Isa 57:15; 66:2).

2. *Mourn*: godly sorrow that grieves over one's personal sins leading to repentance and fully empathizes in the struggles and losses of others (Ps 119:136; John 11:33–36; Rom 12:15; 2 Cor 7:9–11).

3. *Meek*: gentle consideration and treatment of others, never harsh, tyrannical or vengeful (Ps 37:11; Matt 11:29; Jas 3:13).

4. *Hunger and thirst for righteousness*: deep longing for and active pursuit of personal ethical uprightness, as well as the triumph of social justice (Ps 42:1–2; Mic 6:8; Matt 6:33).

5. *Merciful*: compassion for the needy and forgiveness for the guilty, including those who sin against you (Exod 34:6; Ps 72:13; Hos 6:6; Mic 6:8; Matt 6:12; 9:13; 12:7).

6. *Pure in heart*: inner moral purity, not just ceremonial cleanness, nurtured by an undivided focus upon God and his kingdom (Ps 24:3–4; 73:1; Matt 6:33).

7. *Peacemaker*: ambassadors of vertical peace with God through spreading of the gospel of peace and proclamation of the Prince of peace (Isa 9:6–7; 52:7; 2 Cor 5:20), and agents for horizontal reconciliation between people through the removal of strife and bitterness (Ps 34:14; Rom 14:19; Jas 3:17–18).

8. *Persecuted for righteousness' sake*: courageous stand for God's truth and patient, even joyful, endurance of hostility that arises from one's identification with Jesus, amplified in vv. 11–12 (Acts 5:41–42; 1 Pet 3:14; 4:12–19).

The rewards are provisionally received in the present life, but reach their full realization in the consummated kingdom following the return of the glorious Son of Man. In the new heaven and the new earth God's people will receive the kingdom (first and last beatitudes), be comforted, inherit the earth, attain full righteousness, be shown mercy, see God, and be called the sons of God (Rev 21:1–9, 22–26; 22:1–5). In summary, Jesus exhorted his leaders-in-training to give first priority to their interior life. These attributes would transform them into blessed ones and bring inestimable rewards both now and in the future.

⇨ Read Galatians 5:22–23 and James 3:17–18. Compare the eight beatitudes with the nine-fold "fruit of the Spirit" and the nine qualities of the "wisdom from above."

BLESSED REVERSALS OF FORTUNE

(Luke 6:20–26)

Unlike Matthew's eight beatitudes, Luke records four blessings and four woes, with the rewards stated in the second person plural of direct address. Promise and warning, then, bring the moral symmetry of confidence and reverence, trust without presumption, to bear on those entering God's kingdom. The adjective "blessed" (or happy, fortunate) is applied elsewhere in Luke to those who willingly submit to the authority of King Jesus and thus make their zealous pursuit those character qualities that reflect his rule in their lives (Luke 1:45; 11:28; 12:37–38; 14:14–15). Luke is drawing on the usage of the same word in the Septuagint, the Greek Old Testament, to describe the pious or godly person who trusts in the Lord and comes under his loving care (Ps 1:1; 2:12; 32:1–2; 34:8; 41:1; 84:4–5, 12; 94:12; 112:1; 119:1–2; 128:1). Jesus, then, is referring not to subjective feelings of happiness, emotional well-being, or material security, but to the blessed state of being that enfolds the person who is rightly related to God.

Luke's focus on one's economic and cultural circumstances does not contradict Matthew's ethical emphasis. Poverty, hunger, sorrow, and mistreatment incur blessing not because they are meritorious conditions in themselves but because, under God's transformative rule, they nurture the virtues of contriteness, godly sorrow, meekness, uprightness, mercy, purity, peaceableness, and courage (to borrow from Matthew's list). The four woes are the negative restatement of the four blessings. Again, there is nothing intrinsically evil about being rich or comfortable. However, wealth, satiation, mirth, and social honor easily lead to arrogance, self-centeredness, politicizing and frivolity which obstruct repentance and submission to the will of God.

In both sets of statements there is a contrast between the "now" and the future. Surprising reversals take place under God's providential hand of redemption and judgment (Luke 1:50–55). Those who suffer a marginalized present will gain a magnificent future; those whose present life lacks nothing but God will suffer an end to their privileged but ephemeral estate. The promises encourage the faithful to hold on; the warnings urge the rebellious to wake up.

The *blessings* promise incomparable rewards to those who embrace an eternal perspective:

1. The poor will receive the kingdom.

2. The hungry will be satisfied.

3. Those who weep will be comforted.

4. Those who are hated, rejected and insulted for the Son of Man's sake will find great reward.

The corresponding *woes* are a prophetic way of warning the complacent (Isa 5:8–23):

5. The rich will receive no more comfort.

6. Those who are well fed will go hungry.

7. Those who are laughing will mourn and weep.

8. Those who are honored are like the false prophets who were treated favorably in their day.

The kingdom citizen must stay focused on God's promises for the future, for there is no guarantee of insulation from hardship in this life. In fact, in many cases the economic deprivation or personal rejection is the result of one's open identification with their Lord. Jesus called his disciples to share his cruciform pattern of existence now and await the glorious sequel when he returns (Luke 9:23–27).

⇨ One's social and economic circumstances are often the product of one's ambitious pursuits, which in turn reflect one's governing values. Does your life reflect kingdom-centered values and pursuits, trusting in him to provide for your material needs?

BECOMING SALT AND LIGHT

(Matthew 5:13–16)

Kingdom virtues, as expressed in the Beatitudes, are not to be cultivated in monastic isolation from the world. The final blessing upon those persecuted for righteousness' sake assumes the disciple is actively engaged in promoting kingdom interests far and wide. Hatred, insults, slander and rejection will be the common lot of witnessing disciples. Using two rich metaphors, salt and light, Jesus shows how God's transforming rule over believers is designed for impact.

1. *Salt of the earth* (5:13)

   Salt was regarded, along with wine and olive oil, as one of the basic staples of life in the Mediterranean world. Salt is abundant in Israel, gathered from deposits around the Dead Sea, also known as the Salt Sea (Num 34:3, 12). Two of the primary uses of salt were to add flavor to food and to preserve substances from spoiling. The latter function is the sense here. Jesus warns against the salt losing its saltiness, which occurred when the salt was mixed with impure substances making it stale and ineffective as a preservative. As the "salt of the earth," the disciple must be a moral force in the world, a holy irritant that challenges, penetrates and transforms people through the gospel of the kingdom. If the witness loses his/her distinctive character or dilutes the offensive gospel that demands repentance, the power of impact is lost. Domesticated disciples and equivocating churches are useless, like un-salty salt not even fit for a manure pile (Luke 14:34–35). The language here is stronger: such salt is "thrown out and trampled under people's feet." An insipid, palatable gospel becomes an object of scorn even to unbelievers. If all that is offered is a masquerade of religiosity covering over a secular framework, the world simply responds, why bother? One has only to observe, as one example, the empty churches across England and Germany to see the tragic effects of several generations of incre-mental compromise, both doctrinally and morally, where Reformation fires once burned brightly.

2. *Light of the world* (5:14–16)

Homes in the ancient world tended to be dark, damp places often with only one small window. Light was provided at night by flickering oil lamps. In order to illumine a dark world the disciples must display their moral character for all to see. "Good works" are the rays of the inner light of an illumined heart. Even as the oil lamps of elevated ancient towns would shed their glow over the surrounding area, kingdom citi-zens must display their virtue through visible acts of service. In this way the invisible majesty of God, his glory, can be manifested for unbeliev-ers to see and embrace. Like salt that has lost its saltiness, so is the lamp that is placed under a "bushel," a wooden grain measure in the shape of a bowl that would quickly snuff out the flame. Rather, the lamp is placed on a lampstand so that its shining effect is magnified. Jesus is the light of the world (John 8:12; 9:5) and believers are his reflective shining lamps.

In Jesus' final intercessory prayer he speaks of believers as sent "into the world," living "in the world," but not being "of the world" (John 17:14–19). Believers are admonished not to be conformed to the world (Rom 12:2), love the world (1 John 2:15) or be friends of the world (Jas 4:4). In short, kingdom citizens are to be active doers of good, neither retreating into separated fortresses nor sacrificing their core convic-tions to the spirit of the age.

⇨ What does it mean to be "in the world" but not "of the world"? How can believers become actively involved with unbelievers while remaining a distinct and peculiar people? Are you a salty, light-bearing witness for Christ?

TRANSFORMATIVE RIGHTEOUSNESS

(Matthew 5:17–20)

The interpretive framework for the Sermon on the Mount is found in the programmatic passage, Matthew 5:17–20. The inauguration of the kingdom through Jesus is no innovation, but the intended goal of the first stage of God's progressive self-revelation in the Old Testament, here abbreviated as the Law and the Prophets. The Old Testament is a record of God's mighty acts and the interpretive word. All of its rich narrative typology (e.g. the Passover lamb [John 1:29, 36]) and its numerous prophetic predictions (e.g. Isa 7:14 [Matt 1:22-23]) point toward Jesus. In this sense Jesus "fulfills," rather than "abrogates" or "sets aside as of no effect," the Old Testament (5:17). Matthew's important term "fulfill" has two meanings: (i) To "fill up" in that Jesus brings the Old Testament adumbrations, typological patterns, and direct predictions to their intended conclusion. The entire preparatory record culminates in Jesus and thus successfully completes its course, just as a race ends when the finish line is crossed. (ii) To "fill to the full" in that his teaching provides the deeper intended meaning of much of the content of Old Testament ethical commands and prohibitions such as the Decalogue.

The authority and relevance of the Old Testament, even to its minutest details, will be vindicated in the rule of Jesus over his new covenant people (5:18). Further, dishonor and reward in the dawning kingdom will be accorded respectively to those who disobey or obey the prescripts of the Old Testament as they are fulfilled in Jesus (5:19). New covenant disciple-makers are accountable to align the content of their exposition of the Old Testament to its hermeneutical key, the Lord Jesus. Kingdom scribes, then, are those who bring out the meaning of the old in light of the new (Matt 13:52). This teaching of Jesus as it fulfills the Old Testament is called by the Apostle Paul the "law of Christ" (1 Cor 9:21; Gal 6:2). Thus Jesus sets himself forth, in the first person singular, as the intended goal and authoritative interpreter of the Old Testament. He is the key that unlocks its meaning, both in his words ("fill to the full") and works ("fill up"). Augustine captures the way Jesus and Paul view the unfolding progress of redemption: "The Old Testament is the New

Testament concealed; the New Testament is the Old Testament revealed."
One must shine the light of the teaching of Jesus and his apostles on the Old
Testament record to uncover its full significance and, in so doing, vindicate
its abiding relevance.

Jesus concludes this section with a warning: "Unless your righteousness
exceeds that of the scribes and Pharisees, you will never enter the kingdom
of heaven" (5:20). On one level he sets the bar impossibly high, requiring
absolute righteousness and perfect holiness (Matt 5:48) if disciples are to
live under God's rule. But here he is simply setting forth the standard that
kingdom citizens are to strive after. It is the Apostle Paul who will expound
the way such righteousness is initially gained, namely, by grace through faith
in the crucified and risen Lord Jesus Christ. It is left to the Upper Room
Discourse (and Paul) to explain the resource by which such righteousness
will be subsequently empowered, namely, the Holy Spirit. Jesus' kingdom
demands a transformative righteousness, one that rules the deepest recesses
of the personality. External conformity to the Ten Commandments, even
precise concentration on the minutest details of Pharisaical tradition, can
only compel an outward show of piety. The kingdom of the heavens compels
not a rigorous scrubbing of the body but a transplant of the heart.

⇨   How is it that freedom from the binding authority of the law, and its
    precise commands, actually leads to a life of higher spiritual excellence
    and moral virtue in the kingdom?

SIX ANTITHESES FOR NEW COVENANT ETHICS

(Matthew 5:21–48)

Jesus contrasts his approach to the Old Testament as its fulfiller with the
misreading of Scripture the disciples inherited from their religious teachers.
With six antitheses ("You have heard that is was said . . . , but I say to you
. . .") Jesus expounds the true direction in which the Old Testament points,
namely, to a mind-renewing freedom that produces holiness in thought,
motive and action. Whether he intensifies the literal command to a deeper
level (first two antitheses), replaces accommodating measures with more
radical standards (next three antitheses), or corrects rabbinical distortion
of the original text (sixth antithesis), Jesus makes his own interpretation the
standard that possesses binding authority in the new covenant community.

1. *Murder and anger* (5:21–26)

   Not only is murder, violation of the sixth command (Exod 20:13), prohibited, but so is murderous hatred toward another even if it does not lead to the physical act. To say, literally, "Raca" is a degrading insult of a person's intelligence, something like "stupid idiot." To call someone a "fool" has a moral tone, denigrating their character as godless or bankrupt. Jesus warns of eternal judgment to one who allows such retaliatory bitterness to fester and grow.

   The solution is expressed through two illustrations. First, a believer should postpone an act of worship, such as bringing a thanksgiving offering to the altar, if a fellow believer ("brother") harbors anger against them for some offense. This is a case when it is your fault and there is a just claim against you (Matt 18:15–17 takes up the case where it is the other person's fault). Though the principle here applies to all human relationships, it must first be true of those who profess to live under God's rule. Reconcile quickly, Jesus says, then come back and resume your worship. Only then will the offering be acceptable to God. In God's kingdom vertical and horizontal relationships are inextricably bound together (Mark 11:25; 1 Pet 3:7; 1 John 5:2). The second analogy is a law court where one's adversary, with a just claim, is suing you for damages. Just as a debtor should seek an out-of-court settlement lest one be thrown into jail until all debts are paid, an impossibility for one incarcerated and unable to work, so one should settle matters early on, lest extended relational discord produce irreparable spiritual damage.

   ⇨ Can you identify a person who harbors resentment toward you for some untoward word or unjust action? Go and settle matters, if it is possible (Rom 12:18), once and for all.

2. *Adultery and lust* (5:27–30)

   Not only the physical act of adultery, violation of the seventh command (Exod 20:14), is forbidden, but so is lustful intent in one's heart, even if the physical act does not follow. Jesus is not suggesting that anger or lust is just as evil or destructive as murder or sexual intercourse outside of marriage, but that new covenant morality begins with purity of the heart not just ethical practice. To prevent sexual attraction, which is not intrinsically sinful, from turning into controlling fantasies that in turn lead to immoral acts, Jesus mandates radical spiritual surgery:

the physical organs behind looking (eye) and touching (hand) must be ruthlessly controlled; offending members, not the organs themselves but the accessories that enhance the members' opportunity to offend (e.g. online computer access if internet pornography is a stumbling block), must be forcefully removed. The glancing look becomes a stare and the innocuous greeting leads to a suggestive embrace. The heart is the "wellspring of life" (NIV) and must be guarded (Prov 4:23).

⇨ What are your vulnerabilities in the area of sexual temptation? What radical steps need to be taken to prevent compromises and to actively pursue personal holiness?

3. *Marriage and divorce* (5:31–32)

The disciples had been taught the provision in the Mosaic economy where a husband was permitted to divorce his wife for "some indecency in her" (Deut 24:1–4). The ambiguous language sparked an interpretive debate between the two rabbinical schools of Hillel and Shammai over permissible causes for divorce. The more liberal school of Hillel sanctioned divorce for "any good cause," which could include poor cooking. The conservative Shammaites allowed divorce only for adultery. In fact, Jewish law required divorce after adultery. First century legislation uniformly accorded the right of divorce to men, not to women.

Jesus took an independent line. First, Jesus allowed for divorce in the case of adultery (Matt 5:32; 19:9), but did not mandate it. In God's kingdom where grace is the operative principle, even the unfaithfulness of one's spouse can be repented of and forgiven, leading to full reconciliation. That was the very point of the second antithesis (above). Second, in Jesus' teaching the man and woman are mutually responsible for preserving the marriage bond (Mark 10:11–12). Peter draws on Jesus' elevation of the dignity of the wife in exhorting married couples to a happy and holy life together (1 Pet 3:1–7). Third, and most importantly, in the new covenant economy a higher standard is demanded, one which stems from the original divine mandate of one man and one woman for life (Gen 2:18–25). The Deuteronomic divorce code was a temporary accommodation to human weakness. Marriage is to be a permanent, inviolate covenant of two people not to be broken. The disciples should begin not with the question of what is permitted, but with what is pleasing to God.

⇨ As a wife, are you submitting to your husband even as the church submits to Christ? As a husband, are you loving your wife as Christ loves the church (Eph 5:22–33)?

4. *Oaths and truthfulness* (5:33–37)

The disciples knew that the Old Testament required that vows to God and vows to others, especially when citing God's holy name, must be kept (Num 30:2; Deut 23:21–23; Eccl 5:4–6). Oaths were taken to support a person's assertion in order to guarantee its truthfulness, often with an appeal to God as witness. Over the centuries the rabbis sought to regulate oath-taking by establishing varying degrees of binding authority depending on the name or place cited in the pledge. An entire tractate in the Mishnah, Shebuoth or "Oaths," is devoted to this taxonomy. Jesus again sets the bar higher. Uncomplicated, thorough and consistent truth-telling must be the mark of the kingdom heir. Oaths with varying levels of authority easily become clever tricks to mitigate faithfulness to one's word. An oath that places relative valuations on certain places cited in the pledge overlook that God is the sovereign Lord and owner of all things, whether heaven, earth, Jerusalem or the very hairs of one's head. The person under God's rule must build a reputation as one whose unadorned word can be trusted. Jesus' teaching can not be taken as proscribing oath-taking of every form and in every situation. Paul did at times appeal to God to witness to the truthfulness of his assertions, especially since his integrity was frequently under attack (Rom 1:9; 2 Cor 1:23). There is a time to defend one's integrity and a time to leave the vindication to God. The principle here is that a person of integrity, whose honest words express sincere intention, needs no formal assurances to lend weight to their credibility (Eph 4:15, 21, 25).

⇨ Politicians often "flip-flop" on issues in order to ingratiate themselves with voters to get elected. Are you a person whose yes and no can be trusted, whose truthfulness is consistent and unwavering, yet always tempered by love?

5. *Non-retaliation* (5:38–42; Luke 6:29–30)

Old Testament criminal law was embodied in the *lex talionis*, "eye for eye, tooth for tooth" (Exod 21:24; Lev 24:20). This law of retribution was designed not to justify personal payback, but to ensure that the punishment would fit the crime of one guilty of injuring another person or damaging their property. With due process and clearly specified penalties the need for personal vendettas would be eliminated. Once again, as with the matters of divorce and oaths, Jesus demands of his disciples a higher standard of conduct than was prescribed for theocratic Israel.

The one under God's rule is to return generosity and forbearance for ill-treatment and personal offense. Jesus gives four concrete examples of what it means to "not resist" an evil person: (i) turn the left cheek for an additional blow when struck on the right one; (ii) offer the shirt (tunic) as well to one who would sue you for your coat (cloak); (iii) if conscripted by Roman soldiers to carry their baggage one mile, go two miles; (iv) do not refuse beggars or borrowers in need. From Jesus' language comes the expressions "turn the other cheek" and "go the extra mile." This language is hyperbolic, neither to be over-literalized nor emptied of its force. Jesus calls for extreme actions in order to get his disciples' attention and to drive home the importance of showing forbearance rather than vindictiveness in dealing with adversaries of the kingdom.

⇨ Is there a person who has been resistant, even hostile, to your attempt to commend Christ to them? Pray for a forbearing spirit and for wisdom in how to break down barriers through sacrificial consideration of their concrete needs.

6. *Love for enemies* (5:43–47; Luke 6:27–28, 32–35)

The final antithesis corrects a distortion of Old Testament teaching. Only the first half is biblical (Lev 19:18); the second half is well-attested in the writings of the Qumran sect who commanded love for the sons of light and hatred for the sons of darkness. Jesus, in what has now become his characteristic approach, demands a more intense and internally driven standard than that required by the Old Testament. The higher ethic is more than passive non-retaliation, but proactively seeks the welfare of one's adversaries. Disciples are to love unconditionally, to do good to, bless, and pray for those who hate and mistreat them. Two reasons are given. First, sons must imitate their Father who extends his common grace to all people, including the evil and unrighteous. Second, new covenant ethics transcend the conventional morality of non-believers who preserve good relations with their family and friends as a matter of common decency and for mutual benefit. Forbearing love that extends to one's determined enemies sets them apart as people under God's rule.

⇨ Think of an individual who has slandered your character or done something harmful to you or a loved one. Pray for a forgiving spirit and ask for wisdom in how you might "overcome evil with good" (Rom 12:21).

7. *The summative command* (5:48; Luke 6:36)

The final command integrates all six of the antitheses into the framework of God's character. "You therefore must be perfect, as your heavenly Father is perfect." Luke replaces "perfect" with "merciful" or "compassionate" (6:36) which can be seen as God's central attribute (Exod 34:6). The comparative clause that supports the command ("as your heavenly Father . . .") rules out the translation "mature" or "complete." The entire Old Testament, as it is interpreted by and fulfilled in Jesus, points to the very perfection of God himself. To conform to, live in the light of, and reflect the character of the Heavenly Father is at the heart of the kingdom.

⇨ Scholars have termed the Sermon on the Mount "absolutist ethics." Would Jesus command his disciples to do that which is impossible for them? If so, why? To what degree and through what enablement can the final command become a reality in the present life?

AN AUDIENCE OF ONE

(Matthew 6:1–8, 16–18)

Jesus identified the three "acts of righteousness" (6:1 [NIV]) commonly practiced by pious Jews: giving of alms to the poor, prayer and fasting. He assumes that his disciples will regularly practice these disciplines, but from a different motivation than what lay behind the hollow piety of the religious leaders. The governing principle concerns the motive behind one's actions. Once again Jesus reminds his followers that the kingdom is all about the heart. The Pharisees and Sadducees performed many of their religious duties for the sake of human recognition and for this reason forfeited all prospects of divine reward. Kingdom living, which encompasses all activities, not just those placed in the artificial category of the 'sacred' (1 Cor 10:31), must be directed to an audience of one, to please the Father rather than people.

1. *Giving of alms* (6:2–4)

    With practically no social safety net in the ancient world, the destitute depended on the generosity of more favored members of society for survival. Almsgiving then as now was greatly valued. People could enhance their status by being recognized as benefactors (Luke 7:4–5). Jesus tells his disciples that the person who calls attention to their giving is like an actor who plays a dramatic role and views the world as the stage of performance. This is the original meaning of the term translated "hypocrite," that is, one who pretends to be something other than what one, in reality, is. Some would advertise their giving by throwing their coins so that they rattled around the trumpet-shaped donation receptacles in the temple. Rather than "blowing one's own horn," the kingdom citizen should give as the natural outflow of a generous heart that loves God and seeks to help people.

2. *Prayer* (6:5–8)

    Jesus warns the disciples against prayer that is no more than public posturing to draw attention to one's piety, and against lengthy and formulaic prayers that are designed to impress the listeners, especially God. Pagan prayer often took the form of an extended retinue of nonsensical sounds, nothing more than lengthy babbling to extract favors from a capricious deity. But, as Luther reminds us, "Prayer is not overcoming God's reluctance; it is laying hold of his willingness." The prayer life begins with secret, undistracted, personal communion with God the Father, listening to his voice and articulating one's concerns from the heart. Public prayer takes its cue from the vitality of one's private prayer life, never sermonizing, but supplicating an omniscient Father who knows his people's needs and calls them individually and corporately to draw near and ask.

3. *Fasting* (6:16–18)

    As with trumpet-announced almsgiving and ostentatious prayers, so the hypocrites fasted with grief-laden countenances to publicize their self-denial. Jesus says that when a person chooses to voluntarily fast it should be with a rested and joyful countenance so that no one would detect anything unusual from one's normal activity of eating and drinking. Since it is rarely mentioned as a practice in the new covenant (Matt 9:15; Acts 13:2–3; 14:23), it is unlikely Jesus is prescribing fasting for his disciples. His deeper concern is the motive behind these voluntary disciplines. Authentic piety becomes the natural, inconspicuous good works of the kingdom citizen whose life-focus is the glory of God.

⇨ Why are you doing what you are doing in ministry? Ask God to remove all performance-driven motivations so that pleasing the Lord becomes your all-consuming passion.

THE DISCIPLES' MODEL PRAYER: PART ONE
(Matthew 6:9–15)

What is commonly termed the "Lord's prayer" could more accurately be labeled the "disciples' prayer." The designation "Lord's prayer" more accurately applies to the profound intercession that Jesus offered for his disciples on the night before his death (John 17:1–26). Jesus must have taught his disciples this prayer on various occasions, for its abbreviated form is given again after their request, "Lord, teach us to pray" (Luke 11:1–4). Jesus, then, sets forth this prayer not as a rigid formula to be recited, but as the manner in which kingdom citizens should approach the King.

1. *"Our Father in Heaven"*

   God is the Father of disciples, yet dwells in heaven distinct from and above his creation. Thus he is transcendent, sovereign, invisible, yet personal, approachable and caring. Calling upon God as "Abba," the intimate term in Aramaic for one's father (English "dad" or "daddy"), was the most distinctive feature of Jesus' approach to prayer, one that stunned the disciples and transformed their understanding of God (Rom 8:15; Gal 4:6). There is no evidence that anyone before Jesus employed this tender designation to address God. None of the other major world religions approaches God on such intimate terms. Even when the term "Father" is used of God in the Old Testament, it takes on the corporate sense of Israel as God's adopted son (Exod 4:22; Jer 31:9; Hos 11:1). This familial intimacy between a Father and his children is the fulfillment of the recurrent promise that unites the entire program of redemption: "I will be their God and they shall be my people" (Jer 31:33b; cf. Lev 26:12; Ezek 37:27; 2 Cor 6:16, 18; Rev 21:3, 7).

2. *"Hallowed be your name"*

One's name encapsulates the essence of the whole person, their essential being and character. This is a request that the God who is holy may be recognized and honored as such by all people and in every sphere of existence. This opening request sounds the doxological chord.

3. *"Your kingdom come"*

This is the petition that God's saving power might be extended now in bringing people to joyfully submit to his lordship. It also looks forward to the consummation of the kingdom when God's unrivaled sovereignty will be manifested over the created universe (1 Cor 15:24–28; Phil 2:9–11). The benedictory prayer of the Bible echoes the same note: "Amen. Come, Lord Jesus" (Rev 22:20).

4. *"Your will be done, on earth as it is in heaven"*

In parallelism with kingdom, "will" refers to God's desiderative will—that which he desires, in accordance with his character, rather than what he decrees. Jesus prays that people will voluntarily yield to his saving rule. The petition is that earth will imitate the scene in God's heavenly throne room where angels and the spirits of perfected saints embrace God's rule and celebrate his majesty (Rev 4:1—5:14).

The preeminent concern of the opening half of the prayer is God's name, rule and will. The disciple begins by aligning the course of one's life into conformity with God's character and revealed purposes. God the Father is the gravitational center of kingdom living.

⇨ Do you often rush into God's presence with your myriad of personal requests without pausing first to remember into whose presence you are entering and for whose glory the granting of such requests is designed to serve? Do you need a priority check-up?

THE DISCIPLES' MODEL PRAYER: PART TWO

(Matthew 6:9–15)

After this theocentric alignment, the prayer now turns to supplication for personal needs. God is both King and Father. He delights in satisfying the needs of his children, especially when they ask with persistence. He will always give them what is for their benefit, even if it does not correspond exactly with what they think they need (Matt 7:7–11).

5. *"Give us this day our daily bread"*

   God promises to supply the needs, not greeds, of his children (Phil 4:19; Jas 4:3). Literally, the supply is "bread for the coming day," that is, the next day's provisions. Daily reliance on the Lord who has provided in the past buttresses one's confident expectation of supply for one more day. Anxiety among believers regarding adequate income for a future retirement or one's long term financial stability is far removed from the spirit of this request. The prayer presupposes contentment with what the Father supplies (Phil 4:11–13). How God will provide, whether through work (1 Thess 3:10), a miracle (1 Kgs 17:6), or the generosity of fellow believers (2 Cor 9:12), is not the child's concern. The need, of which the Father is acutely aware (Matt 6:32), is simply requested in faith and the provision anticipated in faith.

6. *"Forgive us our debts, as we also have forgiven our debtors"*

   Sin is viewed as a debt owed to God (Luke 11:4), placing us in need of forgiveness. This is God's specialty—the climactic promise of the new covenant, the forgiveness of sins (Jer 31:34). Not only at the moment of salvation, but as an ongoing need, the believer undertakes daily repentance and seeks cleansing from sins of commission and omission (John 13:10; 1 John 1:9). The first of Luther's famous ninety-five theses reads: "When our Lord Jesus Christ proclaimed, 'Repent, for the kingdom of the heavens is at hand,' he thereby declared that the entire life of the believer should be one of repentance." The famous reformer recognized that just as repentance is the precondition for entering the kingdom, so it is the governing principle for the ongoing life of the kingdom citizen.

   Forgiveness is the hallmark not only of Christian theology but also of Christian ethics. The comparative adverbial phrase, "as we have forgiven our debtors," does not introduce the necessary condition of God's forgiveness, but the accompanying attitude and posture toward others of one who recognizes the enormity of their sinfulness and the magnitude of God's forgiveness. Forgiven people should and must be people who can readily forgive those who have wronged them (Luke 7:47; Eph 4:32). This is the only portion of the disciples' prayer that Jesus expands on (6:14–15), because forgiveness is so counter-cultural.

7. *"And lead us not into temptation, but deliver us from evil"*

While recognizing one's proclivity to sin, there is also a moral commitment to obedience (1 John 1:8—2:2). The Greek term can be rendered both "testing" and "temptation." Temptation or enticement to sin never originates with God (Jas 1:13–15). Yet the Spirit led Jesus into the wilderness where he was tempted by the devil (Luke 4:1–2). Here is the intersection of both good (test) and evil (temptation) purposes in the same event. This lends weight to seeing a permissive nuance to the request: "Preserve us in the midst of our testings, designed by the Father to refine our character, from being enticed to sin by Satan." This final request combines a deep sense of one's vulnerability to moral failure, yet confidence in God's enablement to triumph over every temptation (1 Cor 10:12–13).

⇨ Identify a person who has hurt you. Consider the cross and forgive them unconditionally.

TWO TREASURES, TWO VISIONS, TWO MASTERS
(Matthew 6:19–24)

From a severe denunciation of contrived religious behavior, that is, hypocritical posturing masqueraded as "acts of righteousness," Jesus turns to the more seductive pull of material possessions. The pursuit of wealth can become an idol that replaces God. Anxiety over material needs can sap one's energy to promote God's kingdom, which is to be the central pursuit of disciples (6:33).

1. *Where the heart is* (6:19–21)

Jesus' laser-like focus remains on the heart and what captures its affections (6:21). The word customarily rendered "heart" is pervasive in the record of Jesus' teaching preserved in the Synoptic Gospels (thirty-seven times). It is Jesus' definitive term for the center of the human personality, the place where God addresses a person, and the place where a person can either respond with faith and repentance, or refuse those overtures of grace and become dull and darkened. A "treasure" is an object of affection, what is deemed precious and of great worth, which a person will make secure at all costs. Treasures become dominant in one's thoughts, desires and dreams. This is not a blanket condemnation of planning for the future or saving a portion of one's income, both of which are commended in Scripture (Prov 6:6–8; 1 Tim 5:8). Rather, Jesus compels his disciples to make the kingdom of God, the extension of his redemptive rule over individuals, communities and nations, their singular pursuit rather than transitory material things. Clothing can be eaten by moths, precious metals ruined by rust, and all valuables stolen by thieves. To pursue God's rule over one's life and to promote his rule among one's contemporaries has lasting significance, like a treasure that can be laid up in heaven, secure and eternal. As a wealthy business man, who has made it his life's work to use his money to support kingdom enterprises, says: "I cannot take it with me, so I will send it ahead."

2. *The lamp of the body* (6:22–23)

    Jesus compares the eye to the lamp that illumines the dark inner rooms of an ancient home. In the present analogy it is the body that houses the inner recesses of the conscience, mind and will. The eye is the window to the soul, allowing the beatific vision of God and a panoply of virtue to enter and purify the mind or permitting degrading scenes of moral compromise to darken and corrupt it. Just as Matthew 6:23 warns against the destructive potential of one's vision, so Luke 11:36, its positive counterpart, promises that moral excellence will illumine the soul of the one who maintains a "sound eye" (Amplified). The disciples must understand how critical for their spiritual health is the careful supervision of the eyegate (Job 31:1; Prov 27:20; Eccl 4:8; Matt 5:28–29; 1 John 2:16).

3. *Master of the soul* (6:24)

    Behind the decision of where to lay up treasures and the decision of where to fix one's eyes resides the still more basic decision of what master one will serve. With Jesus there are always two mutually exclusive choices, in this case to serve God or money. Ancient and modern people are more sophisticated, clever to craft a *via media* that seeks the best of both worlds. But one's allegiance, Jesus says, can really only be in one place, just as a slave can only belong to one master. Either God is served with one's undivided loyalty or he is not served at all. There is no such thing as partial lordship.

⇨   Compare your patterns of giving and spending over the past three months. Do these patterns reflect sacrificial investment in kingdom concerns or selfish spending on perishable items far beyond one's needs? Where does your true treasure lie, on earth or in heaven?

THE FOOLISHNESS OF WORRY

(Matthew 6:25–34)

The inferential conjunction "therefore" establishes the connection of this paragraph with the set of commands that precede it: heavenly-stored treasure, a sound eye, and undivided commitment to God liberate a person from anxiety over transient, material needs. Worry can be defined as an unhealthy fixation on one's personal concerns that imagines oneself rather than God the real provider. It is thus the opposite of trust in God's ability and faithfulness to supply one's needs. The same Greek verb is used in the New Testament for "be anxious about" and "care for." Negatively, it can denote, as it does six times in this passage, an unhealthy anxiety that saps one's energy and pulls the heart away from God. Positively, it can refer to a proper concern or care for that which is worthy of one's attention (1 Cor 7:32, 34; Phil 2:20). There is thus a fine line between appropriate concern and destructive worry.

The basic physical needs of food, drink, and clothing are in view here. Jesus uses two examples from the natural world that demonstrate the faithfulness of the great Provider. The metaphors are not intended to discourage hard work or saving for the future. Each example concludes with a lesser to greater logical appeal. First, the birds are fed without fretting and storing up in barns supplies for the winter. How much more will God supply the needs of his children, of much greater worth to him than the birds. Anxiety can not add one year to a person's life, in fact, it does the opposite. Second, the lilies of the field do not toil like a laborer or spin their own clothes, but are more gloriously arrayed than King Solomon. How much more will God care for his children who are far more valuable than plants that are pulled up and used for fuel in the oven. The root cause of worry is "little faith," a paucity of confidence in the loving intention and full ability of the Heavenly Father to supply everything his children need.

Such faith-induced freedom from anxiety should be a mark that distinguishes believers from pagans who spend their time and energy passionately pursuing their material needs and greeds. Even when successful, their anxiety then fixes upon how they might preserve what they have acquired. This is not an indictment of the honest acquisition of wealth, but a warning against making material possessions the center of one's value system and the driving objective of one's vocation. The believer, whether rich or poor, is to be characterized by resting in a Father's care, in One who knows our needs and whose love moves him to act upon his knowledge (1 Pet 5:7).

Kingdom citizenship, however, entails more than refraining from worry, but active pursuit of personal ethical righteousness and the extension of God's saving rule in the world (6:33). The guarantee of "all these things," that is, the necessities of life such as food, clothing and shelter, is predicated upon making the kingdom the "first" pursuit of one's life. Paradoxically, by not making "all these things" the singular pursuit, they are in the end abundantly provided.

The summary conclusion ("therefore") reiterates the petition, "give us our bread for the coming day" (Matt 6:11). Focus on your needs one day at a time, Jesus is saying. The present day has enough "trouble" of its own to fully challenge one's faith (6:34). It is foolish to borrow future troubles, starting from tomorrow, and save them up in a storehouse of anxiety. Worry is unnecessary and illogical, for worry borrows its strength from an indeterminate tomorrow which, if it arrives, will find its needs more than met by the God who has satisfied the needs of today.

⇨ Do you inwardly churn about matters, beyond your control, which produces a paralyzing anxiety? Write down the two or three things that you worry most about; then exchange your anxiety for God's peace through supplication with thanksgiving (Phil 4:6–7).

CRITICAL DISCERNMENT, NOT HYPOCRITICAL JUDGMENT

(Matthew 7:1–6; Luke 6:37–42)

A commitment to the exacting standards of righteousness demanded by the King (Matt 5:20; 6:33) brings with it the danger of adopting a censorious attitude toward people who fail to measure up to those standards. Jesus prohibits the disciple from standing in the place of God who is the sole lawgiver and judge (Rom 14:4; Jas 4:11–12). The command here is not to suspend one's critical powers, something that is enjoined in verse 6, but to renounce the presumptuous ambition to usurp God's sole prerogative as judge. It is helpful to identify from this and related passages those principles that should govern one's critical assessment of others, the motives behind it, and the limitations that surround such assessment.

1. A *judgmental attitude* toward others, especially when based on an external taxonomy of spirituality (John 7:24), must be guarded against. How we treat others will be reciprocated, whether with harshness or generosity (Matt 7:1–2; Luke 6:37). Luke records the analogy of a measuring jar filled with a "good measure" of grain or corn pressed down to fill the measure to its full capacity, then shaken together to make it settle into every available space, before being poured into the recipient's fold of a garment used like a pocket to hold the allotment (6:38). This is how a person will be requited who treats others with grace and forbearance.

2. Believers are to cease and desist from *hypocritical judgment*. We must remove the "log" that impairs our own vision before attempting to remove the "speck" from the eye of our brother (Matt 7:3–5). Otherwise we become, like the Pharisees, blind leaders leading blind people into a common pit (Luke 6:39). This allows for correcting a brother once one's own eye is clear to see. Disciples must be "fully trained" students who learn from the one Teacher whose assessments were without a trace of hypocrisy (Luke 6:40).

3. Believers have the responsibility, for the sake of the purity of the church, to *administer discipline* to professing believers who fall into sin. But the manner of judgment must be gentle and the purpose remedial (1 Cor 5:5; Gal 6:1).

4. Severe and *forthright condemnation* is appropriate when the gospel is threatened by false teaching and its destructive moral effects (Gal

1:8–9; Phil 3:2). This requires that leaders are able to apply biblical truth to *unmask false prophets* who masquerade as servants of God through impressive gifts and oratory (Matt 7:15–20; 2 Cor 11:13–15; 1 John 4:1). Again, leaders do not engage in a search and destroy mission, but act to preserve the church's integrity.

5. Disciples must *exercise caution* in situations where incorrigible opponents seek to undermine the mission of promoting the kingdom. Jesus frames his admonition in a chiastic arrangement: dogs—pigs—(pigs) trample—(dogs) tear to pieces (Matt 7:6). Dogs and pigs represent those who treat the precious gospel of the kingdom with utter contempt. Just as he enjoins the disciples to shake the dust off their feet as a symbol of judgment on an unwelcoming town (Matt 10:14), and to leave blind guides well enough alone (Matt 15:14), so Jesus commands them to show thoughtful restraint in promoting the kingdom among those whose proven agenda is to block its advance.

⇨ These five principles balance generous appraisal with critical discernment, a "moral symmetry" attested, in addition to Matt 7:1–6, a number of times in the New Testament (Matt 10:16b; Rom 16:19b; 1 Cor 14:20; cf. Prov 9:8). What happens when either of the two poles of this healthy tension (wisdom of serpents—innocence of doves [Matt 10:16b]) collapses into the other?

PRAYER AND THE GOLDEN RULE
(Matthew 7:7–12; Luke 6:31)

1. *Persistence in prayer* (Matt 7:7–11)

Prayer can guide the disciple through the confusing maze of situations and personalities encountered in the course of kingdom ministry. To strike the balance between generous forbearance and cautious discernment (7:1–6), one must seek God's wisdom. The present tense verbal forms in 7:7–8 carry a durative or continual force: the promise of answered prayer is given to the one who keeps on asking, seeking, knocking. Jesus often put the accent on persistence when instructing his disciples in the art of prayer (Luke 11:5–13; 18:1–8). Think of the finest example of an earthly father. He would never ignore his children's needs or give them anything that might harm them, like a stone to eat or a snake that bites. Remember, Jesus says, to whom your prayers are directed: not to a stingy miser whose reluctance must be overcome, but a gracious Father who delights to provide his children with the "good gifts" that are beneficial to them (7:11). These provisions are, first and foremost, the attributes of kingdom citizenship expounded in the sermon—righteousness, truthfulness, purity, humility, love, freedom from anxiety. They are effectualized in the disciple's life by God's greatest gift, the Holy Spirit (Luke 11:13).

2. *Golden maxim* (Matt 7:12; Luke 6:31)

The conjunction "so" or "therefore" links this maxim to the wider context of the sermon, likely 5:17—7:11. Thus in this simple canon— "Whatever you wish that others would do to you, do also to them"—the content of the Old Testament ("Law and Prophets") as interpreted by Jesus finds its fulfillment. The "Golden Rule," then, must be interpreted within in its present kingdom setting and not isolated as an abstract underpinning for humanistic morality. Love for God and love for one's neighbor comprise the ethical framework of the Old Testament as fulfilled in Jesus (Matt 22:37–40; cf. Rom 13:8–10; Gal 6:2; Jas 2:8), which this simple maxim helps apply in a myriad of situations.

The Golden Rule was not unique to Jesus, but when framed by others it is nearly always stated in negative form. Rabbi Hillel said: "What is hateful to you, do not do to your neighbor: that is the whole Torah, while the rest is commentary thereon; go and learn it." When Confucius was asked, "Is there one word which may serve as a rule and practice for all one's life?," the Master replied, "Is not 'reciprocity' such a word? What you do not want done to yourself, do not do to others." Stated negatively, the maxim could justify isolated passivity, the avoidance of things that would have an adverse effect on others. But when stated positively, it demands constructive action that proactively looks for ways to benefit others, a far higher standard than the absence of offensive conduct. The difference between the sheep and goats in Matthew 25:31–46 is that the former fed the hungry, clothed the naked, ministered to the sick, and visited the prisoners, while the latter observed the same needs and did nothing. Only the sheep applied the Golden Rule in its positive form.

This maxim is not a utilitarian principle of reciprocity that reads, "Do good to others in order that they might return the favor." Jesus is already on record that this common value among pagans (Matt 5:46) is far below the standard required of disciples. New covenant morality brings the heart into ethical decisions by making the welfare of others one's priority.

⇨ Think of your spouse, a friend, or co-worker. What burden do they have that you could relieve? Consider what you would appreciate in that situation. Go and do that for them.

TWO GATES, TWO TREES, TWO BUILDERS
(Matthew 7:13–27; Luke 6:43–49)

Jesus brings his sermon to a conclusion by demanding, through a series of contrastive metaphors, that the listeners choose between two alternatives. The ambivalent multitudes have started to gather and need to hear, along with the disciples, that faith and obedience are inextricably bound together in the kingdom of God. Jesus disallows any notion of two tiers or two categories of kingdom citizens, one of whom is obedient and rewarded, the other of whom is disobedient and unrewarded. Rather, Jesus sets forth an integrated pattern of progressive discipleship under his authoritative direction: decisive commitment to enter the inaugurated kingdom, perseverance in faith in the midst of adversity, and final arrival as heir of the consummated kingdom. This set of three contrasts—narrow versus wide gate and road, good versus bad tree and fruit, wise versus foolish builder—does not distinguish spiritual from carnal Christians, but rather those who hear the word, obey it and receive eternal life from those who hear, fail to obey and experience eternal judgment. Kingdom citizens are obedient disciples and obedient disciples inherit the kingdom.

1. *Two gates* (Matt 7:13–14)

   There are two gates to enter (narrow and wide), two roads that extend from the gates (difficult and easy), and two destinations at the end of the roads (life and destruction). The crucial decision is which gate to enter, for the respective roads and destinations stretch out before the traveler after the choice is made. A narrow gate to life means that the restrictive path must be chosen from the outset, which accounts for the fewer number who enter that gate. Repentance is both the precondition of entering God's rule and the principle that governs the ongoing journey toward the glorious inheritance.

2. *Two trees* (Matt 7:15–23; Luke 6:43–46)

    Jesus warns the disciples against false prophets that will arise and attempt to pull the kingdom community away from Jesus' authoritative teaching. They will be like "wolves in sheep's clothing," that is, their benign appearance will disguise their corrupt character. They will profess allegiance to the King and even prophesy, exorcise demons, and perform miracles in his name. However, the evidence to establish their claims to legitimacy, namely, obedience to the will of God, will be missing (Matt 7:21). Their words and actions reveal the condition of their hearts just as fruit, good or bad, shows the health of the tree (Luke 6:45). Good trees do not produce good and bad fruit in alternative seasons. Disciples, then, must carefully assess the moral character of those who claim to speak for God. The precondition for entry into the kingdom is not impressive outward piety, fine-sounding confession, or dynamic miracle-producing ministry, but a vital relationship that produces obedience.

3. *Two builders* (Matt 7:24–27; Luke 6:47–49)

    The one who hears and obeys is like a wise builder who erects his house on a rock foundation so that it withstands surging floods and beating winds. The one who hears and does not obey is like a foolish builder who constructs his house on the sand so that it collapses under the torrential rains. "These words" are the authoritative declarations of King Jesus who brings his rule to bear on the hearts of those who prove the authenticity of their faith-repentance by obedience.

⇨   Some propose a radical distinction between accepting Christ as Savior and submitting to him as Lord (two tiers or two levels of genuine Christian experience). Does this passage bear on that issue?

7

Middle Galilean Ministry

Popular Acclaim and Official Rejection

MARVELOUS FAITH OF THE CENTURION

(Matthew 7:28—8:13; Luke 7:1-10)

IN THE SERMON ON the Mount Jesus made astounding claims in the first person, setting himself up as the definitive fulfiller of the Old Testament, that is, its goal and interpreter (Matt 5:17–20). Superior to the Old Testament prophets who voiced "the word of the Lord" and certainly unlike the rabbis who cited other rabbis, Jesus claimed that obedience to his words would determine the destiny of his listeners, eternal life or perdition (Matt 7:21–23). Such authoritative declarations stunned the listeners. This was not academic theology to be parsed, but truth to be obeyed (Matt 7:28–29). The large crowds that had gathered in the hills north of Lake Galilee now followed him to Capernaum. Jesus' popularity has reached its apex as he begins the *Middle Galilean* phase of his ministry, which extends from the end of the Sermon on the Mount to his northern withdrawal outside the borders of Israel proper. During this approximately eight month period (*late Fall AD 28–early Summer AD 29*) his popularity will fade as conflict with the religious leaders intensifies. As a result, Jesus turns his attention more and more to those outside of Israel whose openness to the supra-cultural offer of the kingdom anticipates a universal harvest.

A Roman centurion stationed in Capernaum knew all about authority. As an officer commanding 100 soldiers, he issued orders and they were followed. Like many, a crisis brought him to Jesus. A highly valued servant was stricken with paralysis and was near death. The centurion, a respected benefactor for his gifts to support the synagogue, sent Jewish elders who

117

would have a better chance, he thought, of eliciting Jesus' help. When Jesus came near to his house, the centurion sent a delegation of friends, imploring Jesus to heal the servant by a spoken word from a distance. He is respectful, addressing Jesus as Lord, and contrite, confessing his unworthiness to receive such an honored guest. The centurion reasoned from his own experience of delegated authority. Though he operated under the direction of the division commander, the Roman governor, and ultimately the emperor himself, the centurion issued orders to rank and file soldiers under his authority and was obeyed without dispute. He believed that Jesus ministered under God's authority and as such was vested with ability to heal diseases by his powerful word. It is likely that the earlier healing of the royal official's son in Capernaum, also a miracle of distance, convinced him of Jesus' supernatural power (John 4:46–54).

Jesus was astonished at the centurion's simple request, free from manipulation or coercion, and the forthright expression of confidence in his ability to command a healing. This Gentile's faith contrasted with the unbelief of the Jewish leaders. Only with this centurion and later with the woman of Syrophoenicia (Matt 15:28), both Gentiles, does the faith of an individual cause Jesus to marvel (Matt 8:10). Jesus sees here a harbinger of multitudes of Gentiles, from the east and west, flocking to the Jewish Messiah and taking their seats, along with the patriarchs, at the messianic banquet which signals the consummation of God's kingdom (Ps 107:3; Isa 25:6–9; Rev 19:9). By contrast, the "sons of the kingdom," those who claim their places at the table by virtue of their racial connection to Abraham, will be excluded and consigned to judgment (Matt 8:11–12). This centurion's faith previews the conversion of another centurion, Cornelius, which will even more clearly signal the dawning of God's redemptive blessing on the Gentiles (Acts 11:18). The Lord honored the centurion's faith whose servant was healed instantaneously by Jesus' spoken word.

⇨ Are you, like the religious leaders, so accustomed to circumscribing God in a theological box that there is no room for faith? Imitate the humility, boldness and even desperation of the centurion by bringing your problems to the Lord, believing his ability to solve them.

A WIDOW'S RESTORED HOPE

(Luke 7:11–17)

Jesus came to the village of Nain, six miles southeast of Nazareth in the plain of Jezreel. Nain was just east of the hill of Moreh, famous in Israel's history as the place where the Midianites encamped when attacked by Gideon's band of warriors (Judg 7:1). Just to the west of Moreh, in the village of Shunem, eight centuries earlier the prophet Elisha had raised a boy from the dead and returned this only son to his mother (2 Kgs 4:32–37).

As Jesus approached the town gate, he encountered a funeral procession. A young boy, the only son of a widow, was being carried in an open coffin or bier to the place of his burial. In the warm climate of Palestine the body was quickly anointed with spices to counter the stench of rapid decomposition, wrapped in strips of linen, and then interred in a family tomb. The Lord was deeply touched at the sad plight of this widow, whose future would be very fragile without a husband or child to care for her in old age. A severe form of ritual uncleanness would result from direct or even indirect contact with the corpse, through touching the bier, judged from the elaborate red heifer ceremony required to remove such impurity (Num 19). Jesus ignored such concerns, as when he touched the leper (Luke 5:13). He interrupted the procession, touched the coffin, and commanded the dead boy to get up. Immediately the boy sat up, began to talk, and the Lord tenderly restored him to his mother.

The crowd responded with awe and praised God for sending among them a great prophet. The resurrection of a dead boy reminded them of the exploits of Elijah who had raised the son of the widow of Zarephath (1 Kgs 17:17–24), as well as the Shunammite's son by Elisha. There would be other resuscitations of dead people by the Apostles Peter (Acts 9:36–42) and Paul (Acts 20:7–12). But this was more than a prophet or an apostle. This was the Messiah whose raising a boy from the dead was just the climax in a whole series of miraculous works that attested to his identity, as Jesus will need to remind John the Baptist's disciples (Luke 7:22). Not only is he the Messiah, he is the Lord of life and only Son of his Father whose raising of Lazarus will testify to his authority to grant eternal life and becomes a faint glimpse of his own resurrection (John 11:25–27). The eyewitnesses to this event seem to grasp its deeper significance when they confess that God has indeed visited his people (7:16), an expression not only of divine concern but of the divine presence (Luke 1:68, 78).

Once again we are reminded that Jesus' healing ministry is a pastoral rather than strategic one. He prefers obscure villages like Nain and Cana to the high-profile centers of influence like Tiberius and Sepphoris. To one desperate widow in a poor village he elects to demonstrate his grace and power. The movement of an individual from helplessness to hope through the intervention of divine power, with a sequel of praise, is the recurrent pattern of Jesus' ministry. Though it is not mentioned, one can assume that the resulting fanfare surrounding this miracle made Jesus uncomfortable and led to another, probably failed, attempt to withdraw from the crowds.

⇨ Do our feelings of compassion for people in desperate conditions move us, like Jesus, to act on their behalf? We do not have the power to directly solve the problem, as Jesus did in this case, but we can give of our time and resources to help alleviate the suffering of those on the margins of society.

DOUBTS OF THE FORERUNNER

(Matthew 11:2–6; Luke 7:18–23)

For the past year of Jesus' ministry in Galilee, John the Baptist has been languishing in prison. John had confronted Herod Antipas over his marriage to Herodias, whom he enticed to divorce his own half-brother, Philip I (Luke 3:19–20). This was a brazen violation of Jewish law (Lev 18:16). Antipas shut John away in the desert fortress of Machaerus, east of the Dead Sea. Reports came to John of Jesus' miraculous works of healing and exorcism. But John began to have doubts and sent several of his disciples to ask Jesus whether he is indeed "the one who is to come," a messianic title (Ps 118:26), or whether, like John, he is a preliminary figure and someone else will fulfill the role of Israel's deliverer.

John had called Israel to repentance in preparation for Messiah's arrival and then confessed Jesus to be the Lamb of God, the eschatological Spirit-baptizer, the sinless One whose sandals he is unworthy to stoop down and untie. How could the miracle boy of Zechariah and Elizabeth, consecrated as forerunner and final prophet, possibly question Jesus' messianic credentials? That such a shocking development is hardly believable, many scholars, including some of the leading early church fathers, posit that the doubts here are not of John himself but of his disciples whom John sends to Jesus for their strengthening. But that is not the natural sense of Matthew's account.

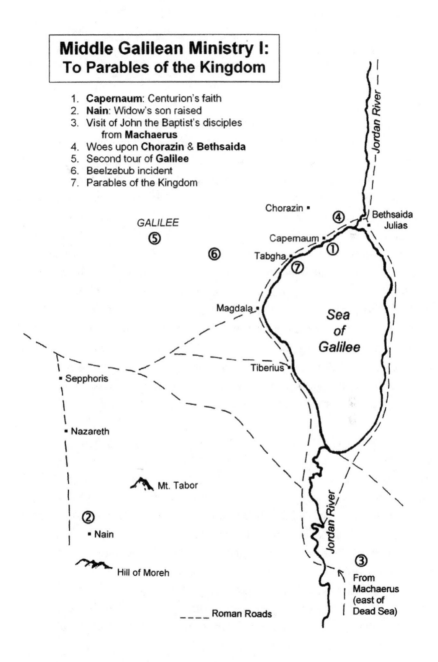

Middle Galilean Ministry I:
To Parables of the Kingdom

1. **Capernaum**: Centurion's faith
2. **Nain**: Widow's son raised
3. Visit of John the Baptist's disciples
   from **Machaerus**
4. Woes upon **Chorazin** & **Bethsaida**
5. Second tour of **Galilee**
6. Beelzebub incident
7. Parables of the Kingdom

GALILEE
⑤

⑥

Chorazin ▪
④   ╱ Bethsaida
       Julias

Capernaum ▪
Tabgha ▪   ①
⑦

Magdala ▪

Sea of Galilee

▪ Sepphoris

Tiberius ▪

▪ Nazareth

🛆 Mt. Tabor

②
▪ Nain

Jordan River

Jordan River

③
From
Machaerus
(east of
Dead Sea)

Hill of Moreh

---- Roman Roads

Doubt born of a demoralization fueled by false expectations has the power to assail the strongest of God's servants. Elijah himself, whose ministry John's is patterned after (Luke 1:17, quot. Mal 4:5–6), became disillusioned when, after the dramatic victory over the prophets of Baal on Mount Carmel, Jezebel vowed to kill him. Afraid for his life, the prophet ran to Beersheba, sat down under a broom tree in the desert and prayed that he might die (1 Kgs 19:1–5).

So Jesus told John's disciples to take back to the discouraged prophet a clear report of his miracles, widely attested to by others as well as performed before their very eyes: the blind are made to see, the lame walk, the lepers are cleansed, the deaf can hear, dead people are brought to life, and the good news of the arrival of the kingdom is proclaimed and confirmed by these attesting works. These are the signs that Isaiah prophesied would signal Messiah's arrival (Isa 35:5–6; 61:1–2). While John had grasped the dual role of Jesus as both suffering Servant and conquering King, he failed to perceive the temporal gap that would separate the former's redemptive death from the latter's consummative judgment. He expected the fire-baptism of judgment to follow the Spirit-baptism of redemption. He failed to see the quiet, effectual emergence of the kingdom in the small band of Jesus' disciples. How could such inauspicious beginnings, coupled with the antagonism of the religious establishment and the immoral actions of the tetrarch, possibly square with the prophetic portrait of a kingdom that would overthrow evil and subdue the universe under its righteous domain (Isa 26:11; 66:15–16, 22–24)?

So John is called to maintain faith in God's unfolding purposes in Jesus even if he cannot put it all together in his head. He and his disciples must not be "offended" (literally, "scandalized") by the delayed timing of God's final overthrow of evil. They must reexamine their presuppositions, partly conditioned by the prevailing understanding of Messiah as a national liberator. They must shed their cultural lenses and listen carefully to Jesus as he expounds the Old Testament prophecies in light of his self-revelation.

⇨ How prone are we, like John, to interpret the ministry of Jesus through the lens of our own experiences? What danger is there in identifying Jesus with a particular form of domestic political ideology? How can we prevent such cultural conditioning?

THE UNSTOPPABLE ADVANCE OF THE KINGDOM

(Matthew 11:7–15; Luke 7:24–30)

John's inquiry revealed a misunderstanding of the delayed timing of the full manifestation of the kingdom. Jesus quickly turned to the crowds, with his own disciples listening in, to disabuse them of any notion that John's faith was suspect or that his earlier witness was faulty. Of his three rhetorical questions, the first two expect a negative answer and the final one an affirmative. The crowds did not stream through the desert of Judea to the Jordan valley to see a vacillating religious figure, like a reed swayed by the wind, or a pampered king like Antipas, royally attired and dwelling in a palace. No, they went to hear a prophet whose dress and diet were a visual protest against such indulgence and whose courageous rebuke had now landed him in prison. John's vacillation is uncharacteristic, the kind that assailed many of the Old Testament prophets who struggled to understand the nature and timing of their own prophecies (1 Pet 1:10–11).

John, in fact, is the final and greatest prophet because he is the messenger of Yahweh prophesied in Malachi 3:1, commissioned to prepare the way for Messiah. Yet John, the last and greatest figure of the preparatory stage of salvation history, assumes a lesser status than even the humblest citizen in the kingdom of heaven. Those who live in the inaugural stage of the kingdom experience the "better promises" of Jeremiah's new covenant: the indwelling of the Spirit, familial intimacy with God the Father, a universal and transcultural brotherhood, and the forgiveness of sins (Heb 8:6–13). John is on the outside looking in at the surpassing glory of the privileges of the new era (2 Cor 3:7–18). Though John's ministry overlaps with the transitional period where the kingdom is beginning to dawn, the formal in-breaking of God's rule comes with Jesus' death and resurrection.

The two main statements of Matthew 11:12 can be translated in several ways (author's renderings):

1. "The kingdom of heaven has been forcefully advancing and violent people are trying to stop its advance."

2. "The kingdom of heaven has been forcefully advancing and forceful people (i.e. its enthusiastic adherents) lay hold of it."

3. "The kingdom of heaven is suffering violently and violent people are attacking it."

Though all three renderings can find adequate lexical support, the second translation has the best contextual fit. Jesus says that from (since but not including) the time of John's ministry God's dynamic lordship is being extended to more and more people, like the Samaritans, the Roman centurion, and preeminently the twelve apostles. Though it demands repentance and radical submission to the King, God is drawing passionate disciples to live under and to promote his rule in the world. Its forward advance is unstoppable and one day the tiny kingdom community will, through its sacrificial proclamation of the gospel, reap a worldwide spiritual harvest from every tribe and nation.

John is not only the messenger of Malachi 3:1, but also the "Elijah" of Malachi 4:5–6 who comes to prepare the hearts of God's people for the arrival of the King in both salvation and judgment. John comes not as the literal reemergence of Elijah (John 1:21), but "in the spirit and power" (Luke 1:17) of that great prophet of old to call the nation away from its lifeless traditions to a living faith in the Lamb of God who has come to bear the sins of his people.

⇨ "He who has ears to hear, let him hear." Do we heed this warning to let the Word of God 'sink in' when we hear it expounded? What does it mean to listen but not hear?

PLAYING GAMES AND WATCHING MIRACLES
(Matthew 11:16–24; Luke 7:31–35)

Jesus launches a set of stinging rebukes to his complacent countrymen. His contemporaries are a generation that cannot be satisfied by John's stern warnings or by Jesus' gracious promises. They are a generation that loves the benefits but hates the demands of the kingdom. Jesus calls his listeners to see their present life in light of a coming day of accountability. John's baptism of repentance has created a divide between those who recognize their bankruptcy and those who congratulate themselves for being separate from tax collectors and other law breakers (Luke 7:29–30).

1. *Childish games*

   This generation is compared to children playing games in the marketplace. The children taunt their playmates who refuse to dance at the playing of the flute and refuse to lament when they sing a dirge.

They pout when the normal rules of the wedding and funeral games respectively are not being followed. Similarly, Jesus' contemporaries are a childish generation that cannot be satisfied. When John appears as the austere prophet demanding a fruit-producing repentance and warning of judgment by fire for those who refuse to hear (Matt 3:1–12), the children play the flute and expect him to dance. Relax, they say, don't be so self-denying and radical; celebrate the blessings of your Jewish heritage. When Jesus enjoys the company of repentant sinners (Matt 9:10–11), prefers wine and food to fasting (Luke 5:33–34), and speaks of a messianic banquet with the patriarchs (Matt 8:11), the children switch to singing a dirge and expect him to mourn. You are too lax in your associations, they say, and play loose with the traditions; take a more serious line with those who would corrupt Israel's heritage.

Both men in different ways embody a kingdom that is unpalatable to the ethno-centric and tradition-minded religious leaders and the multitudes under their influence. John's ministry signifies the necessity of heart-searching repentance as the prerequisite for entering life under God's rule. Jesus' ministry promises the joy of a life lived out under God's governance. The final proverb, "wisdom is justified by all her children" (or "deeds" in Matthew's paraphrase), means that John and Jesus will be vindicated by the fruit of their labor, the transformed lives of kingdom citizens. By contrast, those who ridicule the need for repentance and deride all expressions of joy, will find themselves excluded from both.

2. *Miracles galore*

Jesus levels his severest rebuke for people who remain obstinate in the face of the most convincing evidence. Chorazin (NW), Bethsaida (NE) and Capernaum formed a triangle of towns privileged to witness Jesus' miracles in abundance during the Early Galilean ministry. Clearly miraculous healings and exorcisms, even of the most dramatic kind, have no inherent power to change a person's heart. But with privilege comes responsibility (Luke 12:48b). At the final judgment these people who have seen firsthand the attesting signs of the Messiah and refused his kingdom offer will be judged more severely than the ancient Phoenicians (Tyre and Sidon) whose arrogant smugness was unmatched (Ezek 26–28) and the town of Sodom whose disgusting immorality was proverbial (Gen 18–19).

John the Baptist wondered why Jesus Messiah had not performed his baptism with fire. Here Jesus announces it is coming, yet not only on Gentiles but also on unbelieving Jews. As Paul later writes, the Jew is first in salvation but first also in judgment (Rom 1:16; 2:9; cf. Amos 3:2).

⇨ What lessons are there in this passage for Western Christendom where the gospel is widely known, but the response is often superficial, devoid of repentance and joy?

THANKSGIVING TO THE FATHER

(Matthew 11:25–27)

Approaching the mid-point of his Galilean ministry, Jesus is facing stiff resistance on many fronts. The Pharisees have rejected John's baptism and Jesus' gracious overtures (Luke 7:30). The multitudes, under the influence of the religious leaders, are an unsatisfied generation likened to children playing games (Matt 11:16–17). Towns where his miraculous works have been most visible have failed to profit from the exposure (11:20–24). Even the forerunner, imprisoned for the past year by the immoral tetrarch of Galilee, has begun to entertain doubts (Matt 11:2). Jesus does not panic, but prayerfully entrusts himself to the sovereign purposes of his Father.

Jesus first offers praise to the Father, Lord of heaven and earth. God is not frustrated by the setbacks nor caught off guard by the opposition. In fact, the polarized response—hostility from the learned Rabbis and repentance among those who enter the kingdom like little children—is an outworking of God's purposes. "These things" (11:25) encompass the entirety of God's kingdom program, the present redemptive rule over dependent, trusting individuals which one day will extend to unrivaled supremacy over the universe. The Father has concealed "these things" from the self-sufficient and revealed them to the teachable. Everything is unfolding according to the predetermined good pleasure of the Father, from the tiny, vulnerable community of true disciples, to their determined opponents, to the fickle crowds.

Following his affirmation of God's careful superintendence of history, Jesus solemnly declares his absolute Sonship, one that is in perfect union with the Father. Though planned by the Father, the redemptive mission ("all things" [v. 27]) has been committed to the Son to carry out through his perfect life and vicarious death. Scholars often point out that the Synoptic Gospels primarily set forth a functional Christology with the focus on Jesus' mission, that is, what he came to accomplish. Nevertheless, a higher, onto-logical Christology occasionally protrudes the functional surface, like the tip of an iceberg, and discloses who this Person is who executes the redemp-tive plan. Matthew 11:27 is ontology, approximating many of the definitive Christological texts in John's Gospel where Jesus' preexistence, divine nature and eternal Sonship are front and center (John 1:1–2, 18; 3:35; 5:17; 8:19, 58; 10:15; 14:9; 16:15). Jesus speaks of himself as the Son in an absolute, unmodified sense (Matt 24:36; 28:19). The intimacy of this Father-Son rela-tionship includes a comprehensive mutual knowledge which makes the Son the exclusive agent of the Father's revealed truth. This reciprocal knowledge shared only by Father and Son ensures that what the Son discloses about the Father is truthful.

The self-contained world of Father and Son means that one must lis-ten to the Son if the Father is to be known (John 14:9), hence the Father's repeated plea for human beings to turn their attention to the beloved Son of his good pleasure (Matt 3:17; 17:5). Just as the redemptive program is planned according to God's good pleasure (11:26), so the disclosure of the saving knowledge of God the Father to people is in accordance with the Son's sovereign choice (11:27b). The elective element does not mitigate the demand for faith and repentance. In the 'mystery of providence' divine sov-ereignty and human responsibility complement each other, though in a way that transcends human comprehension. Who Jesus is, the divine Son and second person of the triune Godhead, makes his sacrifice sufficient for all who place their trust in him.

⇨ Is this a period where you are buffeted by doubt or gripped with anxi-ety? Find peace and joy through acknowledgement of God's sovereign lordship over your circumstances.

AN INVITATION TO REST

(Matthew 11:28–30)

Following his self-disclosure as the eternal Son of God and exclusive revealer of the Father, Jesus invites any and all who are "weary and burdened" (NIV) to come to him for rest. The invitation is to a relationship—"come to me"—which renews the soul. Weariness can be physical exhaustion from a long trip (John 4:6) or from working all night (Luke 5:5). But here the weariness denotes the mental and spiritual toll incurred from the futile pursuit of a conformative righteousness based on the law and oral traditions (Matt 5:20). Such people become "heavy laden," that is, weighed down by their chronic inability to attain to the standards demanded of them. Jesus condemned the scribes and Pharisees for placing heavy loads on people's shoulders that they could not bear (Matt 23:4). The invitation to rest, then, comes to those yearning for release from all binding taxonomies ("if ..., then ...") of performance-driven attempts to please God.

The rest that Jesus offers, like the kingdom itself, is both present and future. As the disciple draws near to Jesus, the Lord grants heart refreshment, a state of inner peace free from all burdens of a self-generated striving for God's acceptance. Jesus draws on the agricultural metaphor of the "yoke," a crossbar with two U-shaped pieces that encircled the necks of a pair of oxen, mules or other draft animals for plowing the field. Rather than being yoked to the demands of the Mosaic law, which the Judaizers sought to place upon the necks of the Gentile disciples (Acts 15:10; Gal 5:1), the weary and burdened ones are yoked to Jesus in order to learn from the meek and humble One how to please and glorify the Father. Or, taking into account the preceding context (11:27), the believer is tied to Jesus as a pair serving the Father's redemptive purposes in the world. Though exalted in position and authority as the exclusive Son of the Father, in heart and character Jesus is the humble Servant who provides rest for the souls of those released from the yoke of the law and bound to him (Matt 12:18–21; 21:5). The language of soul-rest is taken from Jeremiah 6:16. There the prophet commands the people of Judah, facing imminent judgment, to stand at the crossroads of a glorious past and an uncertain future and to inquire after the "ancient paths," and once again walk in the "good way" of the patriarchs and godly kings like David. Faith and obedience, then, will result in "rest for your souls." Jesus is not reinstating the worn out provisions of the old covenant, which Israel failed to keep, but, like Jeremiah (31:31–34), inaugurating a new covenant in solidarity with the unconditional Abrahamic covenant of blessing. He himself is the mediator of the new order which centers on a cleansed conscience at peace with God through the forgiveness of sins (Matt 26:28; Heb 8:6).

Though Jesus' demands are soul-accosting and rooted in the very perfection of God himself (Matt 5:48), they are not burdensome (1 John 5:3) because the disciple is paired with a humble Servant in the service of a loving Father. Thus Jesus' yoke "fits perfectly" (NLT) and the resulting burden is, paradoxically, light. This is not the rest of inactivity. Believers yoked to Jesus bear the burdens of others in fulfilling the law of Christ which is sacrificial love (Gal 6:2). In so doing they provide spiritual refreshment for fellow pilgrims in the hard journey toward the kingdom of God which lies just over the next horizon (1 Cor 16:18; 2 Cor 7:13; Phlm 7, 20).

⇨ Are you weary and burdened by addiction to a performance-based approach in your relationship with God? Like "Christian" in John Bunyan's *The Pilgrim's Progress,* let the crushing weight of such false expectations tumble off your back at the cross of Christ. Listen intently to Jesus' invitation: "Come to me . . . and I will give you rest."

MUCH FORGIVENESS, MUCH LOVE

(Luke 7:36–50)

Jesus gladly accepted invitations to meals, whether the host was a tax collector (Mark 2:15), a leper (Mark 14:3) or, as in this case, a Pharisee named Simon. He could mix it up equally with social outcasts as well as religious sophisticates. The invitation was probably to an afternoon meal after the synagogue service on the Sabbath. Simon was so impressed by Jesus' knowledge of the law that he overcame any scruples over inviting to his home one known as a "friend of tax collectors and sinners" (Luke 7:34). As Jesus reclined at the table with his feet spread out away from the low table, a sinful woman, a local prostitute, entered and approached Jesus from behind. She was allowed entrance, in the custom of oriental hospitality, to allow the needy to receive the leftover scraps after the meal was completed. She brought with her a long-necked alabaster bottle full of fragrant ointment. She began to wet his feet with her falling tears, wipe them with her hair, kiss them, and apply the ointment, which was normally intended for the head (Mark 14:3). Her attention to the dusty feet of the Galilean traveler, remaining in the background without words, only tears, revealed a penitent heart. Jesus silently accepted the woman's act of gratitude, but Simon's logic was one of guilt by association—a true prophet, as the people are acclaiming him to be (Luke 7:16), would have perceived the character of the woman touching him and never allow such a thing!

But with prophetic insight into Simon's thoughts, Jesus engaged his host with the parable of the two debtors. One man was forgiven an obligation of 500 denarii, while another's fifty denarii debt was cancelled. When asked which of the two would love the master more, Simon replied cautiously because he could see where Jesus was heading: "The one, I suppose, for whom he cancelled the larger debt." Jesus directed Simon's attention to the actions of the woman. Love, Jesus says, is the active response of the forgiven one to grace bestowed. Loving service is how gratitude is expressed. The implications of the parable became painfully clear to Simon as Jesus applied it to the present situation. Simon had performed the normal duties of hospitality, but this woman had offered to Jesus lavish devotion beyond all expectations—washing his feet with tears, then wiped with her hair, kissing the feet, and pouring expensive perfume on the feet, not head. The entire scene is one of self-giving devotion to one she had come to love deeply. This woman, whose sins were great, loved more because she had felt the release of so great a burden on her soul. On the other hand, one who has been forgiven little, because of the delusion of self-righteousness, is capable of little love. Jesus does not mean that Simon, or others who compare themselves favorably with blatantly immoral outsiders, needs only a small measure of forgiveness, but that he has failed to recognize the magnitude of his sin and has thus underestimated his need for forgiveness. A deep consciousness of one's egregious violation of God's holy law, which merits swift and severe judgment, is surely one of the Spirit's greatest gifts (John 16:8–11).

Jesus pronounced the woman forgiven and sent her away in peace, completing the chain of salvation which began with her pursuit and discovery of Jesus: faith—forgiveness—gratitude—love—peace. Simon would have rightly understood these words to be a claim to an exclusively divine prerogative (Luke 5:21). The other guests, probably including some disciples, were left to ponder: "Who is this, who even forgives sins?"

⇨　From the pen of the former slave-trader, John Newton, came the familiar words: "Twas grace that taught my heart to fear, and grace my fears relieved. How precious did that grace appear, the hour I first believed." Is God's grace "amazing" to you?

THE TRUE FAMILY OF JESUS

(Matthew 12:46–50; Mark 3:20–21, 31–35; Luke 8:1–3, 19–21)

For the second time Jesus toured Galilee (first tour: Mark 1:39), this time traveling through towns and villages with the twelve apostles. This was a systematic campaign of evangelism in the countryside with the accent on the proclamation of the kingdom. Three prominent women were among the "many others" that accompanied them and helped provide financial support for the itinerant band. Jesus rose above the gender-based discrimination of his day to welcome women as vital contributors to the kingdom enterprise. Mary Magdalene is characteristically named first, and thus was the leader of these Galilean women. She had been delivered from seven demons (Luke 8:2), continued to serve him all the way to the cross (Mark 15:40; John 19:25), witnessed his interment in Joseph's tomb (Matt 27:61), was the first to visit the tomb on Sunday morning, bringing news to Peter and John that the stone had been rolled away (John 20:1–2), and saw the risen Lord in the garden at the tomb later in the morning (John 20:10–18). Two other women are named: Joanna, wife of Chuza, a high official of Herod Antipas, and who accompanied Mary to the tomb early Easter morning (Luke 24:10); and Susanna, otherwise unknown.

The successful extension of the kingdom during the second tour brought with it determined opponents. Upon his return to Capernaum, Jesus met with fierce opposition both from his earthly family and from visiting Pharisees from Jerusalem. Mark's Gospel brackets the account of the dispute with the Pharisees over the origin of his exorcising authority (Mark 3:22–30) with this visit of his earthly family (Mark 3:20–21, 31–32). His mother and brothers accused him of being out of his mind and sought to restrain him from further embarrassing them. Mary had long struggled to understand her son's mission (Luke 2:19, 48, 51; 11:27–28; John 2:3–4), while Jesus' brothers did not believe in him until after the resurrection (John 7:5; Acts 1:14). When they arrived they were unable to enter Peter's house due to the pressing crowd. To the report that his family was outside waiting to speak to him, Jesus returned a stunning question: "Who are my mother and my brothers?" (Mark 3:33). He then proceeded to answer his own question: my true family members are those who do the will of the Father. The character and makeup of the family of Jesus is wholly unrelated to ethnic identity, religious affiliation, or even direct blood ties. Submission to the Father's will is what identifies and substantiates that one is a member of the family of Jesus, presently represented by the small group of disciples. Through the new birth people become children of the Father and fellow brothers joined to their elder brother, Jesus (John 1:12–13; Matt 23:8–9; 25:40; 28:10). Here is the fulfillment of the new covenant promise: "I will be their God and they shall be my people" (Jer 31:33b). The kingdom community is a royal family formed on the basis of heart loyalty to the King.

No relationships are more endearing, nurturing, and formative (assuming an intact family structure, which was largely the case in first century

Palestine) than one's ties to father, mother and siblings. It is in this area that some of Jesus' hardest sayings emerge. The four fishermen were called to leave family and occupation to follow him into itinerant ministry (Mark 1:16–20). Jesus warned his followers that at times persecution would originate from their closest relatives (Mark 13:12–13). Love for the Master must be so absolute that, by comparison, a true disciple will appear to disavow (literally, "hate") one's earthly family (Luke 14:26).

⇨ Read Peter's question in Matt 19:27, empathizing with Peter's sense of loss. Now read the Lord's reply in 19:28–30 and be encouraged by the incomparable rewards for the one willing to sacrifice for the kingdom.

PLUNDERING THE POSSESSIONS OF THE STRONG MAN

(Matthew 12:22–29; Mark 3:22–27)

A blind and mute man whose debilitation was due to demon possession was brought to Jesus, who exorcised the demon and restored the man's ability to see and to speak. The astonishment of the people elicited speculation whether Jesus might be the Son of David, a popular designation for the Messiah. However, any celebration of, or further reflection on, this man's healing was quickly drowned out by the theological controversy that followed. When the Pharisees heard of the miracle, they immediately credited it to demonic causation. Jesus was driving out demons by the power of Beelzebub, a derisive epithet for Satan, prince of the demons (Matt 10:25). This perverse charge, attributing the miraculous works of the Son of God to Satanic empowerment, became the stock in trade accusation of the religious leaders who were unable to deny the miracles themselves (Matt 9:34; 10:25; John 7:20; 8:48, 52; 10:20).

Jesus launches a defense by exposing the circular, and thus self-defeating, logic of his accusers. First, he reminds them of the well understood general principle that a kingdom, city or household divided against itself can not stand. Then, he applies the principle to the kingdom of Satan. If Satan is behind this exorcism, then he is using his authority to undermine his own dominion, a patently absurd situation. The presupposition of Jesus' argument is that Satan, though evil and ultimately self-destructive, would brook no dissent among his demonic subjects and immediately crush any division among the ranks. Being the adversary of God and man, he would never work to restore a man from the debilitating effects of demon possession. Before his opponents can attempt a refutation, Jesus asks one further question: "By whom do your sons cast them (the demons) out?" Jewish exorcists were active during this period (one example is the sons of Sceva in Acts 19:13–16). While the Pharisees would have answered that, unlike Jesus, Jewish exorcists were empowered by God, the question forces the wavering multitude to decide who is on God's side, the loving healer or his cynical accusers.

Now Jesus takes the offensive. He posits that if, as is the case, it is by the Spirit of God that he is rolling back the forces of darkness, then God's kingdom has effectively arrived. God's dynamic rule over those who repent is beginning to dawn. The healing and exorcising ministry of Jesus is an initial assault on the dehumanizing activity of the evil one and a harbinger of his sure defeat at the end of the age. Jesus employs the analogy of a thief who enters a person's home, ties up the owner, and then robs his house. In his kingdom ministry Jesus is binding the strong man, Satan, in order to plunder his possessions, which represent human beings subject to his enticement and destructive influence. The binding of Satan in the present age, however, is with a long rope. He is still active in the world, wrecking lives and attempting to thwart the advance of God's rule. But he is a defeated foe whose doom is sure (John 12:31–32). His activities in the world are like the convulsions of a snake whose head has been cut off.

The "already" aspect of the kingdom has been compared to D-day, June 6, 1944, when the allied troops stormed the beaches in Normandy on their way to liberating France. The success of D-day led to V-day (the "not yet" aspect) approximately one year later when Germany offered an unconditional surrender to end World War II. Between D-day and V-day there were still several fierce battles which resulted in heavy casualties on both sides. But the backbone of the German army had been broken and the outcome of the war was certain.

⇨ How does this passage shed light on the nature of spiritual warfare in the present interim age between the kingdom inaugurated and the kingdom consummated?

THE UNFORGIVABLE SIN

(Matthew 12:30–37; Mark 3:28–30)

With the forces of darkness under full assault from the kingdom of light, this is no time for neutrality. Jesus makes the divine claim to be the eschatological harvester of souls: "Whoever is not with me is against me, and whoever does not gather with me scatters." This is directed at the wavering crowd. Indifference aligns itself on the side of those who oppose the kingdom. The inverted saying, "the one who is not against us is for us" (Mark 9:40) is spoken later to correct the myopic attitudes of his disciples who are forbidding a man to exorcise demons in Jesus' name because "he was not following us" (Mark 9:38). Taken together, these proverbs demand exclusive and unwavering commitment to Jesus free of narrow, sectarian divisions, that is, forbearance without compromise. Here is the tension in Christian discipleship.

Then comes a warning concerning blasphemy against the Spirit, which can never be forgiven, either in the present age or in the age to come. What is this unforgivable sin, which is set apart from all other blasphemies, even speaking against the Son of Man, all of which can be forgiven? In its historical context Jesus is addressing people who have, in the face of overwhelming evidence, rejected his messianic claims and attributed his miracles to demonic empowerment. With the Pharisees there is a deliberate and repeated repudiation of his person and Spirit-attested work that has produced an obduracy so pervasive that repentance is rendered impossible. Though the historical situation cannot be reproduced, there is still the possibility that a person in any age can reject the gospel with such determined resistance that they pass a point of no return. The limit is not placed on God's ability to forgive, but on the capacity of a person to repent. Just as in the Old Testament, to sin defiantly, literally with a fist of anger thrust upward toward God's face, meant swift and irrevocable judgment (Num 15:30–31), so to blaspheme the Spirit is to place oneself beyond the sphere of forgiveness. On a formal level, one can compare this to the many New Testament warnings, beginning with Jesus (Matt 10:22; 24:13), directed toward believers which make perseverance in faith a necessary condition for final salvation (Rom 8:11; 11:22; 1 Cor 9:27; 2 Cor 13:5; Phil 2:12; Col 1:23: Heb 2:3; 3:6, 14; 6:4–8; 10:26–31; 12:25; Rev 2:7; 21:7). Nevertheless, the warning against the blasphemy of the Spirit is directed toward people who never entered or even professed to enter the community of faith. A sensitive believer who fears that he or she may have committed this sin demonstrates by their very concern that they have not blasphemed the Spirit.

The true test of spiritual life in the new covenant is not profession, impressive displays of power (Matt 7:16–20), or, in this case, biblical sophistry, but a transformed character that produces Christlike behavior. The Pharisees are labeled a "brood of vipers," bad trees with rotten fruit, corrupt hearts that produce worthless words. As the fruit reveals the condition of the tree, so one's words disclose what is stored up in one's heart. Jesus concludes with a sobering description of the final judgment sure to grab the attention of all aspiring disciples: each one will give an account "for every careless (i.e. without positive effect) word they speak." The implication is clear. One must approach the challenge of controlling one's tongue from the inside-out, allowing the Spirit to cleanse the heart from which will flow wholesome speech. This will meet with God's approbation, promised by the One who possesses authority to forgive sins (Luke 5:20; 7:48).

⇨ Take the warning of Matthew 12:36–37 seriously and pray from the heart David's prayer in Psalm 141:3: "Set a guard, O Lord, over my mouth; keep watch over the door of my lips."

THE SIGN OF JONAH

(Matthew 12:38–45)

The scribes and Pharisees demanded that Jesus authenticate his claims with a miraculous sign, a blatant example of a "careless word" (12:36) since this entire episode began with his healing of a deaf and mute man. His opponents have already rejected his miracles as performed under demonic causation. Their request, then, is self-defeating since they are not open to demonstrable evidence. Miracles can never compel faith (Luke 16:31) because of the remarkable capacity of people to explain them away. Jesus excoriates the miracle-on-demand mindset of his generation, for like money to a covetous person, more will never satisfy.

Nevertheless, there is one signifying work that will prove beyond all doubt, to those with eyes to see, the truth of Jesus' claims to be the Messiah and Son of God. Though unable to overcome stubborn unbelief, miracles are designed to strengthen a weak faith. The "sign of the prophet Jonah" will do this for the disciples. Just as Jonah was inside the belly of the great fish three days and three nights before being vomited onto dry land at the Lord's command (Jonah 1:17; 2:10), so the Son of Man will die, be interred in the tomb, and be raised to life by the Father on the third day. Jonah's experience interpreted typologically by Jesus is the clearest prediction of his death, burial and resurrection up until this time.

As the resurrection will vindicate the suffering Servant as the Son of God (Rom 1:3–4), so it will seal the judgment of those who reject his claims.

Once again Jesus underscores the principle that greater opportunity brings with it a deeper level of accountability (Matt 11:20–24). The Ninevites who repented at the preaching of Jonah will rise up at the final judgment to testify against this generation which has turned its back on one greater than Jonah (Jonah 3:1–10); the Queen of Sheba who came from a great distance to listen to Solomon's wisdom and returned to her country praising the Lord God of Israel will condemn this generation for failing to heed the wisdom of one greater than Solomon (1 Kgs 10:1–13). This comparison must have been particularly galling for the religious leaders who thought of themselves as the rightful heirs of the kingdom, while repentant Gentiles (Ninevites and the Queen) would be at best second class citizens.

Jesus returns to the action that sparked this controversy in the first place, the exorcism of a demon. Three features of demonic behavior are disclosed (12:43–45). First, demons have an affinity for arid places, such as the desert of Judea where Satan assaulted Jesus, but most of all seek humans to inhabit. Second, repossession is a grave danger if the formerly possessed person does not experience spiritual transformation. That person's heart is likened to a house, swept clean, put in order, but left unoccupied. Physical and emotional restoration, even moral reform, is no substitute for heart commitment to Jesus. In the new covenant such allegiance to the King brings regeneration and a new indwelling presence in the person of the Holy Spirit, who stamps the believer with the seal of ownership and claims the body as his holy temple (John 14:17: Rom 8:9, 11; 1 Cor 6:19–20; Eph 1:13–14). Jesus' words further serve as a warning to the man who has been healed to discover the meaning beneath the miracle. Third, demons prefer to inhabit together and, given the opportunity, to intensify their dehumanization of the individual. For a generation privileged with direct exposure to the Son of God, the implications are terrifying.

⇨ Are we afraid to warn our contemporaries of disdaining a radical commitment to the Lord for a domesticated form of moralistic religion? How can we arrest the attention of people and help them see the danger of neutrality?

8

Parables of the Kingdom

Now and Not Yet

MYSTERIES OF THE KINGDOM SPOKEN IN PARABLES

(Matthew 13:1–3a, 10–17, 34–35; Mark 4:1–2, 10–12; Luke 8:4, 9–10)

AFTER THE BITTER BEELZEBUB controversy with the Pharisees, "that same day" Jesus went down to the shore of Lake Galilee and began to reveal "secrets" about the kingdom of God. He employed as his pulpit a fishing boat in which he sat to address the gathering crowds. The traditional location of Tabgha, or the Sower's Cove, was west of Capernaum and formed a natural amphitheatre in which his voice could project from the lake. Jesus spoke in parables, real life settings with extended metaphors, designed to communicate spiritual truths. Though he had spoken on occasion using parables (Matt 7:24–27; Luke 5:36–39; 6:38), his choice here to employ exclusively parabolic language surprised his disciples who wanted to know why he would address the crowds in such enigmatic terms.

Jesus replied that the parables were intended both to conceal as well as to reveal "secrets" (ESV) or "mysteries" (NASB) about the kingdom of heaven. The Greek term rendered "mystery" is drawn from an Aramaic word used in Daniel to refer to God's hidden purposes for the future which he later discloses according to his sovereign pleasure (Dan 2:18, 19, 27, 28, 29, 30, 47). In the New Testament era of prophetic fulfillment, "mystery" takes on the sense of a truth about the kingdom of God that, heretofore being secreted away in the divine counsels, is unveiled to those with receptive hearts (1 Cor 4:1; Eph 3:3, 4, 9; Col 1:26–27). Jesus made a sharp distinction between the crowds and the disciples ("to you . . . to them"). This distinction emerges from the principle enunciated in verse 12, namely, that revelatory light is given in proportion to the heart response of the listener. The parabolic stories were designed to reveal knowledge of mysterious features of the kingdom to the disciples, but to conceal such knowledge from the crowds, whose ambivalence has disqualified them from receiving further insight. The distinction, then, is not one of intellectual capacity, but of spiritual sensitivity. Jesus is a person who compels either submission or rejection; he denies the middle ground to those seeking a benign religious figure. The parables actually deepen the polarization that has developed around his words and works. The present writer's Hebrew Professor used to say, "God places his choicest cookies on the top shelf so that his children have to stretch for them." The parables test the heart condition of the listeners, challenging the eager student to reach higher, while preventing the casual observer from further understanding.

Matthew and Mark see human culpability and divine determinism respectively behind Jesus' choice of parabolic teaching. On the one hand, the obstinate response of Israel to prophetic truth over the long course of her history continues with the spiritual callousness of the religious leaders (Isa 6:9–10). That is the reason (Matt 13:13) Jesus conceals truth, by way of parables, from a nation that has forfeited her right to further understanding (Rom 1:24–28). But the parables also have as their purpose (Mark 4:12) the judicial hardening of the nation so that redemptive blessings can be transferred to the Gentiles (Rom 11:7–10, 25). However, the disciples, by submitting their wills and stretching their minds after God's truth, are accorded the inestimable privilege of seeing and hearing what prophets and sages only longed to experience. Like Asaph who narrated Israel's history in Psalm 78 and interpreted its enigmatic parts, so Jesus is here disclosing "what has been hidden" in earlier stages of revelation (13:34–35). The "mysteries" fill in the shadowy images of the messianic kingdom sketched in the Old Testament.

⇨   Are you willing to stretch for God's "choicest cookies?" Pray with the Psalmist, "Open my eyes, that I may behold wondrous things out of your law" (119:18).

PARABLE OF THE SOWER

(Matthew 13:3b–9, 18–23; Mark 4:3–9, 13–25; Luke 8:5–8, 11–18)

So what is the content of the "secrets of the kingdom?" One must recall the setting in Jesus' ministry to grasp the content and to appreciate their impact. The Lord is approaching the midway point of his public ministry.

The initial excitement of the disciples in this faith adventure has long worn off. They have left family and promising vocations for encounters with hostile Pharisees, schismatic Samaritans, and throngs of sick and demonized people seeking relief. Their Master constantly confuses them with his affinity for social outcasts, repeated withdrawals from the spotlight, enigmatic sayings, and intimations of coming suffering, even death. Yet they remain undaunted in their commitment to one whose messianic claims are ridiculed by the religious leaders and increasingly doubted by the impressionable multitudes. They must have wondered, if the leading theologians (Pharisees) and priestly ruling class (Sadducees) in Israel are vehemently denying Jesus' claims to be sent from God as Redeemer and Messiah, how can the kingdom of God really be dawning? The nine parables that follow are designed to strengthen the disciples' confidence in Jesus and his unfolding kingdom program.

The disciples' dilemma was in large part due to the incomplete understanding of the kingdom that they inherited from their religious instructors. They were expecting the kingdom to arrive in accordance with Daniel's apocalyptic imagery, an overwhelming outburst of divine power that would displace the present social order, destroy Satan's hegemony, and introduce the everlasting rule of the Ancient of Days (Dan 7:9–14). The parables, however, disclose that the age to come is dawning in a totally unexpected, yet divinely planned, manner. The kingdom first arrives in the form of internal rule over repentant hearts; only in the future will its advance over the entire socio-political order be realized. Our method follows a four-fold analysis: (i) the details of the parable proper; (ii) interpretive keys hidden in the language of the parable; (iii) the "mystery" about the kingdom of God now being disclosed; (iv) application(s) of the parable to those with ears to hear.

1. *Details of the Parable of the Sower*

   (i)   A farmer goes out to sow and begins to scatter the seed.

   (ii) Some of the seed falls "along the path," picked up and eaten by birds or trampled upon.

   (iii) Other seed falls on "rocky ground." Due to the hard shallow ground, a plant springs up quickly but when the sun beats down it is scorched and withers, having no deep roots to bring moisture to the plant.

   (iv) Still other seed falls among "thorns." When the plant begins to grow, it is choked by the growing thorns and fails to bear fruit.

   (v)   Finally, some seed falls on "good soil" and produces a crop, multi-plying thirty, sixty or even one hundred times.

2. *Interpretive keys to the parable*

The reader is not dependent on uncovering subtleties in the language of the parable of the sower because it is one of three parables for which Jesus provides the interpretation (Matt 13:18–23). Here, then, is the hermeneutical framework that can be applied to the other unexplained parables. Jesus' interpretation does not squeeze a hidden meaning from every detail, but neither is it limited to a single point. This indicates the parables are restrained allegories in which incidental features are part of the story line, but also where one or more truths can be profit-ably extracted from the dominant features or repetitive elements of the story. From the interpretation emerges a core mysterious insight about the kingdom that has been secreted away in the divine counsels but is now disclosed for all to embrace.

   (i)   The farmer is the disciple and the scattering of the seed is the preaching of the gospel of the kingdom, that is, God's saving rule over the one who repents and believes. The farmer is not to blame for the seed that seems wasted; he is employing the ancient method of broadcast sowing where the seed is scattered in all directions as he walks up and down the paths separating his fields. The four kinds of soil in which the seeds fall represent varying types of heart response to the proclaimed word.

   (ii) The seed sown along the path represents the person who hears the message but before it penetrates the mind with understand-ing Satan moves in and quickly distracts the person from further consideration of the truth.

  (iii) The seed that falls on rocky earth signifies the person who initially receives the word with joy but, because he is not grounded in the saving word, falls away when trouble or persecution arises.

   (iv) The seed that falls among thorns is the person who hears the word, but anxiety over earthly matters and the deceitful attraction of material wealth begin to dominate one's thinking, stifle spiritual growth and prevent fruitfulness

(v) The "good soil" represents the person who hears the word, under-
stands it, embraces its life-transforming effects, perseveres in faith
and bears good fruit. Even among those who bear fruit there are
differing levels of fruitfulness, represented by the thirty, sixty and
hundred-fold crops.

3. *"Mystery" of the kingdom*

The central truth of this initial parable is that the proclamation of the
kingdom will meet with partial success, but for the one who faithfully
proclaims the gospel of the kingdom there will be a measure of lasting
fruit (John 15:16; 1 Cor 15:58).

The parable of the lamp, inserted here in Mark and Luke, is a call to
recognize Jesus as the lamp from God who brings to light the blessings
of the kingdom (Mark 4:21–23; Luke 8:16–17). Presently his glory is
veiled as the Son of Man who first comes to die. Those with hearing
ears will understand that the present obscurity of the Servant will one
day be exchanged for the majesty of a King. The parable of the measure
in this context (Mark 4:24–25; Luke 8:18) underscores that only those
who embrace the redemption provided by the Servant will enjoy the
blessings of the King when he establishes his rule over the universe.

4. *Applications of the Parable of the Sower*

- The gospel of the kingdom must be proclaimed in order for its saving power to be effected in the lives of people. Faith comes by hearing the Word of God (Rom 10:17).

- There will be a variety of responses among the listeners. The division
is between the first three categories and the last one. While on one
level mere exposure ("along the path") and temporary profession
("rocky ground" and "thorns") are distinguishable, the main way of
differentiating saving faith from superficial faith is fruit-bearing,
an important theme in Matthew's Gospel (3:8, 10; 7:16–20; 12:33;
21:43). Faith alone saves, but the faith that saves is not alone; it is
accompanied by a persevering faithfulness.

- For the crowd the call is to be a good listener. One must hear, understand, believe, persevere in the midst of persecution and worldly
enticements, and bear fruit. God's saving rule is effected in the comprehensive process of discipleship.

PARABLE OF THE SPONTANEOUSLY GROWING SEED

(Mark 4:26–29)

The second parable is also from the agricultural domain. In the first parable the focus is on the soils into which the seed falls; in this parable the focus shifts to the quality of the seed itself.

1. *Details of the Parable of the Seed*

    (i) A farmer scatters seed on the ground.

    (ii) As time passes in the normal course of daily activities (at night when he sleeps, during daytime while he is active) the seed sprouts and grows—first the stalk, then the head, then the full kernel in the head.

    (iii) The farmer "knows not how" the seed grows into a full plant.

    (iv) The soil "produces by itself" or, literally, "of its own power."

    (v) When the plant is ripe, the farmer thrusts the sickle to harvest the grain.

2. *Interpretive keys to the parable*

    The two expressions, "he knows not how" and "the earth produces by itself," indicate there is a resident life-germinating power in the seed itself. The sower is also the reaper. Though he is involved in the entire process, it is the seed which guarantees a crop to harvest. The human instrument plays its part faithfully, but the divine initiative and activity is what guarantees fruitfulness. How sowing ensures reaping is beyond the comprehension of the kingdom witness.

    The sickle thrust into the grain at the harvest is a metaphor for eschatological judgment taken from Joel 3:13a.

3. *"Mystery" of the kingdom*

    The central truth of this parable, unique to Mark's Gospel, is that the message of God's transforming rule through repentance has intrinsic power to penetrate the human heart and draw a person into submission to King Jesus. God is at work as the gospel of the kingdom is proclaimed by the human instrument. A community of faith is formed that will stand the final judgment and enter the consummated kingdom.

4. *Applications of the Parable of the Seed*

- As in the parable of the sower, the kingdom witness must faithfully call people to submit to Jesus' lordship in order for the saving power of the message to have its effect. The gospel is the power of God for salvation to all who believe (Rom 1:16).

- Because of the power resident in the kingdom message, proclamation of that word guarantees fruit. There is organic continuity between the sowing and the reaping (John 4:36–38). Both are undergirded by the supernatural work of the Spirit of God. The kingdom witness relies on the power of the Word, not one's abilities, resources or strategies (1 Cor 2:1–5).

PARABLE OF THE TARES

(Matthew 13:24–30, 36–43)

The third agricultural story also involves sowing and reaping, but makes a radical distinction between two kinds of plants that spring forth. Unlike the first two parables where one kind of seed is sown by the same person, here two kinds of seeds, one good and one bad, are sown by different sowers.

1. *Details of the Parable of the Tares*

    (i) A man sows good seed in his field.

    (ii) While everyone is sleeping, an enemy secretly sows tares among the wheat and departs.

    (iii) The servants discover the wheat and tares growing up together.

    (iv) Informed by his servants, the owner recognizes the mixed field as the work of the enemy.

    (v) The owner instructs his servants not to separate them now, lest he damage the wheat crop, but to wait until the "harvest," at which time the reapers will gather the weeds for burning and the wheat for storing.

2. *Interpretive keys to the parable*

    This is the second parable for which Jesus provides the meaning of the details. Once again there are multiple truths, but also many undeveloped details that are simply part of the story line.

(i)   The sower of the good seed is the Son of Man.

(ii)   The field is the world (not the church).

(iii)   The good seed which grows into wheat represents the sons of the kingdom, the people over whom God rules.

(iv)   The tares represent the sons of the evil one, those under Satan's domination.

(v)   The enemy who sows the tares is the devil.

(vi)   The harvest is the end of the age when final separation and judgment will take place.

(vii)   The reapers sent to separate wheat from tares at the harvest are the angels.

3.   *"Mystery" of the kingdom*

The "mystery" is disclosed in vv. 40–43 which describes the eschatological separation and judgment. This description unpacks the surprising turn in the parable itself when the owner tells the servants to hold off from attempting to separate wheat from tares until the designated harvest season. The main point of the parable, then, is a delay of indefinite length between the inaugural period of the kingdom, where the sons of God and the sons of the devil live together in the world, and the consummation of the kingdom when angels will separate believers from unbelievers, for salvation and judgment respectively.

This parable deals with eschatology not ecclesiology. The field is not the church but the world. Human society will continue its normal patterns of existence with unbelievers living side by side with the people transformed by God's saving rule. Only at the consummation will unbelief and evil be uprooted. Then the righteous ones will inherit a glorious kingdom where they will shine like the sun reflecting the radiance of their Father (Dan 12:2–3).

4.   *Application of the Parable of the Tares*

The church is to be a counter-cultural witness to the coming Son of Man during the present age. The church is not called to legislate Christian morality to unredeemed people, or to be caught up in endless protestations against the immorality of the godless. Kingdom citizens proactively point people to the Son of Man, the one who first comes to suffer a redemptive death and will return as Judge and King.

PARABLE OF THE MUSTARD SEED

(Matthew 13:31–32; Mark 4:30–32)

1. *Details of the Parable of the Mustard Seed*

   (i)   A farmer plants a mustard seed in his field.

   (ii) Though it is the smallest seed planted by Palestinian farmers, it grows into the largest of all garden plants.

   (iii) The mustard tree becomes so large that the birds come and perch in its large branches for shade.

2. *Interpretive keys to the parable*

   The central feature is the stunning contrast between the tiny size of the mustard seed when it is planted and the vast mustard plant when it is full grown. The spreading branches that provide shade to the birds of the air is prophetic language for the extensive growth and impressive magnitude of the mature plant (Ezek 17:23; 31:6; Dan 4:12). The organic life shared by mustard seed and plant is what determines and guarantees undeterred extension.

3. *"Mystery" of the kingdom*

   Though the kingdom of God dawning in Jesus is at present unimpressive, weak and vulnerable, it is destined for greatness. The tiny beginnings in Palestine with the disciples of Jesus will issue in a glorious worldwide reign of God spanning the globe and encompassing people from all cultures. The successful extension of God's rule is ensured by the organic continuity that binds the small beginning to its vast expansion.

4. *Application of the Parable of the Mustard Seed*

   Evangelists and church planters who toil in resistant cultures where small groups of believers struggle to make headway can take great encouragement from this parable. They are a part of a worldwide kingdom enterprise destined to succeed. They sow in faith, confident that a glorious day of harvest will come.

PARABLE OF THE LEAVEN

(Matthew 13:33)

1. *Details of the Parable of the Leaven*

    (i) A woman took yeast and mixed it into a large amount of flour.

    (ii) The yeast worked effectively until the entire batch of dough was leavened.

2. *Interpretive keys to the parable*

    Leaven, often a symbol of evil (Matt 16:6), did have positive uses as when yeast accompanied stipulated offerings (Lev 7:13; 23:15–18). Its central image is its power to spread and influence.

    In this case, a small amount of leaven works through a large batch of dough, estimated at twenty-two liters, producing bread enough to feed up to 100 people.

3. *"Mystery" of the kingdom*

    God's rule operates quietly but effectively from small beginnings to spread its transforming influence over larger portions of the human race until one day, at the return of Christ, it will prevail and displace all rival sovereignty.

4. *Application of the Parable of the Leaven*

    Though kingdom citizens must avoid triumphalistic notions of the Christianization of the entire world through evangelization and social work, their ministries should be inspired by a vision for the harvest, confident in the one who promises to build his church (Matt 16:18).

PARABLE OF THE HIDDEN TREASURE

(Matt 13:44)

1. *Details of the Parable of the Hidden Treasure*

    (i) A treasure is lying hidden in a field.

 (ii) A man discovers the treasure and quickly hides it again.

 (iii) Rejoicing, he sells "all that he has," and purchases the field in which the treasure is buried.

2. *Interpretive keys to the parable*

The treasure, of incomparable worth, represents the kingdom. That the man sold "all that he has" to purchase the entire field, made valuable by its holding the buried treasure, means the kingdom is a precious treasure worth sacrificing everything for. The point is not that the kingdom can be purchased, for redemption is a free gift received by faith and repentance.

3. *"Mystery" of the kingdom*

The parable illustrates the inestimable value of the kingdom. Nothing that a person owns or aspires to compares to the rule of God over one's life and the promotion of the rule of God over the lives of those presently dominated by sin and the devil. It is an enterprise that deserves one's entire life, possessions, resources, talents and energies.

4. *Application of the Parable of the Hidden Treasure*

Like the four fishermen, Levi and the other apostles, the obedient disciple is called to joyfully, not with grudging disdain, offer to God one's family, possessions, vocational prospects, societal standing and all other normal human spheres of involvement so that the kingdom of God can be one's singular, all-consuming ambition (Matt 6:33).

PARABLE OF THE VALUABLE PEARL
(Matthew 13:45–46)

1. *Details of the Parable of the Valuable Pearl*

 (i) A merchant is actively looking for fine pearls.

 (ii) His eager pursuit is rewarded when he discovers a pearl of great value.

 (iii) He departs, sells "all that he had," and uses the money to purchase the precious pearl.

2. *Interpretive keys to the parable*

As with the hidden treasure, the valuable pearl represents the incomparable worth of the kingdom of God. It is worth sacrificing anything for. If there is a slight distinction in the two parables, it lies in the detail that here the merchant is actively looking for pearls, while the hidden treasure was an unplanned sudden discovery. Thus Jesus brings people into his kingdom through both sudden conversions and lengthy earnest periods of searching.

3. *"Mystery" of the kingdom*

The pearl of great price symbolizes the kingdom that is of great value. All that one has or aspires to have is worth sacrificing in order to enter and to promote this kingdom. There is nothing like it in the world.

4. *Application of the Parable of the Valuable Pearl*

Like Paul, knowing Jesus Christ as one's Lord is of such surpassing worth that all other past allurements and sources of boasting become rubbish. To know Him and to make him known becomes the defining pursuit of one's life (Phil 3:7–10).

PARABLE OF THE FISHING NET

(Matthew 13:47–50)

1. *Details of the Parable of the Fishing Net*

    (i)   A fishing net was cast into the lake and caught fish of "every kind."

    (ii) When the net was full, the fishermen pulled it up on shore. These dragnets, spread over a wide area of water, could contain such a large haul that at times they had to be pulled to shore by several boats (Luke 5:4–7; John 21:6–8).

    (iii) The fishermen then collected the good fish in baskets, but threw the bad fish away.

2. *Interpretive keys to the parable*

This is the third parable, along with the parables of the sower and the tares, for which Jesus provides the interpretation. Jesus relates this parable to the final separation of people at the end of the age, just as with the parable of the tares (13:39–43). However, while the tares represent unbelievers who live alongside the kingdom community throughout human history (the field is the world not the church [13:38]), in this case the good and bad fish together caught in the net represent the mixed community created as the kingdom proclamation goes forth. Unlike the parable of the tares, this parable has an ecclesiological application. "Every kind" of fish, in addition to including good and bad fish, may also imply every ethnic category, that is, both Jew and Gentile.

3. *"Mystery" of the kingdom*

The community created by the proclamation of the kingdom in the present age is a mixed one, composed of true believers and superficial professors. At the future judgment a thorough distinguishing of authentic believers from false disciples will take place.

4. *Applications of the Parable of the Fishing Net*

- Because faith-repentance is the sole precondition for entering the kingdom, one must be cautious about making confident assessments regarding who is and who is not a truly regenerate subject of the King. The transforming reality of an internal spiritual transaction is ultimately known only to the person and to God. Fruit-bearing, which Jesus sets forth as the proof of spiritual life (Matt 7:17–20), can be slow to develop and at times difficult to detect because the transformation may be at first in the hidden recesses of one's values, thoughts and motives before it finds expression in external behaviors. All attempts at creating the pure church in the interim period by weeding out suspected professors are not only misguided but will ultimately fail. Each person must be vigilant to test their own profession of faith and leave the definitive separation to God at the final judgment.

- Nevertheless, the apostles commanded the churches to practice discipline. When the spiritual welfare of the church is threatened by members who violate the doctrinal, moral or relational standards set forth in Scripture, disciplinary measures, even excommunication, are imperative. The goal, however, is always the repentance and restoration of the offender (Matt 18:15–20; 1 Cor 5:1–13; 2 Cor 2:5–11; Gal 6:1; 1 Tim 1:19–20).

PARABLE OF THE HOUSE OWNER

(Matthew 13:51–53)

Before relaying the final parable, Jesus asks the disciples whether they have understood "all these things." As the exemplary teacher who has crafted nine stories to reveal truth to his true followers, he is concerned that they grasp the "secrets of the kingdom." Their quick and unqualified affirmative once again shows the apostles' tendency to overestimate their perception, as well as their courage (Matt 15:16; 20:22). It will soon become clear that they have no clue how to fit his predictions of the suffering Servant into God's kingdom program (Matt 16:21–23).

1. *Details of the Parable of the House Owner*

    (i) The subject is identified as "every scribe who has been trained for (the benefit of) the kingdom of heaven."

    (ii) This kingdom scribe is likened to the owner of a house who brings out from his storeroom (literally, "treasure") new things and old things.

2. *Interpretive keys to the parable*

    The subject is one who is trained in the kingdom teachings of Jesus and who in turn can make disciples of others. Jesus gives his disciples the benefit of the doubt that they have been listening with perceptive hearts, even if their affirmative reply to his initial question is a bit overstated. The "treasure" in the homeowner analogy is the heart (Matt 6:21) in which is stored up a set of truths gleaned from stage one of salvation history in the Old Testament, now illumined by the fulfillment of the types, promises and predictive prophecies in Jesus.

3. *"Mystery" of the kingdom*

    The commitment to discipleship, which involves training under the Master, leads to a transformed understanding of how the new fulfills, and thus illumines, the old. The promissory-prophetic revelation of the old covenant culminates in the new covenant inaugurated by Jesus (Matt 5:17–20) and is expounded by his kingdom disciple-teachers as they carry out the Great Commission (Matt 28:18–20).

4. *Application of the Parable of the House Owner*

This final parable contains an implicit exhortation for kingdom citizens to move from commitment to understanding to teaching. Serious study of both Testaments, with special focus on how Jesus and the apostles interpret the Old Testament, is paramount.

SUMMARY OF THE PARABLES OF THE KINGDOM

The comprehensive sense of the "secret/mystery of the kingdom," then, is its initial arrival in a veiled manner that works secretly but powerfully in the hearts of people. One day, however, this provisional beginning will break out in apocalyptic power to bring the universe, human and subhuman, under the lordship of God. The kingdom theology of their Lord equipped the disciples to align themselves with God's purposes, free from both triumphalism on the one hand and marginalization on the other. They had committed themselves to the King who with authority was even now establishing his rule over repentant hearts. Though the community is small and the opposition is intense, the ultimate triumph of the enterprise of which they are a vital part is certain.

⇨ Do your activities point toward a singular focus on God's mandate—the discipling of the nations—or are other competing agendas displacing a kingdom perspective with an organizational or programmatic one?

9

Middle Galilean Ministry

Call to Sacrifice, Promise of Harvest

POWER TO STILL THE STORM

(Matthew 8:18, 23–27; Mark 4:35–41; Luke 8:22–25)

JESUS DECIDED TO WITHDRAW to the east side of Lake Galilee. He needs physical rest from the exhausting Galilean ministry, seen in his deep sleep in the boat that even a storm cannot disturb. He states his intention to "go over to the other side," traveling from the north to the southeast side of the lake in the region of Gadara. With hills to the east and west ascending abruptly to 2,000 feet above sea level and the lake situated like a bowl 680 feet below sea level, there was a natural condition for sudden storms. Cool air masses rushed down the steep slopes causing violent eruptions that overwhelmed small craft, even those piloted by experienced fishermen.

The squall erupted as the group made their way across the lake. When the boat began to fill with water from the storm-tossed waves, the disciples frantically woke their sleeping Master, questioning whether he cared at all for their safety. In the crisis they had the faith to call upon him for help, addressing him as "Lord" (Matt 8:25), but not to sustain their confidence in him as the Messiah who could not possibly lose his life in a storm while his mission remain unfulfilled. Did they think that his kingdom program, so boldly expounded in the nine parables at Tabgha, could be thwarted by the turbulent forces of nature? Mark's Gospel, drawn from Peter's eyewitness recollection, records his sternest rebuke: "Why are you so afraid? Have you still no faith?" (4:40). Jesus reproved them for allowing unbelief to settle in their hearts and grow into fear. Matthew Henry comments: "He does not chide them for disturbing him with their prayers, but for disturbing themselves with their fears." How often the Lord will have to command his disciples, "Do not fear" (Matt 10:28; 14:27; 17:7; 28:10).

Jesus rebuked not only his disciples' unbelief but also the raging storm. At his command the wind ceased and the waters became calm, a double miracle. Nature is bowing before its Creator. Jesus exhibits the same control over the natural world that Yahweh performed in the Old Testament (Ps 107:23–32). Amazed and terrified, this time with a holy awe, the disciples responded with the right question, "Who then is this, that he commands even winds and water, and they obey him?" (Luke 8:25). Matthew's Gospel places the unqualified commitment to discipleship alongside this demonstration of Jesus' lordship (8:19–22). This nature miracle is meant to focus attention first and foremost on the identity of the One who harnesses the sea. The final rhetorical question invites the response of faith: This Jesus is the Creator and Redeemer, the sovereign Lord whose majesty compels worship and whose authority demands submission.

⇨   Do you believe in a Lord who both rules over the universe and is at the same time concerned for the very details of your life? In prayer reconfirm your trust in his ability and willingness to still the storms that threaten your peace or to direct the storms, even as they continue to rage, to effect their good purposes in your life (Rom 8:28).

ASSAULTING SATANIC STRONGHOLDS IN THE DECAPOLIS
(Matthew 8:28–34; Mark 5:1–20; Luke 8:26–39)

After the boat landed, and the storm had been stilled, Jesus was immediately confronted by a demoniac inhabited by a legion of evil spirits. In the Roman army a legion consisted of 6,000 military personnel, but in this case probably means a large number which have assumed complete domination of the personality. Matthew refers to two demoniacs, while Mark and Luke take up only the more prominent individual. Jesus entered the Decapolis, a territory north and east of Perea, named after its ten autonomous Greek cities. Gadara, five miles southeast of Lake Galilee, was one of these cities and gave its name to the surrounding territory which stretched to the villages on the shore, including Gerasa to the east of the lake. This accounts for the different designations in the Synoptics. This was a largely Gentile area in New Testament times. Ritual defilement (pigs, tombs), from the Jewish perspective, pervades the entire scene.

Jesus earlier warned against the horrors of multiple demonic possession (Matt 12:43–45). The picture is one of total degradation as the demons
seek to efface, even destroy, the image of God in the person. The man was
isolated, living among the ancient tombs on the hillside near Gerasa. Tombs
were often subterranean caves in which a person could find shelter. He was
naked, possessed supernatural strength so that he could not be permanently
chained or fettered, a threat to others, and especially self-destructive, cutting
himself with stones and crying out in anguish.

The demoniac ran toward Jesus from a distance, fell at his feet, acknowledged him as the Son of God, and asked, "Have you come here to torment
us before the (appointed) time?" The church father Theophylact comments:
"While the men in the boat are doubting what manner of man this is, that
even the winds and the sea obey him, the demons come to tell them." The demons have independent knowledge of Jesus' identity and apparently recognize that God is beginning his successful assault on the kingdom of darkness
and that they are destined for eternal torment. But they fail to recognize the
delay before the final judgment that will afford them an indefinite period of
limited freedom (Matt 12:28–29). Their direct address to Jesus as "Son of the
Most High God" (Mark 5:7) is the animistic technique of gaining mastery
over an opponent by uttering one's precise name. But Jesus dominates this
encounter by demanding their name, which is Legion.

Next comes a strange plea. When Jesus commands them to depart
from the man, the demons ask to enter the herd of about two thousand pigs
that are grazing on the hillside. While tombs and pigs defile Jews, they are
desirable habitations for unclean spirits. By granting permission to their
request, Jesus precipitates a spiritual test for the townspeople. The possessed
swine lose control, rush down the steep bank into the lake and are drowned.
Demons once again prove their destructive nature, both to those they inhabit
and to themselves, which seems to be the main point of this bizarre incident.
But they are effective in removing Jesus from the Decapolis when the townspeople, stung by the loss of their property, ask Jesus to depart. They lament
the loss of their pigs while expressing no joy at the salvation of the formerly
demonized individual.

The restoration of this man is complete—from a violent, uncontrollable,
naked, self-destructive wretch to a calm, clothed, sane, bold witness to the
person of Jesus throughout the Decapolis. In this case there is no command
to secrecy, perhaps because this was not a Jewish area where his messianic
authority would be interpreted in socio-political terms. Jesus commands the

man to return to his family and to proclaim the saving mercies of the Lord toward him.

⇨ Have you declared to your family and neighbors how much the Lord has done for you?

JESUS RESPONDS TO THE FAITH OF THE DESPERATE

(Matthew 9:18–26; Mark 5:21–43; Luke 8:40–56)

Jesus and the disciples acceded to the request of the Gadarene townspeople to leave their area and crossed by boat "to the other side" of the lake, apparently back to Capernaum. There he was met by one Jairus, the ruler of the synagogue, an influential Jewish layperson who looked after the building and supervised the Sabbath worship. This prominent individual came and knelt at Jesus' feet, supplicating help for his twelve year old daughter who was near death. He expresses faith that Jesus' personal touch can heal his daughter and thus implores Jesus to come to his home. Was Jairus strengthened in faith and drawn to Jesus by the earlier healings in Capernaum of the royal official's son (John 4:46–54) and the centurion's servant (Matt 8:5–13), though they were both miracles from a distance?

As Jesus, pressed by a large crowd, makes his way to Jairus' home, another desperate person approaches him. A woman subjected to an incurable bleeding condition, probably chronic hemorrhaging between her regular menstrual flows, thought to herself, "If I only touch his garment, I will be made well" (Matt 9:21). Her desperation was compounded not only by the perpetual ritual uncleanness caused by her condition (Lev 15:25–27), but by the mounting medical expenses that had reduced her to poverty. She is an example of a person who, having exhausted all other means, finally turns to the One who alone has the power to help. She clearly entertained magical notions about the power released by making physical contact with the Lord's garment. While Jesus accommodated her weakness and released his healing power to the instantaneous cessation of her blood flow, he would not let her disappear into anonymity with such a faulty faith. Unable to escape the Lord's search, she fell at his feet trembling with fear and made a full confession of her bold act. There is no rebuke, just a gentle but firm word of confirmation that her faith, not her touch, is what beckoned the divine response. Her touch merely bridged faith with the person of Jesus and that is what made it effective.

The healing of the woman would have served as a pledge to Jairus that Jesus' touch, if received by faith, could also produce his daughter's recovery. But that faith was immediately tested as his servants arrived to announce the death of his precious one. It is too late, death being irreversible, they reasoned, and thus there is no need to bother the teacher any more. But Jesus had earlier raised the son of the widow of Nain (Luke 7:11–17) and would later return Lazarus to life. If he will not fear but believe, Jesus promises Jairus, he will see his daughter restored. Upon their arrival, professional hired mourners, including flute players and wailing women, had turned the home of Jairus into a boisterous scene. Their mourning was clearly artificial since the tears were soon exchanged for mocking laughter when Jesus expressed hope for the girl's restoration. After forcibly removing the crowd, Jesus, her parents and the inner circle of Peter, James and John entered the girl's room. With calmness restored, Peter heard and remembered the two Aramaic words that the Lord uttered, *Talitha koum*: "Little girl, arise." Her spirit returned to the dead girl, she arose and received some food. Unlike the Decapolis, Galilee was swirling with eager crowds and politically-minded zealots who would co-opt Jesus to an earthly mission. So he issued his characteristic command to secrecy. Jesus wanted to nurture radical trust in his person, not ostentatious acclaim as a miracle worker or passionate aspirations for a social revolutionary.

⇨   Why is it that severe trials often have the power to wake people up to their need for God? Should this inform the way we pray for people who do not know Christ?

DEEPENING HOSTILITY AND A FINAL VISIT TO NAZARETH

(Matthew 9:27–34; 13:54–58; Mark 6:1–6a)

Two desperate blind men cried out for mercy, addressing Jesus by the Jewish messianic title, Son of David. Jesus' healing of blind people was an attestation of his Messiahship (Isa 35:5–6), cited earlier to John the Baptist when he was assailed by doubts (Matt 11:5; Luke 7:21–22). As with Jairus' daughter, Jesus performs a private miracle inside the house, perhaps Matthew's, and calls for faith on the part of the seekers: "Do you believe that I am able to do this?" (Matt 9:28). Their unhesitating affirmative reveals a faith directed toward Jesus and his power to reverse the most irreversible of maladies. Jesus declares healing in accordance with their faith, not a mechanical *quid pro quo* response to the measure of faith they possess, but a promise of God's mercy mediated through their faith, no matter how faulty or limited. The healing is followed up by a stern warning not to publicize the miracle to others. But the excitement of these men whose sight was restored cannot be contained. Once again the command to secrecy fails to stem the tide of popular enthusiasm for a miracle-working Messiah and threatens to impede his mission as the suffering Servant.

As he was leaving the house, a dumb and deaf man was brought to Jesus. Unlike the Gadarene who cried out with a loud voice (Mark 5:7), in this case demon possession manifested itself in the impairment of the victim's speech and hearing. The demon bowed to the authority of the King and the deaf man spoke. Earlier the exorcism of a demon from a blind and mute man sparked the Beelzebub controversy where the Pharisees accused Jesus of acting under Satanic empowerment (Matt 12:24). This time the Pharisees repeat the charge, which will become their standard apologetic in the face of undeniable healings and exorcisms (Matt 10:25; John 7:20; 8:48; 10:20). The crowds, recognizing the unprecedented magnitude of the miracles, were amazed. Thus hostility from religious quarters and popular excitement were growing side by side. Emotions were high on all sides, a ferment of cynicism and wonder.

Jesus decided to make one final visit to his hometown of Nazareth. At the outset of his Galilean ministry Jesus had preached in the synagogue there. He incited the anger of the townspeople when he expressed God's concern for the Gentiles, but had providentially escaped their murderous intentions (Luke 4:16–30). Now about one year later the instinctive anger seems to have abated, but not their skepticism. The people with whom he grew up were amazed at the reports of his miracles, as well as the wisdom with which he taught the Scriptures. Neither his education nor family upbringing could account for his authority in speech and in deed. Jesus had apparently lived a very ordinary life as the eldest son of Mary and the carpenter Joseph, alongside his numerous siblings. Though they could not deny his wisdom or works, they "took offense" (literally, "were scandalized" [Matt 13:57]) at him, a term used by the Gospel writers for the profound discomfort felt by people repelled by his forceful claims on their lives and destinies (Matt 11:6; 13:21; 15:12; 24:10; 26:31, 33; John 6:61; 16:1). Jesus saw in this response the fulfillment of the familiar proverb that a prophet is only without honor in his own hometown and among his family (John 4:44; Luke 4:24). In contemporary idiom, familiarity breeds contempt, or to state it more directly, those who gain prominence also gain envy. Jesus' inability to do miracles in Nazareth (Mark 6:5) was a self-imposed limitation related to his mission. Miracles-on-demand performed in the context of deeply-rooted unbelief would only serve to justify the artificial substitute of fascination for faith, emotion for repentance, and a wonder-worker for a Servant.

⇨ Why is it that family members and lifelong friends often prove the most difficult to witness to of one's new life in Christ? What is the best approach to these loved ones?

LABORERS FOR THE HARVEST

(Matthew 9:35–38; Mark 6:6b)

In recent weeks Jesus has demonstrated his authority over nature's fury (storm), multiple demon possession (Gadarene), incurable disease (hemophiliac), irreversible maladies (blindness and dumbness), and death itself (Jairus' daughter). Then comes a final visit to Nazareth where, due to stubborn unbelief, Jesus "could do no mighty work" (Mark 6:5). The diverging lines of acceptance (faith responders), ambivalence (crowds), and rejection (religious leaders) intersect as the narrative progresses. The disciples' growth in understanding is not a neat linear one. They are often overwhelmed by the events and even Jesus questions the stability of their faith (Mark 4:40). Their shaky confidence in Jesus seems at times perilously close to the total absence of faith of the people of Nazareth (Matt 13:58). People plunged into desperate situations, like the hemorrhaging woman, the synagogue ruler, and the two blind men, find physical healing and, almost certainly, eternal salvation through faith in Jesus (Matt 9:29; Mark 5:34, 36). The crowds are either amazed (Matt 9:33) or scandalized (Matt 13:57), preferring the blessings of the kingdom over its demand for repentance. The Pharisees are entrenched in their defensive positions, assessing his miracles as the works of the devil (Matt 9:34).

Matthew records a summary statement of Jesus' Galilean ministry (9:35). Three major activities have consumed his energies: (i) preaching in the open air in the towns and villages; (ii) formal teaching in the synagogues on the Sabbath; (iii) healing of people with physical diseases. In this transitional paragraph Matthew identifies the driving incentive behind Jesus' missionary activity to this point, as well as his plans for a third tour of Galilee with the disciples (9:36–38). He is driven by a compassion for the ordinary people of the land who were like sheep without a shepherd to guide them. This was an indictment of the religious leaders who had acted as false shepherds or hirelings unconcerned for the spiritual welfare of the sheep under their care (John 10:11–12; cf. Jer 23:1–4; Ezek 34:1–10).

Then, addressing his disciples, Jesus shifted metaphors from sheep farming to the familiar symbol of the wheat field (Matt 13:24–30; John 4:35–38). He instructed them to pray for workers who will go out and reap a ready harvest of souls for the kingdom. Not only compassion for the lost, but commitment to the holy enterprise of extending God's saving rule in the world moved Jesus to impart to his disciples a harvest perspective. His strategy for accomplishment of the mission started with prayer, not for the harvest field but for laborers. The "Lord of the harvest" guarantees fruit, but the sowing and reaping will be through, and only through, willing human vessels. The disciples' prayerful concern, then, should be for more workers to take advantage of the existing opportunities. Jesus saw many among the faceless, harassed multitude ready to be reaped for the kingdom. The disciples were being trained to be instruments for kingdom advancement, and were to pray that the Lord who ensures the harvest will produce through them even more harvesters.

⇨ Are you being obedient to the Lord's command (which is actually a call to corporate rather than individual prayer [Matt 9:38: "you all pray"]) to regularly pray for more committed and trained (Matt 13:52) workers to go to the unreached peoples of the earth? Are you willing to be the answer to your own prayer?

COMMISSIONING THE HERALDS OF THE KINGDOM
(Matthew 10:1–16; Mark 6:7–11; Luke 9:1–5)

The call and training of the disciples has come in stages. Four fishermen abandoned their career and accompanied Jesus through Galilee (Mark 1:16–20, 39). A tax collector, Levi, made the same decision (Mark 2:14). These and seven more were designated his "apostles" after a night of prayer (Mark 3:13–14). A second tour of Galilee followed (Luke 8:1). Jesus imparted to the disciples the theology of the already-not yet kingdom (Mark 1:15; Matt 11:11–13; 12:28–29; 13:1–52; Mark 4:26–29). Now he will formally commission them to proclaim his kingdom, first within Israel, but with a view to evangelizing the nations of the world. The gospel of the kingdom

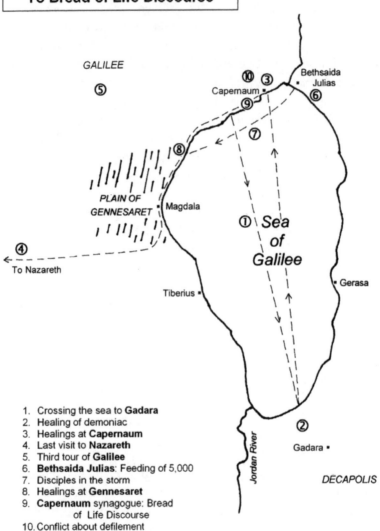

**Middle Galilean Ministry II:
To Bread of Life Discourse**

GALILEE

⑤

⑩ ③   Bethsaida
Capernaum ▪   Julias
⑨   ⑥

⑦

⑧

PLAIN OF
GENNESARET ▪ Magdala

④
← - - - - -
To Nazareth

① Sea
of
Galilee

Tiberius ▪

▪ Gerasa

1. Crossing the sea to **Gadara**
2. Healing of demoniac
3. Healings at **Capernaum**
4. Last visit to **Nazareth**
5. Third tour of **Galilee**
6. **Bethsaida Julias**: Feeding of 5,000
7. Disciples in the storm
8. Healings at **Gennesaret**
9. **Capernaum** synagogue: Bread
         of Life Discourse
10. Conflict about defilement

Jordan River

②

Gadara ▪

DECAPOLIS

is, in Paul's words, "to the Jew first and also to the Greek" (Rom 1:16). The stream of salvation history is a Jewish one that eventually overflows its banks and waters the Gentile world (Mark 7:24–30; John 4:21–24). The mission to the lost sheep of Israel (Matt 10:6) was designed to gather laborers who will harvest the Gentiles for the kingdom (Matt 10:18). The redemptive focus on a man, a family, and a nation is meant to reverberate into universal blessing (Gen 12:1–3). Jesus' blueprint combines in perfect tension a belief in the vast potential for kingdom advancement, while underscoring that its promoters will be required to make tremendous sacrifices.

The commission proper (10:1–16) sets forth parameters for the accomplishment of the initial, particularized stage of the mission, the proclamation of God's saving rule to the Jewish people.

1. The apostles' *authority* is a delegated one as representatives of Jesus. Like him, they are to engage in proclaiming the nearness of the kingdom as the incentive for repentance, authenticated by the miracles of healing and exorcism (Luke 9:1).

2. Their *sphere of ministry* is not Gentiles or even Samaritans, but only Jewish people who are like lost sheep wandering after false shepherds (Matt 10:5–6).

3. Their *message* is the same as that of John the Baptist (Matt 3:2) and of Jesus (Matt 4:17): "The kingdom of heaven is at hand" (Matt 10:7).

4. Four representative miracles are to provide *attestation* of the arrival of the kingdom and to demonstrate the delegated authority of the heralds in solidarity with Jesus (Matt 10:8a).

5. They are to serve without mercenary *motives* (Matt 10:8b). The apostles are to be unencumbered by *material possessions* and dependent on God to supply their needs through the hospitality of his people (Matt 10:9–11).

6. Confidence in God's sovereignty must govern their *responses* to those who are receptive and to those who are hostile to their Lord. The Christological core of their message, delivered with clarity and courage, must be undiluted, for the eternal destiny of people depends on their response to Jesus. The apostles are learning that promotion of the kingdom is divisive and at times meets with violent opposition (Matt 10:12–15).

7. Their *mental posture* must exhibit a moral symmetry: "wise as serpents and innocent as doves" (Matt 10:16). Prudence and caution toward determined opponents is to be combined with pure motivation free from guile. To be realistic without becoming cynical, strategic but never suspicious, is the delicate balance required of spiritual warriors storming fortresses of darkness.

To summarize, the apostles are being sent forth with authority to boldly proclaim the arrival of God's saving rule in Jesus Messiah. Their total dependence on God and his people for food, shelter and clothing is a lifestyle that communicates the grace character of the message. Their summons to repentance sifts the listeners' hearts, creating a polarized response.

⇨ How does one apply the axiom "wise as serpents, innocent as doves" in ministry today?

PREPARATION FOR PERSECUTION
(Matthew 10:17–31)

After the commission proper, the manual of instruction is designed to prepare the apostles for the persecution that they will face as heralds of the kingdom of God. The principle of harvest through sacrifice is an unbreakable law of the kingdom that Jesus imparts to his representatives with great repetition and intentionality.

1. The apostles will be arrested and brought before religious and secular authorities. This will provide opportunity for witness to Gentile magistrates (10:17–20). They should not be anxious because the "Spirit of your Father" will guide the testimony. Jesus indicated that the source of the initial persecution would be Jewish, but he anticipated an extended period of witness beyond Jewish parameters. Suffering becomes the context for worldwide extension of the kingdom (Acts 8:1–4; 11:19–21; chs 24–26).

2. Bitter division over the kingdom message and the king himself, his claims and demands, will take place even among family members (10:21–22). Jesus demands total allegiance, one that transcends family bonds. The kingdom heirs must show endurance to the end of life or to the end of the age, whichever comes first, to prove the reality of

their confession. Perseverance is the seal of one's true kingdom identity (10:22b; cf. Matt 24:13).

3. The witness to the Jewish people and, by extension, to Gentiles will continue until the end of the age signaled by the glorious return of the Son of Man to consummate his kingdom program (10:23; cf. Matt 24:30; 25:31; 26:64).

4. The heralds should not be surprised by how harshly they are treated, for they are in solidarity with the King, who is being accorded the same (10:24–25). The blasphemous accusations leveled against the teacher, the master and the head of the household will surely translate to rejection for the student, the servant and the member of the household. It is a badge of honor for the servant to bear the branding marks of his Lord (Gal 6:17).

5. The apostles must continue their faithful proclamation regardless of the cost. Intimidation has the power to silence and thus incapacitate God's servants who then begin marking time rather than making an impact (10:26a). The exhortation to fearless public confession is supported by theological propositions. First, the truth will ultimately emerge and be vindicated. Thus it needs to be boldly declared now to provide an opportunity for those who do have ears to hear (10:26–27). Second, God is to be feared, not Satan or people, because he alone has authority to destroy both soul and body in hell (10:28). Jesus implies that martyrdom is the price some of the heralds will pay for their allegiance to his kingdom. Third, the disciples can trust their heavenly Father whose providential care covers the tiniest details of life and thus encompasses those of the greatest magnitude as well (10:29–31).

In summary, at the center of the kingdom message is the demand for repentance (Mark 6:12). A great distinguishing work is taking place and the apostles out of compassion for people and reverence for God must courageously fulfill the task of the herald. The eternal fate of people rests upon their response to Jesus and his kingdom offer. Faithfulness to Jesus' mission will invite opposition, suffering, and maybe even death. They can trust their Father with whatever consequences follow, for his final approbation will outweigh every kind and level of sacrifice.

⇨ Proverbs 29:25 reads: "The fear of man lays a snare, but whoever trusts in the Lord is safe." Pray that the Lord will release you from fear so that you may take your place as a clear and bold witness of the Lord Jesus Christ.

COSTS OF DISCIPLESHIP

(Matthew 10:32–42)

Anyone who aspires to become Jesus' disciple must be informed that they are taking on a life-absorbing commitment. At the center of the kingdom message is the demand of repentance that accosts the entire personality of the listener and initiates a comprehensive transformation of beliefs, character and destiny. The costs are high, but the rewards are even greater.

1. *Public acknowledgment of the Son* (10:32–33)

   Open and unashamed confession of Jesus as the only Son of the Father, sent to be the Redeemer whose death and resurrection alone provides the basis of eternal life, is evidence of one's true relationship with Jesus (Rom 10:9–10). Public confession of Jesus before people now will be vindicated at the final judgment with the Son's acknowledgment of his faithful confessor-disciple before the Father. Forthright denial, or timid equivocation short of clear confession, will result in final condemnation before Father and Son. There is no middle ground. The unequivocal language of Jesus is a warning of exclusion for all those who do not explicitly confess Christ, not a window of opportunity for those who, never having heard the gospel, do not explicitly deny him.

2. *Unrivaled love for Jesus* (10:34–37)

   Those who believe and repent often encounter bitter division with family members whose expectations and values run counter to one's new allegiance to the King. Jesus bequeaths to his followers inner peace (John 14:27; 16:33), but external turmoil in a world that rejects him, including one's own family. Like Jesus, the disciple may face the hostility of one's earthly family (John 7:3–5), but enters the greater family of the Father that creates bonds stronger than blood ties (Matt 12:48–50). To love anyone or anything more than the Lord Jesus, including even one's beloved parents or children, is to engage in idolatry. One's governing affections and priorities must reside preeminently in Jesus and in no other.

3. *A cross to bear* (Matt 10:38)

The cross was an instrument of torture and death. Crucifixion may not have been the most excruciatingly painful way to execute a criminal (flailing the skin or burning slowly were ancient inventions for maximizing the level of sheer pain), but it was unparalleled as a method for shaming the victim with prolonged naked exposure to insults and mockery. Sacrifice, self-denial, suffering and, in some cases, death, emerging from one's intentional identification with Jesus, are the willing experiences of the worthy disciple.

4. *A life to lose* (Matt10:39)

The one who "finds his life," that is, determines to spare it from such hardships, will forfeit all reward; the one who "loses his life," that is, pours it forth as a sacrificial offering (Rom 12:1) to promote the Son ("for my sake") will be abundantly rewarded. Jim Elliot, the martyred missionary to the Auca Indians of Ecuador, framed Jesus' paradoxical statement this way: "He is no fool who gives what he cannot keep to gain what he cannot lose."

The concluding words of the commission promise incomparable reward to those who promote the kingdom, as well as those who actively support its heralds. The promise of reward is based on the continuity between Jesus, his disciples, and those who receive them as the king's emissaries, thus becoming his disciples by receiving their message (Matt 10:40–42).

⇨ How can the disciple love God first, as well as seek to honor one's parents (Exod 20:12), when the parent seeks to hinder one from walking the path of true discipleship?

THIRD JOURNEY THROUGH GALILEE IN A CONTEXT OF OFFICIAL HOSTILITY

(Matthew 11:1; 14:1–12; Mark 6:12–30; Luke 9:6–10a)

With a mandate to carry out and a manual to guide them, the disciples set out on a *third tour* of Galilee. On the first tour Jesus had traveled with his first four disciples (Mark 1:39). On the second tour the twelve apostles accompanied him and many other followers, including three prominent women (Luke 8:1–3). This time he sent the twelve ahead two by two through the villages and towns where they preached the good news of the kingdom, commanded repentance, and healed the sick (Mark 6:7, 12–13; Luke 9:6). Jesus followed them and carried out the same ministry in the towns (Matt 11:1). After their tour the disciples returned, reported and rested. Their training to be people of impact for the kingdom followed a familiar pattern: concentrated instruction regarding the nature of discipleship; intense activity in itinerant evangelism; return and debriefing (Mark 6:30); and withdrawal from the demands of the crowd for rest and further teaching (Mark 6:31–32). They reported the results of their work because they were accountable to Jesus as his authorized representatives.

Jesus' growing fame arising from the third tour of Galilee caused concern to Herod Antipas, tetrarch of Galilee. Reports of a powerful preacher attested by miraculous signs came to Antipas who resided in the capital of Tiberias on the southwest shore of Lake Galilee. His initial fears, fueled by the speculation of others, were that this was the reappearance of John the Baptist risen from the dead. Mark provides the most detailed account of John's death at the hands of Antipas, which is the sequel to the earlier brief mention of his imprisonment (Mark 1:14a; Luke 3:19–20). This has been called the first Passion narrative of the Gospels, which points to the climactic Passion of the Lamb of God who takes away the sin of the world, of which John testified (John 1:29, 36).

About eighteen months previously, at the end of Jesus' Early Judean ministry, Herod Antipas had imprisoned John, according to Josephus, at Machaerus, east of the Dead Sea. This was because John publicly rebuked Antipas for taking Herodias as his wife, at the time married to his half-brother Philip I. This was a clear violation of the law and merited the prophet's condemnation (Lev 18:16; 20:21). Herodias nursed a grudge against John, but Antipas was restrained from executing John due to his prophetic acclaim among the people and by his own superstitious fears of one whose moral character commanded his respect. Herodias found the opportune time at the banquet on Antipas' birthday, arranging for her daughter to dance before the dinner guests. The infatuated Antipas promised the girl on oath whatever she wished "up to half of my kingdom." Herodias' conspiracy succeeded as she instructed her daughter to request the head of the Baptist on a platter. The wimpish tetrarch, bound by a foolish oath and tricked by his vengeful wife, ordered John to be executed. John's head was delivered to the girl who brought it as a trophy to her mother; the body was then claimed and buried by his disciples.

The unjust execution of the forerunner of Messiah was the result of an arrogant, malicious demand from one who despised the kingdom ethic of repentance. Even the Roman authorities, pledged to rule justly, were subject to manipulation. To silence the message required that one kill the messenger. The entire incident presages the climactic Passion event toward which the life of Jesus has been moving since its inception.

⇨ What implications does Jesus' fourfold pattern of training the disciples—concentrated instruction, itinerant evangelism, debriefing and reflection, withdrawal for rest and further teaching—have for leadership training today? How should curricula in Bible Schools and Seminaries be reshaped in order to reflect this?

FEEDING THE FIVE THOUSAND

(Matthew 14:13–21; Mark 6:31–44; Luke 9:10b–17; John 6:1–13)

At the conclusion of the third tour, Jesus' took the disciples by boat across the lake northeast to Bethsaida Julias, east of where the Jordan River empties into Lake Galilee. The purpose of the withdrawal was rest and renewal away from the pressing multitudes, hostile religious leaders and capricious political authorities. But the familiar cycle began again as the crowds, like sheep without a shepherd, discovered his location and thronged the hills north of Bethsaida. The fields were beginning to green during rainy season just before Passover in early *Spring, AD 29* (Mark 6:39; John 6:4), one year before his final Passover.

Jesus' teachings, authenticated by healings, held a powerful attraction to the crowd, even more than their physical hunger. They remained until evening hanging on his every word. The disciples express concern that the people be sent back to the villages so they will not be stranded at night in a desolate place without food. The disciples' sole focus at this point is the human dilemma, much like Mary's attitude at the wedding in Cana when the wine was running out (John 2:3). The Lord then characteristically tests his disciples' faith by commanding them to provide food for the multitude. Their spokesman, Philip, responds incredulously that 200 denarii, or the equivalent of eight months' wages for a laborer, would not be sufficient to purchase enough bread for this many people. Simon Peter announces he has discovered five loaves of bread and two fish carried by a small boy for his family's needs, a token provision that only serves to underscore the impossibility of complying with Jesus' command. The disciples have apparently forgotten their Lord's ability to meet critical needs through his supernatural intervention, as when he transformed water into an abundant supply of wine for the wedding feast (John 2:9).

Here, however, the miracle is one of quantity not quality. Jesus engages the disciples to organize the crowd into companies of fifty and one hundred, blesses God for the loaves and fish (surrendered by the boy?), and multiples food for the crowd. No one sees the miracle itself, only its effects as loaf after loaf and fish after fish is placed in the hands of the disciples to distribute to the hungry multitude. With 5,000 men present, the total number of people, including women and children, was probably around 15–20,000. The leftover fragments of fish and bread filled twelve wicker baskets, confirming an abundant supply that fully satisfied the hungry recipients.

What is the meaning of this important miracle, one recorded in detail in all four Gospels? First, the background is the Lord's miraculous provision of manna during Israel's wilderness wanderings (Exod 16). Matthew and Mark describe the area to which Jesus attempted to withdraw as desolate or desert-like. Just as Jehovah provided manna to sustain his old covenant people in the desert, so Jesus satisfies the physical needs of those who come to him. The focus is not so much on the spiritual character of wilderness Israel or of the fickle multitude, but on the identification of the Lord Jesus with Jehovah as a supernatural provider. Second, the bread of life discourse which follows this incident in the fourth Gospel surely provides its interpretive key. Jesus himself is the bread of life who when appropriated by faith provides eternal life (John 6:27, 33, 35). Third, the banquet in the hills anticipates the coming messianic feast when his new covenant people, Jew and Gentile, will celebrate his public coronation as King and their eternally binding marriage to him as Lord (Matt 22:1–14; 25:10; Luke 13:29; 14:15; cf. Isa 25:6; Rev 19:9). The twelve baskets symbolize the twelve apostles of the new Israel.

⇨ Do you find Jesus to be the ultimate satisfier of your physical, emotional and spiritual needs? If not, where else are you looking the fill the voids only he can fill?

ANOTHER TEST ON LAKE GALILEE

(Matthew 14:22–33; Mark 6:45–52; John 6:14–21)

The multitude seemed to recognize the miraculous way they were fed and immediately proclaimed Jesus as the eschatological prophet of Deuteronomy 18:15, clearly a messianic designation. Jesus, however, knew that the popular understanding of Messiah was that of a conquering king who could rally Israel, drive out the Romans, and cleanse the priesthood. Gamala, the headquarters of the anti-Roman zealot movement, was not far from Bethsaida. Jesus withdrew from the growing pressure of the people, influenced by nationalistic aspirations for political freedom, to be their king. Yes, he was the King of Israel (John 1:49), but his kingdom was not the kind of earthly rule that would threaten the Romans (John 18:33–37). In order to stay the course of the Servant, Jesus forcefully dismissed the crowds, sent the disciples ahead first to Bethsaida, then by boat toward Capernaum, and withdrew to the mountain to pray.

Meanwhile the disciples made painful headway westward on the lake against a strong contrary wind which blew them off course. They had traveled 3–4 miles over a 9–12 hour period, probably placing them half way across the nine-mile lake heading toward the western shore. Having dismissed the crowds and dispatched the disciples in early evening (approx. 6:00 p.m.), Jesus spent the next several hours in private prayer (Matt 14:23). Now in the early morning hours of the "fourth watch" in Roman time, that is, 3:00–6:00 a.m., Jesus approached the boat, walking on the water and intending "to pass by them" (Mark 6:48). He was testing their faith. Would they recognize him as transcendent over nature, one who had already turned water to wine, raised two people from the dead, stilled a storm, and just the day before fed the multitude from a few loaves and fish? Terrified at the sight of a figure moving across the lake, the disciples screamed out, "It is a ghost." The latter term denoted a hazy apparition or the disembodied spirit of a dead person. The Lord calmed their fears and said, "It is I," or literally, "I am," the same profound expression found often in John's Gospel signifying his deity (8:58). Drawing on Exodus 3:14, Jesus is declaring his equality with the eternal, self-existing Lord who revealed himself to Moses at the burning bush. Along with Matthew 11:25–27, this is the strongest self-assertion of divinity by Jesus to this point of his ministry.

Matthew alone records the bold act of Peter as he requests Jesus to bid him come to him on the water (14:28–31). To attempt to analyze the logic of Peter's words and actions is a futile exercise (Mark 9:5–6; John 21:7). The New Testament portrays the chief of the apostles as a bundle of conflicting thoughts and emotions so tangled as to defy any attempt at classification. What seems clear is that Peter wants to be with Jesus. His faith is firm enough to get him up, out of the boat and on to the water, but too weak to bring him through the storm to Jesus. He looks in two directions at the same time, to Jesus and to the wind-blown waves, and begins to sink. But the Lord reaches out and takes his servant's hand, reproves his "little faith," stills the winds, enters the boat, and brings them all safely to the western shore.

The response of the disciples is a complex one. Matthew's appraisal is more positive, while Mark is characteristically more critical. They worship, confessing that he is surely the Son of God (Matt 14:33); they are amazed but prevented by hardened hearts from learning lessons from the feeding of the multitude or the miracle on the lake (Mark 6:52). The Gospels tell it like it is: the disciples before the resurrection are a mixture of faith and doubt, of comprehension and misapprehension, struggling to fully trust the One in whom they have come to believe.

⇨ Do you see in the disciples a reflection of yourself, believing but at times not trusting?

"I MYSELF, AND NO OTHER"

(Matthew 14:34–36; Mark 6:53–56; John 6:22–25, 35, 48)

Jesus and the disciples landed at Gennesaret, a fertile plain on the northwest shore of Lake Galilee, half way between Capernaum and Magdala. This was called the garden spot or paradise of Galilee by the Rabbis, where grapes, figs, olives, various grains and vegetables were grown, with trees and wild flowers in abundance. Just to the south was Tiberius, the capital of Galilee since AD 18 when it replaced Sepphoris. Tiberius was a largely Gentile town where Herod Antipas had his palace. The main road from Capernaum to Tiberius ran close to the shore through Gennesaret. Jesus' reputation as a healer preceded him and people from the surrounding towns and villages brought their sick to him hoping just to touch the fringe of his garment. His compassion released healing power even to those who, like the woman with the blood issue (Matt 9:20–22), mixed genuine faith in his person with animistic views of the intrinsic power of physical contact with his cloak.

John mentions the search for Jesus by people from Tiberius who traveled by boat first to Bethsaida, then on to Capernaum, where they finally located him (6:22–24). They wondered how and when Jesus had come to Capernaum since it was relayed to them by the crowds at Bethsaida that the disciples alone had boarded the only boat available and embarked without him. Probably Jesus traveled from the Gennesaret plain to Capernaum by foot, ministering to the sick in the rural areas en route (Mark 6:56). Jesus did not answer their question but delivered an extended discourse on the bread from heaven that when received provides eternal life. At the heart of the discourse is Jesus' claim in a solemn first person singular statement to be the bread of life (John 6:35, 48). This is the first of seven "I am" declarations in the fourth Gospel that are implicit claims to deity. In each case the sense is "I, myself, and no other." The theological import of this seven-fold testimony can best be felt when seen collectively.

1. I am the bread of life (John 6:35, 48).

2. I am the light of the world (8:12).

3. I am the door (or gate) of the sheep (10:7, 9).

4. I am the good shepherd (10:11, 14).

5. I am the resurrection and the life (11:25).

6. I am the way, the truth and the life (14:6).

7. I am the true vine (15:1, 5).

The massive range of Jesus' provisions for his new covenant people as the exclusive mediator of God's redemptive blessings is impressive: enduring satisfaction of the yearnings of the heart for spiritual nourishment; illumination of the path of life that pleases God; entrance into God's secure keeping; guidance and correction by a loving protector; resurrection after death to eternal life; assurance in finding the true way to the Father; and life-sustaining communion that produces lasting fruit. These statements could be called practical ontologies, that is, majestic assertions which bring the grace of God to bear on the entire life of the believer and thereby authenticate Jesus as the only Son of the Father. Jesus is saying, I myself and no one else possesses the full array of prerogatives that compel confession and worship. You need look nowhere else.

⇨ How can we set forth the exclusivity of Jesus Christ with persuasive power in this postmodern age of toleration and religious pluralism?

"I AM THE BREAD OF LIFE"

(John 6:26–47)

The bread of life discourse began as a corrective response to the crowds who asked how and when he came to Capernaum (6:25). He exposed them as miracle-seekers rather than inquirers after the meaning behind the miracle of the feeding. Other portions of the sermon were delivered in the Sabbath service in the synagogue (6:59). John brought the material together into a unitary discourse. The message develops four crucial theocentric propositions.

1. *The work of God is to believe in the One whom God sent and on whom he has set his seal of approval* (6:26–29). Jesus rebukes the motives of his interrogators. They are seeking him not from earnest hearts but because he filled their stomachs. His command to labor for the food that does not perish is an accommodation to their performance-directed approach to God. However, Jesus quickly defines the "labor" as receiving by faith the gift of eternal life from one whom God has authenticated, both audibly at his baptism (Matt 3:17) and through his attesting "signs" (John 2:11; 4:54; 6:14). The performance-oriented and prosperity-driven mindset of the people is not easily uprooted. They remain focused on what Jesus is requiring that they do. Jesus displaces their works (pl.) with God's work (sg.). The latter removes the need and basis for the former. To believe in the one sent by God is the single work that God requires and, in fact, faith itself is a response originating in God's gracious enablement.

2. *The bread of God is the one who comes down from heaven and gives life to the world* (6:30–33). The crowd's demand for a "sign" like the miraculous provision of manna long ago to wilderness Israel is more than surprising in the immediate aftermath of just that kind of sign in the feeding of the 5000 near Bethsaida. Signs alone, then, no matter how many and how dramatic, have no power in themselves to produce faith. The wilderness manna and the Bethsaida multiplication of loaves are material metaphors for a deeper spiritual reality, the appropriation by faith of Jesus Messiah, the heaven sent bread of God who gives eternal life.

3. *The will of the Father is to preserve unto eternal life all who look in faith to the Son* (6:34–40). Jesus is not frustrated by the spiritual dullness of his inquirers. He is confident in the purposes of the Father who has graciously chosen and bestowed upon him the gift of believing disciples, all of which will come and be welcomed and none of which will ever be driven away or lost. To believe on the Son is to receive eternal life now and the assurance of resurrection life after death.

4. *Only those who are drawn by the Father and are taught by God come to the Son* (6:41–47). Jesus' claim to being sent from heaven invites complaint from those who know him as the son of Joseph and Mary and nothing more. Jesus knows that only the divine power can overcome such recalcitrant unbelief. He assigns salvation to the activity of the Father from start to finish. God draws people to the Son and effectually teaches people about the Son. This teaching is the work of God through his Spirit in the hearts of his chosen new covenant people, prophesied in Isaiah (54:13), Jeremiah (31:34a), Ezekiel (36:26–27) and Micah (4:2).

⇨ Observe in John 6 how the invitation to believe, come to, look to and feed on Jesus complements the emphasis on divine election and prevenient, that is, preparatory grace. Do you maintain the balance of human responsibility and divine choice in your theology?

EATING HIS FLESH AND DRINKING HIS BLOOD

(John 6:48–71)

For the second time Jesus solemnly declares that he is the bread of life (6:35, 48). The interchange with the crowd now is dominated by the language of eating the bread from heaven, who is Jesus himself. The wilderness manna was a physical provision to sustain Israel in her wilderness journeys, but it did nothing to prevent an entire generation from dying in the desert. Anyone who eats this living bread from heaven will live forever. Then Jesus for the first time equates this bread with his "flesh," which he gives for the life of the world (6:51b). It is clear that the bread which is Christ himself is, more specifically, the crucified Christ as the basis of the gift of eternal life. Flesh is the metaphor for his sacrificial death for sinners (the world) and eating is the metaphor for personal appropriation by faith of the benefits of that sacrifice.

Jesus would have known that such stark language, eating someone's flesh, would have invited a sharp reaction. But when his listeners protest, Jesus speaks even more severely: "Unless you eat the flesh of the Son of Man and drink his blood, you have no life in you" (6:53). Ingesting blood was taboo for the Jew (Gen 9:4; Lev 17:10) and evidently such language for the moment shocked his listeners into silence. In the biblical worldview, the life of a created being is in the blood. The shedding of the blood of a sacrificial victim offered in one's place was required to provide atonement for sin, that is, one life for another (Lev 17:11; Heb 9:22). In speaking of his flesh and blood as distinct elements, Jesus is anticipating his substitutionary death on the cross as the basis of the forgiveness of sins. In the language of eating and drinking, Jesus challenges his listeners to embrace that death, violent and offensive as it is, as the gift of God to them. Personal appropriation by faith of the crucified and risen Jesus brings not only resurrection life in the future but the Lord's abiding presence now. This is Jesus' mission from the Father—to communicate the fellowship he enjoys with the Father to his new covenant people. There may be a secondary reference here to the Lord's Supper which commemorates Jesus' death, though in the Synoptics and Paul it is his "body" not his "flesh" that is uniformly cited in the Eucharistic passages (Matt 26:26; Mark 14:22; Luke 22:19; 1 Cor 11:24).

The cryptic language was designed, like the parables, to stimulate faith among truth seekers but to shield the truth from those whose attachment to Jesus was superficial. The test served to effectively sift the listeners. Now one year before his final Passion, Jesus pressed the growing crowds of "disciples" for a decision. Will they follow him to his intended destination as the suffering Servant born to die? John 6:66 is one of the saddest verses in the New Testament: "After this many of his disciples turned back and no longer walked with him." As these loosely attached followers who possessed a faulty faith (John 2:23–25) began to evaporate, Jesus turned to the twelve: "You do not want to leave too, do you?" (author's rendering). With mounting suspense, Peter stepped forward to speak for the others: "Lord, to whom shall we go?" This is the response of a thinking person. In the light of Jesus' difficult sayings that portend a difficult way ahead, the disciples have contemplated the alternatives. But, despite their faulty grasp of his self-revelation, they remain confident that he is the Holy One of God, a messianic title. Peter's representative confession, like its reconfirmation at Caesarea Philippi a few weeks later

(Matt 16:16–17), springs not from human insight, but from Jesus' election of the twelve, except for Judas Iscariot.

⇨ When Peter confesses, "We have believed, and have come to know" (6:69), he uses the perfect tense which signifies both past conviction and present confidence. Does your confession spring also from a settled assurance in the Lord that is growing even when it is severely tested?

TRADITIONS OF MEN OR THE WORD OF GOD?

(Matthew 15:1–20; Mark 7:1–23; John 7:1)

The setting was a private house in Capernaum, probably Peter's, where Jesus and his disciples were enjoying a meal together. A delegation of Pharisees from Jerusalem arrived and observed some of the disciples eating without washing their hands in the prescribed way. They immediately charged Jesus with allowing his disciples to transgress "the tradition of the elders" (Matt 15:2). The Pharisees had earlier clashed with Jesus over the issue of Sabbath observance (Mark 2:24; 3:2; John 5:10, 16, 18). Now they precipitated conflict over another area of difference, hand washing before meals. Mark explains the Jewish custom for his Roman readers (7:3–4). The "tradition of the elders" refers to the massive body of rabbinical rulings passed down orally for several hundred years and later codified around AD 200 in the Mishnah. An entire tractate of the Mishnah, Yadaim or "hands," is devoted to the area of hand washing before meals. Anyone who violated the prescribed method of washing hands, as well as for the cleansing of eating and cooking utensils, would contact ritual defilement, which would render them unfit members of the covenant community.

Jesus shot back with a stinging rebuke for his accusers. They were guilty of replacing the clear commands of Scripture with man-made doctrines (Mark 7:8). The Pharisees had elevated their traditions to the level of canonical status, which became extra-biblical standards for judging the behavior of others. Isaiah's denunciation of the hypocritical leaders of his day for creating a lips-heart chasm (Isa 29:13) applied equally to them. Legalism removes the heart from one's worship and replaces it with conformity to a set of external rules. In the same vein, Jesus had repeatedly enunciated the principle of "mercy over sacrifice" from Hosea 6:6 (Matt 9:13; 12:7).

Jesus then provided a concrete example of how traditions have ended up nullifying the ethical force of the Old Testament law. The fifth command states: "Honor your father and your mother" (Exod 20:12). This is supplemented by a severe warning: "Whoever curses his father or his mother must be put to death" (Exod 21:17). Jesus interpreted this divine command as laying responsibility on children to care for parents in their old age. But the rabbinical traditions allowed a son to declare money saved for parental care to be "*Corban*," that is a gift devoted to God and, at one's death, paid into the temple treasury (Mark 7:11). It is unclear whether such a vow could later be annulled. What is clear, and Jesus' central point, is that the tradition negated the force of the clear command of God. A pretentious claim to piety, giving money to support the temple ministry, became the means to justify dishonoring one's parents.

Jesus made this an object lesson for his disciples on the nature of uncleanness. That which enters the body from the outside, food, does not make a person unclean. Mark adds that in this statement Jesus "declared all foods clean" (7:19b). Jesus rescinded the old covenant category of ceremonial purity and replaced it with its new covenant fulfillment, purity of heart (Jer 31:33b; Ezek 36:26). What defiles a person, rather, is the panoply of evil words and actions that spring from the heart. Consecration or defilement is a moral not ritual category. What a person truly is—hidden character, thoughts, motives—determines what one says and does. Only by stripping away the layers of oral tradition could Jesus help his disciples recover the unadulterated teaching of Scripture and bring their lives under its transforming authority.

⇨ How do churches today often, like the Pharisees, show scrupulosity over matters of little import, but indifference to areas vital to biblical integrity? Specify some extrabiblical traditions that are elevated and other clear biblical teachings that are neglected?

10

Later Galilean Ministry

Harbinger of Gentile Salvation

OFFERING CRUMBS TO DOGS

(Matthew 15:21–28; Mark 7:24–30)

THE *LATER GALILEAN* MINISTRY begins with Jesus' withdrawal from Israel proper to itinerate in Gentile areas like Phoenicia (NW), the Decapolis (SE), and Caesarea Philippi to the far north. This phase extends over a four month period, *Summer-Fall, AD 29*. We are dependent on the Synoptic Gospels for this period, since John's Gospel moves from the feeding of the 5,000 and the subsequent bread of life discourse in the Spring (John 6:4: Passover, AD 29) to Jesus' trip to Jerusalem for the Feast of Tabernacles in the Fall (John 7:2). John adds the helpful note that during these final months in Galilee, and its surrounding environs, Jesus remained in the north because the Jewish leaders in Judea were plotting his death (7:1). His popularity with the crowd has waned, the wider group of "disciples" has dissipated, and the hostility of official Judaism is implacable. The lines have formed which will lead to the Passion in less than one year.

Jesus first travels northeast to the region of Tyre and Sidon, thirty and fifty miles respectively from Capernaum. These Phoenician cities were historical foes of Israel (Isa 23; Ezek 26–28) and the ancestral home of Jezebel who helped import Baal worship to the north when she married King Ahab (1 Kgs 16:31). Matthew underscores these associations by identifying the woman who comes to Jesus as a Canaanite (Matt 15:22). She implores him as the Son of David to show mercy upon her demonized daughter. While the Jewish leaders attack him for breaking their oral traditions (Matt 15:1–2), this Gentile woman, a descendant of Israel's ancient military and spiritual enemies, beseeches the Jewish Messiah for grace.

Before he can respond to her request, Jesus must test the tenacity and refine the purity of her faith. When the disciples urge the Lord to deal with and dispatch this irksome woman, he reminds them, and probably the woman who is listening in, that he has been sent to the lost sheep of Israel. The time would come for the Gentile mission (Matt 10:18), but only after the present period of the kingdom offer to Israel was complete (Matt 10:5–7). Undeterred, she approaches Jesus again, humbly kneeling before him, and this time addresses him as "Lord." The Lord's response, though, is even harsher than before: "It is not right to take the children's bread and throw it to the dogs" (Matt 15:26). The covenant children are the Jews, while dog was a common metaphor for unclean, uncovenanted Gentiles. The former have a prior promissory claim on the bread, a symbol for the blessings of the kingdom, that is, the forgiveness of sins and physical healing. Jesus is reminding this woman brought up in the absorptionist religion of Phoenicia that he will not countenance being added to her Canaanite pantheon (John 4:22).

The woman responds with yet a renewed plea for undeserved mercy from one whose grace, she believes, can encompass a Gentile dog like herself: "Yes, Lord, yet even the dogs eat the crumbs that fall from their masters' table" (Matt 15:27). There is no defensive maneuver or clever counterstroke here, as with the kosher Pharisees, but a sincere admission of spiritual bankruptcy that can make no claim on God. She will be satisfied if the leftover crumbs of his kingdom blessing might release her daughter from darkness. Jesus is amazed at the faith of this woman who boldly and tenaciously places her confidence in the limitless mercies of one she now surrenders to as Lord. Only this woman and the Roman centurion evoke approbation for a great faith, both of whom were Gentiles and both of whom saw their beloved ones healed instantaneously from a distance (Matt 8:10, 13).

⇨   How does this passage apply to contemporary mission practice? Can a Buddhist, for example, continue to practice ancestor worship and become a follower of Christ?

MIRACULOUS HEALINGS AND FEEDING
IN THE DECAPOLIS

(Matthew 15:29–38; Mark 7:31—8:9a)

Mark describes Jesus' long circuitous journey from Tyre north to Sidon along the Mediterranean coast, then along the ridge routes skirting the mountains of Lebanon eastward to the Jordan valley and south to the Sea of Galilee, before arriving at its southeastern shore in the region of the Decapolis (7:31). It would be difficult to interpret this any other way than a deliberate avoidance of Jewish areas due to rejection by the religious leadership (John 7:1) and a consequent offer of kingdom blessings to Gentiles. Matthew refers to the many people afflicted in various ways—lame, blind, mute and crippled—who greeted him upon his arrival (15:30). Had his reputation as Savior preceded him due to the widespread testimony of the former Gadarene demoniac in this area (Mark 5:20)? Jesus amazed the people with his healing ministry, fulfilling here in the Gentile Decapolis the same kinds of attesting miracles, in fulfillment of biblical prophecy (Isa 29:18; 35:5–6), that he had among his Jewish kinsmen (Matt 11:5). As a result the Gentiles glorified the God of Israel.

Mark focuses on the single healing of a deaf mute, one of only two miracles peculiar to that Gospel (blind man at Bethsaida [8:22–26]). In both instances, Jesus removes the individual from the crowd and employs a bizarre method of healing. He put his fingers into his ears, spat, touched the man's tongue with the spittle, and commanded in Aramaic, *Ephphatha*, meaning "be opened." The command was performed in conjunction with a heavenward look and a deep sigh, expressing his dependence on God's healing power through him—stressed in the shockingly personal method employed here—and a spirit exhausted by the incessant demands of people seeking physical wholeness more than spiritual wellness. The instantaneous healing was followed by an unsuccessful command to secrecy. What was intended to be a private miracle became another occasion of expanding his reputation as a miracle worker among the impressionable crowds.

Jesus felt compassion for these people who were desperate for a word or touch from God, even to the point of remaining with him for three days without sufficient food. Along with the 4,000 men were women and children (thus a total crowd of 10–12,000?) who might faint from protracted hunger if sent home without nourishment. There are many parallels, as well as differences, with the earlier feeding of the 5,000 near Bethsaida. Both

Matthew (16:9–10) and Mark (8:19–20) distinguish these as two separate incidents. It is surprising, though not uncharacteristic, for the disciples to once again see only the human extremity after they earlier experienced the Lord's multiplication of loaves and fish in Galilee. But such is the case even with believing disciples to forget past mercies and to doubt the Lord in a fresh crisis. With seven loaves and a few fish, Jesus proved once again that a little becomes more than sufficient when placed in his hands. This time seven, not twelve, baskets of fragments of leftovers were gathered. Seven is the number of completion and probably signifies the universality of the new covenant community. What he has previously done among his Jewish kinsmen in Galilee he now performs for the Gentiles in the Decapolis. Jesus is the bread of life for the whole world. His sacrificial death, the flesh broken and the blood shed on the cross, is the basis for the free gift of eternal life to any and to all who believe (John 6:54, 56: "Whoever … ").

⇨ How can we learn to remember God's faithful provision in times past in order to remain calm and trusting in present crises? What is the remedy for spiritual forgetfulness?

RENEWED ENCOUNTER WITH PHARISEES AND SADDUCEES
(Matthew 15:39—16:12; Mark 8:9b–26)

Jesus and the disciples returned to Galilee, this time crossing the lake from east to west landing in the area of Magadan (Matt) or Dalmanutha (Mark). The former is probably the same as Magdala, home of Mary Magdalene, just north of Tiberius on the western shore of Lake Galilee; Dalmanutha was the territory south of Gennesaret which included the town of Magdala. After a period of ministry outside of Jewish territory during which a Canaanite woman embraced the Jewish Messiah as her Lord (Matt 15:27) and Gentile crowds praised the God of Israel (Matt 15:31), Jesus returns to Israel proper and is met by Pharisees and Sadducees who demand proof of his authoritative claims with a "sign from heaven." Their earlier insistence on a miraculous sign was met by a stinging rebuke and the promise of the sign of Jonah, that is, vindication after his suffering by being raised from the dead (Matt 12:39–40). By adding "from heaven" to their demand, they are mandating an even more impressive display of apocalyptic power than just healings or exorcisms, both of which they attribute to demonic agency. The Pharisee-Sadducee alliance, here formed for the first time, reveals the depth of the hostility of official Judaism toward Jesus, for these were antagonistic rivals with little theological affinity (Acts 23:6–8).

Jesus has already fulfilled, both in Jewish and Gentile territory, the array of signs prophesied of Messiah's coming (Matt 11:4–5; 15:29–31), so he castigates his self-appointed judges for being better at predicting the weather than in discerning the signs that presage the arrival of the kingdom. They know that a red tinge to the evening sky without clouds points to fair weather the next day and the tinge with clouds in the morning signals coming storms. One is reminded of the maritime proverb: "Red sky at morning, sailors take warning; red sky at night, sailors' delight." These religious leaders are better meteorologists than they are theologians. They have overlooked the clear testimony of the Old Testament that Messiah will come not only as a heavenly conqueror (Dan 7:13–14), but as a servant and sacrifice (Ps 22:1–18; Isa 52:13—53:12). The sign of Jonah alone will be given to this generation. His resurrection from the dead on the third day will exalt the suffering Servant to the place of supreme lordship.

The sequel to this unpleasant encounter is a warning to his disciples, as they travel by boat back to the east side of Lake Galilee, to be on guard against "the leaven of the Pharisees and Sadducees." Mark inserts an additional warning against the leaven of Herod. At first they wonder whether this is a rebuke for not bringing enough bread for the trip. This invites a stinging rebuke in the form of seven rapid-fire rhetorical questions (Mark 8:17–21). Could Jesus not multiply their one loaf to satisfy the team of thirteen when he had filled multitudes from a few loaves and fish in recent days? Further, have they not learned from the bread of life discourse that they must penetrate the surface meanings of his terms (i.e. leaven) for the spiritual lesson? When he repeats the warning for a second time they finally grasp that leaven is a symbol for the perfidious spreading influence of the doctrines of the Pharisees, Sadducees and Herod, namely, binding legalistic traditions, rationalistic interpretation of Scripture, and political acquiescence respectively. Jesus does not fit into any of the religious or political groups of his day because his focus is not ideology but the heart. The episode of the blind man at Bethsaida, unique to Mark (8:22–26), is the only case of gradual healing in Jesus' ministry, underscoring that the kingdom's advance will at times be inexorably slow.

⇨ What danger is there in identifying the gospel of Christ with a particular form of domestic religious or political ideology, either on the right or on the left?

PETER'S CONFESSION AND DIVINE REVELATION

(Matthew 16:13–17; Mark 8:27–29; Luke 9:18–20)

Jesus again withdrew with his disciples from Jewish territory, taking them to the far north in the region of Caesarea Philippi. This city, twenty-five miles northeast of the Sea of Galilee and fifty miles southwest of Damascus, was built by Herod Philip II on the ancient village of Paneas, named for the Greek god Pan which was worshipped there. Shrines to Pan were carved in the niches of the rocky cliffs of Mt. Hermon just to the north, at 9,200 feet the highest mountain in the environs of Israel. Philip II, tetrarch of the northeast territories (Luke 3:1), renamed the city in honor of Augustus Caesar and himself. Devout Jews would normally avoid such places, but it is in the dark corridors of idol-infested Syro-Phoenicia, Decapolis and Caesarea Philippi that Jesus chose to prepare his disciples for a worldwide missionary enterprise.

Jesus had chosen his twelve apostles after a night of prayer (Luke 6:12) and he now came to the conviction in prayer (Luke 9:18) that the time was right for him to test the disciples' understanding of his person. When he inquired what the popular estimate of him was, they referred to a number of opinions that were circulating: John the Baptist raised from the dead, which was Antipas' fear (Matt 14:2); Elijah, due to his prominent role in hastening the day of the Lord (Mal 4:5–6); Jeremiah, who suffered greatly for boldly confronting Israel's leaders; or one of the other prophets. There was clearly no consensus and no one, apart from a few marginal and desperate individuals (Matt 9:27; 15:22), was publicly confessing him to be the Messiah. Earlier he tested their loyalty in the face of the disillusionment of many "disciples" (John 6:66–67). Now, away from confused crowds and scoffing Pharisees, Jesus directed to them the collective question: "But what about you (pl.)? Who do you (pl.) say that I am?" (NIV). Once again Peter answered for the group: "You are the Christ (Messiah), the Son of the living God" (Matt 16:16). The earliest disciples had arrived at the conviction that Jesus was the promised Messiah when they were first introduced to him by John the Baptist (John 1:41, 45, 49). But their understanding of Messiah's role had to be radically altered in light of Jesus' self-revelation as the suffering Servant. They struggled

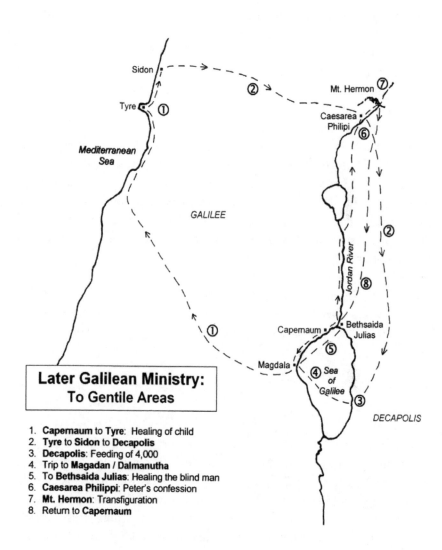

Later Galilean Ministry:
To Gentile Areas

1. **Capernaum** to **Tyre**: Healing of child
2. **Tyre** to **Sidon** to **Decapolis**
3. **Decapolis**: Feeding of 4,000
4. Trip to **Magadan / Dalmanutha**
5. To **Bethsaida Julias**: Healing the blind man
6. **Caesarea Philippi**: Peter's confession
7. **Mt. Hermon**: Transfiguration
8. Return to **Capernaum**

THE PASSION OF THE SERVANT

to overcome the triumphalistic tones of a conquering liberator who would fulfill Israel's national aspirations. Here in Peter's confession, a reaffirmation of his earlier one (John 6:69), is the dawning of real understanding. Jesus was not only the promised Messiah of prophetic Scripture, but also stood in a unique relationship with God as his Son. Soon it will become apparent that Peter's understanding of Jesus' mission remains faulty. He still does not fully grasp how the Messiah can be a servant and sacrifice. Nevertheless, this is the first unambiguous and measured confession in the Synoptic Gospels of Jesus' Messiahship and divine standing on the lips of a human being.

The Lord immediately affirmed Peter's words as divinely imparted revelation. This confession springs not from human initiative, intuition, or the processes of inductive logic, but rather from insight imparted by the Father who alone can reveal the Son (Matt 11:27). He will now take his closest followers and future bearers of his legacy to the next step with an unmistakable disclosure of his redemptive mission to suffer, die and to be raised from the dead. The apostles have passed one more crucial stage in the painful process of maturation.

⇨ What do we learn in this interchange about the way Jesus deals with his followers when they take forward, even if faulty, steps in the journey of faith? What implications might this have in our discipling of others?

THE ROCK OF THE CHURCH AND THE KEYS OF THE KINGDOM

(Matthew 16:18–19)

After pronouncing a blessing on Peter for his God-given insight into his person, Jesus makes a wordplay on the name Peter (Gk. *petros*) and announces that he will be the "rock" (*petra*) upon which Jesus will build his church. While many interpreters take the rock-foundation of the church here to be Christ himself (1 Cor 3:10–11) or Peter's confession regarding Jesus, Messiah and Son of God (Rom 10:9–10), the natural sense of Jesus' language is that Peter himself is the rock who will become the foundational apostle of the new community. Though there are two distinct Greek words in Matthew's account (*petros-petra*), the spoken Aramaic words behind them (*kepha'*) would have been identical and the wordplay more direct. Peter is granted salvation historical primacy, not special ecclesiastical status, as the apostle who, in the aftermath of Jesus' death and resurrection and the descent of the Spirit at Pentecost, becomes the special instrument of God in proclaiming the gospel to Jews and Gentiles (Acts 2:14–41; 3:6–10; 3:12–26; 4:8–12, 19–20; 5:1–11; 5:29–32; 8:20–25; 9:32–43; 10:1—11:18). In the early chapters of Acts we see the Apostle Peter, once snared by the fear of man, now standing as a rock, boldly proclaiming the gospel to crowds in the temple courts (3:11–12), to hostile priests and Sadducees (4:7–8) and before the powerful Sanhedrin (5:27–29). The religious leaders are at a loss to explain the boldness of Peter and John, except that "they had been with Jesus" (4:13). Peter and John set the spiritual tone for the growing church, leading it in praise, prayer, holiness, joy in adversity, and bold witness (2:42–47; 4:23–31; 5:11, 41–42).

The Greek term for "church" (Matt 16:18; 18:17) is drawn from the Hebrew term for an assembly of worshippers on redemptive mission. The mission of the new covenant community is to live under and to promote God's saving rule in the earth through Jesus Christ. In the formative years of this missional community, Peter is in the vanguard as the church storms the "gates of hell," the citadel of defense manned by Satan and his demonic forces to bind people under their reign of darkness (Matt 12:28–29). Jesus promises Peter, the apostles, and those who follow in their train as church-planters that their work will prevail because Jesus is determined to build his church.

As the foundational apostle, Peter is given the keys of the kingdom to bind and to loose on earth. The language derives from Isaiah 22:22 where Eliakim, the palace administrator under Hezekiah, controlled entrance to the royal palace. Ultimately it is Christ who possesses the keys to the kingdom, ushering in or excluding people based on their response to him (Rev 3:7). Peter is the *primus inter pares*, the first among equals, the keys signifying his authority to exclude or permit entrance to salvation, through the forgiveness of sins (John 20:23), based on response to his preaching. The verbs that express heaven's role in the binding/loosing activity are in the future perfect passive tense: "shall have been bound in heaven . . . shall have been loosed in heaven" (Matt 16:19). Thus the church on earth proclaims the destiny of people determined according to heaven's decrees, not the heavenly councils ratifying the church's pronouncements. The apostles (Eph 2:20; Rev 21:14), and believers of all ages, represented by Peter, are entrusted with proclaiming the gospel of the kingdom, warning of exclusion and judgment, offering entrance and forgiveness. It is in this sifting process, founded upon the authority resident in Christ himself (Matt 28:18), that they become instruments in building the church.

⇨ When sharing the gospel do you lovingly yet faithfully clarify what is at stake in their response—salvation or judgment? Pray for courage to speak the truth in love.

FROM VEILED HINTS TO DIRECT PREDICTIONS OF THE PASSION

(Matthew 16:20–21; Mark 8:30–31; Luke 9:21–22)

The charge to secrecy that follows Peter's majestic confession can only be understood in the subsequent interchange. Peter and the apostles still do not grasp that Jesus is to be a suffering Messiah. Therefore, they must not publish abroad—Messiahship/Sonship—what they themselves do not fully understand. Jesus is following the divine blueprint and schedule and will not be shifted off course by wrongheaded fervor or misguided messianic conceptions, even from his disciples.

The confession of Peter now leads Jesus to clarify his identity and mission that until now has been communicated in adumbrations, vague hints and veiled allusions. "From that time," Matthew inserts in the narrative as the turning point in Jesus' self-disclosure, the Lord begins to predict his coming Passion in stark and unmistakable terms: the Son of Man *must* go to Jerusalem, suffer at the hands of the elders, chief priests and teachers of the law (three groups that comprised the Sanhedrin), be killed and on the third day be raised to life. In one sense this is the culminative explanation of the cryptic references to his Passion to this point, especially those voiced during the past eighteen months of his Galilean ministry:

1. Jesus takes up his people's infirmities and bears their diseases (Isa 53:4), linked to the vicarious sacrifice portrayed so graphically in Isaiah's fourth servant song (Matt 8:17).

2. The friends of the bridegroom, an allusion to the disciples who are reproved for not fasting, will one day mourn when the groom is taken from them. At that time fasting will be an appropriate vehicle for their sorrow (Matt 9:15).

3. In his tender healing of the sick, Jesus fulfills the first servant song of Isaiah (42:1–4) who prophesies the coming of the Spirit-empowered Servant who causes justice to triumph for the weak and vulnerable (Matt 12:18–21).

4. The only sign that will be granted to this miracle-demanding generation is the sign of Jonah—as the prophet was in the belly of the fish three days and nights, so the Son of Man will be three days and three nights in the heart of the earth (Matt 12:39–40).

5. The fate of a Master and Teacher who has been accused of casting out demons by the power of the prince of demons will be shared by those who belong to his household as servants and students (Matt 10:24–25). The plots of the Pharisees to kill him (Matt 12:14) and the prediction of Judas' betrayal (John 6:70–71) fit the ominous tone of this passage.

6. Only a disciple who takes up his own "cross" is a worthy disciple of Jesus (Matt 10:38).

7. The death of John the Baptist, the forerunner and preeminent witness of Jesus, has been called the first Passion narrative, since it is a harbinger of the death of the one John pointed to, the Lamb of God who takes away the sin of the world (Matt 14:3–12; cf. John 1:29).

8. One must eat the flesh and drink the blood of the Son of Man in order to receive his gift of eternal life. The personal appropriation of Christ's substitutionary death on the cross—believing that "he died for me in my place"—is the means of receiving the benefits that accrue from that death, the forgiveness of sins and transfer from death to life (John 6:53–58).

All three Synoptics underscore the divine necessity ("must") of Jesus' appointed path of suffering and vindication, though its redemptive meaning is not filled out until the last ascent to Jerusalem (Matt 20:28) and on the final night before his death in the institution of the Lord's Supper (Matt 26:26–29).

FROM DIVINE INSIGHT TO SATANIC MANIPULATION

(Matthew 16:22–26; Mark 8:32–37; Luke 9:23–25)

Peter represented the others with his confession: "You are the Christ, the Son of the living God." Jesus affirmed Peter's words as God-given revelation. The faith of the disciples germinated early in their journey with Jesus (John 1:41, 45, 49), but their progress in understanding the nature of his Messiahship was slow and torturous during the long process of exposure, correction and further reflection. Rather than celebrate this dawning of insight, Jesus immediately turned the conversation toward his impending suffering, death and resurrection.

Peter is caught off guard by such dire predictions and soundly rebukes his Lord in the most emphatic terms: "Far be it from you, Lord! This shall never happen to you" (Matt 16:22). The Son of Man is not only the sovereign King of Daniel 7:13–14, but also the suffering Servant of Psalm 22 and Isaiah 53. Peter has apprehended the former, but has no thought of the latter. Jesus turns toward Peter in a face to face confrontation: "Get behind me, Satan. You are a hindrance (literally, stumbling block) to me. For you are not setting your mind on the things of God, but on the things of man." The command to depart given to Peter here was earlier issued to Satan at the conclusion of the three temptations in the desert (Matt 4:10). Once again Jesus detects the insidious activity of the evil one. Peter is being manipulated by Satan to turn Jesus aside from the cross-way of the Father's will. Peter is blocking Jesus from his ordained path, exalting him as King, but without recognizing him as the suffering Servant. Jesus' radically different assessments of Peter in this interchange are shocking. The chief of the apostles moves from a confession that springs from divine revelation to active opposition to the purpose of God in unconscious alignment with Satan. Far from being a foundation stone, Peter has become a stumbling block. His understanding of Jesus' identity is not conditioned by the life and teaching of Jesus in his self-disclosure, but by popular Jewish expectations. This mixture of insight and confusion will mark the apostles until the risen Lord appears to them.

Turning to the disciples, Jesus succinctly states three governing values of the worthy follower. It is his method to reiterate earlier teachings because of the disciples' remarkable capacity to forget (Matt 10:38–39).

1. *Self-denial and cross-bearing*

   Sacrifice of personal 'wants' and 'likes' and public identification with the crucified Lord are central to the life of one who walks behind Jesus. Luke includes the adverb "daily" to indicate this is a decision that must be renewed continuously (Luke 9:23).

2. *Losing in order to gain*

   The paradox of discipleship is that the one who loses most gains the most, for true life consists of submission to the rule of God whose benedictory presence falls upon the servant. Sacrifice is costly and faith always undertakes an element of risk. The true disciple places at the foot of the cross the ambitious pursuit of fortune, prominence, vocational success, recognition, status, security and comfort.

3. *Forfeiting the world, gaining one's soul*

Only the blood of Christ can ransom a person's soul from judgment. That is the costly (to him) but free gift of God (to us). History is replete with tragic examples of those who, having gained wealth and fame, forfeited their very souls in the pursuit. They are remembered for a life that was spent rather than invested.

⇨   In what ways is your walk with Christ characterized by the values of self-denial, forfeiture (of the ephemeral), and investment (in the eternal)?

A GLORIOUS SEQUEL AWAITS

(Matthew 16:27—17:8; Mark 8:38—9:8; Luke 9:26-36a)

Jesus' intentional focus on his coming death in the aftermath of Peter's confession is balanced by corresponding promises of glory and vindication. Not only will the Son of Man be rejected and crucified, he will also be raised to life. Beyond his death and the disciples' own sacrifices as heralds of the suffering Servant, the Son of Man will return in glory to reward the faithful (Matt 16:27). What follows is an enigmatic prophecy: "There are some standing here who will not taste death until they see the Son of Man coming in his kingdom" (Matt 16:28). This may be a direct reference to the transfiguration event that follows. However, the apocalyptic accent of the preceding verse on a glorious appearing of the Son of Man with the angels to vindicate his people more likely indicates Jesus is speaking here of his second advent (Matt 10:23; 26:64). At that time he will consummate the kingdom that was inaugurated in his death and resurrection. The ones who are "standing here" is a prophetic foreview of the final generation of witnesses who stand in solidarity with the first witnesses, the apostles. The Lord anticipates a period of indefinite duration in which his servants will proclaim to all nations the suffering Servant and coming King. Some will even live to the arrival of the King. This promise of a glorious sequel supports the call to self-denial which precedes it (Matt 16:24–26). The disciples, then, must understand that all of their sacrifices—loss of possessions, physical hardship, persecution and even death—pale in comparison to the glorious kingdom that will be their inheritance.

About one week later the inner circle of Peter, James, and John accompanied the Lord up a high mountain, probably Mt. Hermon. Here they were given an advance viewing of the coming glory when Jesus was transfigured (literally, "metamorphosized") so that "his face shone like the sun, and his clothes became as white as light" (Matt 17:2). The dazzling brilliance of the sun and the whiteness of his raiment symbolize his majesty and holiness, the regal splendor unveiled for all to behold at his return to earth (Rev 1:7, 13–18). But for now, the glory is veiled in the flesh of the one destined to die. The apostles need this self-disclosure from their Lord and the authenticating voice of the Father that, as at his baptism (Matt 3:17), urges them to pay heed to his beloved Son, Isaiah's suffering Servant (42:1) and the Psalmist's Ruler of the nations (2:7). Moses and Elijah appear and converse with Jesus about his coming "departure" to be fulfilled in Jerusalem (Luke 9:31), certainly a reference to his mission-culminating death. As the major representatives of the old order of the law and the prophets, their testimony finds its fulfillment in the death and triumph of the Son (Luke 24:27, 44). The apostles are reassured that the kingdom, one for which they are challenged to sacrifice everything, holds a future beyond the darkening present. The religious authorities have accused him of being demon-possessed. His earthly family has accused him of mania. The crowds are growing distant from the healer who prefers the loneliness of the hills to their company. Jesus' language of eating his flesh and drinking his blood has offended many of the more promising followers. Now Peter has been soundly scolded for trying to disabuse Jesus from these depressing thoughts of suffering, betrayal and death.

The Transfiguration event, bracketed as it is by two Passion predictions (Matt 16:21; 17:9, 12), discloses that the One who will suffer a degrading death is God's Son, possessor of kingdom authority and majestic deity. Beyond the cross of shame—his and theirs (Matt 16:24)—will be a crown of glory.

⇨　How does Jesus' teaching in this entire episode (Matt 16:21—17:8) serve as a corrective to those who teach that faith in Christ is the way to personal success and prosperity?

THE COMING OF ELIJAH

(Matthew 17:9–13; Mark 9:9–13; Luke 9:36b)

At the time the three disciples appeared to grasp very little of the significance of the Transfiguration. Peter's words about building tents for Moses
and Elijah were the ramblings of a frightened observer (Mark 9:6). When
the cloud representing the divine presence enveloped them and the audible
voice of the Father announced his pleasure in the Son, the disciples fell face-
down to the earth in terror. Years later, Peter will recall the majesty of the
Lord transfigured before them and the audible voice of the Father (2 Pet
1:16–18). But for now they must remain quiet about their experience. For the
fifth and final time in Matthew's Gospel, Jesus issued the command to tell no
one what they had seen (8:4; 9:30; 12:16; 16:20; 17:9), but this time it is made
a temporary injunction, operative "until" the Son of Man is raised from the
dead. The disciples simply cannot put it together yet, how their conviction of
Jesus as Messiah fits with predictions of suffering and death. The resurrection will fill out the Lord's enigmatic self-disclosure during his lifetime and
then a full-orbed revelation of the Son as suffering Servant and coming King
can be boldly proclaimed to the nations.

The disciples are further confused by the scribes' insistence, based on
the prophecies of Malachi (3:1–4; 4:5–6), that Elijah must come to prepare
for the arrival of Messiah. If Jesus must suffer, as he is predicting, and is the
anointed one of God, as they have confessed, how can it be that Elijah comes
in advance to signal the great and terrible day when the Lord returns as a
refiner's fire to judge the wicked and to vindicate his people? Jesus' answer
is that Elijah will come and has come. This is the same already-not yet tension resident in John's announcement of Messiah's twofold baptism "with the
Holy Spirit and with fire" (Matt 3:11). A portion of Malachi's predictions
have been fulfilled in John the Baptist and another part awaits fulfillment in
the coming of Elijah just before the great and terrible day of the Lord (Rev
11:3–6). Though John was not literally Elijah risen from the dead and now
reappearing (John 1:21, 25), he is the "Elijah who is to come" (Matt 11:14)
because he ministered "in the spirit and power of Elijah" (Luke 1:17) to prepare the people for Messiah's coming. Further, John's treatment at the hands
of Antipas is a harbinger of the suffering of Jesus at the hands of Caiaphas
and Pilate; the first Passion narrative presages the climactic Passion. Even as
the imprisonment and execution of John, foreshadowed in Elijah's rejection
by Ahab and Jezebel (Mark 9:13; cf. 1 Kgs 19:2, 10), does not disqualify him

from fulfilling the role of Elijah (Mal 4), so Jesus' coming rejection does not discredit him as being the triumphant Son of Man (Dan 7). Finally, it clicks that Jesus is referring to John the Baptist, though the disciples' understanding of Jesus' destiny to suffer, die and rise is still very limited.

⇨ What accounts for the disciples' slowness to grasp Jesus' mission to die, even when given detailed, unmistakable predictions? How can we avoid the same insensitivity to his clear teachings?

DEPENDENT FAITH AND BELIEVING PRAYER
(Matthew 17:14–20; Mark 9:14–29; Luke 9:37–43a)

One day after the Transfiguration, Jesus and the three disciples descended Mt. Hermon and approached the town of Caesarea Philippi. From the glorious metamorphosis on the mountain they returned to the demon-scarred lives of real people. As they entered the town, they observed the other nine disciples surrounded by a large crowd and engaged in heated debate with some teachers of the law. The controversy was over the disciples' inability to exorcise a demon from a young boy who had since childhood been thrown into convulsions and robbed of his speech. The demon attempted to dehumanize, dominate and even destroy the boy, reminiscent of the terrible plight of the Gadarene demoniac (Mark 5:3–5). The boy's father pleaded with Jesus to take pity on the boy. He had implored the disciples to help, but "they were not able" (Mark 9:18).

The disciples were delegated the authority of exorcism in their formal commission to proclaim the kingdom (Matt 10:1, 8). Until now they had experienced unbroken success in casting out demons, evidenced by their request for an explanation of their powerlessness in the present case. Had they begun to view their authority as some kind of magical property to be used apart from dependence on God's power? Jesus lamented the perverseness of his generation, one that demanded miracles but refused to probe beneath the signs for their deeper meaning. This was a generation that never seemed to learn that the singular pursuit of the outwardly spectacular would never satisfy because with miracles, as with money, more is never enough.

Before responding, Jesus called the desperate man to believe in the God who is able to perform the impossible. To the father's "if you can do anything, . . . help us," Jesus replied "what is this 'if you can?'" (Mark 9:22–23 [author's rendering]). One must move beyond weighing possibilities, even

192

probabilities, based on the testimony of others to a stance of confident trust in God's power operative through Jesus. The man admits to a mixture of faith and doubt—how many times had he been disappointed in the past?—but inclines his heart to the former, pleading for help to overcome his unbelief (Mark 9:24). At Jesus' authoritative command to depart for good, the demon left with one final violent convulsion. There was no coaxing or protracted struggle with this particularly recalcitrant evil spirit.

Taking the disciples indoors for a private debriefing, Jesus attributed their failure to lack of believing prayer. Some forms of demon possession are so deeply rooted that they can only be overcome through prayer. Even a small faith directed to the mighty God can break the most tenacious demonic strongholds, symbolized by the imposing Mt. Hermon. Jesus draws on a variety of proverbial expressions at different times to underscore the centrality of believing prayer for extending the kingdom of God in enemy territory: uprooting a mulberry tree and replanting it in the sea (Luke 17:6); casting a mountain in the sea (Matt 21:21; Mark 11:23); or, as here, moving a mountain from here to there (Matt 17:20). Each analogy speaks of overcoming seemingly impossible difficulties through audacious prayer for God's powerful intervention.

The disciples must steadfastly embrace the potentials for kingdom breakthrough even in the darkest corridors of human depravity and satanic oppression. They must also remember that exorcism, like healing and all deliverance ministry, is a kingdom task performed through dependent prayer, not a mechanical ability they now possess in isolation from its divine source and doxological purpose.

⇨ Identify an obstacle you are presently facing in your life, the removal of which would be occasion to magnify the grace of God. Ask him in faith, for his glory, to intervene. Do not forget to record the answer to your supplication when it comes and to offer praise.

PAYING THE TEMPLE TAX

(Matthew 17:22–27; Mark 9:30–32; Luke 9:43b–45)

Jesus returned to Galilee with his disciples and for the second time predicted with clarity his upcoming Passion. The Transfiguration event, bracketed as it is by two Passion predictions, was meant to preview a glorious sequel to the terrible events that awaited Jesus in Jerusalem. Exaltation will follow humiliation; the crown of glory will be placed upon the sacred head of him who first bore the crown of thorns. All of this is implied in the promise of resurrection on the third day, but the disciples were still "greatly distressed" at the words (Matt 17:23). This was a sorrow born not out of understanding the necessity of the Passion, but out of their utter failure to figure it all out. They were even afraid to ask for clarification. No longer did they object to Jesus' fixation on his impending death; they were resigned to it. Luke adds that the meaning was divinely concealed from them due to their incapacity to embrace a suffering Messiah (9:45b).

Having returned to Capernaum, a strange episode follows. The Mosaic law mandated that Jewish males, aged twenty to fifty (of military age), pay an annual tax of a half-shekel to support the tabernacle, now the temple, and its services (Exod 30:11–16; 38:25–26). The half-shekel was paid with a two drachma coin which was the equivalent of two days' wages (i.e. one drachma = one denarius, laborer's daily wage [Matt 20:2]). The collectors of this revenue came and asked the disciples whether Jesus regularly paid the temple tax. This was a divine tax incumbent upon devout, law-keeping Jews but not enforced by Roman law. They responded in the affirmative.

The Lord used this as a teaching moment for the disciples, now gathered in Peter's house. With a series of questions Jesus draws out from Peter that earthly kings collect taxes and tribute from "others" but that their own "sons" are exempt from the obligation. Slaves, freedmen who have not attained citizenship, and conquered peoples were required to pay taxes and tribute to the Emperor, but members of the royal household and full citizens gained exemption as "sons of the empire." Next comes the theological lesson: Jesus, as God's unique Son, is free from the mandate to pay the half-shekel temple tax of the Father, as are the sons of his advancing kingdom bound to Jesus by faith. Further, it is his death and resurrection that will render the temple worship with its animal sacrifices obsolete. Sons under the rule of the crucified and risen King will be free from the binding obligation of the Mosaic law.

Jesus then commands Peter to cast his line into the waters of the Sea of Galilee. The omniscient Son knows which single fish has swallowed a four drachma coin, directs it to the hook on Peter's line, and the fish is reeled in. This coin is then extracted and paid to fulfill the annual temple tax for Peter and Jesus, not out of legal obligation but in order "not to give offense to them" (Matt 17:27). In order to commend the gospel of the kingdom to the Jewish people the Lord and his disciples voluntarily submit to the Mosaic mandate. Even though he is the glorious Son, confessed by Peter (Matt 16:16) and disclosed in his Transfiguration (Matt 17:2, 5), and the Lord of nature (calms storms, multiples bread, produces a coin from the fish's mouth), he is also the humble Servant who disdains causing needless offense that might keep seeking hearts among his Jewish kinsmen from heeding his invitation to enter the kingdom (Matt 11:28–30; 12:18–21). In a few short years a Jewish rabbi-turned-apostle will apply the same principle of 'sanctified expediency' in commending the gospel to Jews, Greeks and Romans (1 Cor 9:19–23).

⇨ Are we, like Jesus and Paul, sensitive to the cultural context of the people to whom we are witnessing, commending Christ while avoiding unnecessary offenses that might make it harder for them to hear our message?

A KINGDOM FOR LITTLE CHILDREN

(Matthew 18:1–5; 19:13–15; Mark 9:33–37; 10:13–16; Luke 9:46–48; 18:15–17)

Now less than a year from his Passion the Lord is determined to spend more concentrated time with his disciples away from popular pressures (Mark 9:30–31a). These select men will be his legacy, leaders and mobilizers in the great kingdom enterprise he inaugurates through his death and resurrection. In the fourth great discourse recorded in Matthew's Gospel (5:1—7:29; 10:5–42; 13:1–52; 18:1–35) Jesus sets forth those attitudinal qualities that must govern their practice of leadership, their relationships with one another, and their approach to outsiders: humility, generosity, seriousness, purity, compassion for the lost, reconciliation and forgiveness, prayerful agreement and unity.

The discourse begins in response to a question from the disciples: "Who is the greatest in the kingdom of heaven?" The question was not an academic one. Piecing the Synoptic accounts together, it appears that Jesus detected their rivalry for elevated positions in the kingdom (Luke 9:46), challenged and silenced their argumentativeness (Mark 9:33–34), whereupon they blurted out their question (Matt 18:1). Jesus' priority—his coming Passion—and the disciples' driving ambition—kingdom status—were completely at cross-purposes. So for his object lesson Jesus chooses a little child, perhaps Peter's if this took place in his house (Matt 17:25). He summoned and stood the child in their midst and then declared that a person must humble himself like a child both to enter the kingdom, as well as to attain greatness within it. When Jesus refers to the one who is "the greatest in the kingdom" (Matt 18:4), he is not using the term in the sense of elevated status/position meant by the disciples in their dispute, but greatness in the sense of meeting the standards for divine approval. Obviously Jesus is not commending qualities that children often demonstrate such as naivety or playful foolishness. A child, however, has not yet mastered the arts of manipulation, self-aggrandizement, and selfish maneuvering. There is a trust, a simplicity of motive free from concern for social status, in a child that the disciples must study and imitate. To those with childlike hearts God reveals his hidden treasures of wisdom (Matt 11:25) and promotes to places of unexpected and unsought prominence.

Not only must disciples become like little children, they must also be generous in welcoming those who enter Jesus' kingdom through a childlike faith, regardless of their age (Matt 18:5). A "little child" or "little one" becomes, then, a descriptive term for disciples, especially young and vulnerable ones whose spiritual ruin can be caused by needless offenses (Matt 18:6, 10, 14). The disciples quickly forget this lesson when they step in to rebuke some people who are bringing their children to Jesus for his blessing (Matt 19:13). Jesus is angered by their protective attitudes and commands his disciples to stop hindering the children from drawing near to him (Mark 10:14). His kingdom is comprised of those who receive his rule like a child, that is, with humility and trust (Matt 19:14). The dissembling of the multitude, the pride of the religious leaders, and even the ambition growing among his closest followers run contrary to the kingdom values of faith and repentance. It will take much more than the object lesson of a child to drive out the deeply rooted desire for exalted position in the kingdom from the hearts of the disciples, but at least the process has begun.

⇨ Observe carefully the small children around you, especially your own child, or your neighbors' children. Write down a few of the commendable qualities they exhibit in their daily life. Ask God for help to "become like" them.

EXTREME CARE FOR "LITTLE ONES"

(Matthew 18:6–14; Mark 9:38–50; Luke 9:49–50)

John informed Jesus that they encountered an individual outside their circle who was exorcising demons in Jesus' name. Maybe the disciples expected to be commended for ordering the man to stop. However, Jesus has just commanded them to welcome "little children" who are drawing near because to do so is to welcome him (Matt 18:5). The strange exorcist may well have been a person who was moving toward Jesus with a childlike, faltering but growing, faith, though not yet given to a full commitment. There is no suggestion that the exorcist was in any way exploiting the name of Jesus for personal gain like the false prophets in Matthew 7:15, 21–23, or the seven sons of Sceva in Acts 19:13–16. Are not John and the others in danger of excluding a "little one" who bears his name and thus potentially doing irreparable damage to his spiritual development? The subsequent warning against causing offenses is issued, at least in part, as a response to this incident (Mark 9:42).

Jesus gave three reasons to support his command to stop hindering the exorcist. First, such a person will no longer be negatively disposed to Jesus (Mark 9:39b). At least this person recognizes Jesus' authority and places himself on the side of God's kingdom, against Satan. This recognition will lead to deeper conviction and must not be quenched. Second, "the one who is not against us is for us," that is, one cannot drive out Satan by proclaiming Jesus' name and at the same time be opposing Jesus' kingdom (Mark 9:40). There are two opposing forces, with no neutrality possible, and this individual has chosen to align himself with the forces of good against evil. It must be remembered that the converse saying, "Whoever is not with me is against me, and whoever does not gather with me scatters" (Matt 12:30), was spoken concerning those actively opposing Jesus' mission. Third, all who serve the disciples of Jesus because they bear his name will be rewarded (Mark 9:41). Even small sacrifices, in this case supporting the kingdom mission by exorcising demons in Jesus' name, call forth God's approbation. The disciples must shed their myopic outlook and give special care for people who are moving toward Jesus but still have a distance to travel.

Jesus followed up his lesson with a severe warning not to cause offense toward "these little ones who believe in me" (Matt 18:6). The "little ones" (Matt 18:6, 10, 14) refer not only to literal children who desire to be near Jesus (Matt 18:2, 5), but also to all who humble themselves like a child (Matt 18:3–4; 19:14), believe in him, enter his reign, and bear his name. To cause grave spiritual harm to young, vulnerable believers, or seekers, invites the severest judgment. It would be better if such a potential offender's life was taken from him, such as being drowned in the sea by being cast in with a heavy millstone hung around his neck, than for such an offense to occur. Such offenses that lead people into sin and away from God are inevitable in our fallen world, but those who aspire to kingdom leadership must take the most radical steps to avoid being the cause of another's spiritual ruin.

In this context the metaphor of removing one's hand, feet and eye refers to the eradication of any attitudes or actions, especially pride, exclusivism and sectarianism, which would hinder people from entering Jesus' reign. Jesus used a series of expressions to warn of eternal punishment for those who cause such offenses: eternal fire (Matt 18:8); the Gehenna of fire (Matt 18:9); Gehenna, the unquenchable fire (Mark 9:43); the place where "their worm does not die and the fire is not quenched" (Mark 9:48); salted with fire (Mark 9:49). Gehenna is the transliteration of the Hebrew for the "valley of Hinnom," the valley south of Jerusalem where infants were sacrificed to pagan gods (2 Kgs 16:3; 21:6; Jer 7:31), later desecrated by godly King Josiah (2 Kgs 23:10), and which became a trash dump (worms/smoldering fire). The expression came to denote the place of eternal punishment for the wicked in Jewish theology.

Jesus is holding his aspiring kingdom leaders up to the most searching standards regarding how their ministry will influence others, either toward or away from the rule of God. The disciples must maintain their role as moral preservatives, symbolized by salt, in a corrupting world where offenses are frequent (Mark 9:50). Not only overt actions but subtle attitudes such as despising or looking down on tender believers can cause offense (Matt 18:10a). This final warning is given support: the Father has deep concern for these little ones by dispatching guardian angels to watch over them (Matt 18:10b). The Father is a shepherd who rejoices over the recovery of even one lost sheep (Matt 18:12–14). How can anyone who aspires to share the Shepherd's heart not guard their hearts, lips, hands and feet from any fault that might cause another to stumble and fall?

⇨ Do you detect any sectarian attitudes in your own heart which cause you to "look down" on brothers who differ with you on minor theological issues? Obey Jesus' final command in this section: "Be at peace with one another" (Mark 9:50b).

COURAGE TO REBUKE AND HUMILITY TO FORGIVE

(Matthew 18:15–35)

The loving unity of the kingdom community commends the gospel and has the power to arrest the attention of unbelievers (John 13:34–35; 17:20–23). Conversely, a community spoiled either by the tolerance of moral impurity or by refusal to offer reconciliation to its fallen members who repent brings the kingdom message into disrepute and repels those who might otherwise embrace its liberating promises. Jesus has already addressed the case where "your brother has something against you" (Matt 5:23). In that instance the disciple should temporarily suspend the act of worship and quickly reconcile, if possible, with the estranged brother (Matt 5:24–26). Now Jesus addresses the other case where "your brother sins against you" (18:15a). Reconciliation rooted in repentance, in this case the other person's, is again the rule with a four-step process to be followed:

1. The initial step is private reproof "between you and him alone," with the redemptive purpose to win the offending brother over, that is, lead to repentance and effect his restoration (18:15). The offended brother takes the initiative in seeking truth-based reconciliation.

2. If the offending brother refuses, the offended brother is to take two or three others and expand the circle of confrontation, in line with the law of confirmation by two or three witnesses (18:16; cf. Deut 19:15).

3. If the brother remains recalcitrant, the matter should be brought before the local congregation of believers as a whole (18:17a). Each successive step is triggered by the offending brother's refusal to listen.

4. The final stage is excommunication, that is, the severance of formal ties and community privileges: "let him be to you as a Gentile and a tax collector" (18:17b). The binding and loosing in this context refers to disciplinary expulsion and the restoration of the offending brother respectively (18:18). As two or more believers come to prayerful consent about the judicial matters raised in the confrontation, God will respond to preserve the purity of the community, which is the motivation behind all disciplinary measures (18:19). Jesus who is present in the gathered, unified prayer team will, as divine judge, ratify the decision of the offended brothers and move to defend the integrity of the congregation against unrepentant offenses (18:20). God's answer to the prayers of the

brothers is due to his commitment to the mission of the community that bears his Son's name.

Peter wondered whether there might be some limit to the amount of times a repeat offender should be offered forgiveness. The rabbinic consensus was that an offending brother was to be forgiven up to three times; the fourth repeated offense relieved one of the responsibility to forgive. Peter was more generous and suggested a limit of seven times. Jesus offered the number seventy-seven times, which means without limit. Lamech's principle of revenge (Gen 4:24) was transformed into a principle of forgiveness. In the kingdom community forgiveness is to have no bounds with respect to frequency or quantity. All disciples have been forgiven by God far more than they could ever forgive another person.

This is the point of the subsequent parable of the unforgiving servant (18:23–35). A servant was relieved of an enormous debt by his gracious master. Ten thousand talents translated to nearly 200,000 years of work for the average day laborer. The number represents crippling debt that could never be paid off. Relieved of his oppressive burden, that servant showed appalling callousness toward a fellow servant who begged to be given time to pay back his much smaller debt (100 denarii or about four month's wages). When the other servants protested to their master about the unforgiving servant's actions, the master condemned him, delivered him to the jailers, cancelled his earlier promise of remission, and commanded that the unforgiving servant be tortured and jailed until he paid back all he owed.

Jesus made the lesson of the parable clear: the Father will severely judge his servants who, having experienced God's unlimited forgiveness, do not forgive from the heart those who sin against them (18:35). God's forgiveness of sins is the climactic promise of the new covenant (Jer 31:34b). The people over whom God reigns will model forgiveness in their relations with one another. Here we encounter once again the moral symmetry in Jesus' teaching. On the one hand, there must be ecclesiastical discipline for unrepentant offenders. There can be no full and satisfying reconciliation apart from the repentance of the guilty party. On the other hand, frayed personal relations should never be the cause of personal vendettas. Nor should a wronged brother allow a root of bitterness to grow and spread. The need to confront and discipline offending members must not degenerate into harsh measures that prevent restoration. Because the church is a redeemed community, it must also be a redemptive one.

⇨ Is there a family member or friend whose words or actions in the past deeply hurt you so that it is difficult to forget, let alone forgive? Recall how the Lord has relieved you of your 10,000 talent burden of sin and forgive "from your heart" the one hundred denarii debt owed you.

11

Later Judean Ministry

Sharpening Lines of Acceptance and Rejection

JESUS' FACE RESOLUTELY SET ON JERUSALEM

(Luke 9:51–56)

L UKE'S GOSPEL RECORDS THE decisive turning point, now about six months
before his Passion, where Jesus "resolutely set his face to go to Jerusalem"
(9:51b [NASB]). The final stages of his ministry, in Judea and Perea, will lead
to the culmination of his life's purpose in Jerusalem, not only his death on
the cross, but also his resurrection and ascension to heaven (9:51a). Jesus is
conscious of his final destination, anticipating the glory after the suffering
(Isa 53:10–12; Phil 2:9–11; Heb 12:2). Luke 9:51—19:28 is often called the
"central section" or "travelogue" of Luke's Gospel. The opening verse does not
specify one final journey to Jerusalem but rather the determined focus on
his coming Passion which is to be fulfilled in the Holy City. That is where he
is inexorably heading, though the route will be circuitous as he moves north
to south on three itineraries during the *Later Judean* and *Perean* stages of
ministry:

1. Luke 9:51/John 7:2 refers to his trip to Jerusalem for the Feast
   of Tabernacles in early Fall, AD 29. From then until the Feast of
   Dedication in Winter, AD 29, where we again find him in Jerusalem
   (John 10:22–23), Jesus ministers in the towns of Judea. This *Later Judean*
   period, from Tabernacles to Dedication (three months) is recorded in
   Luke 9:51—13:21 and John 7:2—10:39.

2. Luke 13:22/John 11:17 indicates Jesus once again headed toward
   Jerusalem, having gone north for a period of ministry in the towns and

villages of Perea (John 10:40–42). This *Early Perean* ministry, recorded in Luke 13:22—17:10 and John 10:40—11:53, culminates with his trip to Bethany to raise his friend Lazarus from the dead.

3. Luke 17:11/John 12:1 refers to the journey to Jerusalem, by way of Bethany, for his final Passover, Spring AD 30. This follows a second period of ministry in Perea after withdrawing north to a village called Ephraim (John 11:54) and traveling through the area bordering Samaria and Galilee (Luke 17:11). The *Later Perean* ministry, recorded primarily in Luke 17:11—19:28, with slight coverage in Matthew (19:1—20:34) and Mark (10:1–52), ends with his arrival in Bethany six days before Passover (John 12:1).

Jews traveling from Galilee to Judea normally avoided contact with the schismatic Samaritans and went the long route eastward across the Jezreel valley, down the Jordan valley to Jericho, where they ascended the steep ridge route along the Wadi Qelt to Jerusalem. But this time Jesus took the disciples on the more direct course through the heart of Samaria. The religious tensions between Jews and Samaritans had a long history (John 4:9) and, as was often the case, the group met a nasty reception as they passed through a Samaritan village. James and John reacted with vengeful indignation, showing how faint their grasp of the lessons of humility and forgiveness the Lord had set forth in recent days (Matt 18:1–9, 21–35). Overly impressed with their own delegated apostolic authority, the explosive "sons of thunder" viewed themselves as prophetic spokesmen like Elijah and asked Jesus if they might call fire down on their adversaries, as Elijah had to the captains under evil King Ahaziah (Luke 9:54; cf. 2 Kgs 1:10–12). Jesus rebuked them because they utterly failed to discern that Jesus' mission was not to destroy but to seek and save the lost, whether Jew, Samaritan, or Greek (Luke 19:10; John 4:23–24). The issues at stake now and in Elijah's day were utterly different. Elijah was defending the claim of Yahweh to Israel's exclusive loyalty; the disciples are suffering from injured pride.

⇨ How do you feel about the multicultural character of this twenty-first century global village in which we are living? Do you view people of different ethnic and religious backgrounds as a threat or as the mission field at your doorstep?

RENEWED TEMPTATION FROM FAMILIAR SOURCES

(John 7:2–9)

The time for the annual Feast of Tabernacles (late September/early October, AD 29) is drawing near. Jesus remained in Galilee for the first part of the seven-day celebration. Tabernacles commemorated God's goodness to Israel during the forty years of wilderness wanderings, reenacted by constructing leafy shelters on roofs or in the courtyards of houses to live in during the month of Tishri, days 15–21. It was also a time to give thanks for the completion of the harvest season (Exod 23:16b; Lev 23:33–36; Deut 16:13–15).

Jesus' unbelieving brothers pressured him to ascend to Jerusalem and to openly manifest his miraculous powers. They appear frustrated by his relative obscurity during the past six months of withdrawals outside of Israel proper. Earlier his family had traveled from Nazareth to Capernaum to get his attention, charging that he had lost his mind (Mark 3:21). His brothers share the skeptical viewpoint of the religious leaders—a messianic claimant must prove his claims by authenticating works (Matt 12:38; 16:1). Where better to prove yourself than in the Holy City to the vast crowd of pilgrims gathered for this summative feast in Israel's calendar. Though John's Gospel does not record Jesus' three temptations in the desert, there are compelling parallels in John 6–7 to that Synoptic narrative:

1. *John 6:15*: After the feeding of the 5000, the crowds attempted to make him King by force, just as Satan offered him all the kingdoms of the world (Matt 4:8–10).

2. *John 6:30–31*: The popular Jewish expectation was that Messiah would provide once again the bread from heaven, the manna God provided to wilderness Israel. The listeners to his bread of life discourse in the synagogue demanded that he signify his messianic credentials by producing the manna. This parallels Satan's temptation of Jesus to turn stones into bread to satisfy his deep hunger (Matt 4:3–4).

3. *John 7:3–4*: His brothers' demand that he show himself to the crowds in Jerusalem parallels Satan's enticement to jump from the pinnacle of the temple to prove God's providential care (Matt 4:5–7).

In the wilderness of Judea and now here at the close of the Galilean ministry Jesus is being tempted to act prematurely and to use his divine prerogatives independently of God's will. To rally the multitudes and anti-

Roman zealots from nearby Gamala around himself in a call for a new Maccabean revolt for independence, to reenact the wilderness miracle of manna from heaven, to storm Jerusalem with awe-inspiring demonstrations of supernatural power—such actions would amount to aborting his mission as the suffering Servant and the veiled self-disclosure that beckons worthy disciples to surrender of the heart. The Lord will not be distracted from his mission nor thrown off the divine timetable. "My time" is not "your time," he tells his brothers. As part of the rejecting world, his earthly family marks time in meaningless succession because they are outside of and unrelated to the Father's plan. The Servant submits, both in timing and in method, to the Father's direction. He waits in Galilee for the appointed hour, not joining the family caravan.

⇨ Do your loved ones sometimes attempt to pull you away from following God's will for your life? Graciously explain to your family that Christ is now your Lord and you are committed to making your life count for him.

EXCUSES OF WOULD-BE FOLLOWERS

(Matthew 8:19–22; Luke 9:57–62)

A few days after his family headed south to celebrate Tabernacles, Jesus embarked quietly for Jerusalem on the direct route through the Samaritan heartland, then along the patriarchal ridge route from Shechem, arriving in the Holy City halfway through the seven-day feast (Luke 9:52; John 7:10–14). Along the way Jesus invited others to follow him, just as he had called the four fishermen and the tax collector. One by one these would-be followers offered reasons why they could not make such a commitment. Three excuses are singled out for special attention.

1. *Earthly comforts*: One man, a teacher of the law, offered to follow "wher-ever you go," but turned back when Jesus spoke of a nomadic life with few earthly comforts, the absence of social prestige, and no offer of financial security. The man did not reckon with all that was involved in "wherever you go." Crowds, miracles and excitement were in his mind in the offer to follow Jesus. Along with those things, Jesus said, would be deprivation, loneliness, hostility, and no permanent home to retreat to and feel secure.

THE PASSION OF THE SERVANT

⇨ How important are personal comforts to you? A quick check of your recent expenditures could be painfully revealing in this regard.

2. *Strategic priorities*: A second man, identified as a "disciple" (Matt 8:21; cf. John 6:66), heard the invitation to follow and replied, "Lord, let me first go and bury my father." In light of his father's death the request for a delay seems like a reasonable one. Jesus' reply comes across as harsh and unloving: "Leave the (spiritually) dead to bury their own (physically) dead. But as for you, go and proclaim the kingdom of God" (Luke 9:60). However, the uncompromising demand of Jesus is what was needed in this man's case, even as the rich young ruler was told to sell all of his possessions or their grip on his heart would remain (Luke 18:22). Behind the term "first" Jesus detected one whose supreme priority was filial allegiance. To become a true disciple there must be a decisive transfer of loyalties so that God's kingdom become one's "first" pursuit (Matt 6:33).

⇨ Do you allow demands from work or family to usurp all your energies so that nothing is left for investing time and resources in the kingdom?

3. *Defining relationships*: Another offered to follow, but only after he "first" returned home and said goodbye to his family. Jesus again perceived behind this 'reasonable' request a division of loyalty, a lack of resolve, the pull of earthly ties over kingdom values. Just as it is impossible for the farmer who "puts his hand to the plow and looks back" to run a straight furrow, so the disciple must maintain an undivided focus on the mandate to submit to God's lordship over the entire course of one's life. Jesus knew from recent personal experience that one's family members, without allegiance to the King, could apply the strongest and most subtle of pressures to dissuade one from following him on the cross-way of the Father's will.

⇨ Are there personal relationships that govern your decisions more than God's Word?

Those who aspire to enter the Jesus way have to do so through a gate that is narrow at the outset of the journey (Matt 7:13–14). These terse interchanges, overheard by the twelve disciples, served as a reminder to them that, along with promises of future reward, the pursuit of the kingdom in the present age will be a hard one.

⇨   In light of the three questions above, do some self-assessment and reca-
    librate your priorities.

STREAMS OF LIVING WATER

(John 7:10–52)

The *Later Judean* period extends from the Feast of Tabernacles (John 7:2, 11) to the Feast of Dedication (John 10:22), three months of *Fall AD 29*. The first phase is recorded in John 7:2—10:39 and the second phase in Luke 9:51—13:21. One can trace in John 7 the three divergent lines of response to Jesus among the sectors of population gathered in Jerusalem for the feast.

1. *Line of acceptance*: The apostles appear only as silent observers. Nicodemus, a Pharisee and member of the Sanhedrin, courageously steps forth to protest the treatment of Jesus who is being condemned without a fair hearing. In the vignettes that John provides of Nicodemus, we see a person moving toward deeper levels of commitment to Jesus: a private conversation at night in which he is confused about Jesus' teaching on the new birth (John 3:1–15); his rebuke of fellow Pharisees for subverting the normal judicial process that allows a person to speak in self-defense and then requires objective evidence to establish guilt (7:50–52); open identification with the crucified Lord, standing alongside Joseph of Arimathea to provide Jesus a proper burial (John 19:39–42).

2. *Line of ambivalence*: The crowds, confused and impressionable, waver back and forth without reaching a definitive conclusion. Some say he is a good man (7:12a); some marvel at his miracles and on one level believe in him (7:30–31); some speculate that he is a prophet or the Messiah (7:40–41a). Others say he is a deceiver (7:12b), that he is demon-possessed (7:20), and deny that a Galilean could be the Messiah (7:41b–42). Intimidation from the authorities prevents the crowd from making a commitment to follow Jesus (7:13); they are bullied into sub-mission and ridiculed by the Pharisees (7:49). The crowds that are native to Jerusalem carefully weigh the official assessment of Jesus (7:25–27).

The temple guards, impressed by his powerful teaching, are quickly silenced (7:45–47). Thus the people as a whole remained divided (7:43).

3. *Line of rejection*: The religious authorities have now hardened in their resolve to seize and kill Jesus (7:1, 11, 19, 25, 30, 32, 44). Largely overlapping terms for sections of the religious establishment are: the Jews (7:1, 11, 13, 15, 35); the rulers or authorities (7:26, 48); the Pharisees (7:32, 45, 47, 48); and the chief priests, predominantly Sadducees (7:32, 45). At every juncture the authorities crush dissent, pressuring the crowds to keep silent (7:13), making attempts to arrest Jesus when popular sentiment swings in his favor (7:32), ridiculing the temple guards (7:47–48), the crowds (7:49), and Nicodemus (7:52) when they offer positive comments about Jesus. Yet even the authorities could not account for Jesus' profound exposition of Scripture (7:15). They are not able, for the present, to move against him because "his hour had not yet come" (7:30).

Jesus is up to the moment. He addresses recalcitrant Pharisees and chief priests, fickle crowds, and true disciples with authoritative declarations in the first person singular. On three distinct occasions during the seven-day feast, at the halfway point (7:14), a day or two later (7:28), and on the last and greatest day (7:37) Jesus proclaims loudly to worshippers gathered in the temple courts his messianic identity and mission. We summarize this self-testimony.

1. *Jesus' teaching originates from God the Father, seeks to honor him and is wholly truthful* (7:16–18). This accounts for Jesus' wisdom and distinguishes him from the teachers of the law who draw on rabbinical tradition for their ideas. The reason for the Jews' rejection is not academic but moral. Faith-obedience must precede spiritual discernment. Recognition of the truth follows submission to God's will. Anselm famously captured this axiom, "I believe, therefore I know." Or as the Hebrew poet framed it: "The fear of the Lord is the beginning of wisdom, and the knowledge of the Holy One is insight" (Prov 9:10).

2. *Jesus is sent by the Father and after the fulfillment of his work at the appointed hour will return to the Father* (7:29, 30, 33). Commission, humiliation and exaltation are the three moments of his redemptive task, each fulfilled according to the Father's will. Neither his teaching nor his mission is self-generated. He moves forward according to his

appointed "hour." John records Jesus' statement of destination (7:33) which Luke made a hinge point in his narrative (9:51): as his Passion nears, he anticipates reunion with the Father, just as Isaiah's servant contemplated the light of life and the justification of many sinners after his sacrificial death (53:10–12). The human plots do not threaten the accomplishment of the Father's plan; the unfolding conflict is not a human tragedy but the divine strategy. When Jesus speaks of his departure to a place beyond his enemies' reach, they speculate that he is planning to disappear among the Greek-speaking Jews in order to propagate his message in their synagogues. Ironically, the proclamation of the gospel following Pentecost "to the Jew first and also to the Greek" (Rom 1:16b) will begin in the Hellenistic synagogues, to Jews as well as Greek god-fearers. Written in the final decade of the first century, when the Christian faith had spread in such manner throughout the eastern Mediterranean world, John's narrative anticipates the worldwide extension of the salvation proclaimed through the death and resurrection of Jesus.

3. *After his glorification Jesus will mediate his life-giving presence to his covenant people through the gift of the Holy Spirit* (7:37–39). To any person ("whoever") who heeds the invitation to come to Jesus in faith, the Spirit becomes not only a thirst-quenching well (John 4:13–14), but streams of living water flowing forth from within to provide spiritual refreshment to others. During the week-long Feast of Tabernacles, climaxing on the seventh day, there was a procession of priests and worshippers from the temple court to the pool of Siloam. The designated priest filled a golden pitcher with water, returned to the court of the priests, and poured out the water at the base of the bronze altar of burnt offering. The act commemorated God's miraculous provision of water for Israel during their forty years of forced wandering in the desert, but more profoundly symbolized eschatological cleansing from sin and the outpouring of the Spirit in the new covenant. Jesus cried out with the offer of a satisfying inner spring of water that would gush forth into streams of blessing to others. By this, John notes, Jesus was speaking of the gift of the indwelling Spirit that would follow his glorification, fulfilling numerous predictions in the Old Testament prophets (Isa 12:3; 55:1; 58:11; Jer 31:33b; Ezek 36:25–26; 37:14; 39:29; 47:1, 12; Joel 2:28–32; 3:18). Jesus has already spoken of this gift to the Samaritan woman

(John 4:13–14) and makes the coming of the Spirit one of the themes of his Upper Room Discourse (John 14:16–17, 26; 15:26–27; 16:7, 12–15). The New Testament apostles celebrate this distinctive provision of the new covenant (Acts 2:32–33; 1 Cor 15:45; 2 Cor 3:17–18).

Calvary is the prelude to Pentecost as the benefits of Christ's death, vindicated in resurrection, flow to the believer through the Spirit who mediates the vital presence of the exalted Lord to his people. Believers quench their thirst in the cleansing blood of Calvary, then, through Spirit-energized words and works draw others to come and drink the water of life freely (Rev 22:17).

⇨ Are you, like the Dead Sea, a stagnant pool that takes in but never flows out? Or are you, like the Jordan River, supplying life-giving water to the thirsty souls around you?

"BEFORE ABRAHAM WAS, I AM"

(John 8:12–59)

Jesus and the Pharisees now faced off in open confrontation in the temple court of the women where the thirteen trumpet-shaped offering boxes were located (8:20). They traded accusations in a fierce volley of charges and countercharges. Throughout this interchange Jesus is clearly on the offensive: the Pharisees do not know God the Father (8:19, 47, 55); they will die in their sins banished from God's presence (8:21); they belong to this world, which is Satan's domain (8:23); they will face him as judge (8:26); far from being Abraham's true descendants, they are the children of the devil, imitating their father as a murderer and a liar (8:37–45, 55).

The Pharisees counter that Jesus' testimony is invalid (8:13), suggest he is going to kill himself (8:22), imply he is illegitimate (8:41), revile him as a Samaritan and as demon-possessed (8:48, 52), assert he is delusional for claiming to overcome death and to know Abraham (8:52–53), and finally threaten to stone him (8:59). The conflict explodes out of the claims that Jesus makes regarding his divine origin and authority. The essential divide between Jesus and the religious leaders is not the Sabbath, fasting, food laws, table relations with Gentiles, or the washing of hands and cooking utensils. These are extrinsic matters that exacerbate tension originating from his intrinsic claim to be the Son of God and Messiah. Here he makes seven astounding declarations in the first person singular.

1. *Jesus is the light of the world, illumining the path to God for all who follow him* (8:12). The Old Testament typology of the wilderness years of Israel continues: just as the manna previews the true bread from heaven whose sacrificial death brings life (Exod 16; John 6:32–35, 51), and as the water from the rock points to the purifying work of the Spirit of the glorified Lord (Exod 17:1–6; John 7:37–39), so the pillar of fire illumining Israel's path at night anticipates the light who illumines the walk of the believer through a dark world (Exod 13:21–22; 40:36–38).

2. *Jesus is in perfect accord with the Father whose audible testimony at his baptism and Transfiguration authenticates his Son's divine prerogatives* (8:14–18). Earlier Jesus appealed to multiple witnesses who attested to his authority (John 5:31–47), but his final appeal all along has been the Father (John 5:31–32, 37–38). Jesus stands alongside his Father as judge of the human race, executing a true judgment based in the character of the God who is the source and norm of all truth (John 7:28; 17:3).

3. *Jesus is the heavenly sent Redeemer, apart from whom people have no hope of forgiveness and without which they will die in their sins* (8:23–24). There is an inseparable gulf between the Pharisees and Jesus. They belong to the world of thought and values of which Satan is overlord and sin is the operative principle. Sin is properly defined as the violation of God's moral character in thought, word or deed, expressed in concrete transgressions of his holy law, preeminently the mandate to love him with all of one's heart, soul and strength and to love one's neighbor as oneself (Lev 19:18; Deut 6:5; Matt 22:36–30). Jesus is of heavenly origin and thus thinks about, speaks of and reveals the Father to people. Apart from faith in a heaven-sent, divine Redeemer, people will remain under sin's hegemony, the penalty of which is eternal death.

4. *Jesus is the Son of Man whose oneness with the Father will be vindicated when he is "lifted up"* (8:27–29). Jesus' uplifting, previewed in the raising of the bronze snake on a pole by Moses (Num 21:4–9), is a complex redemptive event, beginning with his literal crucifixion on the tree and culminating in his exaltation at the right hand of the Father (John 3:14; 12:32, 34; cf. Acts 2:33; Phil 2:9). Jesus' true identity and character as the suffering Servant (Isa 53)—Son of Man (Dan 7) will be disclosed in

that singular event, one which encompasses shame and glory, humiliation and exaltation.

5. *Jesus is the eternal Son who speaks the truth that has the power to liberate people from bondage to sin into the full rights of adopted sons in the family of God* (8:31–36, 51). Cognitive acceptance of Jesus' testimony must lead to habitual obedience to his authoritative teaching for one to be a true disciple (8:30–31). Only that kind of faith, adhering faith, liberates one from the operative principle of sin. New covenant liberty, then, is cancellation of the penalty of sin—death or separation from God—and victory over the controlling influence of sin in one's bodily members. Freedom found in one's connection to the Son transfers a person from the deprivation of a slave to the full rights of an adopted son, empowered to serve in God's household.

6. *Jesus fulfills all of the salvation historical aspirations of the Old Testament, beginning with Abraham* (8:54–56). Physical and spiritual kinship to Abraham, the progenitor and conduit of Israel's covenantal privileges, are two disparate relationships. The former constitutes one a member of empirical Israel, to the Pharisees a badge of honor (8:33, 39). The latter, unrelated to ethnicity, is entered into by faith in the Savior who Abraham himself strained to see through the long, dimly lit corridor of revelation. He eagerly looked forward, drawing on the covenantal promises (Gen 12:1–3; 15:4–5; 17:4–7; 18:10–14), to the coming of the son/Son who will bring redemptive blessing to all nations (Gal 3:6–9; Heb 11:10, 13–16).

7. *Jesus is the preexisting, eternal Lord who became at the opportune moment the incarnate Son of God* (8:58). Characteristically misinterpreting his words about Abraham—he "rejoiced that he would see my day. He saw it and was glad." (8:56)—in a strictly literal fashion, the Pharisees charged the not yet fifty year old Jesus with being delusional. With that came the summative declaration, bringing together all of Jesus' majestic claims in this interchange in the temple court: "Before Abraham was (born), I am (existing)." Drawing on the language of Exodus 3:14 where God introduced himself to Moses at the burning bush as the eternally self-existent Lord (Yahweh), Jesus distinguished his eternality and preexistence from that of Abraham whose life began at his birth. This is consonant with the way John introduces Jesus as the eternal Logos, fully divine and yet distinct from the Father (1:1–2). It is difficult to conceive

how Jesus could have made a more direct and unmistakable claim to being divine than in the language of this declaration. His listeners understood the nature of the assertion. Either one must fall prostrate and confess with Thomas, "my Lord and my God" (John 20:28), or take up stones to eliminate the blasphemer. Unwilling to do the former, they did the latter.

⇨ Notice the sequence in 8:30–32: a cognitive belief must translate itself into obedience to Jesus' teaching to constitute true discipleship, which in turn produces freedom from the controlling influence of sin. Is discipleship in this sense properly understood in the contemporary church? More importantly, by this criterion can you call yourself a disciple of Jesus?

I ONCE WAS BLIND, BUT NOW I SEE

(John 9:1–41)

Providing sight to blind people was the single most frequent category of miracle performed by Jesus, probably because it symbolized the removal of spiritual darkness. This kind of miracle, the work of God alone (Exod 4:11; Ps 146:8), was to be an authenticating sign of the Messiah (Isa 29:18; 35:5; 42:7). Near the entrance to the temple courts as worshippers filed in during the Feast of Tabernacles (or possibly the Feast of Dedication [John 10:22]), Jesus saw a man blind from birth. The disciples combined a Jewish determinism with traces of animistic superstition when they asked whether his misfortune was caused by his own sin or that of his parents. Jesus rejected such a rigid connection between personal sin and tragedy. Though sin is sometimes the direct cause of one's suffering (John 5:14), such is rarely the case (Luke 13:2–5). Jesus holds a providential worldview and sees behind the tragedy a divine plan with a merciful intent: God has permitted this misfortune in order to display his glorious power. The light of the world has a short time left to shine and so he works with urgency to accomplish the Father's purpose.

Employing the method of spittle mixed with clay placed on the man's eyes (Mark 7:33; 8:23), followed with a washing in the pool of Siloam, Jesus restored the obedient man's sight. Neighbors and other observers familiar with this blind beggar provided multiple, independent confirmation that the person now seeing is the same as the former blind man. For the first of many times (9:10, 15, 19, 21, 26), the man, or his parents, were asked how he came to see, and in each case, until his patience wore thin (9:27), he offered a straightforward recital of the events: "The man called Jesus made mud and anointed my eyes and said to me, 'Go to Siloam and wash.' So I went and washed and received my sight" (9:11).

When it was discovered that the miracle took place on the Sabbath, the man was quickly escorted to the religious inspectors. Among the Pharisees were hardliners who dismissed Jesus as a Sabbath violator and moderates who wondered how such a work could be performed by a law-breaker. Unconvinced that such a miracle has really occurred, they question his parents who identify their son, confirm the removal of his congenital blindness, but make no pronouncement on its causation. Their caution is attributed to the threat of excommunication from the synagogue for any one who openly confesses that Jesus is the Messiah. Frustrated, the Pharisees conduct a second interrogation of the blind man which leads nowhere. Amidst accusations against Jesus and personal attacks on his own character, the man remains firm in his testimony that this Jesus has performed a miracle like no other and so must be of God. The authorities do not show a trace of compassion for this fellow human being whose suffering has been alleviated, only threats and insults for challenging their cherished presuppositions. The callousness is appalling.

Jesus quietly reappears and summons the healed man, now excommunicated, to a living faith. The man's estimation of Jesus progresses throughout the narrative: he is just a man called Jesus (9:11), a prophet (9:17), one who is worthy of a disciple's allegiance (9:27), one who is from God (9:33), the Son of Man (9:35), and, climactically, Lord, whom he confesses and worships (9:38). The healing of the blind man represents the paradoxical principle that salvation comes to those who recognize their need for spiritual sight, while judgment descends upon those who claim they can see even while turning away from the light of the world (9:41).

⇨   What are some ways that we, in reliance upon the convicting work of the Spirit (John 16:8–10), can help people to recognize their spiritual blindness?

THE GOOD SHEPHERD

(John 10:1–21)

The Old Testament prophets lamented the priests and false prophets of their day as blind watchmen and selfish shepherds who led Israel away from her covenantal obligations (Isa 56:9–12; Jer 23:1–4; Ezek 34:1–10). Jesus has just denounced the Pharisees, trained to be practitioners and teachers of Israel's law, for spiritual blindness (John 9:39–41). Now he provides a figure of speech (10:6), followed by an interpretation, which is a portrait of the good shepherd.

Figure of Speech (10:1–6)

1. The thief does not enter the sheep pen by the gate but climbs over the walls to enter.

2. The shepherd enters by the gate, calls his own sheep by name, and leads them out to the fields. He goes ahead of the sheep and speaks to them in familiar tones.

3. The watchman opens the gate for the shepherd to enter.

4. The sheep recognize the shepherd's voice, clearly distinct from the voice of strangers from whom they run away, and follow the shepherd.

Interpretation (10:7–18)

1. The thief is the false prophet or teacher who enters the church, not by believing in Jesus, but by some other way, and seeks to scatter, harm, and even destroy God's flock. The hired hand is a professed custodian of the flock, but flees when danger comes, allowing the marauding wolf to attack and scatter the believers. The wolf is Satan and the hired hand is the religious leader who stands firm in time of safety, but abandons his post when threatened with danger or persecution. The Pharisees must be in the background here.

2. Jesus is the gate of the sheep pen. The pen is the sphere of salvation and security. The fields are the paths of danger and temptation in the world into which God's people are directed and protected, following Jesus. Jesus is the good shepherd who comes to bring abundant life.

3. The Father, who is the watchman, loves the Son, who is the good shepherd. In accordance with the Father's mandate, the Son lays down his

life for his people. With divine authority Jesus makes his life a sacrificial offering and takes his life up again in resurrection.

4. The sheep are the people of God, secure in their salvation, careful in their ability to distinguish the shepherd from strangers or hirelings, obedient to listen to and follow the voice of the Lord Jesus. There are sheep already in the fold and "other sheep" not yet gathered who will comprise "one flock." Jesus anticipates a universal people of God, Jew and Gentile, bound together by their common allegiance to Jesus.

Theological Implications

1. The people of God face real danger from the destructive purposes of Satan (wolf), dedicated legalists and heretics (thief), and cowardly pastors who work for money and lose their nerve when pressured (hireling).

2. Jesus Christ is the exclusive way to salvation. There is no alternative path to the Father.

3. Believers are secure in the faithful care and loving guidance of the Good Shepherd. Through God's Word they avoid false teachers and are preserved in faithful obedience.

4. The Father and Son cooperate in the redemptive plan. The means by which the redemption of God's people is secured is the sacrificial death and resurrection of Jesus.

Again there is a division of response, even among the Pharisees. Some denounce Jesus as a demonized lunatic; others wonder how a demon could give sight to a man born blind (10:19–21).

⇨ What kinds of people do the wolves, thieves and hirelings represent in the church today?

SEVENTY MISSIONARIES

(Luke 10:1–24)

The twelve apostles were the foundational representatives of Jesus. They proclaimed the kingdom of God throughout the villages of Galilee on three separate tours (Mark 1:38–39; Luke 8:1–3; Luke 9:6). They had been instructed to pray for more laborers for the harvest (Matt 9:37–38). The Lord of the harvest now answered their prayers and expanded the laborers to seventy, which included the twelve (Luke 22:35). These seventy emissaries correspond to the number of names in the table of nations in Genesis 10. The symbolism seems to be that Jesus is sending out missionaries of the kingdom that equal the number of (ethnic) nations on earth and are thus a harbinger of the coming universal proclamation of the gospel (Luke 24:47–49; Acts 1:8). It is clear that Jesus enlisted and authorized kingdom workers far beyond the initial twelve. Even these seventy, like the twelve earlier, were enjoined to pray for still more laborers for the harvest (10:2). The seventy went two by two through the villages of Perea and Judea to prepare for the Lord's follow-up visit.

The practice of ministry of these seventy corresponds to the earlier instructions give the twelve at their formal commissioning (Matt 10:5–16), except that they are no longer explicitly precluded from evangelizing Gentiles or Samaritans. The congruity of the two instruction manuals (Matt 10; Luke 10) points toward normative principles designed to govern the manner in which kingdom workers go about their task, even if the context of ministry is a particular one.

1. *Simplicity of lifestyle* (10:3–4): Like lambs among wolves, they enter a mission fraught with danger. No money bag, knapsack, or extra pair of sandals means they will be dependent on God and his people for their basic needs. To refrain from salutations signifies the urgency of their message that must be delivered without distraction.

2. *Authoritative message* (10:5–15): Their message is "the kingdom of God has come near to you," one authenticated by healing miracles. A benediction of peace is to be pronounced on receptive towns and homes, but a warning of strict judgment on those whose refusal to grant hospitality reveals their spiritual obduracy.

3. *Missional solidarity* (10:16): The ground of their authority is the representative continuity between the Father, Jesus and the disciples. They are mediators of the kingdom mission committed to them by Jesus and to Jesus by the Father. Theirs is thus a derived authority. The disciples must maintain fidelity to the teachings passed on to them by their Lord. As disciples accurately proclaim revealed truth, the listeners possess a grave responsibility to hear with their hearts, not just their ears, for their eternal destiny depends on it.

Jesus followed the seventy disciples to the towns of Perea and Judea that they first visited in their teams of two. He then gathered them for a debriefing session regarding the results of the tour. The disciples exulted in their power to exorcise demons "in your name" (10:17). Jesus detected here the danger of misplaced priorities, success-driven arrogance, and a propensity for power encounter over truth encounter. His rebuke, however, is gentle. In the exorcisms, both his and theirs, Jesus saw the sacking of Satan's kingdom, one being displaced by the dawning of the messianic rule (10:18; cf. Matt 12:28–29). This was a prelude to the defeat of Satan at the cross (John 12:31; 16:11) and his final vanquishing at the second coming of Christ (Rom 16:20). Jesus has delegated to his missionary-disciples authority to dispel the enemy's death-dealing hold on human beings. They need not fear harm from Satan's minions, symbolized by stinging scorpions and biting snakes, for they are secure in the Father's providential care (10:19; cf. Matt 10:29–31). The Lord does not discourage his disciples' joy, but redirects it and purifies it. Their deepest level of satisfaction should spring not from their ability to command the submission of evil spirits, but from the security they possess as God's beloved ones whose names are listed in the heavenly recording of the redeemed (10:20). This registry, often called the "book of life," is a common thread woven into the tapestry of redemption (Exod 32:32; Ps 69:28; Dan 12:1; Phil 4:3; Rev 20:12, 15; 21:27).

Jesus' greatest joy comes from his relationship with the Father and the gracious work of the Father in securing the fellowship of believers with him in the inaugurated and soon to be consummated kingdom (10:21–22). Jesus wants his disciples to share this joy. He reminds them of the inestimable privilege that is theirs of standing on the threshold of the kingdom, yearned for by prophets and kings, though it comes in a unexpected form, namely, God's reign operative in the lives of people mediated through the sacrifice of the suffering Servant (10:23–24).

⇨ Are you caught up with the success of your work more than your relationship with the One for whose glory and by whose grace you serve? Where does your deepest sense of fulfillment reside? Remember Jesus' warnings in Matthew 6:1–8: even good and noble activities can be pursued with wrong motivation.

PARABLE OF THE GOOD SAMARITAN

(Luke 10:25–37)

An expert in the interpretation of the Old Testament law approached Jesus with a question: "Teacher, what shall I do to inherit eternal life?" The question was not an honest inquiry, but a test designed to discredit Jesus. In the mind of this scholar "doing" was the precondition for receiving eternal life. The Lord kept the conversation on the legalist's plane of thought in order to drive home the futility of such an approach to God. Jesus reminded him of the two summative commands of the law, to love God from one's entire being and to love one's neighbor to the extent one naturally loves oneself (Lev 19:18; Deut 6:5). Whoever fulfills these commands in their entirety, Jesus posited, will be granted eternal life. Jesus, and Paul later (Rom 10:5; Gal 3:12), saw in Leviticus 18:5 a hypothetical offer of life to the one who obeys the law perfectly.

Unwilling to face the spiritual bankruptcy that such an unattainable standard exposes, the scholar sought to evade the implications of Jesus' counterquestion (10:26) and command (10:28). Feeling the need to justify himself, he responded with a further question: "And who is my neighbor?" The question was an attempt to quiet his conscience by stimulating a dispute over the meaning and range of the word "neighbor." If he could shift the conversation away from the applicational force of the law's command to one of theological disputation, he reckoned he would gain the upper hand over the uneducated Galilean.

Jesus reframed, by means of a parable (or an actual incident), the lawyer's question from "Who is my neighbor?" (10:29) to "To whom am I acting as a neighbor?" (10:36 paraphrase). The seventeen-mile steep decline from Jerusalem (3,000 ft. above sea level) to Jericho (-1,000 ft.) was a rugged and rocky road around cliffs that straddle wadis. Robbers, hidden in hollow places, attacked a traveler who was robbed, stripped, beaten, and abandoned. Two officials, a priest and a Levite, were returning to Jericho, likely after performing their duties in the Jerusalem temple, and came upon the "half dead" man. Each one "passed by on the other side." Such callous disregard was a clear violation of the law, which enjoined mercy for those in need (Exod 23:4–5; Lev 19:34; Mic 6:8). Precise attention to carrying out the duties of their religious vocation had obscured the "weightier matters" of the law, namely, justice, mercy and faithfulness (Matt 23:23). Finally, a despised Samaritan came by, saw the helpless victim, and was moved with compassion. He went to him, bound up his wounds, pouring on oil and wine, took him to an inn on his own donkey, cared for him, paid two denarii for lodging, and pledged to repay whatever expenses were incurred to nurse the stranger back to health.

Now Jesus moved to the probing interpretive question and its direct application. The original passive question of interpretation, "Who is my neighbor?," is restructured into an active question of engagement: "Which of these three . . . proved to be a neighbor?" (10:36). Unable to evade any longer, the lawyer answered correctly: "the one who showed him mercy." The one who began the conversation with a precondition of "doing" to gain eternal life was told to "go and do likewise" (10:37b). To love one's neighbor as oneself meant to seek proactively the welfare of the person in distress who crosses one's path. Did the light begin to dawn in the darkened mind of the Torah scholar that such a command was impossible to obey perfectly and that he must abandon every attempt at justifying himself before God? There is no recorded sequel.

⇨ James reminds us that the concrete expressions of our faith are more revealing about its reality than are verbal professions (Jas 1:27). Recall some of the practical ways you have served the practical needs of others, especially those in physical distress.

THE GOOD PORTION

(Luke 10:38–42)

Jesus and his disciples came to the home of his friends, Mary, Martha, and Lazarus, in the village of Bethany on the eastern slope of the Mt. of Olives just two miles from Jerusalem. This was their favorite place to lodge when they traveled to Jerusalem (Matt 21:17; John 11:17–18; 12:1–2). The two sisters were quite different in temperament. Martha was the aggressive personality (John 11:20, 21, 28; 12:2), while Mary was quiet and contemplative (John 12:3–8). In this instance Martha threw herself into the preparations for her thirteen guests as a model oriental hostess, while Mary "sat at the Lord's feet and listened to his teaching" (10:39).

Martha became irritated at her sister for not pulling her share of the load, and even at Jesus for not reproving Mary: "Lord, do you not care that my sister has left me to serve alone? Tell her then to help me" (10:40). Martha found herself in the place of issuing a command to her Lord. Jesus' gentle

Later Judean Ministry

1. Last journey from **Capernaum** to **Jerusalem**
2. **Jerusalem**: Feast of Tabernacles
3. Ministry of 70 in **Judea** and **Perea**
4. Visit to **Bethany**
5. Last ministry in **Judea**
6. **Jerusalem**: Feast of Dedication

Capernaum

Sea of Galilee

GALILEE

Scythopolis

①

SAMARIA

Shechem

Jordan River

Lebonah

PEREA

JUDEA

Mediterranean Sea

③

Jericho

Jerusalem

⑤

⑥②   Bethany

④

Dead Sea

rebuke that followed must have stung, especially since it came from one who was to enjoy the lavish meal she was feverishly preparing. The Lord reproved Martha for being anxious and troubled about the many lesser, unnecessary things. He had come to Bethany more for the fellowship than the food. Mary, on the other hand, is commended for having chosen the "one thing (that) is necessary," "the good portion," that is, to sit with Jesus and to give heed to his word (10:42). The truths gleaned from drawing close would have greater lasting impact than the finest meal. The priority was worship over work, listening before doing, relationship over service. The happy sequel to this incident will come when Jesus visits Bethany again the Friday before Passion Week (John 12:1–8).

⇨   Are you busy and distracted by activities that, good and noble in them-selves, usurp daily time that should be given to meditation on God's Word and prayer? Refocus your schedule so that "the good portion" will regain its rightful priority.

IMPORTUNATE PRAYER
(Luke 11:1–13)

One day when Jesus was engaged in prayer, the disciples interrupted him with a request: "Lord, teach us to pray, as John taught his disciples" (11:1). The request reveals the degree to which they were impressed by the Lord's manner of prayer to his Father. Behind the request was a yearning for such relational intimacy with God. He had earlier imparted to them a model prayer in the Sermon on the Mount (Matt 6:9–13), which he repeats here in abbreviated form (11:2–4). The disciples' broad request ("teach us to pray"), however, was not only a search for the manner of prayer, but for its hidden character, the kind of prayer that prevails with God the Father. The parable of the importunate friend provided the latter.

An unexpected guest arrived at midnight and there was no bread to serve for a late meal. The host went to a friend's house to borrow three loaves of bread, but was refused because the latter would have to disturb his sleep-ing family. However, the friend eventually got up and gave him the bread because of the supplicant's "shamelessness" to keep knocking and asking despite the late hour and embarrassing circumstances. This colorful term is used in the New Testament only in Luke 11:8 and is rendered in a variety of ways: boldness (NIV); importunity (AV); persistence (NASB); impudence

(ESV). The Amplified Bible paraphrases it: "shameless persistence and insistence," which is an attempt to capture the audacious and obtrusive nature of the action described by this word.

The parable contains an implicit lesser to greater argument: if an earthly friend will extend help under pressure rather than from sympathy, how much more will the heavenly Father abundantly extend grace to his children who earnestly continue to seek his face. The interpretive words that follow confirm that importunity in asking, driven by trust in a benevolent Father, is the central point of the parable (11:9–13). The parable clearly does not mean that God is a reluctant giver who must be coaxed against his will to grant our wishes. Rather, Jesus exhorts the disciples to persevere in asking even when the heavens are silent, though the request would appear to be in line with God's will and assured by his promises (1 John 5:14–15).

⇨   Is your prayer life characterized by bold determination to keep seeking, asking, and knocking until the request is granted? Think of a long-standing prayer that remains 'unanswered.' Bring it once again to your Father with 'reverent audaciousness.'

PRINCIPLES OF SPIRITUAL WARFARE

(Luke 11:14–36)

About one year earlier in Galilee Jesus exorcised a demon from a blind and dumb man and was accused of being empowered by Beelzebub, the prince of demons. This sparked a heated exchange over his identity and authority (Matt 12:22–30). Now in Judea a similar healing of a dumb man brings the same charge and reply. As the Passion draws nearer, the battle lines between Jesus and the religious authorities are drawn more sharply. This is more than a clash of worldviews, but a conflict of cosmic proportions. They view him as demon-inspired, a deceiver of the people, a false prophet. Jesus, however, expounds his mission as a direct assault on Satan's counterfeit kingdom, his exorcism of demons "by the finger of God" a dawning of the kingdom of God (11:20). The Son of Man—suffering Servant who will one day be Ruler of the universe—is assailing the strong man, removing his protective armor, and plundering his goods. This is a metaphor for the evil one, his demonic minions, and the human souls subject to his rule of deceit. Satan's defeat is anticipated in Jesus' ministry, secured at the cross and consummated at the return of the Son of Man in glory (Matt 12:28; John 12:31; Rev 20:7–10).

Luke records a number of Jesus' sayings that in the present context delineate principles that must govern the manner and message of those engaged in spiritual warfare:

1. *A person must align himself for or against Jesus.* There is a call to undivided allegiance; neutrality places oneself on the side of those who reject the King (11:23; cf. Matt 12:30).

2. *Moral reformation without spiritual transformation leads to personal and national ruin.* Unless the divine presence fills the void left by the departed demon, it will be replaced by more defiled inhabitants. This may be a metaphor for Israel's religious leadership, a house swept clean by the Assyrian and Babylonian exiles from idolatry, but replaced with a lifeless and tradition-bound religion so debauched that when the Messiah himself arrives they mistake him for Beelzebub, the prince of demons (11:24–26; cf. Matt 12:43–45).

3. *God's favor rests on the one who both hears and obeys his word.* A woman in the crowd burst forth with a word of blessing on the mother who bore Jesus. This was not a Mary-centered theological confession, but an emotional response at the beauty and power of Jesus' words. Jesus responded with a gentle corrective: those blessed or favored by God are not those who are moved by oratory or personal charisma, but those who hear and continue in obedience to the authoritative word of God (11:27–28; cf. Luke 8:21).

4. *Repentance alone can avert God's judgment and bring one under God's saving rule.* Some people in the crowd demanded a "sign," remarkably just after the healing of the dumb man (11:16). Here the "sign of Jonah" promised by Jesus is not a resurrection sign (Matt 12:40), but the warning of judgment and the demand for repentance that makes Jonah a type of Christ (Jonah 1:1–2; 3:1–10). The gravity of repentance is underscored by the identity of the one demanding it, one wiser than Solomon and one more powerful than Jonah (11:29–32; cf. Matt 12:41–42).

5. *One must allow the light of God's truth to penetrate the heart so that its darkness is uncovered, confessed, and cleansed. Then the heart can be renewed by God's Spirit.* The analogy of the lamp, placed on a stand to magnify its illuminating power, is a call to not obstruct the penetrating

force of Jesus' works and words. The eye is the window that allows the "light of the world" to enter in, purify and recreate the inner person into conformity with God's truth (11:33–36; cf. Matt 5:15; 6:22–23).

⇨ Are you engaged in this kind of spiritual warfare, one that is radical, uncompromising and soul-accosting?

OUTWARD VERSUS INWARD CLEANSING

(Luke 11:37–54)

Jesus was invited to dine at an unnamed Pharisee's house. Hosted by one who placed great store in matters of ritual purity, Jesus' failure to properly wash his hands before the meal must have been intentional, designed to precipitate a debate. Jesus' laxity in such matters explains the relaxed attitudes of his disciples which earlier invited censure (Mark 7:1–5). Knowing he has caused offense, Jesus confronts the Pharisee about misplaced priorities: the concern for proper washing of hands and eating utensils is not matched by a pursuit of personal holiness (11:37–41). The Old Testament laws of purity were external regulations intended to underscore the holiness of God and the need for his people to be consecrated in every aspect of existence, beginning with the interior life (Lev 11:44). With six woes Jesus condemns a ceremonial purity that masks moral corruption, three each against the Pharisees and the teachers of the law respectively.

1. *Perversion of priorities* (11:42)

   Perfunctory matters are scrupulously attended to, such as the tithing of even garden herbs, yet the weightier matters of the law, namely, social justice and love for God, are neglected. The Old Testament prophets lamented this lifeless religion with the same contrast (Isa 1:10–17; 58:1–8; Amos 5:21–24; Mic 6:6–8).

2. *Prideful desire for human praise* (11:43)

   The Pharisees coveted the "best seat" in the synagogue, which was in the front, facing the congregation, next to the person leading in prayer or reading from the Hebrew scroll. To be greeted "Rabbi" by admiring laymen was a sign of status. A desire for recognition displaced the central motives of authentic ministry—the glory of God and the spiritual welfare of people.

3. *Pretension of piety* (11:44)

   Graves were whitewashed before festivals like Passover to prevent pilgrims from becoming ceremonially defiled by accidental contact with unmarked tombs. The Pharisees are like unmarked graves which spiritually defile those who come under their influence.

4. *Prejudicial hypocrisy* (11:45–46)

   Now the teachers of the law, many but not all of them belonging to the party of the Pharisees, are the target of the denunciation. These experts in the Mosaic law had skillfully exempted themselves from many of the binding regulations they forced on others. They were harsh on others and easy on themselves.

5. *Persecution of God's prophets* (11:47–51)

   The religious leaders invested vast resources in rebuilding the tombs of the Old Testament prophets. Yet in memorializing the prophets, Jesus detects a sinister irony: they testify to their own solidarity with their forefathers who killed the true prophets of God, from Abel, son of Adam, to Zechariah, son of Jehoiada the high priest under Josiah (Gen 4:10; 2 Chr 24:20–22). The entire span of redemptive history, recorded in the Hebrew canon (Genesis—2 Chronicles), testifies to the wicked treatment of God's prophets by Israel and now the generation that rejects God's greater Prophet and Son is memorializing those deeds.

6. *Prevention of others from entering the kingdom* (11:52)

   By obscuring God's grace with a synergistic interplay of divine election and human merit, the teachers of the law withhold the "key of knowledge" which would open the kingdom to people. By encrusting God's truth with layers of human tradition, the scribes deflect the penetrating force of Holy Scripture which alone has the power to prick the conscience leading to repentance. Now the keys to open and to shut, to loose and to bind, will be passed to faithful apostles who proclaim the saving rule of God (Matt 16:19; John 20:23; Rev 3:7).

Once again a meal in a Pharisee's home has become the occasion for an explosive confrontation (Luke 7:36–50). The Pharisees and teachers of the law lie in wait for evidence to use against him, as if they are hunting wild animals (11:53–54). God in his wisdom is working out his redemptive purposes in the persecution of prophets and apostles and preeminently in the death of his Son, the greatest apostle and prophet (11:49).

⇨ Which of the above characteristics of legalism, if any, have you detected in the contemporary church? How does one nurture a culture of grace among God's people?

WARNING AGAINST HYPOCRISY AND EXHORTATION TO COURAGE
(Luke 12:1–12)

Luke's record of the *Later Judean and Perean* ministries includes many teachings of Jesus that appear in different settings. Clearly the Lord repeated familiar sayings at various times, sometimes with distinct applications. As opposition from the various strands of the religious leadership in Israel begins to congeal, the Lord concentrates on preparing his disciples to carry on his legacy after his departure (Luke 12:1, 22). His approach is a perfect balance of warning and exhortation, admonition and promise, severity and tenderness.

1. *Be on guard against the hypocrisy of legalists* (12:1–3; cf. Matt 10:26–27; 16:6). As the preceding woes make clear, the Pharisees are engaged in play-acting where outward appearance and inward disposition are dichotomous. Such pretentious piety is a "leaven" that spreads its pernicious influence due to the affinity of people for a performance-oriented approach to God (12:1). The antidote, Jesus says, is to remember that God searches the heart, its inner thoughts and motives, as well as one's words which express its character. A day is coming when thoughts and words will be fully disclosed and assessed in the searchlight of God's holiness (12:2–3). Integrity—a heart-hands congruity—is nurtured by a deep sense of accountability before God.

2. *Overcome the fear of man by reverential trust in a sovereign and loving Heavenly Father* (12:4–7; cf. Matt 10:28–31). Jesus has just predicted that some of his emissaries will face persecution and even death as they

represent him (Luke 11:49). Disciples must fear God alone, for man can only kill the body, while God arbitrates the soul's eternal destiny. For the believer, God is not only the sovereign Judge but also the loving Father who superintends the tiniest details of his child's life. Trust in God has the power to release one from the fear of man (Prov 29:25).

3. *Maintain a courageous witness for the Lord Jesus Christ in preparation for future judgment* (12:8–9; cf. Matt 10:32–33). Jesus binds together the disciple's faithful confession of his Lord before people in this age to the Son's acknowledgment of people before the Father at the final judgment. One's public confession is evidence of the genuineness of personal faith (Rom 10:8–10).

4. *Pay careful attention to the testimony of the Holy Spirit, taking special precaution not to resist, or even revile, his gracious operations* (12:10; cf. Matt 12:31–32). The Pharisees are a terrifying example of people who, when exposed to the truth, resist the Spirit's convicting work and incrementally build up a callousness that eventually leads to decisive repudiation of the Son of God, even attributing to him demonic em-powerment. The disciples are warned against starting down the path that leads to ruin (Heb 3:12).

5. *Rely upon the Holy Spirit to guide your words when you are called to tes-tify before religious or secular authorities* (12:11–12; cf. Matt 10:19–20). Arrest and inquisition before the Sanhedrin and before secular magis-trates will provide a wider opportunity for witness. Here is a promise of the Spirit's help at the opportune moment, enabling disciples to give the "reason for the hope that is in you" without anxiety (1 Pet 3:15).

⇨ Does reverence for God so condition your life that fear of people and anxiety over circumstances have little ability to dampen your enthusi-astic witness for Christ?

THE RICH FOOL

(Luke 12:13–34)

A stranger emerged from the crowd and interceded with Jesus to interfere in an inheritance dispute. This man felt his brother was cheating him in the settlement of the family estate. Rabbis were sometimes called in to settle such disputes. Jesus refused to intervene: "Man, who made me a judge or arbitrator over you?" (12:14). Jesus detected that behind the request lurked greed, not a sincere desire for justice. He then issued a wider warning against "all (manner of) covetousness" (12:15a). This term literally means "the thirst for more," yet more can never satisfy. It is like attempting to quench one's thirst by drinking saltwater which only creates more thirst. The warning is supported by a principle: "One's life does not consist in the abundance of his possessions" (12:15b). True worth is not measured by the value of one's material holdings.

To illustrate the danger of greed Jesus gave a parable, one of fifteen parables peculiar to Luke's Gospel. The focus is on the internal dialogue of the rich man (12:17, 19). A farmer's land produced an abundant crop that could not be stored in his small barns. So he decided to build bigger barns to store the grain and to house the goods purchased from the extensive prof- its. Such prosperity, he thought to himself, would enable him to secure his long-term future with many good things to consume and enjoy. His motto was: "Relax, eat, drink, be merry" (12:19). There was no thought of God, the source of such blessing, nor of sharing with others who were less fortunate. He thought only of expending his riches for his own comfort and enjoyment. He acts as if he is the captain of his soul, the determiner of his destiny (Jas 4:13–17). The parable ends with God rebuking the man as a fool, for his life is about to prematurely end and he will have to give an accounting of the way he spent, rather than invested, his days. All of his wealth will remain behind to be consumed by others.

Jesus presses home the central lesson of the parable—a fool is a person that leaves God out of his/her thinking (Ps 53:1) and shrinks into a self- lover ("I/my" occurs eleven times in vv. 17–19). The problem is not with wealth per se or with the sound business principle of saving for the future, which is commended elsewhere (Prov 6:6–8). Rather, the spiritual cancer is this person's godless, material-centered value system. Money was the object of his trust and the source of his security. Though the story ends with the announcement of his imminent demise, one wonders if the rich fool left behind a family in discord, fighting over the spoils of the estate, much like the individual whose request sparked this interchange in the first place.

Jesus then turned to his disciples and pressed home familiar teaching regarding the importance of being free from anxiety over one's material needs and pursuing the lasting riches of the kingdom of God (12:22–34; cf. Matt 6:19–21, 25–34). Unique to Luke's account is 12:32: "Fear not, little flock, for it is your Father's good pleasure to give you the kingdom." If their Heavenly Father has brought them under his saving rule (past) and will lead them safely to an eternal inheritance (future), why should his children entertain fearful doubts about his ability and commitment to provide their present needs? The radical command that follows—"sell your possessions, and give to the needy" (12:33a)—is not to be interpreted in an overly literal fashion, as if disciples are to be propertyless, but is a mandate to give sacrificially to those in need, especially fellow believers (1 Cor 16:1–2; 2 Cor 8:1–9; Gal 6:10).

⇨ What characterizes your inner dialogue? Do your thoughts and desires revolve around extending God's kingdom or expanding your financial portfolio?

PREPAREDNESS FOR THE MASTER'S RETURN

(Luke 12:35—13:21)

Jesus is already looking beyond his Passion to his glorious return as the Son of Man (12:40). With a variety of images he underscores the urgency of the kingdom enterprise and the need to be prepared, at an unknown hour, to give an account of one's stewardship.

1. *The faithful and wise steward attends to his Master's business and is alert, ready and engaged when the Master returns* (12:35–48). A servant who is prepared for his master's return from an evening wedding banquet keeps his oil lamp trimmed, filled, and burning and tucks his long outer robe into the belt so that when his master knocks he can quickly find his way to the door and open it. A householder keeps his home locked and possessions guarded against the surprise visit of a thief.

   A chief steward cares for the needs of the servants under his charge and diligently manages the affairs to the benefit of the master. The principle of accountability is that with greater privilege comes increased responsibility: "to whom much was given, of him much will be required" (12:48b). The most compelling image of reward is of the master who reclines with and waits upon his faithful servants (12:37).

2. *The true disciple maintains fidelity to the crucified Savior and coming Judge, swearing an allegiance that transcends even the most intimate of earthly relationships* (12:49–53; cf. Matt 10:34–36, 38). Before bringing

the fire of retributive judgment upon mankind, the Lord completes his appointed baptism, a metaphor for the agony of his coming Passion. The exclusivity of the kingdom message—the promise of exemption from judgment only through the Servant's death—is divisive and radically countercultural.

3. *The servant of Christ, like his Master, confronts the spiritual lethargy of his generation and challenges people to be reconciled to God* (12:54–59; cf. Matt 5:25–26; 16:2–3). The multitudes fix their attention on earthly matters, like predicting the weather, but fail to prepare for coming judgment. The procedure of the law court and resulting incarceration for the offender—accuser, magistrate, judge, officer, prison—speaks in the present context of a person's guilt before a holy God. The warning in v. 59 is a closing appeal to be reconciled with the Master before he returns in judgment.

4. *The proclaimer of the kingdom, like his Master, does not round off the sharp edges of the message to make it palatable, but demands repentance—one that is proved by fruitbearing—and warns of judgment* (13:1–9). The common Jewish view was that calamity is visited upon people for their personal wickedness (Job 22:5–10; John 9:1–2). Jesus cites two incidents, otherwise unknown, to support his conviction that individual sin and suffering are not in an unbroken cause-effect relationship. Conversely, prosperity is no sign that all things are well with one's soul. The Galileans killed by Pilate in the temple courts and the eighteen people crushed when the tower in Siloam fell on them were no worse or better than others who were spared such calamities. Further, God's patience has its limits. In the parable of the barren fig tree, one more year is granted to produce fruit; if by next summer, when figs ripen, the tree fails to produce, it will be cut down. The composite lesson is clear: Repentance is incumbent upon all (13:1–5) and must not be delayed (13:6–9).

5. *In the face of hostility, especially in the religious realm, the disciple remains confident in the triumph of God's kingdom* (13:10–21; cf. Matt 13:31–33). Opposition from religious quarters forms again after a healing on the Sabbath. Jesus labels his opponents "hypocrites," censuring their willingness to water a beast of burden on the holy day while condemning the healing of a woman bent over for eighteen years with an arthritic spine. After the admonitory and judgmental tones of the preceding

context, Jesus reminds his listeners through two familiar parables that his kingdom will grow to worldwide proportions. The mustard seed that becomes a large tree in which the birds of the air can perch signifies the expansion of God's rule over many peoples and nations in the aftermath of Israel's rejection. The leaven means that God's rule will spread its transforming influence over larger portions of mankind until, at the return of Christ, it prevails over all opposition.

⇨ Does the return of Christ—though it has been delayed for over 2,000 years since these words were spoken—motivate you to energetic service in the kingdom? What are the practical benefits of maintaining a vivid focus on his soon return (1 John 3:2–3)?

THE SHEEP OF GOD'S PASTURE

(John 10:22–39)

The time is the Feast of Dedication, also known as Hanukkah or the "festival of lights." This eight-day feast, from Kislev (mid-December) 25, commemorated the purification of the temple by Judas Maccabeus in Kislev 164 BC after its profanation by the Seleucid King Antiochus IV (1 Macc 4:59). The place is Solomon's Colonnade, a cedar roofed portico with twenty-seven-foot-high stone columns on the eastern edge of the court surrounding Herod's temple. One of the chambers served as a meeting place for the early church (Acts 3:11; 5:12). Here Jesus is surrounded by Jewish religious authorities who demand that he speak more plainly if he is claiming to be Messiah. Jesus rejects their assertion that he has been anything but clear. His miracles have "signified" his messianic identity (John 2:11; 4:54; 5:9; 6:14; 9:16b) and the "I am" statements that follow are unmistakable testimony of one claiming to share the divine nature with the Father (John 5:17; 6:35; 8:12, 58; 9:5; 10:7, 9, 11, 14).

The problem is not a lack of clarity in his self-revelation but the unbelief of the Jewish leaders, which Jesus attributes to divine election: they are not the chosen sheep whom the Father has drawn to the Son (10:26; cf. John 6:37, 44; 10:29a; 17:6a; 18:9). Jesus returns to the shepherd-sheep analogy (John 10:1-18) to remind his listeners of his mission from the Father—to gather and secure a community of believers who hear his voice and carry out God's will (10:27–29).

1. The shepherd knows his sheep, speaks to them, and grants them eternal life.

2. The sheep hear the shepherd's voice and follow him. They shall never perish because they are doubly secure in the firm grasp of the Son and of the Father.

3. The omnipotent Father has given the sheep to the Son.

Jesus complies with the Jews' request for clarity with a claim to unparalleled authority: "I and the Father are one" (10:30). This is not meant to confuse the distinct identity of their persons, Father and Son, but to express their inviolable intimacy and shared pledge to secure the welfare of the sheep, the community of believers. As in the prologue to John's Gospel (1:1–2, 14, 18), there is an equality of prerogative of Father and Son in the redemptive purposes but a distinguishing of their personhood. Once again the Jewish theologians accurately grasp the implications of the language and take up stones to eliminate the blasphemer who is claiming to be God (10:31; cf. John 5:18; 6:41; 8:59).

Jesus recites Psalm 82:6 where ancient near eastern rulers, especially those of the covenant nation Israel, were addressed as "gods" because they represented the will of the one true God and King. The logic follows a lesser to greater comparison: if the term "god" (Gk. *theos*) can be applied in one sense to human rulers, how much more fitting is it to apply the term to the Son of God, one in nature and purpose with the Father (10:30), set apart as mediator of redemption (10:36), and vindicated by his attesting miracles (10:37–38). That Jesus here is in no way mitigating the force of his claim to possess divine authority is evidenced by the sequel: the Jews attempt to arrest him on a charge of blasphemy but are prevented by Providence (10:39). Only after the Passover meal will their long-planned ambush coincide with the divine timetable.

⇨ Does your sense of security as a believer flow from your feeble grip on Jesus or from the firm hold that he and the Father have on you? Can a disobedient believer—one who refuses to listen and obey the Shepherd's voice—claim these promises for himself? Observe the balance of divine sovereignty and human responsibility in John 10:27–30.

12

Early Perean Ministry

Grace for Sinners and the Promise of Resurrection

WHO ARE THE TRUE KINGDOM CITIZENS?

(John 10:40–42; Luke 13:22–30)

The final three months of Jesus' ministry leading to Passion Week, from the Feast of Dedication (John 10:22), *December AD 29, until* Passover in *Spring, AD 30*, take place in Perea or, as it is called in the Old Testament, "Beyond the Jordan" (i.e. Trans-Jordan). This period is covered primarily by Luke (13:22—19:28). During Jesus' life the Trans-Jordan area from just south of Pella, the southernmost city of the Decapolis, to just south of Machaerus on the border of the Nabatean kingdom was governed by Herod Antipas, tetrarch of Galilee and Perea (4 BC—AD 39). The *Perean* period can be divided into two parts:

1. *Early Perean* ministry (Luke 13:22—17:10; John 10:40—11:53): Jesus' movements were to Perea, Bethany, Jerusalem and then a brief withdrawal north to Ephraim, probably the same as Ophrah, fifteen miles north of Jerusalem (John 11:54), covering a period of six to eight weeks in *Winter, AD 30*.

2. *Later Perean* ministry (Luke 17:11—19:28; Matt 19:1—20:34; Mark 10:1–52): From Ephraim Jesus then went further north to areas along the border of Samaria and Galilee (Luke 17:11), probably to join the pilgrims making their way south to Jerusalem for Passover by way of Perea and Jericho.

The response to Jesus in Perea will be in sharp contrast to the hostility he has encountered in Jerusalem. In the area where John the Baptist conducted his ministry of preaching and baptizing, probably Bethany beyond Jordan (John 1:28), many believed in Jesus, fulfilling the purpose of John's witness (John 10:40–42; cf. John 1:6–7; 3:30).

Jesus had now left Judea and was traveling with his disciples through the towns and villages of Perea on his way to Jerusalem (Luke 13:22). In recent days Jesus had spoken about judgment for those who fail to heed his call to repentance (Luke 13:1–9), as well as the incredible expansion of the kingdom which will follow its inconspicuous beginnings (Luke 13:18–21). The admonitory tones, however, filled the mind of an unnamed listener who brought forth the question: "Lord, will those who are saved be few?" (Luke 13:23). The listener must have witnessed the bitter clash of values between Jesus and the Pharisees (Luke 13:10–17) and reasoned as follows: If the majority of people in Israel, especially the leaders trained in the law, are re-fusing Jesus' offer of the kingdom, how few there must be who will ultimately be ushered into that kingdom.

The Lord did not answer the question with theological abstraction, but confronted the listeners with the urgency of the kingdom offer. "You (pl.) strive to enter," he commanded, for the door of entrance is narrow and the opportunity for entrance is of limited duration. At an appointed time the door will be shut. Entrance is conditioned on a repentant and believing heart, not on Jewish lineage. The true kingdom citizens are those of the line of faith with Abraham, Isaac, and Jacob, not merely ethnic descendants of the patriarchs. Jesus anticipates people from the four corners of the earth streaming to join the messianic feast, one of his favorite metaphors for future kingdom blessing (Luke 13:29; cf. Matt 8:11–12; 25:1–13; 26:29; Luke 14:7–24). Surprising reversals of destiny will characterize God's final sifting of the human race. Those who are last now, uncovenanted Gentiles, will be first then; those who have the privilege of hearing the kingdom offer first, the people and leaders of the chosen nation of Israel, will be last.

The quantitative question has thus been given a qualitative answer. It is not a matter of how many will be saved, but who will be saved. Jesus, and John before him, has consistently made faith-repentance the sole condition for kingdom citizenship, not physical lineage or religious sophistry (Luke 3:3–18; 4:25–27; 6:46–49; 7:9; 8:4–15; 10:25–37; 11:29–52). Over time and through painful experiences the ethno-centric disciples will come to under-stand and embrace this matter of utmost importance to their Lord, namely, that the kingdom is all about the heart (Acts 10:34–35).

⇨ If Jesus had directly answered the question posed to him in a quantitative manner—How many people will be saved?—how do you think he would have answered, in light of the just given parables of the mustard seed and the leaven (Luke 13:18–21)?

LAMENT OVER JERUSALEM

(Luke 13:31–35)

The Pharisees attempted to frighten Jesus by relating a supposed plot by Antipas to ambush him in Perea. They wanted him to leave this area under Antipas' jurisdiction for Judea where their influence was stronger. Jesus calls Herod a "fox," meaning a crafty, scheming politician whose actions are always self-serving. His prevaricating behavior both in the arrest and death of John the Baptist (Matt 14:3–12) and at the trial of Jesus (Luke 23:6–12) justify the label. In fact, though he will move at his own pace, Jesus affirms that Jerusalem is his destination, a motif that drives forward Luke's narrative (9:31, 51; 13:22; 17:11; 18:31; 24:47)—"today and tomorrow and the day following" is a symbolic expression for "very soon" (13:32–33). Jesus is on a divine mission and will only reach his goal in the city known for its persecution of God's prophets.

Jesus voices an emotional lament for the Holy City which, due to the inveterate hardness of the temple hierarchy and Sanhedrin, continues its long history of rejecting God's "sent ones." This is not an imprecatory prayer but a cry of grief from a Savior who yearns for the salvation of his people, yet is like a mother hen turned away by her own chicks. Jesus' pleading heart for his kinsmen is shared by two other great lovers of Israel, Moses (Exod 32:32) and Paul (Rom 9:1–3; 10:1). For now Israel's house will be left desolate, a foreshadowing of the destruction of the temple, city and nation in AD 70—physically trampled by the Gentiles (Luke 21:20–24) and spiritually broken off and cast away for the sake of the Gentiles (Rom 11:17–21). But desolation is not the final word for the covenant nation. Just prior to Christ's second advent, Israel will come to recognize her Messiah, repent, and joyfully acclaim as blessed the One who comes in the name of the Lord (13:35, quot. Ps 118:26).

⇨ Though the Jewish people worldwide and the modern state of Israel, except for a believing remnant, remain hostile to the Christian gospel, their future is as bright as the promises of God. Will you pray for the peace of Jerusalem (Ps 122:6)?

BANQUET FOR THE POOR AND AFFLICTED

(Luke 14:1–24)

Jesus often used provocation to press home his kingdom theology. Dining as a guest at the Sabbath meal in the home of a prominent Pharisee was not the diplomatic choice for a healing miracle. With the Pharisees "watching him carefully," Jesus healed a man with dropsy, an accumulation of fluids that damaged vital organs. The Pharisees for the moment held their tongues (14:4, 6), even when upbraided by Jesus for a callousness that valued legal technicalities of greater weight than the suffering of a fellow human being. Jesus then spoke three brief parables drawn from the context of communal meals of various kinds.

1. *Parable of the honored guest* (14:7–11)

   A guest invited to a wedding feast should not take the place of honor, the center position at the base of a U-shaped curve where guests reclined around the low table. If a more distinguished guest should arrive, then the initial guest would be displaced and shamed. Rather, one should sit in a lower position where he will be honored when asked to move up. The Pharisees who sought to polish their image by scrambling for recognized seats of honor around the table embodied pretense rather than humility.

   - *Lesson*: The kingdom of God demands self-humbling and seeks to elevate others. Humility before honor is an unbreakable law of the kingdom (Luke 18:14b; Jas 4:6; 1 Pet 5:5–6).

2. *Parable of the blessed host* (14:12–14)

   One is to apply the virtues of sacrifice and impartiality when drawing up a list of invitations to a special luncheon or dinner. A host who limits his guest list to rich friends and family members is expecting to be repaid in kind. Rather, hospitality should be offered to the poor, blind, crippled and lame, that is, people who truly need the provisions and have no way to return the favor. God himself models this approach in his gracious call of sinners into his kingdom (14:21).

- *Lesson*: When God's rule is operative, a person delights in sacrificial giving without hidden motives of future reciprocity; such values are nurtured by an eternal perspective.

3. *Parable of the great banquet* (14:15–24)

   The third parable is sparked by a fellow guest's spontaneous blessing upon the person who is privileged to attend the messianic banquet, a common biblical figure for the initial event of the consummated kingdom (Isa 25:6; Matt 8:11; 26:29; Luke 13:29; Rev 19:9). Preparations were made for a great banquet and invitations sent out to the preferred guests. Those who were invited accepted the offer initially, but then, at the last minute, offered excuses why they could not attend, namely, concerns over material possessions, career prospects, and family relationships. So the angry master sent his servant out again with fresh invitations for the poor, crippled, blind and lame. They were literally taken by the hand and brought in, not out of coercion but because they believed themselves unworthy to enjoy such a sumptuous feast. Then the servant was sent to remote places to compel all that were willing to join the banquet until all the seats at the table were filled. The opportunity for the disenfranchised and distant ones was due to the forfeiture by the original invitees of their places at the banquet. The master wanted his house to be filled to capacity with guests.

- *Lesson*: Jesus' final interpretive comment provides the key to the parable—"none of those men who were invited shall taste my banquet" (14:24). All who respond to God's gracious invitation to submit to his reign over their lives, making his kingdom their foremost priority, freely partake of redemptive blessing. Those first invited and first to refuse represent the Jewish nation. The original particularized mission to the lost sheep of Israel (Matt 10:5–6) is giving way to the universal summons of "whosoever will."

⇨ Do you embody these principles of the kingdom—humility, sacrifice and impartiality—when you both provide as well as receive the gift of hospitality? Note how often this ministry, literally "love of strangers," is enjoined in the New Testament (Rom 12:13; 1 Tim 3:2; 5:10; Titus 1:8; Heb 13:2; 1 Pet 4:9; 3 John 5–8).

COUNTING THE COST OF DISCIPLESHIP

(Luke 14:25–35)

The Perean ministry had attracted wide attention. Many had believed in Jesus on some level (John 10:42) and large crowds were following him (14:25). He turned toward these 'followers' in order to test their commitment and to sift real disciples from superficial enthusiasts. The conditions of discipleship are radical and that means one must first count the cost before setting out on the arduous journey behind Jesus.

1. *Preeminent allegiance* (14:26): To "hate" one's most intimate family members, in fact one's own life, speaks of undivided allegiance. One must nurture a consuming affection for God and his concerns, with every other earthly loyalty submitted to this central governing relationship. "Not to hate" is to "love more than" (Matt 10:37); to hate is to love less. When becoming an American citizen, an alien takes the oath of loyalty, renouncing allegiance to one's native land. So it is with citizens of the heavenly commonwealth.

2. *Sacrificial obedience* (14:27; cf. Matt 10:38): The cross is the image of a condemned criminal who is forced to carry his instrument of death to the place of execution. Earlier Jesus stated this demand in the positive form (Luke 9:23). Personal attachment to and public identification with Jesus—"come after me"—brings with it the hostility and hardship that attended his way.

3. *Parable of the foolish builder* (14:28–30): The two parables that follow support Jesus' demands for total allegiance and obedience. A disciple, then, must be one who counts the cost, contemplates the sacrifice involved, and willingly surrenders one's entire life to the Lord. A builder begins to construct a tower, either a watchtower for the vineyard or a farm storage tower. However, after laying the foundation he cannot complete his project because he failed to estimate its true expense. He ends up being an object of ridicule, his unfinished tower standing as a witness to his foolishness.

4. *Parable of the reckless king* (14:31–33): A king launches a military campaign but upon realizing that he has overestimated his strength, and underestimated the enemy's forces, seeks to reconcile with his enemy before overtaken by certain disaster. The summative demand is for the

surrender of everything one owns (v. 33). The attitude of release rather than the literal disposal of possessions is in view here, since later Jesus urges his disciples to use their worldly wealth to promote the kingdom (Luke 16:9). Disciples are stewards who recognize that material possessions are on loan from God and are to be wisely administered for his glory and for the benefit of others.

5. *Distinctiveness for impact* (14:34–35; cf. Matt 5:13; Mark 9:50): Both of the primary uses of salt in the ancient world provide the backdrop, that is, to add flavor to food and to act as a preservative to keep food from spoiling. The disciple must retain his "saltiness" if he is to impact others as a moral force and a winsome agent for the kingdom.

⇨ How many contemporary Christians, particularly in the prosperous Western church, can be called "disciples" based on Jesus' radical way of defining that term here?

HEAVEN'S JOY OVER THE SINNER WHO REPENTS

(Luke 15:1–32)

To eat with someone meant, in the noble tradition of oriental hospitality, to accept them, to treat them with dignity, to relish in their company without preconditions. Jesus clearly enjoyed sitting down to a meal with "tax collectors and sinners" (Luke 5:29–30; 7:34, 39; 11:37–38; 14:12–14). To the Pharisees and legal scholars that criticized such associations Jesus delivered three parables (15:1–2). First, a lost sheep (one of 100) is earnestly sought and found. Its return to the fold becomes the source of great personal and communal rejoicing (15:3–6). Second, one of ten silver coins is lost. The woman lights a lamp, sweeps the house, and diligently searches for the coin "until she finds it." She invites her neighbors to celebrate with her the recovery of the lost coin (15:8–9).

Third, a father distributes shares of his estate to his two sons. The younger son departs and squanders his portion on immoral living, so that he is reduced to the verge of starvation as a keeper of swine. For a Jewish son in a privileged family, this degraded condition is unimaginable. At his lowest point he comes to his senses and decides to return to his father. As he makes his way back, he plans his confession of guilt before God and his father. He will make a humble plea for forgiveness, not restored status. Seeing his silhouette in the distance, the father is moved by compassion, runs to, embraces (literally, "falls on his neck") and kisses his son. He celebrates the son's return with the gifts of a robe of distinction, a signet ring of authority, sandals to distinguish the freeborn son from a slave, and a fatted calf, only sacrificed for special occasions. The eldest son is angry with his father, protesting that his own faithfulness has gone unrewarded while "this son of yours" who squandered the inheritance is lavished with gifts! The father defends his action. It is fitting to celebrate, he replies, for "this your brother" was lost and is found, was dead (separated) and is now alive (reconciled) (15:11–32).

Jesus provided the interpretation to the first two parables and left the listeners to figure out the meaning of the third. The parables of the lost sheep and the lost coin symbolize the joy that fills the heart of God when a sinner repents, that is, when a person alienated by sin is brought into his fellowship and under his rule (15:7, 10). The searching shepherd and housewife represent God the lover of souls who will do whatever it takes to find and bring back the lost. By analogy, the prodigal son and the father represent the lost sinner and the forgiving God respectively. In all three parables the theme is the Heavenly Father's yearning love for lost people (15:7, 10, 20–24, 32). The offer is not just restoration, but a summons to heartfelt repentance as the way to restoration (15:7, 10, 18–19, 21). Jesus does not compromise his call to repentance, faith and surrender by his association with sinners. But neither does he make oral traditions based on the old covenant concept of ritual purity a precondition for genuine friendship and table fellowship. The first and last parables contain inferences that condemn the exclusivist attitudes of the Pharisees: ninety-nine righteous persons who do not need to repent (15:7b); the older son who pouts over his father's treatment of his restored brother (15:28–30). The real prodigal sons, he implies, are the religious leaders. The tragedy is that they see no need to repent and return.

⇨ Do you share the heart of the Father and the heart of his Son (Luke 19:10) for the salvation of lost people? Do your prayers, verbal witness, and investment of time and resources reflect the priority of the evangelization of those who do not know the Savior?

USING MONEY FOR KINGDOM PURPOSES

(Luke 16:1–13)

Jesus has cautioned his disciples against allowing concern for material things to sap their spiritual vitality (Matt 6:19–34). The parable of the rich fool reminded them of the futility of storing up goods while forgetting God (Luke 12:13–21). Now, with another parable, he turns the financial motive into a positive lesson: money can be used to promote God's kingdom in the world if managed wisely.

A rich man called the manager of his estate to give an account when he received reports the manager was squandering the possessions entrusted to him. The manager felt too proud to beg and too weak to do manual labor, so he devised a scheme to secure his future when his employment ended. In his final act as official steward he called in a number of his master's debtors and reduced the amount that they owed. These tenant farmers made their livelihood out of the annual produce from their rented fields and were glad to relieve their heavy debts. They quickly wrote out promissory notes to the manager, one who cultivated olive trees relieved of half of his debt and another who grew wheat given a 20% reduction. The master surprisingly commended the manager for his shrewdness (16:8a). Though he had squandered part of the estate, and even engaged in what appears to be fraudulent business transactions without the owner's consent, the manager secured his own future by ingratiating others who could be a source of help in the uncertain days ahead. Jesus was impressed that the "sons of this world" pursue their earthly interests more shrewdly than the "sons of light" pursue heavenly concerns (16:8b). Shrewdness in this context must mean wise or prudent in the positive sense of exploiting a legitimate opportunity for noble use.

Now to the lesson of the parable: the sons of light should use material wealth to promote the kingdom. Those who are then brought under God's redemptive rule through such sacrificial giving will form a joyous welcoming party for the givers when they leave behind their earthly habitation and enter their eternal dwelling place (16:9). Money has the power not only to control the heart (Luke 18:22–25) and to divide family members (Luke 12:13); it also possesses the potential, if faithfully managed (16:10–12) and ruthlessly controlled (16:13), to promote God's interests in the world.

How one handles material things is a key test of one's integrity. Three areas of stewardship provide the context in which God appraises and rewards faithfulness:

1. *Faithfulness (or dishonesty) in little* will translate into faithfulness (or dishonesty) in much (16:10). That is, faithfulness springs from the intrinsic character of a person (and the opposite the lack thereof), not the amount with which one is entrusted.

2. *Faithfulness in handling material resources* qualifies one to receive and manage the affairs of God's kingdom—the "true riches" which do not pass away (16:11; cf. 1 Tim 3:5).

3. *Faithfulness in managing the property of another* qualifies one to be given property "which is your own" to manage (16:12). This is the golden rule as it applies to material things (Matt 7:12).

At a more fundamental level, the one who proves trustworthy in handling money is a person living under God's rule with the priorities of life in proper order: first God, who alone is to be worshipped, then people who are to be loved, and finally money, which is to be used. The reversal of these priorities is nothing less than idolatry (16:13).

⇨ Does your life reflect this order—worship God, love people, use things? Where is there a need for some readjustment in managing these stewardships of life?

THE RICH MAN AND LAZARUS

(Luke 16:14–31)

The Pharisees had been listening in to Jesus' teaching directed at the disciples (Luke 16:1). Luke censures the Pharisee for being "lovers of money" in spite of their meticulous tithing (16:14; cf. Luke 11:42). Their scoffing at him places them in the category of servants of mammon rather than servants of God (Luke 16:13). Jesus labels them as those who "justify yourselves before men" (16:15), that is, human approval rather than the divine approbation is their governing value. These Torah-centered religious leaders fail to live up to their own standards. The law, in fact, in its preparatory and prophetic function reaches fulfillment in all of its details in the kingdom inaugurated by Jesus (16:17; cf. Matt 5:18). This kingdom era is dawning with bold proclamation and earnest adherents (16:16; cf. Matt 11:12). But the Pharisees fail to grasp the testimony of the law and the prophets to the kingdom. Their approach to the issue of divorce is a case in point (16:18). The ideal of marriage is one man and one woman for life, as Genesis 2:18–25 makes clear. But the rabbinical schools, both Hillel and Shammai, are caught up with rival interpretations of the exception allowed in Deuteronomy 24:1–4. The Pharisees dwell in the shadows of old covenant stipulations rather than in the light of fulfillment where such stipulations anticipate a higher kingdom ethic.

Jesus returns to the motif of material wealth with a parable (or a story of actual people) to correct the Pharisees' notion that material wealth is a sign of God's favor. A rich man indulged his wealth with no concern for the poor. At his gate was a physically handicapped beggar named Lazarus, afflicted by sores, ritually unclean due to contact with dogs, who lived on the scraps discarded from the rich man's table. Death proved to be the great equalizer. Lazarus entered Abraham's bosom, the upper compartment of Sheol where the spirits of righteous people remained during the old covenant era; the rich man descended to Hades, the lower compartment where the wicked were assigned. The rich man saw Abraham from a distance and pleaded with him to send Lazarus to come and relieve his fiery torment with a dip of cool water. The patriarch's reply was that justice has seen fit to reverse their former conditions, the righteous Lazarus comforted after all his afflictions on earth and the rich man judged for spending all of his "good things" on himself. Besides, the chasm between the two compartments is an impassable and irreversible one. So the rich man pleaded with Abraham to send Lazarus to his father's house to warn his still living brothers to repent lest they suffer the same torment. But Abraham answered that if they will not give heed to the written testimony of Moses and the Prophets, whose univocal testimony anticipates the coming Redeemer (Luke 24:27, 44–47), even a warning from Lazarus, risen from the dead, would fail to move them.

One can draw from this story four truths that govern a person's relationship to the saving rule of God.

1. While one's material status in this life, rich or poor, is not in itself a proof of one's spiritual condition, poverty often nurtures dependence (Luke 6:20) while wealth produces self-satisfaction (Luke 18:24–25). When the kingdom is consummated there will be surprising reversals of fortune.

2. There is no reversal of destiny after one's death.

3. No amount of evidence—even the resurrection and testimony of a dead person (a case in point [16:18] being the resurrection of another Lazarus in John 11 which, far from moving the religious leaders to reconsider

the evidence and repent, actually served to deepen their hostility)—will convince a close-minded, wealth-satiated person to repent.

4. The testimony of Scripture is sufficient to render a person responsible for heeding its call to faith and repentance.

⇨ Has your testimony over many years failed to impact beloved family members for the gospel? Consider the gift of a New Testament; then pray for the Spirit to move them to open it and read it. Trust the Word of God to do its saving work (Isa 55:11).

FOUR LESSONS FOR SERVANTS OF GOD

(Luke 17:1-10)

During the Perean ministry Jesus reiterated some of the relational issues he had earlier imparted to the disciples in Galilee.

1. *Warning against causing offense* (17:1–3a; cf. Matt 18:7; Mark 9:42): They must guard themselves against causing the spiritual ruin of "little ones." In this context "little ones" are the poor, vulnerable members of society like Lazarus (Luke 16:20) who respond enthusiastically to the offer of salvation. Better to die an immediate death—the heavy top-stone, drawn by a donkey, used to crush grain, fitted around one's neck and cast into the sea—than to be an offender.

2. *Unlimited forgiveness* (17:3b–4; cf. Matt 18:15, 21–22): One is to openly and honestly reprove one's offending brother, but always be prepared to offer forgiveness if he repents. To put it together, one is to be without offense, and when confrontation is necessary, to be ever forgiving. Such an attitude of continual forgiveness without limit toward a repentant offender would require supernatural faith in God's enabling grace. Thus the request from the apostles is "increase our faith" (17:5).

3. *Faith in a mighty God* (17:5–6; cf. Matt 17:20): Such a request is met with a challenge to exercise the faith that is already theirs, for even a small faith in a great God can effect humanly impossible things such as uprooting and replanting a mulberry tree in the sea.

4. *Dutiful and privileged servants* (17:7–10): The spirit of forgiveness and trust must be accompanied by the attitude of a servant bound by a resolve to obey and overwhelmed with gratitude at the privilege of

serving. Jesus used the analogy of a slave who returned to the master's home after a long day of tending sheep and plowing in the field. Before he could rest and eat, the servant was required to prepare a meal for and wait on his master. In the slave-master relationship of the first century the slave did what the lord demanded without expecting reciprocation or thanks. There is a limit to every analogy. Jesus was not comparing service in the kingdom to slavish obedience to an insensitive Lord performed out of grudging disdain.

The application of the analogy to the disciples comes at the end: even when they have done everything that was commanded, they should confess, "We are unworthy servants; we have only done what was our duty" (17:10). The disciples are being equipped as servants of the King. Their obedience will always, in this life, be partial and imperfect. Still, the Lord chooses to dignify their service with lasting fruit (John 15:8, 16) and to reward their service with an eternal inheritance (Matt 19:27–30). Rewards are gifts of grace like the kingdom itself; they are never a *quid pro quo* type of mechanical repayment for meritorious service. The disciples must view themselves as entirely the products of grace and so serve, from a deep sense of gratitude, a Servant-King who does the unthinkable, waits upon them (Luke 12:37b; 22:27) and washes their feet (John 13:4–5, 12–16).

⇨ What part does the incentive of reward play in motivating Christian service? What does the promise of reward reveal about the character of God?

RAISING OF LAZARUS FROM THE DEAD

(John 11:1–54)

1. *Climactic Sign*

The resurrection of Lazarus is the seventh and climactic "sign" in John's Gospel. The first six are: turning water to wine at the wedding feast in Cana, a miracle of quality (2:1–11); healing of the official's son at Capernaum, a miracle of distance (4:46–54); healing of the thirty-eight year invalid at the pool of Bethesda, a miracle of time (5:1–14); feeding of the 5000 at Bethsaida, a miracle of quantity (6:1–14); walking on the Sea of Galilee, a miracle of nature (6:16–21, 26); the healing of the man born blind at the pool of Siloam, a miracle over congenital misfortune (ch. 9). Though the Synoptics record two other raisings from the dead, the son of the widow of Nain (Luke 7:11–17) and the daughter of Jairus (Matt 9:18–26), the raising of Lazarus is the most dramatic and detailed miracle of Jesus recorded in the Gospels. As "the resurrection and the life" (11:25), Jesus conquers irreversible death and validates his authority to bestow eternal life on the one who believes on him (John 5:24–27; 6:35–40; 10:27–30).

2. *Decisive Event*

According to John, this miracle instigated the chain of events that would lead to Jesus' death. The hardening of the Jewish leaders toward Jesus crystallizes around this crucial event, since in this act Jesus produces definitive evidence of his claims to be the Son of God. There is now nothing left for the Jewish authorities to do but to humbly acknowledge their misguided past assessments and confess him as Messiah or to persist in assigning his works to the devil and eliminate the pretender. Led by the cold calculations of their high priest, they choose the latter (John 11:47–57; 12:37–43). This complements the Synoptic Gospels which ascribe the triumphal entry (Sunday) and the cleansing of the temple (Monday) at the beginning of Passion Week as being the decisive events that sealed Jewish rejection of Jesus. The latter events hasten the inevitable outcome that has been in the concrete planning stage since the raising of Lazarus several weeks earlier.

3. *Announcement of Lazarus' death* (11:1–16)

Jesus had an endearing relationship with this family in Bethany composed of Lazarus and his two sisters, Mary and Martha (11:3, 5, 36; cf. Luke 10:38–42). The sisters sent for Jesus who was in Perea to bring his healing touch to their ailing brother. Jesus sees a divine purpose behind the sickness, one that will issue not in physical death alone, but will reveal God's glorious resurrection power (11:4, 40). The glory of the Son will also be revealed because this catalytic event will lead to the cross where his unconditional love will be placarded before the world (John 12:23; 13:31–32; 17:1). Jesus delayed his trip to Bethany two days in accordance with a foreordained plan—even here his "hour" does not conform to the pressing emergency of his friends. Lazarus evidently died shortly after the messengers left to find Jesus: one day's trip to

Perea, along with the two days' delay and the one day return to Bethany, equals the "four days" Lazarus has been in the tomb at Jesus' arrival (11:17).

The disciples are incredulous that Jesus would return to the environs of his enemies who earlier threatened to stone him (John 10:31, 39). Here is a test for the disciples: will they follow "the light of the world" (John 8:12; 9:5) to witness an unparalleled display of God's life-giving power or will they retreat into their fears and stumble in darkness? Jesus speaks of waking Lazarus from sleep, which is euphemistic language for the death of a believer whose destiny is resurrection. The disciples think of physical sleep until Jesus declares without euphemism, "Lazarus has died" (11:14). He rejoices in the opportunity that awaits him in Bethany, not to heal a sick man but to raise a dead man. Now the disciples are resigned to follow him to death, both his and theirs, though their sincere expression of courage will prove hollow at the critical moment of confrontation in Gethsemane.

4. *Jesus' declaration and Martha's confession* (11:17–27)

The fact that Lazarus has been dead four days when Jesus arrives is significant. The traditional Jewish belief was that the soul left the body permanently and decomposition set in on the fourth day. Thus Lazarus' body was in an irreversibly corrupt state. Jewish friends from nearby Jerusalem came to comfort the sisters over the loss of their brother. Upon his arrival the active Martha sets out to meet the Lord, while the contemplative Mary remains at home. Martha offers a gentle rebuke to one whose power to heal she does not doubt and thus by coming sooner could have prevented her brother from dying. Jesus promises Martha that her brother will rise again to life but because the temporal note is left off she interprets him to mean future resurrection at the last day, not immediate restoration.

But Jesus' meaning is deeper and is expressed in the fifth "I am" statement of John's Gospel: "*I am the resurrection and the life*" (11:25a; cf. 6:35; 8:12; 10:7, 11). He promises the gift of eternal life, which is the life of the age to come enjoyed from the moment a person believes in God's Son. The future is thrust into the present. This includes the gift of abiding fellowship with God that transcends and is untouched by physical death and the certainty of future bodily resurrection when final deliverance from the penalty and power of sin is consummated and a person is made fit for life in the eternal kingdom of God (11:25b–26; cf. John 1:4; 3:15–16, 36; 4:14; 5:21–26; 6:35–40; 8:12; 10:10, 28; 17:3; 20:31). When Jesus summons Martha to respond, she utters a confession that rivals Peter's as the highest acclamation of Jesus' identity on the lips of a human being to this point: "You are the Christ, the Son of God, who is coming into the world" (11:27; cf. Matt 16:16; John 6:69). Surely Martha should be remembered more for her three-part confession of Jesus' messianic identity and divine character than for her weaker moments of worry and complaint.

5. *Sorrow over the death of a beloved brother and friend* (11:28–37)

Martha summons Mary who comes to Jesus just outside the village followed by the friends who were consoling her. Mary falls to her knees and repeats the same expression of faith in Jesus' healing ability and disappointment in his failure to act that Martha expressed earlier. Jesus was "deeply moved in his spirit and greatly troubled" and thus "wept" before proceeding to the tomb (11:33, 35, 38). Here is the full, voluntary self-identification of the God-man with sin, death and grief, in short, all of the conditionalities of space-time existence bound to the fallen order. His redemptive death will establish a new order where righteousness, life, and hope are the operative powers. Rather than paralyzing him, Jesus' grief moves him to compassionate intervention. As they approach the tomb, there is no one who is thinking of Lazarus' immediate restoration. The crowd mimics the disappointment of the sisters that Jesus could have acted sooner, but now it is too late.

6. *Dead man brought back to life* (11:38–44)

The tomb was sealed by a large circular stone set in a groove on a sharp incline which would require several men to move. Because of the unpleasant odor of the decomposing body, Martha objects to Jesus' command to roll the stone away. Jesus ignores her protest and probes her faith. He reminds Martha that the death of her brother will provide the opportunity for the glorious power of God to be manifested through his Son, validating his claim to be "the resurrection and the life." Jesus directs the onlooking crowd's attention away from himself with an audible prayer to the Father so that those with ears to hear will acknowledge he is the one sent by God to fulfill the redemptive mission. In all he does, Jesus acts in dependence on the Father. At Jesus' powerful command—"Lazarus, come out!"—Lazarus clumsily exits the tomb still wrapped in his burial clothes. At Jesus' word the head wrapping and strips of linen binding his hands and feet are removed. Here is evidence that demands a verdict, brought forth only a few kilometers from Jerusalem. How will the religious authorities deal with such incontrovertible proof of Jesus' claim to be the Son of God?

7. *Ruthless calculation and unwitting prophecy* (11:45–53)

Many of the Jewish friends of Mary who had come to console her placed their faith in Jesus because of this signifying miracle. Yet such sign-oriented faith of the "many" is a Johannine theme for a shallow faith that needs deeper roots in order to become a stable trust (John 2:23; 7:31; 8:30; 10:42; 11:45; 12:11, 42). Others, however, reported to some leading Pharisees what had occurred. An emergency meeting of the Sanhedrin was called. This Jewish ruling council was composed of Pharisees, Sadducean priests, and, though not mentioned here, influential members of aristocratic families called elders. This was an informal meeting to deliberate Jesus' growing influence among the Jewish populace, one which would only be fueled by a miracle of this magnitude. The authorities admit that their measures against Jesus to this point have failed. Yet the miracle here as before, almost certainly attributed to demonic agency, only serves to harden their resolve. The sole concern of the members of the Sanhedrin is the preservation of their social status; they fear that the Romans will react swiftly to suppress a messianic uprising and destroy both the temple and their limited autonomy as a theocratic people.

Caiaphas, high priest (AD 18–36) and presiding officer of the Sanhedrin, arrogantly rebukes the council members for underestimating the gravity of the situation. Jesus must be eliminated if the temple and nation are to survive. The cold, ruthless calculation is Caiaphas' application of the principle, 'the end justifies the means:' for one man to die "for the people" (11:50) is far better than that an entire nation should perish under the bewitching spell of a false prophet and messianic pretender. Ironically, the high priest's policy of expediency will fail to prevent Israel's dissolution within one generation (AD 70).

The author comments that Caiaphas' words were a prophetic utterance ultimately originating from the Spirit of God (2 Pet 1:20–21). This 'deeper meaning' (*sensus plenior*) transcended the meaning the author

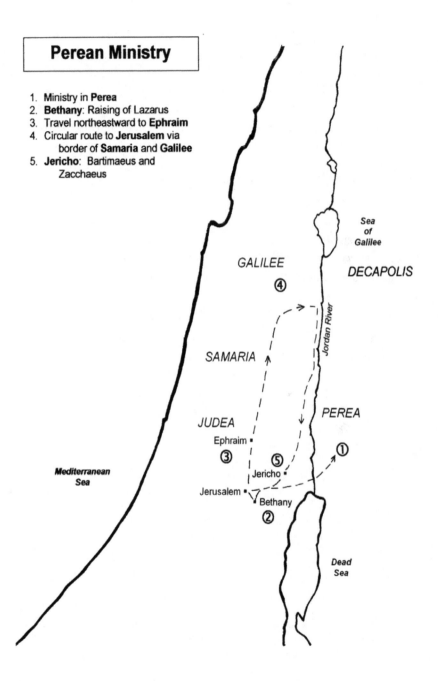

Perean Ministry

1. Ministry in **Perea**
2. **Bethany**: Raising of Lazarus
3. Travel northeastward to **Ephraim**
4. Circular route to **Jerusalem** via border of **Samaria** and **Galilee**
5. **Jericho**: Bartimaeus and Zacchaeus

understood or intended at the time (1 Pet 1:10–12). What Caiaphas spoke as an expression of cruel expediency was a prophecy of the substitutionary death of Jesus both for the Jewish people and for "the children of God who are scattered abroad" to be drawn from all nations and forged into one people united by the cross (11:52; cf. John 10:16; 17:20–23). This counsel from the high priest proved decisive and from that day forward the Jewish leadership was resolute in its determination to kill Jesus, the congealing of a plot that had long been deliberated (John 5:18; 7:1, 25; 8:37, 40, 59; 10:31, 39).

8. *Withdrawal to Ephraim* (11:54)

One final withdrawal brought Jesus north to the village of Ephraim, probably Ophrah fifteen miles north of Jerusalem. He now enters the *Later Perean* period of ministry, approximately six weeks from *mid-February to late March, AD 30*. Jesus will die for the people, as Caiaphas prophesied, but in his own time not that of his enemies.

⇨ Do you recall other Old Testament passages that the New Testament authors interpret with a 'deeper sense' that transcends but does not violate its original historical context? *Hint*: Review our study of the first two chapters of Matthew's Gospel.

13

Later Perean Ministry

Servants of the Servant

A SAMARITAN GIVES THANKS

(Luke 17:11–19)

FROM EPHRAIM, A VILLAGE in a remote district of northern Judea, Jesus went north through Samaria and Galilee, probably to join the pilgrims headed to Jerusalem from Galilee through Perea for the festival of Passover. In an unnamed village, probably in Perea, ten lepers called out from a distance if the renowned healer might show mercy upon them. Their debilitating disease had made them social outcasts, banished from normal participation in community life (Lev 13:45–46; Num 5:2–4; 2 Kgs 7:3–4). All ten men were cleansed from their leprosy when they obeyed Jesus' command to go and present themselves to the priests. Earlier Jesus had healed a leper who then was required to go and perform the elaborate ritual for restoration to ceremonial purity (Luke 5:12–14; cf. Lev 14:1–32). This time, however, the lepers exercised faith to obey Jesus' word and were healed as they proceeded to the temple. Incredibly, only one of the healed men, a Samaritan, returned to offer thanks to his healer. Jesus asked the man incredulously, "Were not ten cleansed? Where are the nine?" They also had been restored to the community, shame and ostracism removed, a painful disfiguring condition healed, but turned no longer to Jesus after relief was provided. Jesus pointed out to his disciples that it was the one foreigner of the group, and a despised Samaritan at that, who acknowledged God's good gift of wholeness and rendered thanks. The Samaritan's faith that "saved" him (17:19; rather than "has made you well" [ESV; NIV]) points toward a relational trust that brought more than cleansing from leprosy but the removal of the deeper stain of sin that the disease symbolized (Luke 7:50; 8:48, 50; 18:42).

This was by no means the first time that Jesus pointed out that spiritual insight bears no connection to physical ancestry or cultural background. He first taught his disciples about the spiritual harvest by engaging an immoral Samaritan woman in conversation, which led to her conversion and that of an entire Samaritan village (John 4:39–42). In the synagogue at Nazareth Jesus angered the Jewish listeners by reminding them that in the days of the prophets Elijah and Elisha God providentially selected a Sidonian widow and a Syrian general respectively to show his favor (Luke 4:25–27). On two rare occasions did Jesus register astonishment at a remarkable display of faith, once of a Roman centurion (Matt 8:10) and once of a Syro-Phoenician woman (Matt 15:28). When asked by a legal scholar about the meaning of "neighbor," Jesus told a parable about a Samaritan who fulfilled the great command to love one's neighbor and two Jewish religious leaders who did not (Luke 10:30–37). At the final judgment, Jesus declared, the Queen of the South, who came to inquire of Solomon's wisdom, and the Ninevites, who repented at the preaching of Jonah, will rise up and condemn this wicked generation of Israelites who have rejected the One who is greater than Solomon and Jonah (Luke 11:29–32). In the case of the lepers it was the lone foreigner who possessed a heart of gratitude, and rendered that most fundamental expression of what it means to be in a right relationship with God, namely, the giving of thanks.

⇨ Is your life characterized by thanksgiving or, like the nine, do you receive benefits from God and quickly forget them? Do you acknowledge Jesus only in moments of crisis or recognize that "every good gift and every perfect gift is from above" (Jas 1:17)?

THE KINGDOM THAT IS NOW AND NOT YET

(Luke 17:20–37)

Jesus was asked by some Pharisees regarding the timing of the arrival of God's kingdom. Clearly their expectations of a visible subjection of the world, and Israel's Gentile oppressors, to the rule of God collided with the proclamation of Jesus and his disciples of the imminent and even present in-breaking of the kingdom in his ministry (Luke 4:43; 8:1, 10; 9:2, 27; 10:9, 11; 11:20; 12:32; 16:16). He answered that the kingdom's arrival will not be accompanied by observable signs or visible displays of power but makes its quiet but effective entrance in the hearts of those who lay down their arms and surrender to the authority of the King. With his statement "the kingdom of God is within you" (NIV; a generic "you" for all who repent and believe, clearly not true of the Pharisees [17:21]) Jesus identifies the kingdom as the internal, transforming rule of God over the whole personality producing the qualities of gratitude (Luke 17:11–19), faith (Luke 18:1–8) and humility (Luke 18:9–14).

Spiritual kingship over people's hearts as the inaugural fulfillment of the Old Testament kingdom prophecies, however, does not mean that there will not be a literal, earthly subjection of the entire world to God's vice-regent, the Messiah, by a supernatural display of power. Jesus must first inaugurate the kingdom through his sacrifice as the suffering Servant (17:25), but some day will return as the Danielic Son of Man to judge the nations, gather his elect and consummate his worldwide rule (Dan 7:13–14).

Jesus informs his disciples about the nature and timing of his second coming:

1. There will be an indeterminate delay between his first and second advents that will create a yearning for his return (17:22). This calls for patience and faithfulness.

2. During his absence false Christs will arise and deceive many people (17:23). This calls for a thorough grounding in revealed truth.

3. The return of the glorious Son of Man will be unmistakable, not hidden or obscure, like the flash of lightning that illumines the entire sky (17:24).

4. In the days before the second advent, people will go about their normal daily activities, with no thought of accountability before God, until the day of judgment unexpectedly overtakes them—as with Noah's generation before the flood and the people of Sodom in Lot's day (17:26–29).

5. The second coming will result in an instantaneous sifting of the human race, the saved taken and the unsaved left behind, whether it occurs at night (in bed) or during the day (grinding grain) (17:34–35). This calls for a commitment to discipleship, which demands the abandonment of self-directed pursuits and an undeterred focus on living life under God's rule. Hesitancy and equivocation at the Son of Man's return disclose the values of a life spent rather than invested (17:30–33).

6. When the disciples ask "where" (rather than "when") such a separation will take place, the Lord speaks a parable: "Where the corpse is, there the vultures will gather" (17:37). The meaning is that the Son of Man's return in judgment will overtake all who are spiritually dead just as vultures appear wherever there is carrion to be devoured. Judgment will be certain and severe, underscoring the gravity of the call to submission to God's rule now.

Jesus thus once again expounds a present-future kingdom with two decisive moments of emergence in the world, an inaugural one through the suffering Servant and a consummative one through the glorified Son of Man. This confirms our earlier comprehensive definition: *"The kingdom of God is the present transforming rule of God over the entire personality of believing and repentant individuals, creating a community over which he reigns, and one day resulting in a redeemed universe that joyfully submits to his sovereign lordship."*

⇨ Does the indeterminate period between the two advents, now nearly 2,000 years, make the second coming of Christ a fading and distant promise? Read 2 Peter 3:8–14 and ask the Lord to give you a sense of urgency to live in light of his imminent return.

TWO PARABLES ON PRAYER

(Luke 18:1–14)

1. *The unjust judge and the persistent widow* (18:1–8)

Drawing near to Jerusalem for his final Passover, Jesus concentrated on preparing his disciples for his departure. The inter-advent period of his absence will find them engaged in promoting the kingdom to both responsive and resistant hearts. During those often difficult and lonely days the disciples will long for his return (Luke 17:22). The antidote to discouragement, of losing heart amidst the disappointments and persecutions, will be persistent prayer (18:1). The parable of the unjust judge illustrates the kind of prayer that prevails with God. An unrighteous judge, moved neither by fear of God nor respect of persons, acts to vindicate a widow who tenaciously persists in pushing her case to the court. She has been exploited by someone who took advantage of her vulnerability. The judge's slowness in judging her case may have been due to hopes of receiving a bribe, which she was unable or unwilling to pay. Regardless of the details of the situation, she literally "beats him down," that is, wears him out with her persistent pleas for justice (18:5).

The limits of the analogy must be recognized: just as God is not a reluctant friend (Luke 11:5–8), neither is he an unjust judge. A lesser to greater argument is implicit in the parable: if an unrighteous judge, who neither fears God nor respects people, is moved by the tenacious demands of a helpless widow, how much more will a just and merciful God act to vindicate his elect who cry out to him day and night for justice (18:6–7). The setting of the prayer is a time of severe persecution and rapid decline of faith as the return of the Son of Man draws near (18:8). As they promote the kingdom in this hostile context, Jesus' disciples are to be bold and persistent in bringing their requests to God.

2. *The Pharisee and the tax collector* (18:9–14)

The central point of the parable of the Pharisee and the tax collector is introduced before the story itself: rebuke for those who look with judgmental disdain on those who fail to measure up to their external taxonomy of righteousness (18:9). In the story there are two people, two prayers and two results. Both men engage in private prayer in the temple. The Pharisee's prayer is self-directed ("to himself" [author's rendering]), self-confident ("standing"), and self-congratulatory ("I thank you that I am not like other men") (18:11). He recites his practice of fasting twice a week, which was far more than the law's requirement of once a year (Lev 16:29). He reminds God of his practice of tithing one tenth of all he possesses, not just wine, grain and olive oil as commanded in the law (Deut 14:22–23), but even garden herbs (Luke 11:42). He singles out the tax collector for special scorn. There is no request, only a rehearsal of religious credentials.

By contrast, the tax collector approaches God with the posture of repentance. He recognizes his unworthiness ("standing far off"), is deeply contrite before a holy God ("would not even lift up his eyes to heaven"), and feels a mournful sorrow for his sin ("beat his breast") (18:13). He makes the humble plea for God to show mercy to a sinner. No excuses are offered and no comparisons are made with others. The tax collector looks into the recesses of his own heart, discovers sin, and feels the need for divine pardon. The Pharisee looks in the mirror and sees a paragon of virtue. Only the former sees himself as God does, a guilty sinner deserving judgment.

The outcome is that the tax collector who made no claim to righteousness went home having been declared righteous by God. The Pharisee who was persuaded of his own righteousness was condemned (18:14a). A principle of paradox embodies the contrastive outcomes: those who exalt themselves will be humbled, while those who humble themselves will be exalted (18:14b). Jesus imparted to his disciples this unbreakable law of the kingdom on a number of occasions (Matt 18:4; 23:12; Luke 14:11). The biblical principle of humility before honor, service before status, suffering before glory, a cross before a crown is given special prominence in the new covenant community where all are brothers and the coming King is first a suffering Servant (Luke 1:48–49; Rom 8:17b; Phil 2:5–11; Jas 4:10; 1 Pet 5:6; cf. 1 Sam 2:3–10; 2 Chr 7:14–15; Job 5:11; Prov 3:34; 25:6–7; Isa 57:15; 66:1–2).

⇨ Humble dependence combined with undaunted persistence brings these two parables into a unified theology of prayer. Keep a notebook of people and concerns that you are praying for; persist in prevailing prayer and record God's answers as they come.

DIVINE BLUEPRINT FOR MARRIAGE
(Matthew 19:1–12; Mark 10:1–12)

At this point the narrative of Matthew and Mark resumes after the long 'interruption' of Luke 9:51—18:14 and John 7:2—11:54, that is, the Later Judean and Early Perean ministries. The *Later Perean* ministry, a period of approximately six weeks from *mid-February to late March* (AD 30), is covered in Luke 17:11—19:28; Matt 19:1—20:34; Mark 10:1–52. Jesus departs Galilee, enters the region of Judea beyond the Jordan, that is, Perea, then moves southward by way of Jericho to Jerusalem for his final Passover.

The Pharisees test Jesus with a question about the inviolability of marriage. Is it lawful, they ask, for a man to divorce his wife "for any cause?" They were drawing him into a long-standing debate between the two leading Pharisaical schools of interpretation. The school of Hillel ruled that a man could divorce his wife for nearly every reason, including poor cooking. The more conservative school of Shammai allowed divorce only for gross indecency, which again placed all authority in the husband to initiate divorce proceedings.

Jesus takes an independent line from both schools, bringing his listeners back to the creation ordinance for marriage, much as he did in his approach to keeping the Sabbath (Mark 2:27–28). While his opponents could cite the Mosaic concession for divorce in Deuteronomy 24:1–4, which allowed a man to divorce his wife for "some indecency in her" (probably close to Shammai's ruling), Jesus keeps the focus on God's original design for marriage in Genesis 1:27–28; 2:18–25. Yes, he admits, God did accommodate himself to the hardness of man's heart brought on by the entrance of sin into the world. However, for those who enter God's rule by faith and repentance the standard is not what may or may not be allowable, but the divine intent for marriage—one man and one woman for life. Divorce is contrary to God's creative purpose for man and woman and is thus rebellion against his will—separating what God has joined together. Thus he issues a resounding "no" to their original question. The sanctity of marriage rests in God's creation of two genders and his ordination of the inviolable covenant relationship.

The Matthean account adds the clause, "except for sexual immorality" (19:9; cf. Matt 5:32), allowing for divorce on the sole grounds of marital unfaithfulness or adultery by one of the spouses. While adultery does not mandate divorce, since forgiveness and reconciliation are always possible through God's grace, Jesus does recognize the dissolution of the marriage when such an egregious violation of the covenantal relationship takes place. The Apostle Paul makes a further concession when a believer is abandoned by an unbelieving spouse in a mixed marriage (1 Cor 7:12–16): the believer is free to let the unbeliever depart and is released from the binding contract of the marriage. But in his normative teaching on marriage, Paul, like Jesus, keeps the focus on the original institution of marriage and the divine intent (Eph 5:22–33). Jesus' words in the Markan account place equal responsibility on husband and wife to maintain marital fidelity.

The disciples clearly caught the force of Jesus' intent (rather than parking on the singular concession), being so astonished at the severity of his answer that they wonder if it might, then, be better to remain single. They were certainly aware that the kingdom ministry was requiring extended periods away from home which had caused the family of Peter, their married teammate, constant strains. But Jesus recommends singleness only to those to whom this gift has been given by God. He identifies three kinds of single men or eunuchs: (i) those who are born eunuchs, that is, the physiologically impotent; (ii) those who are made eunuchs by others, that is, forcibly castrated (e.g. for court positions serving royal women); (iii) and those who voluntarily commit to a life of celibacy for the sake of the kingdom of heaven. To borrow from the Apostle Paul's teaching, for those, and only for those, who can maintain a life of continence while remaining single there are advantages in the freedom from family responsibilities to devote one's entire energies to promoting the kingdom (1 Cor 7:32–35). Paul, like Jesus, endorses singleness for those who are able (1 Cor 7:7–9), but for both marriage is the norm.

⇨ How can we apply Jesus' (and Paul's) approach to marriage to a culture where divorce is now claiming nearly one half of marriages? Since many come to Christian ministers with questions over what is "permissible," why is it so important to solidify one's convictions in this area?

REWARDS THAT DWARF THE SACRIFICES
(Matthew 19:16–30; Mark 10:17–31; Luke 18:18–30)

A young man approached Jesus and asked what he must do to inherit eternal life. He is identified as rich, young, and religious, probably a lay leader in the synagogue. The young man was at least concerned about more vital issues than casuistry over food laws and the Sabbath or rabbinical rulings on divorce and remarriage. However, his mind gravitated toward works and achievement rather than repentance and faith. Jesus kept the conversation on the same plane and demanded that he obey the law's commandments. For the one who can obey the law perfectly, Jesus implied, there is a hypothetical offer of eternal life (Matt 19:17b). The standard of complete obedience is set forth to confront the young man with the stark reality that he is a lawbreaker and must look elsewhere for eternal life. Only when he recognizes that the standard is unattainable and comes to admit his spiritual bankruptcy will he turn from human merit to God's grace. But the young man does not see his failure, only his accomplishments. He claims faultless obedience to the ten commandments throughout his short life, much as Saul viewed himself before being arrested by the risen Lord as he neared Damascus (Phil 3:6b).

Jesus perceives that a deeper issue must be confronted. What hinders the young man from surrendering to God's grace is a heart entangled with the pursuit, enjoyment, and management of his abundant material possessions. He was able to concentrate his energies on the task of external piety, but could not extricate himself from the treasures that held a firm grip on his heart. So Jesus makes the radical demand that he first sell his possessions, give them to the poor, then come and follow him. Jesus' demand saddened rather than angered him, pointing to a divided heart yearning for but unable to find release. Apart from God's saving power, Jesus concludes, it is impossible for a rich person to be freed from the binding distractions that great wealth brings, just as it is impossible for a camel, the largest animal in Palestine, to pass through the eye of a sewing needle.

The disciples were astonished at this final assessment. Their surprise indicates they viewed material wealth as a sign of God's favor. One need only look at the aristocratic members of the Sanhedrin to see how piety and plenty complemented one another. The disciples asked, if the rich cannot be saved, who then can be saved (Luke 18:26)? Jesus replied that all people are potentially redeemable because salvation depends on the ability of God, not on the extremity of the human condition. Peter suddenly interjected into the conversation the great sacrifice he and the other disciples had made when they became his followers: "We have left everything and followed you" (Matt 19:27). He wanted Jesus to acknowledge how different they were from this rich man who could not bear such loss. The Lord did not castigate his disciples (whose sentiments the vocal Peter represented) for such boasting, but gently corrected their shortsightedness. One can never outgive God. Both in the present life and in the life they will enjoy in the consummated kingdom, to be ushered in at the return of the Son of Man (Matt 19:28), there will be incomparable rewards for those who have sacrificed possessions, family ties, comfort and security in order to extend God's rule among people (Luke 18:29–30).

⇨ Do you sometimes feel the weight of the sacrifices involved in being a dedicated follower of Christ? Enumerate the ways that the Lord has already, in this life, rewarded your sacrifices (Mark 10:30). Recall also the incomparable sacrifice he made for you to secure your eternal destiny.

REWARDS DISPROPORTIONATE TO THE SERVICE
(Matthew 20:1–16)

At the time of the final divine accounting, there will be stunning reversals: many who are first (now) will be last (then), and many who are last (now) will be first (then) (Matt 19:30). This saying is repeated, in reverse order, at the end of the parable of the laborers in the vineyard (Mt 20:16). The parable supports the principle that Jesus has just declared, namely, that God's grace will prevail over all human priorities of wealth and status in the allocation of rewards in the kingdom.

With the parable Jesus illustrates what "the kingdom of heaven is like" (20:1). A landowner hired laborers for his vineyard at different times of the twelve-hour workday (6:00 a.m.–6:00 p.m.). He agreed to pay one denarius to the workers who came at 6:00 a.m. Later other workers were added, at 9 a.m., 12 p.m., 3 p.m., and 5 p.m., and in each case the landowner promised to pay "whatever is right." When evening came, at 6:00 p.m., the steward of the landowner paid all the laborers their wages. All received one denarius, from those who were hired last and worked one hour to those who were hired first and worked twelve hours. The early workers began to grumble that those who worked only one hour in the cool of the late afternoon received the same as those who labored all day in the scorching sun. With a series of rhetorical questions, the landowner defended his right to "do what I choose with what belongs to me" (20:15). The early workers were begrudging not the landowner's fairness to them (one denarius was the agreement), but his generosity to others. The parable supports the promise of Jesus that his servants will be rewarded far more than they deserve, and immeasurably more than all of their sacrifices merit (19:29). God will distribute his rewards not based on human notions of fairness, but according to his sovereign, and abundantly gracious, determination. Kingdom rewards, then, depend wholly on sovereign grace and in that grace surprising reversals will take place.

⇨ Rewards are sometimes presented in popular teaching as a kind of *quid pro quo* remuneration for services rendered. Along with this is the common idea that there will be distinctions of status and privilege among believers that persist into eternity (e.g. some dwelling in larger mansions, ruling over more extensive domains, or shining with greater capacity). How does Jesus' teaching in Matt 19:27—20:16 serve as a corrective to such notions?

SERVANTS OF THE SERVANT

(Matthew 20:17–28; Mark 10:32–45; Luke 18:31–34)

Jesus was making his way to Jerusalem for the final time in a circuitous fashion through Perea. For the fourth time he detailed what awaited him in the holy city: arrest and trial before the high priest, condemnation to death, deliverance to the secular authorities where he will be mocked, scourged and crucified, and on the third day he will be raised from the dead (Matt 20:17–19; cf. Matt 16:21; 17:22–23; Luke 17:25). Even after repeated predictions of his coming Passion in unmistakable language, the disciples remained utterly mystified: "This saying was hidden from them, and they did not grasp what was said" (Luke 18:34b). What the disciples did remember, however, was his recent prediction of the return of the Son of Man and his promise that they would share his glorious rule (Matt 19:28). The problem of selective hearing, then, was behind the request of the two sons of Zebedee (Mark 10:35). Urged on by their mother (Matt 20:20), they asked to be granted the most prominent positions in the coming kingdom. Apparently they had forgotten their Lord's earlier teaching that servanthood was central to kingdom elevation (Matt 18:1–4). Though James and John were among his first disciples, and part of an inner circle of privilege along with Peter, they have made little advancement in their understanding of the core kingdom value of deferential humility. Salome, mother of James and John, and sister of Mary the mother of Jesus, supported Jesus' ministry and would be one of four women at the cross (Matt 27:55–56; Mark 15:40; 16:1; Luke 8:2–3; John 19:25–27). Zebedee's wife, then, was Jesus' aunt on his mother's side, and thus was asking special favors for his two first cousins. Though they were misguided, there was also an element of faith behind this request, for they looked forward to a kingdom where they could function as vice regents under King Jesus (justifiably emboldened by the promise in Matt 19:28).

Jesus challenged their presuppositions. They were thinking only of kingdom glory, not of the suffering that must precede its arrival. They envisaged the crown without the cross, which is compared to the "cup" that Jesus must drink (Matt 20:22). The cup is a biblical metaphor for God's holy anger or retributive judgment (Ps 75:8; Isa 51:17, 21–22; Jer 25:15; Rev 14:10; 16:19) and signifies that Jesus would experience God's wrath in his propitiatory death on the cross (Matt 26:39, 42; 27:46). To their overconfident assertion that they were able to drink the same cup, Jesus affirmed that they would indeed suffer because of their identification with him. James, in fact, would be the first of the apostles to make the ultimate sacrifice for his Christian witness (Acts 12:2). Though John will live to a ripe old age, he will be persecuted by the Sanhedrin in Jerusalem (Acts 4:1–22), along with the other apostles (Acts 5:17–42), and later be exiled to the penal settlement of Patmos "on account of the word of God and the testimony of Jesus" (Rev 1:9). Suffering is a gift granted by God to all of his faithful witnesses (Phil 1:29), but favored positions are determined not by Jesus but by the Father, the source of his derived messianic authority (Matt 20:23; cf. Matt 11:27; 24:36; 28:18).

When the other ten disciples learned of the preemptive move of James and John to seize the top positions in the cabinet, they became indignant (Matt 20:24). The disciples had earlier argued among themselves who would be the greatest in the kingdom (Mark 9:33–34) and were told that the method of elevation in the kingdom of God is to take the place of the servant. Now the squabbling degenerated into jealous hostility and threatened to divide the tiny company of the committed. Jesus immediately called them together and reminded them that leadership in God's kingdom is completely different from the kind of leadership practiced in secular society. The latter is authoritarian and hierarchical. Gentile rulers, whether military, governmental, or civic, possess authority due to the positions they hold and demand compliance because of such vested power (Matt 20:25). The possession and exercise of ruling authority is wholly unrelated to the moral character of the leader. The centurion who came to Jesus earlier spoke about the unquestioned obedience his soldiers rendered to him: "I say to one 'Go,' and he goes, and to another, 'Come,' and he comes, and to my servant, 'Do this,' and he does it" (Matt 8:9). In the kingdom of God, however, one climbs only by first descending. One becomes a servant of others before one can be elevated by God to lead others (Matt 20:26–27). This indicates that there are favored positions of delegated authority even in the kingdom of heaven, but they are sovereignly granted, rather than pursued, to those who first qualify as servants. The servant in this context is one who seeks to promote the welfare of one's brother and to sublimate all personal agendas under the all-consuming ambition of promoting God's name and kingdom in the world. This is the opposite of the self-aggrandizing action of James and John and of the ensuing jealousy that threatened to overtake the others.

Jesus pointed to his own sacrificial manner of life and to his coming substitutionary death as the concrete example of what it means to be a servant-leader (Matt 20:28; Mark 10:45). He pointed the disciples to his motivation and to his action. First, as the Son of Man his mission to the world is not to be served like secular officials, but to give of himself to others like a humble servant. Uppermost in the mind of every servant-leader like Jesus, then, is the welfare of others over personal power and perquisites. "*Son of Man*" was Jesus' favorite self-designation and occurs over eighty times in the four Gospels, nearly seventy of which are in the three Synoptics. The historical precedent to the designation Son of Man comes primarily from Daniel 7:9–14. The scene is one of final judgment as the Ancient of Days takes his seat before the court of heaven. One "like a son of man" approaches the throne and is given authority, glory, and sovereign power. He is worshipped by people of all nations and given an everlasting dominion and an indestructible kingdom. Daniel's imagery of a glorious Son of Man who receives authority to rule the nations is clearly behind many of the texts where Jesus refers to the return of the Son of Man to consummate the kingdom (Matt 13:41; 16:27, 28; 19:28; 24:27, 30, 37; 25:31; 26:64; Luke 17:22, 30; 18:8; 21:27). However, in many other places Jesus refers to himself as the Son of Man who walks among people offering redemption to lost sinners, proclaiming God's inaugural rule, and experiencing loss, persecution, and betrayal (Matt 8:20; 9:6; 11:19; 12:8, 32; 13:37; 16:13; Luke 19:10; 22:48). Even more graphic are those passages, such as the present one, where the Son of Man is one who will be betrayed by the religious authorities, suffer the shameful death of crucifixion, and be vindicated in resurrection (Mark 8:31; 9:9, 12, 31; 10:33, 45; 14:21, 41; Luke 9:22; 11:30). How can Daniel's Son of Man, who is an exalted figure with direct access to the heavenly throne and invested with everlasting authority to rule the nations, fulfill the role of an earthly servant who makes authoritative claims, suffers an ignominious death, and is vindicated by being raised from the dead?

The most plausible explanation is that Jesus intentionally poured into the designation Son of Man both phases of his redemptive mission, humiliation from Isaiah 52:13—53:12 and exaltation from Daniel 7:9–14. *The Son of Man, then, is the one who first comes as a suffering Servant to provide redemption through his vicarious death, is raised from the dead, and will some day return in glory to judge and to rule over the nations.* The fourth servant song of Isaiah (52:13—53:12; cf. 42:1–7; 49:1–7; 50:4–11) develops the motif of the suffering of the messianic Servant touched on in the second and third songs (49:4, 7; 50:6–8). The fourth song introduces the servant as one who suffers extreme disgrace, but provides cleansing from sin and is highly exalted by the Lord (52:13–15). The song progressively expounds the servant's lowly demeanor and career of sorrows (53:1–3), his vicarious death as the

Lord places on him the sins of wayward people (53:4–6), his silence before the accusers (53:7–9), and his satisfaction at the results of his death, namely, the justification of many transgressors (53:10–12). The fourth servant song of Isaiah is seen fulfilled by the Gospel writers in many incidents in Jesus' life and preeminently in his Passion.

Isaianic Servant of the Lord	Fulfillment in the Suffering of Jesus
53:1: "Who has believed what he heard from us?"	*John 12:38:* rejection by Israel's religious leaders
53:2: no beauty, no majesty, nothing desirable	*Matt 2:23:* a Nazarene, that is, a despised one (John 1:46)
53:3a: despised and rejected by people	*Mark 9:12:* the Son of Man must suffer and be rejected
53:3b: man of sorrows, and familiar with suffering	*Matt 16:21; Luke 18:31–33:* predictions of his Passion
53:4: "He took our illnesses and bore our diseases."	*Matt 8:17:* healing and exorcising ministry in Galilee
53:5: pierced, crushed, his wounds	*Matt 26:67:* they spit upon him and struck him with fists *Matt 27:26:* Pilate had Jesus flogged
53:6–7: iniquity laid on him; lamb to the slaughter	*John 1:29, 36:* John the Baptist's confession: Lamb of God
53:7a, c: as a sheep before shearers, he did not open his mouth	*Matt 26:62–63a; 27:13-14:* trials before the Sanhedrin and Pilate
53:7b: led like a lamb to the slaughter	*Matt 27:31:* soldiers led him away to be crucified
53:9: assigned a grave with the rich in his death	*Matt 27:57–60:* burial in the tomb of Joseph of Arimathea

53:12b, d: poured out his life unto death; bore the sin of many, and made intercession for the transgressors	*Matt 26:28*: Lord's supper: cup is blood poured out for many for the forgiveness of sins *Matt 26:38–39*: Gethsemane prayers for the cup he must drink, representing the Father's wrath poured out on him
53:12c: numbered with the transgressors	*Luke 22:37*: arrested in Gethsemane as a criminal *Luke 23:33*: crucified between two robbers (Matt 27:38)

At Jesus' baptism and at his transfiguration the Father's voice of authentication declared, "This is my beloved Son, with whom I am well pleased" (Matt 3:17; 17:5). This declaration combines Isaiah 42:1 ("behold my servant … in whom my soul delights") with Psalm 2:7 ("you are my Son; today I have begotten you"). The Father identifies Jesus both as the servant whose faithfulness to the redemptive mission brings God delight, as well as the messianic Son who is exalted as King and Lord at his resurrection (Acts 13:33; Rom 1:4; Heb 1:5; 5:5). As the initial phase of Jesus' Galilean ministry draws to a close, Matthew notes that Jesus' healing ministry fulfilled Isaiah 42:1–4 from the first servant song (Matt 12:15–21). Jesus is the servant upon whom God has poured out his Spirit to fulfill the mission of bringing justice and hope to the nations. The servant does not cry out or quarrel. In spite of intense opposition, he trusts in God and is gentle in heart to reveal the kingdom to his disciples (Matt 11:28–29). He is not harsh toward the weak (bruised reed, smoldering wick), but reveals his salvation to child-like hearts (Matt 11:27). The justice he brings is the present gift of righteousness to the repentant who hope in his name.

The clearest reference in the Synoptic Gospels to the substitutionary nature of Jesus' death is found in the present text where his life is given as "a ransom for many" (Matt 20:28/Mark 10:45). The one who believes and repents is freed from slavery to sin by the payment of Jesus' blood shed on the cross. Though this text anticipates the fuller theology of redemption developed in the New Testament epistles (Titus 2:14; 1 Pet 1:18–19), it occurs here to support Jesus' challenge to his disciples to imitate his pattern of servanthood. Theirs will not be a redemptive, vicarious suffering. The imitation is one of degree not kind: just as he sacrificed comfort, security, and status in order to redeem others, so they must set aside career prospects, monetary gain, personal prestige and other such natural human pursuits for the promotion of God's rule among people. They must constantly remind themselves that they are servants, not lords, and that leadership in the kingdom of God must take on a wholly distinct and contrastive character from leadership in the secular world. Their authority as vice-regents will come later (Matt 19:28). The present age, however, is the salvation historical phase of sacrifice, suffering, and, in some instances, even death to promote first God's kingdom and righteousness (Matt 6:33). Their recollection of the life and death of Jesus, Son of Man, the suffering Servant and coming King, will provide the pattern and motivation to pursue their calling to lead by serving.

⇨ What is the difference between selfish ambition and holy aspiration? Does a believer have to drain one's drive toward personal accomplishment in order to develop the attitude of a servant? How do you apply Jesus' teaching here to your present vocational context?

HEALING AND SALVATION COME TO JERICHO
(Matthew 20:29–34; Mark 10:46–52; Luke 18:35–43; 19:1–10)

Two blind beggars sitting by the roadside were stirred by the commotion of the large crowd accompanying Jesus as he entered the Herodian town of Jericho (Luke 18:35). They addressed him as "Son of David," one with messianic authority to heal their blindness (Isa 35:5). The crowd, composed mostly of pilgrims eager to make their way to Jerusalem for Passover, attempted to quiet the men from interfering in their audience with Jesus, much as the disciples had earlier rebuked children for disturbing the Lord (Matt 19:13b). Bartimaeus, the more vocal of the two, only pleaded more loudly: "Son of David, have mercy on me." Jesus, never deterred by human pressures, stopped and called the blind men forward. Jesus is not so consumed with his mission, soon to reach fulfillment in Jerusalem, that he cannot extend his compassion to two desperate men. Mark records the graphic picture of Bartimaeus excitedly casting aside his cloak and jumping to his feet in the hope of having his sight restored (10:48–49). Faith brings the Healer and their blighted condition together as Jesus touches their eyes and the sight of the two is immediately restored. Does the removal of the blindness of Bartimaeus and his friend symbolize something deeper, the removal of spiritual darkness through the coming Passion of the Servant? The fickle crowd who first hindered the blind men from making their request now are caught up in the enthusiasm of the miracle (Luke 18:43), a harbinger of instability that will show itself even more starkly during Passion Week.

Luke's focus suddenly shifts from the blind beggar to a rich public official. The wealthy chief officer of the tax district of Jericho, named Zacchaeus, wanted to see this Jesus who was attracting so much attention from the crowds. Being short, he climbed up the branches of a sycamore tree to get a glimpse. The evergreen sycamore fig tree had wide-spreading lateral branches which made it easy to climb as well as to be hidden. When Jesus reached the spot, he looked up, called Zacchaeus by name, and invited himself to a meal at the tax official's home. Jesus perceived that the deep desire of Zacchaeus to meet him was more than superficial curiosity. Zacchaeus came down and gladly welcomed him to his home. The religionists murmured about Jesus having table fellowship with this sinner, for tax collectors were viewed as extortionists and traitors. Zacchaeus, keenly aware of the criticisms, defended his integrity by citing his record of generosity toward the poor. He offered to make four-fold restitution to anyone he had defrauded, even though the Jewish law only required double restitution (Exod 22:4, 7, 9). In this offer Jesus detected a repentant heart and pronounced Zacchaeus' salvation as a true son of Abraham, one justified like his forefather by faith (Luke 19:9; cf. Gen 15:6).

Jesus' necessary visit ("I *must* stay at your house today" [Luke 19:5]) to the home of Zacchaeus was a particular act of obedience to his divinely appointed mission "to seek and to save the lost" (Luke 19:10). Jesus was on the Father's ordained path to search for and find those who are lost and bring them under God's saving rule, a salvation grounded in his imminent sacrificial death at Golgotha. The murmurers could only see a civil servant of Rome (just as the crowd only saw in Bartimaeus one more useless beggar), lax to Jewish traditions, greedy for gain, and friendly with the enemy. Jesus saw a lost human being who needed to hear of God's saving mercy.

⇨ Do you share Jesus' sensitivity to those with real needs who cross your path? Is there room in your busy schedule to notice the Zacchaeuses and Bartimaeuses who need an encounter with Jesus Christ?

PARABLE OF THE MINAS

(Luke 19:11–28)

Nationalistic aspirations were often stirred up among the pilgrims crowding Jerusalem during Passover season. With Jesus nearing the Holy City, along the steep ascent straddling the Wadi Qelt from Jericho, the crowds began to speak of the imminent appearance of the kingdom of God (19:11). Jesus had always distanced himself from attempts to co-opt him for a political role (John 6:15) and in recent months had repeatedly predicted his rejection by the Jerusalem authorities (Matt 16:21; 17:22–23; 20:17–19; Luke 17:25). Such messianic fervor, however, was difficult to dampen. If the disciples failed to grasp his coming Passion (Luke 18:34), how much more so the impressionable multitude.

With the parable of the minas Jesus qualifies the timing of the arrival of the kingdom in light of his coming death. A nobleman leaves for a distant country to be crowned king before returning at an unspecified time to establish his rule over the land. Before leaving he calls ten of his servants and distributes to each of them one mina with the instruction to effectively trade with it until his return. One mina was equal to 100 drachma (or 100 denarii) which amounted to approximately three months' wages. However, his future subjects hated the nobleman and sent a delegation to the capital seeking to block the coronation. Their protest failed and the newly crowned King returned home. His first act as king was to call his servants to account for how they handled the money entrusted to them. The first and second servants had multiplied their investment tenfold and fivefold and were given authority over ten cities and five cities respectively. A third servant, however, only hid away his one mina and returned it without interest. He offered excuses about the master's harsh business practices, a recognition that should have motivated him even more to bring some returns to such a demanding lord. The servant was condemned and his one mina taken away and given to the servant with ten minas.

The parable must be interpreted in light of its historical context. After his death and resurrection, Jesus will be exalted to the right hand of the Father, taking his seat on the Davidic throne (Ps 110:1). While the King is absent, his servants are to act as faithful stewards to invest their resources in promoting his interests. In the period of unspecified duration between his departure and return, Jesus' disciples are to invest time, talents and treasures promoting his rule over those who believe and repent. A day of final assessment will follow the King's return when each one will give an account of his/her stewardship. Faithful servants will be rewarded and unfaithful servants condemned.

In light of the Lord's teaching on the gracious character of rewards (Matt 20:1–16; Luke 17:7–10), the distinction between the first two servants, placed over ten and five cities respectively, should not be interpreted as introducing some hierarchical distinction among God's people that will persist in the eternal kingdom. In the related parable of the talents, the first two servants, in spite of differing returns, are praised with identical language and rewarded with the same charge: "I will set you over much" (Matt 25:21, 23). The studied distinction is between the first two servants and the last servant whose profession proves hollow by his failure to obey the master. The principle of 'more invested, even more received' (Luke 19:26) underscores that one is spiritually enriched by sacrifice, but impoverished by hoarding for oneself what is intended for God's glory. The third servant who doubted the master's goodness has aligned himself with those rebellious citizens who rejected his rule and will meet severe judgment upon the King's return. Jesus is clearly speaking of the religious authorities in Jerusalem with whom a final conflict is looming.

⇨ How are you investing your time, talents and treasures in promoting the kingdom of God among your contemporaries? In what ways are you seeking to nurture your skills to be a more effective emissary of the King?

14

Passion Week I

Days of Celebration and Confrontation

ANOINTING FOR BURIAL

(Matthew 26:6–13; Mark 14:3–9; John 11:55—12:11)

JESUS MADE HIS WAY to Jerusalem for his final Passover. Many pilgrims went early to purify themselves before the feast proper on Nisan 15, from Thursday sunset to Friday sunset in the orthodox Jewish calendar. Initial speculation among the swelling crowds (from a settled population of 50,000 to as much as 1,500,000 during Passover) was that Jesus would not come to the feast at all. The Sanhedrin continued in its determination to arrest and charge him with capital crimes (John 11:53, 57). Jesus arrived in Bethany six days before Passover (John 12:1), that is, after sunset on *Friday* (or as late as Saturday) *before Passion Week*. The village of Bethany was just two miles from Jerusalem, on the road from Jericho at the eastern foot of the Mount of Olives. He and his disciples would lodge with his familiar hosts, Mary, Martha, and Lazarus, for the next six nights before proceeding to Gethsemane on Thursday evening (Luke 21:37–38).

Probably on the evening of his arrival, a dinner was given in Jesus' honor at the home of one Simon the leper, with the active Martha waiting upon the thirteen guests. During the meal Mary, known earlier for her worshipful demeanor (Luke 10:38–42), broke open an alabaster jar of perfume made of pure nard, a costly scented oil, and poured it on her Lord's head, as well as on his feet as he reclined away from the table. Mary then wiped the feet with her hair, a humble act of devotion for one whose life she sensed was drawing to a close. Judas Iscariot failed to enter into the spirit of Mary's action, feigning concern for the poor for whom such expensive perfume could have been sold and given. John censures Judas' hypocrisy in light of the later discovery that he often pilfered the money bag of which he was the designated custodian (John 12:6). This is the first time, before his act of betrayal, that Judas' flawed character is exposed. The deepening resolve of the Jewish leaders to seize Jesus will soon be satisfied by the willingness of his covetous disciple to betray him for money.

Jesus relates Mary's anointing to his burial. Normally anointing was associated with joyful festivity, not funerals. Mary has grasped what the disciples have missed (Luke 18:34)—he is about to arrive at the appointed hour where he will culminate his redemptive mission through death. Here is the fruit of Mary's contemplative nature, the closest any human being comes to understanding the cross before that decisive event. She performed a "beautiful thing" (Matt 26:10), "preserving" (literally) the perfume, that is, devoting it for the very purpose she intended, to prepare him for burial (John 12:7). Jesus' commendation of Mary was not insensitivity to the poor, but a validation of Mary's understanding that the opportunities for personal devotion were rapidly fading in light of his imminent departure. As the gospel of the crucified and risen Lord is proclaimed throughout the world, future generations will recall Mary's prophetic action.

Crowds filed to Bethany not only to see Jesus but also Lazarus, whose resurrection from the dead continued to bring popular acclaim to the Galilean. The frightened Sanhedrin now purposed to move against Lazarus as well (John 12:10). When the evidence overwhelmingly supports the opposition, both opponent and evidence have to be eliminated.

⇨ Does your worship cost you anything? What act of self-humbling (wiping the feet) and self-sacrifice (costly perfume) have you offered, like Mary, to the Lord Jesus?

PASSION WEEK

The final week of the earthly life of Jesus, Passion Week, is the extended "hour" toward which his entire life's work has been moving. Nearly 40% of the material of the four canonical Gospels is taken up with the events of this week, from Palm Sunday to Easter Sunday. His death on the cross on Good Friday will culminate his appointed mission from the Father when Jesus cries out, "It is finished" (John 19:30). The eight days of the detailed narrative can be summarized as follows:

Sunday	Day of Celebration
Monday	Day of Confrontation
Tuesday	Day of Controversy
Wednesday	Day of Conspiracy
Thursday	Day of Consecration
Friday	Day of Consummation
Saturday	Day of Cessation (Sabbath)
Sunday	Day of Conquest

Sunday: Day Of Celebration

TRIUMPHAL ENTRY INTO JERUSALEM

(Matthew 21:1–11, 14–17; Mark 11:1–11; Luke 19:29–44;
John 12:12–19)

1. *Colt of a donkey*

On *Sunday morning* Jesus sent two disciples ahead of him from Bethany to the tiny village of Bethphage on the Mount of Olives to secure the colt of a donkey for his mount to Jerusalem. He has meticulously planned the event. The disciples are told they will locate a donkey with her colt tied up and that the owner will grant permission for their use when they relate that "the Lord needs them." Events unfold just as the Lord predicted. Cloaks are placed on the colt who has never been ridden before. The mother donkey probably goes ahead to calm her inexperienced foal which is mounted by Jesus for the slow ride down the slope of the Mount of Olives through the deep Kidron valley into Jerusalem through the northern entrance to the outer court of the temple.

2. *Fulfillment of prophecy*

The initial act of Passion Week fulfills Zechariah 9:9, with introductory words from Isaiah 62:11a: "Say to the Daughter of Zion, Behold, your king is coming to you, humble, and mounted on a donkey, and on a colt, the foal of a beast of burden" (Matt 21:5). Matthew specifies two animals which lines up precisely with Zechariah's prophecy. Isaiah's prefatory command to the people of Jerusalem signals the coming of a Savior who calls to himself a holy and redeemed people (Isa 62:11b–12). Jesus gently rides to Jerusalem on a beast of burden, not on a charger readied

274

for war (Zech 9:10; Rev 19:11). In the Old Testament donkeys were ridden by rulers in times of peace (Judg 10:4; 12:14; 2 Sam 16:2), though the preferred mount for royalty was the mule (2 Sam 13:29; 18:9; 1 Kgs 1:33). The ride to Jerusalem is an acted parable: Jesus offers himself to Israel as a burden-bearing Servant whose mission is to bring peace through his redemptive sacrifice.

3. *Davidic King*

Large crowds gather as the procession moves slowly to Jerusalem from the east. Pilgrims from Galilee and more distant places who arrived early for their ritual purification went out to meet him (John 11:55; 12:12). Many permanent residents of Jerusalem, Bethany and the surrounding areas wanted to see the one whose miracle of raising Lazarus from the dead has been widely reported (John 12:17–18). As he neared the city, the multitudes spread their cloaks and palm branches on the road and hailed him as the Son of David (Matt) and King of Israel (John) who comes to usher in the promised kingdom of his great royal father (Mark). Luke adds a chorus of praise similar to that of the angels at Jesus' birth (19:38b; cf. 2:14). The pronouncements come primarily from Psalm 118:26, a climactic text of the great Hallel (Praise) Psalms (113–118) regularly cited by pilgrims at the major feasts of Passover, Pentecost and Tabernacles. While acknowledged as the Davidic Messiah and King (from such texts as 2 Sam 7:11–16; Ps 89; Isa 9:6–7), there is no understanding of Jesus' mission to provide salvation from sin as the suffering Servant (from Ps 22; Isa 52:13—53:12; Zech 12:10–13). The King of Israel (John 12:13b) comes to establish a heavenly reign not an earthly dominion (John 18:36–37); the one whose coming elicits the praise of angels and crowds is the Savior who brings the good news of the forgiveness of sins (Luke 2:10–11). The tender tones of the acted parable of Messiah riding a beast of burden on a mission of peace (bestowed on the earth [Luke 2:14] through reconciliation with heaven [Luke 19:38b]) are drowned out by shouts of nationalistic fervor.

4. *Lines of response*

The three lines of acceptance, ambivalence and rejection crystallize over the next six days. First, the disciples are overtaken by the events. They are confused onlookers whose faith is about to endure its severest test. Only their encounter with the risen and glorified Lord will provide the corrective lenses to clearly view all that has unfolded before their eyes (John 12:16). Second, the crowds are flush with enthusiasm for the miracle worker and caught up in the cries for a national deliverer. When the tide turns against Jesus and he submits to rather than resists his accusers, they will quickly shift their allegiance to the winning side. Third, the Pharisees are horrified at his growing popularity (John 12:19) and resort to their customary charge of blasphemy when Jesus does not refuse the acclamations (Luke 19:39–40). They will form an alliance with the Sadducees to move against Jesus when an offer of betrayal suddenly arises from unexpected quarters.

5. *Lament over Jerusalem*

A few weeks before, while traveling through Perea, Jesus expressed sorrow over the coming desolation of Jerusalem, though he ended with hope that one day the people of Israel will turn to their Messiah with the confession, "Blessed is he who comes in the name of the Lord" (Luke 13:34–35). Though these very words from Psalm 118:26 are now on the lips of the crowds welcoming him to Jerusalem, the fulfillment of Jesus' prophecy will have to wait. As the city and its imposing temple complex come into view, Jesus once again weeps over the nation that it represents and the redemptive peace that it is about to forfeit (Luke 19:41–42). There is a sinister force conspiring in the city that will soon turn the "Hosannas" of praise into demands for his death. Israel is not ready for a suffering Messiah. Because she does not recognize the time of her divine visitation a terrible judgment is on the horizon. Within one generation (AD 70) Roman armies will surround the city, build their siege works, reduce the city walls and temple structures to rubble, and massacre the inhabitants (Luke 19:43–44).

6. *Testimony of children*

For a final time Jesus engages in a healing ministry in the outer court of the Gentiles where handicapped people could enter (Matt 21:14–16). Children that are present join in voicing "Hosanna" to the Son of David. The priests are incensed at his healing miracles and the adulations of children. To the priests and scribes Jesus is a false prophet deceiving naive minds with demon-inspired miracles. But Jesus rejoices in the wisdom flowing from babes, a fulfillment of Psalm 8:2. In receiving the application to himself of a biblical text that exalts the Lord of Israel, majestic Creator and Ruler of the earth (Ps 8), Jesus is making a bold claim of messianic authority and even deity. By rejecting his claims the Jewish leaders are sealing their own destiny and that of the nation. Jesus returns to Bethany on Sunday evening to rest and prepare for further spiritual warfare the next day.

Monday: Day of Confrontation

CURSING A FIG TREE AND CLEANSING THE TEMPLE
(Matthew 21:18–19a, 12–13; Mark 11:12—18; Luke 19:45–48)

Early on *Monday morning* Jesus and his disciples made the short two-mile trek over the Mount of Olives from Bethany to Jerusalem. Jesus was hungry and noticed a fig tree by the road. Though it was not the season for figs (June), the tree was sprouting leaves, likely due to unseasonably warm weather. A fig tree in leaf meant fruit was present but in this case there were leaves without figs. Jesus issued a shocking command for the tree to be forever fruitless. His control over nature was validated the next morning when the same fig tree was discovered withered from its roots (Mark 11:20). The incident must be interpreted against its Old Testament context and in conjunction with the cleansing of the temple that follows.

The fig tree, whether fruitful or unfruitful, was often a symbol for Israel's spiritual condition (Jer 8:13; 29:17; Hos 9:10, 16; Joel 1:7; Mic 7:1). In the final days of the southern kingdom of Judah, Jeremiah called the faithful remnant carried to exile in Babylon with King Jehoiachin "good figs" and the corrupt officials and supporters who remained with King Zedekiah "bad figs" (Jer 24:1–8). Jesus gave a parable of a farmer who planted a fig tree which bore no fruit for three years. Exasperated, he decided to give the tree one more year to bear fruit before cutting it down (Luke 13:6–9). Together these texts illumine the cursing of the fig tree as an acted parable of judgment on the hypocritical religious leaders of Israel. They make a show of external piety, like the leafy tree, but fail to bear the fruits of a nation in covenant with a holy and loving God. So rotten is the nation at its core that the Sanhedrin is even now plotting the murder of her Messiah. The six woes of Luke 11:42–52 and the seven woes of Matthew 23:13–36 expose an external religiosity divorced from internal purity. Jesus' anger expressed in the cursing of the fig tree and the cleansing of the temple must be balanced by his mournful lament over a people that he yearns to embrace, but are like chicks fleeing from the protective wings of the mother hen and like stubborn children disdaining peace for ruin (Luke 13:34–35; 19:41–42).

On the first Passover of his public ministry (AD 27) Jesus entered the outer court of the temple and confronted the moneychangers who had turned his Father's house into a market. This was Jesus' initial act of confrontation with the Jerusalem authorities (John 2:13–17). Three years later on Monday before his final Passover, Jesus once again enters the temple. The first cleansing failed to put an end to the deeply rooted and profitable business enterprise housed in the court of the Gentiles. This second, culminative confrontation of the temple leaders, who sponsored such activity, makes them furious and seals his destiny as a mortal threat to their vested interests. Four days later they will move to prosecute his death.

The moneychangers were Jewish merchants who converted Greek and Roman currency into the required local currency for the worshippers to purchase what was needed for sacrifices including animals, wood, oil, wine and salt. Others sold pigeons for those too poor to purchase animals (Matt 21:12) and for use in other purification rites (Luke 2:24; cf. Lev 12:6–8; 14:22; 15:14, 29). There was rampant extortion in the exchange rates charged in the currency transactions, an exploitative situation exacerbated by the requirement that the annual temple-tribute required of all Jews and proselytes had to be paid in exact half-shekels. The temple court was even being used as a convenient transit to ship goods from the city to the Mount of Olives (Mark 11:16).

The normally measured anger of Jesus boiled over into a holy rage as he went through the courts driving out merchants and shoppers alike, and overturning the tables of the moneychangers and pigeon hawkers. Jesus borrowed the language of two Old Testament prophets in condemning the officials for turning the house of prayer for the nations (Isa 56:7) into a den of robbers (Jer 7:11). Isaiah described the redemptive purpose for the temple: to mediate God's gracious presence to his people and thereby attract the surrounding nations to draw near the God of Israel for prayer in its outer court (56:7–8). The centripetal missionary witness of Israel was designed to presage the centrifugal witness of the new Israel to all the nations of the earth (Matt 28:19–20). Jesus was moved once again with holy zeal (John 2:17, quot. Ps 69:9) to recover the temple from those who had obscured its intended role to be a distinctive witness to the Gentiles of the holiness of Israel's God and the necessity of cleansing from sin. The provisional paschal sacrifices would soon find their fulfillment in a final efficacious sacrifice, the offering of the temple of his body (John 2:21–22). Ironically, the plot of the paranoid priestly authorities to kill Jesus (Mark 11:18) would precipitate the very event they feared most, the dissolution of a system that had run its course. For the moment, though, they were prevented from moving against him by the crowds who were attracted by his daily teaching in the temple (Luke 19:47–48).

THE SON OF MAN LIFTED UP

(John 12:20–50)

In the court of the Gentiles on *Monday afternoon* some Greeks approached Philip and asked to have an audience with Jesus. From all over the Roman empire Jews and God-fearing Gentiles came during Passover to worship the God of Israel (Acts 2:5–11). Though they disappear from the narrative and there is no recorded sequel, Jesus' reply to the Greeks' request discloses the universal scope of his redemptive sacrifice. At the triumphal entry on Sunday the Pharisees ironically expressed their fear that "the whole world" was being drawn to Jesus because of Lazarus' resurrection (John 12:19 [NIV]). On *Monday* Jesus cleansed the temple, blasting the merchants for making an emporium out of his Father's house of prayer "for all the nations" (Mark 11:17). The spiritual yearning of Greek god-fearers now elicits one of the most profound expositions of the meaning of his coming death recorded in the Gospels, one that anticipates the fuller theology of the cross in the New Testament epistles.

1. *The culminative hour for Jesus to be glorified has now come* (12:23). In spite of the misguided pressures from a loving mother (John 2:4), skeptical brothers (John 7:6), and the attempts of his enemies to prematurely seize him (John 7:30; 8:20), Jesus has continued to march inexorably forward to his appointed "hour." Though the disciples will scatter in fear (John 16:32), this defining moment will result in the salvation of the world and a triumphant return to the Father (John 13:1). The cross is not shame but glory, not tragedy but triumph (John 17:1). Jesus' self-sacrificing, unconditional love and humble abandonment to the Father's will is his glory, that is, manifested majesty.

2. *His death will produce life for people from all over the world who come to believe in him. Jesus' sacrifice is, further, a paradigm for the disciple's cruciform pattern of life* (12:24–26). The kernel of the grain must be

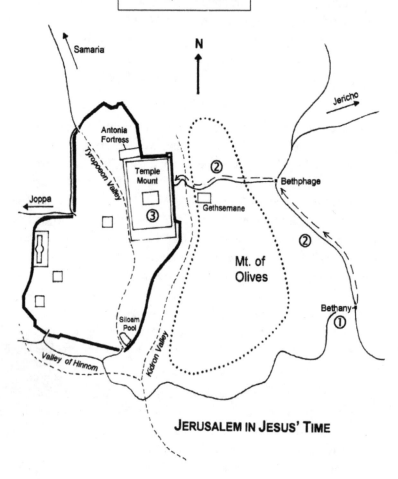

JERUSALEM IN JESUS' TIME

Friday (before Passover Week)   1. To **Bethany**

Sunday <u>Triumphal Entry</u>:   2. **Bethany** to **Bethphage** to**Temple**

Monday <u>Cleansing the Temple</u>:   3. **Bethany** to **Temple**

buried and perish for the wheat plant to spring forth. Jesus' death will reap a spiritual harvest, by "losing his life" he will gain eternal life for others. Disciples emulate Jesus' self-oblation: those who serve him follow the way of the cross in promoting the redemptive purposes of God the Father.

3. *The final intent of Jesus' offering of himself as a sacrifice for sin is that, in redeeming people, God the Father is glorified* (12:27–30). The prospect of the Servant-Son bearing the sin of mankind causes him to recoil from the resultant separation from the Father. J. A. Bengel comments that here "the horror of death and the ardor of obedience are fused together." Jesus' troubled heart anticipates the tormented prayers of Gethsemane as he commits himself one final time to finish his work (Matt 26:36–44). Jesus' prayer is that God's name be glorified, which prayer is answered with the Father's audible reply: "I have glorified it (my name), and I will glorify it again" (12:28). At the cross the Father pours out his holy wrath on a sinless substitute, his beloved Son, so that sinful people can be justified rather than condemned. At the cross God's "steadfast love and faithfulness meet; righteousness and peace kiss each other" (Ps 85:10). This is the third time during Jesus' earthly ministry that the Father breaks the silence, misunderstood by the crowd as thunder or the shout of an angel. On all three occasions that the Father speaks, he validates the Son's mission to suffer. Both at his baptism and at the Transfiguration he identifies the Son as the suffering Servant of Isaiah (42:1) in whom he is perfectly satisfied (Matt 3:17; 17:5). God is determined to glorify himself, to disclose his majestic character, in the redemption of people through the death of the Son.

4. *The cross is the decisive verdict of condemnation for the entire godless world system and its evil prince, the devil* (12:31; cf. John 16:11; Col 2:15). Jesus' death signals victory for those who enter his kingdom and guarantees the final overthrow of the old order governed by the flesh, sin, death, and Satan (Gal 2:19–20; 5:24; 6:14; 1 John 5:4–5). The enemies have been defeated at the cross, anticipated in Jesus' ministry of exorcism (Matt 12:28–29), but are only vanquished when the Son of Man returns (Rom 16:20a; Rev 20:7–10).

5. *By being "lifted up" on a cross in humiliation and later to the right hand of the Father in exaltation, Jesus draws people from all the nations of the*

earth to himself (12:32–34). Through his bloody sacrifice on the cross, the literal placarding of an condemned criminal for a public spectacle, God propitiates his wrath and moves to justify ungodly people (Rom 3:25; 1 John 4:10). Though his visage is marred beyond recognition so that people turn their faces away from the horrific sight (Isa 52:14; 53:3), sinners in need of forgiveness are drawn to look and live at one whose humiliation invites the Father's vindication (John 3:14–15; 8:28; Phil 2:5–11).

6. *Those who place their faith in Jesus no longer walk in spiritual darkness, but walk as sons of light along the path illumined by the light of the world* (12:35–36a; cf. John 8:12; 9:5; 12:46). This is the path of unbroken communion with the Father and the Son secured by the continuous cleansing provided by the blood of Jesus (1 John 1:3, 7).

7. *The claims of Jesus Christ divide people into two mutually exclusive categories—those who refuse to believe face the judgment of God the Father; everyone who believes and obeys receives eternal life* (12:36b–50). The persistent unbelief of the Jewish religious leaders and the muted voices of those sympathetic to Jesus but fearful of speaking out fulfill Isaiah's prophetic foreview of Jesus' glorious death and the response of his contemporaries (12:41). The greatest of the writing prophets predicted Israel's forfeiture of her moment of opportunity (Isa 53:1; cf. Rom 10:16) and divine hardening resulting from and further producing spiritual dullness (Isa 6:10; cf. Acts 28:25–27).

⇨ Locate in a hymnal the well-known hymn by Philip Bliss, "Man of Sorrows, What a Name!" Note how the author captures the complementary phases of humiliation and exaltation of our Lord's ministry. Sing this poem of praise to the Lord.

15

Passion Week II
Day of Controversy

Tuesday: Day of Controversy

MOUNTAIN-MOVING FAITH

(Matthew 21:19b–22; Mark 11:19–25; Luke 21:37–38)

O N MONDAY MORNING JESUS pronounced a curse upon the fig tree which, occurring the same day as the cleansing of the temple, was clearly a symbolic condemnation of the religious leadership of Israel. These leaders pretended to be fruitful tenders of the fig tree of Israel, but were actually purveyors of spiritual death.

The next morning as they retraced their steps from Bethany to Jerusalem, the disciples saw the same fig tree, now withered from the roots. How could a leafy tree become utterly barren in twenty four hours, they wondered? Their surprise was born out of failure to believe Jesus' authoritative command the day before. Rather than develop the theological meaning of the symbolism, Jesus used it as an opportunity to teach his disciples a lesson on the possibilities of faith. His following words are a command: "Have faith in God" (Mark 11:22). As his life is drawing to a close, Jesus wants his disciples to learn to exercise faith in God for themselves, rather than continue to live vicariously through his faith. He specifies several features of authentic faith. First, faith is unwavering trust in God's willingness and ability to do what is humanly impossible, like transporting a mountain from here to there (Mark 11:23). Second, faith is expressed in concrete prayers and in the confidence that God will do the very thing that is requested of him. Jesus viewed prayer not as a subjective exercise to sanctify the attitudes of the one who prays (however much that may be true), but an objective transaction that links the request to its realization (Mark 11:24; cf. John 14:13–14; 15:7; 16:23). Third, the spirit of unforgiveness toward another person saps faith of its energy and short-circuits the power supply that connects the request to the answer (Mark 11:25). Jesus envisioned the kingdom of God being extended into the frontiers of darkness through the audacious faith of his disciples directed toward a mighty God.

⇨ Recall a recently answered prayer, no matter how seemingly trivial. Now trust him for a specific need that only he can meet, make your request to God, and anticipate his answer.

A QUESTION ABOUT AUTHORITY

(Matthew 21:23–27; Mark 11:27–33; Luke 20:1–8)

Tuesday was a long day of conflict in the temple courts. Representatives of the major religious and political parties approached Jesus, one after another, in order to best him in theological debate and to discredit him in the eyes of the excitable crowds. In each case the interchange followed the pattern of confrontation—counterquestion—consternation—cowardice. Jesus responded to the questions designed to trap him with a question for his interlocutors; they then were placed in an unenviable position and, for fear of being discredited themselves, timidly refused to pursue the conversation further. Another group would come forth and the pattern would repeat itself.

The first questioners were composed of the three factions that comprised the Sanhedrin: (i) priests of Aaronic lineage that normally belonged to the Sadducees; (ii) teachers of the law who were, with few exceptions, Pharisees; and (iii) elders, that is, influential members of aristocratic families supporting the maintenance of public order to protect the lucrative temple system. They inquired as to the basis of his "authority" to do "these things." The latter must include Jesus' bold actions of the past forty eight hours: willing acceptance of the acclamations of the multitude and the praises of children during his triumphal entry to Jerusalem; the healings of blind and lame people in the court of the Gentiles; and the cleansing of the temple. Their question is one of substance. The Jewish leaders are right to recognize that the fundamental issue which separates them from Jesus is the legitimacy of his messianic claims and actions. Authority has to do with prerogative and power. In the context of his proclamation of the kingdom of God, Jesus is asserting his right to rule and the power to effect that rule as God's exclusive vice-regent. He has demonstrated his authority to heal infirmities (Matt 9:8) and to exorcise demons (Luke 4:36). His teaching has been marked by authoritative assertions in the first person (Matt 7:28). He claims to possess the authority to forgive sins (Mark 2:10), to arbitrate judgment on the final day (John 5:27, 30), to both offer as well as take up his life again in resurrection (John 10:18), and to grant eternal life to the elect (John 17:2). The entirety of redemptive authority has been granted him by the Father and stands behind the great commission to disciple the nations (Matt 28:18-20).

In this case Jesus issues a question of his own. Was John's baptism of human or divine origin? He will answer their inquiry about his authority if they state their convictions about John the Baptist. This is a masterful reply which lands his cunning questioners in a dilemma. If they reply "from heaven," they will have an answer to their own question, for John testified of Jesus as the Lamb of God, the incomparable One, the Messiah (Matt 3:11–12; John 1:19–36; 3:27–30). If they answer "from man," they fear alienating the multitudes who esteem John as a true prophet from God. So they refuse to commit themselves by feigning ignorance: "We do not know (where it was from)." They refuse to voice their true beliefs—John is a false prophet and Jesus is a messianic pretender—but weigh the outcome of alternative answers. Equivocation trumps conviction. They are calculating politicians rather than caring shepherds of the flock of Israel. The rejection of revelation previously given disqualifies them from receiving more. If the leaders cannot tolerate the lesser light of John, the greater light of Jesus will only blind them. Jesus sees no reason to issue a reply to a question his opponents have already answered in their minds and to which he has already given abundant reply through his claims and actions.

⇨ In commending Christ to people in an age of religious pluralism as well as moral relativism, why is it so important to keep the focus on the authority of Christ as Lord?

PARABLES ABOUT MEMBERSHIP IN THE KINGDOM COMMUNITY

(Matthew 21:28—22:14; Mark 12:1-12; Luke 20:9-19)

Before the next delegation of questioners arrived, Jesus issued three parables about the kingdom of God (Matt 21:31, 43; 22:1). The first two parables conclude with a rebuke for the legal scholars (Pharisees) and the influential priests (Sadducees).

1. *Parable of the two sons* (Matt 21:28–32)

   (i) *Parable proper*: A Father has two sons who are both commanded to go and work in the vineyard. The first son initially refuses but then changes his mind and goes to work; the second son agrees to go but does not follow through.

   (ii) *Probing question and answer*: Which of the two sons did his father's will? The first son (21:31a).

   (iii) *Interpretation*: The tax collectors and prostitutes "go into the kingdom of God before you" (21:31b). The first son symbolizes the unsavory classes of people who openly break God's commands and violate his character but then repent and prove their repentance by obedience. The second son represents the religious leaders who profess obedience but whose external morality masks a self-righteousness that sees no need for repentance.

   (iv) *Rebuke*: In line with the controversy that precedes these parables, Jesus affirms his solidarity with John who proclaimed repentance as a precondition for entering the kingdom of God (Matt 3:2) and demanded that such repentance be proved by a changed life (Matt 3:8–10). John prepared the people for the transformative "way of righteousness" (21:32) without which no one can enter the kingdom (Matt 5:20).

2. *Parable of the tenant farmers* (Matt 21:33–46; Mark 12:1–12; Luke 20:9–19)

   (i) *Parable proper*: A landowner plants a vineyard. He digs a winepress to crush and preserve the juice from the grapes. He surrounds the press with a wall to keep out animals and fortifies it with a watchtower to protect from thieves and fire. The owner then rents it out to tenant farmers who are to tend the vineyard and return to the owner a portion of the produce. At harvest time the owner sends some servants to collect his fruit, but the tenants beat, kill and stone successive delegations of servants. Finally, the owner determines to send his son, reasoning that they would not dare treat the stipulated heir of the estate the way they have treated his servants. But the tenants conspire against the son-heir, reckoning that by killing him they can seize the inheritance for themselves. They kill the heir and cast his body outside of the vineyard in an act of open defiance.

(ii) *Probing question and answer*: When the owner of the vineyard returns from his journey, what will he do to these tenants? He will summarily execute them and rent the vineyard out to "other tenants" who will provide him with his rightful share of the crop at harvest time (Matt 21:41).

(iii) *Interpretation*: Jesus quotes Psalm 118:22–23 and applies it to himself. The stone that has been rejected by the builders has become the cornerstone or "head of the corner," the anchor stone of a city wall or the top stone of a door or arch. The one rejected by his own people will be vindicated by God, whose reversal of man's estimation is marvelous to those who receive him. God is the owner, Israel the vineyard (Isa 5:1–7; Ps 80:8–16), the tenants the designated custodians of Israel's religious life centered in the Sanhedrin, the servants the Old Testament prophets, and Jesus the Son-Heir. The "other tenants" who believe and replace the original tenants are repentant people like the "tax collectors and harlots" of the first parable and include Gentiles.

(iv) *Rebuke*: The kingdom is to be "taken away from you" and given to a people that produce fruit that attests to the authenticity of their repentance (Matt 21:43). Here is the displacement of the religious leaders and the nation held captive to their binding ceremonialism. They end up being crushed by the capstone, as if it were not securely fastened, is shaken from its moorings, and comes crashing down upon their heads. The Pharisees and Sadducees immediately knew the first two parables were directed against them. For the moment they restrain their desires to move against Jesus because they fear the multitudes who esteem him, like John, to be a true prophet of God (Matt 21:46; cf. Matt 21:11, 26).

5. *Parable of the wedding banquet* (Matt 22:1–14)

  (i) *Parable proper:* The story is meant to illustrate truth(s) about the kingdom of the heavens (22:1), just like the parables that precede it (Matt 21:31, 43). A king gives a wedding feast for his son, which in the Jewish context took place on the day when the marriage was contracted before the evening of the consummation. After invitations have been issued to a select number of guests, the king sends his servants to inform those invited that the feast is ready and he desires their presence. But the original invitees refuse to come, ostensibly due to other priorities. Other servants are sent and announce that a sumptuous feast has been prepared, but the intended guests either ignore the second call by attending to their private affairs or, in the case of others, mistreat and even kill the servants. The king is enraged and dispatches his army to destroy the murderers and burn their city.

  The King is determined to have the banquet hall full for his son's wedding. So servants are once again sent, this time with orders to search the streets and invite any and all who are willing to come. This produces a wedding hall filled with guests, "both bad and good" (22:10). When the king arrives to greet his guests, he discovers one man not dressed in wedding clothes. This man is speechless when asked how he gained entrance without the proper attire. At the king's order the man is seized, bound hand and foot, and cast outside into the darkness where there is sorrow (weeping) and horrific pain (gnashing of teeth).

  (ii) *Lesson:* The meaning of the story is captured in the brief aphorism that follows: "For many are called, but few are chosen" (22:14). The King is God the Father and the wedding banquet represents the dawning of the kingdom of his Son, Jesus Messiah (Matt 8:11; 9:15; 25:1; John 3:29), who is calling his new covenant people, his bride, into an eternal, redemptive relationship with himself. The leaders and people of Israel have refused the invitation to submit to the rule of the King, some with indifference and others with determined opposition. Severe retributive judgment awaits those who reject the Son. The wedding garment symbolizes the righteousness with which one must be clothed to enter the kingdom (Matt 5:20; 21:32). The Father's elect people are those who heed the invitation to come and surrender to the authority of King Jesus. The related parable of the great banquet (Luke 14:15–24) places emphasis on the universal range of the invitation—the original invitees are displaced and the opportunity is extended to all who are willing. In this parable the focus shifts from the range of those invited to the norms required of those who wish to have a seat at the table.

⇨ What governing motif binds these three parables together in their exposition of the character of God's kingdom? Remember to locate these parables in the midst of a series of delegations of the Jewish religious leadership who come to inquire of Jesus on this long day of controversy.

LOYALTY TO CAESAR AND TO GOD

(Matthew 22:15–22; Mark 12:13–17; Luke 20:20–26)

A delegation of Pharisees and Herodians approached Jesus. The Herodians were a political party that supported the restoration of the dynasty of Herod the Great, one which would include the elevation of Antipas to the former rule of his father. They would have had some affinity with liberal-minded Pharisees whose vested interests were bound up with preserving the status quo of limited Jewish autonomy under Roman rule (Mark 3:6). The intent of their questioning was to trap Jesus into voicing anti-Roman sentiments which they could file against him in the court of the governor (Luke 20:20). Their initial words of praise for his integrity and piety are insincere flattery designed to weaken his defenses in order to catch him off guard.

Their question centered on taxes and loyalty: Is it right, for law-abiding Jews, to pay taxes to Caesar or not? They frame the question as to demand a yes or no answer. There were several levels of Roman taxation. The poll or head tax, based on the census, was one denarius per year paid by Jewish males aged fourteen to sixty-five. The land tax required one-tenth of the produce of the land from middle class and wealthy farmers. In addition, there were sales taxes. These direct forms of taxation were tribute taxes required by the Roman government and were a grating symbol of Jewish submission to their Gentile overlords. There were also indirect taxes such as customs duties on transported goods. Added to the annual half-shekel tax (or didrachma, equaling two Roman denarii [Matt 17:24–27]) on Jewish adult males to support the temple sacrificial system, these various forms of taxation created a considerable financial strain. The direct taxes had to be paid in Roman currency which bore an image of the emperor's head with the inscription "Tiberius Caesar, son of the divine Augustus" on one side and "pontifex maximus" (high priest) on the other. This offended pious Jews who viewed such images as a violation of the first two commands of the Decalogue (Exod 20:3–6).

Jesus was thus placed squarely in the horns of a dilemma. He perceived the hypocrisy of his questioners. If he denies the lawfulness of such taxes, he will be accused of disloyalty, even treason, against Caesar's authority, a charge that will be falsely raised against him at his trial before the Roman governor (Luke 23:2). If he answers in the affirmative, he risks alienating the teeming crowds who felt the burden of taxation and acknowledged the offensive nature of Roman images in the Holy City. So Jesus, in characteristic fashion, responds to a question with a counterquestion: Whose portrait is inscribed on the face of the denarius? When they answer it is Caesar's, Jesus commands them to "render to Caesar the things that are Caesar's, and to God the things that are God's." Thus he sides neither with the anti-Roman zealots who are seeking to overthrow the political order, nor with those protesting Caesar's taxation system, nor with the temporizing Sanhedrin which often compromised its religious principles to please the occupying authorities. There is a domain of worship which belongs exclusively to God (Acts 4:19; 5:29); there is a socio-political order which, as long as it does not invade God's domain, should be supported by obedience and submission (Rom 13:1–7; 1 Pet 2:13–17).

Though his answer probably ended up satisfying no one entirely, Jesus refused to be co-opted by the political left (Zealots) or right (Herodians), or by the religious left (Sadducees; liberal Pharisees) or right (most Pharisees) wings of the first century spectrum of ideologies. He pointed the way for new covenant citizens to prosecute his kingdom mission free from distraction with socio-political agendas which, while restructuring governmental laws and policies, have no power to transform the interior life of a human being.

⇨ What does the dual principle of Mark 12:17 (and parallels) imply with respect to the Christian's involvement in contemporary political issues and movements?

SADDUCEES INQUIRE ABOUT THE RESURRECTION

(Matthew 22:23–33; Mark 12:18–27; Luke 20:27–40)

A third group of religious representatives took their turn to debate Jesus over what they considered to be the absurd doctrine of bodily resurrection. The Sadducees were enraged at the Nazarene who had for the second time boldly attacked their lucrative business enterprise housed in the outer court of the temple. Unlike the Pharisees, they embraced a Greek view of the afterlife which acknowledged the immortality of the soul but derided as an outmoded supernaturalism such things as angels and resurrection (Acts 23:6–8). They constructed a hypothetical situation around the Mosaic provision of Levirate marriage and then asked Jesus to solve the riddle. Jewish law stipulated that a younger brother was obligated to marry the widow of his deceased brother and to sire children who became legal heirs of the deceased (Deut 25:5–6; cf. Gen 38:8). This provided not only heirs for the deceased man but also guaranteed continuance of the family name and preserved decentralized ownership of the land along family and tribal lines. If a man died without children and each of his six brothers in succession married the widow but then died before producing offspring, whose wife would she be in the resurrection age? One can almost picture the smug countenance of the Sadducees as they waited for Jesus to embarrass himself.

Jesus exposed their limited value system which wrongly presupposed that resurrection life must be of the same kind as present earthly life with marriage relationships and physical reproduction. With their tortured reasoning the Sadducees display ignorance not only of the Old Testament's attestation of the doctrine of bodily resurrection (Job 19:25–27; Ps 16:10–11; 17:15; 49:14–15; 73:23–26; Isa 26:19; Dan 12:2), but also of God's ability to raise the dead to life. First, Jesus countered, there will be no marriage in the resurrection age, but people will be "like angels in heaven." A new order of existence that transcends gender distinctions and sexual procreation will be ushered in by God's power at the final resurrection. This anticipates Paul's more developed teaching on the nature of the resurrection body, one which will in some ways be continuous with the present physical identity but possess new and transformed properties fit for service in the eternal kingdom of God (1 Cor 15:42–44; Phil 3:20–21). Second, their own sacred text (Sadducees venerated the five books of Moses) testifies of God's power to raise the dead. The Hebrew text of Exodus 3:6 with its understood verb in the present tense (translated with the present indicative of the Greek be-verb in the Septuagint) implies the doctrine of resurrection: "I *am* the God of Abraham, the God of Isaac, and the God of Jacob." The Lord speaks of the patriarchs in the present tense to Moses at the burning bush over four hundred years after the death of Jacob. Since God is the God of the living and not of the dead, he speaks of the covenant fathers as living in his very presence in anticipation of their coming resurrection.

Not only were the crowds astonished at his teaching, but some teachers of the law praised Jesus' reply (Luke 20:39), plausibly because they were Pharisees who sided with Jesus' affirmation of angels and resurrection. The Sadducees only embarrassed themselves and would not dare approach him again until they had the upper hand at his trial (Luke 20:40).

⇨ What does the doctrine of the resurrection imply about the stewardship of one's physical body in the present life (1 Cor 6:12–20)?

SUMMATIVE COMMANDS OF THE LAW
(Matthew 22:34–40; Mark 12:28–34)

With the Sadducees silenced, the Pharisees now returned. They put forth one of their own, a trained legal scholar, to ask Jesus: "Teacher, which is the greatest commandment in the law?" (Matt 22:36 [NIV]). This was another attempt by his adversaries to discredit Jesus, though the lawyer seemed to respect Jesus and to have affinity with his answer. Sometimes the Jewish authorities disagreed among themselves about Jesus, with a minority of moderating, even sympathetic, voices of dissent (John 7:45–52; Acts 5:33–39). After reciting the Shema, Israel's confession of God's oneness (Deut 6:4), Jesus quoted the Old Testament commands to love God with the entire being and to love one's neighbor as oneself (Lev 19:18; Deut 6:5). "On these two commandments," Jesus stated, "depend all the law and the prophets" (Matt 22:40). In other words, these are the two essential commands that incorporate all other teaching into their framework to produce an integrated whole. If one does not love God and one's neighbor, then, regardless of the precise fulfillment of the ceremonial requirements, the law is being violated.

The lawyer registered his wholehearted agreement with Jesus' answer. He added that he understood and endorsed Jesus' implied elevation of the love ethic over animal sacrifices, a comparison commonly preached by the Old Testament prophets (Deut 10:12; 1 Sam 15:22; Isa 1:1–18; 43:22–24; Hos 6:6; Amos 5:21–24; Mic 6:6–8). From their position in the outer court of the temple could be heard the bleating of the sheep being sold and led off for sacrifice in the court of the priests. Jesus returned the compliment: "You are not far from the kingdom of God," a kingdom that centers not on perfor-mance but on the heart (Mark 12:34). Earlier Jesus had quoted to another expert in the law these two summative commands in order to drive home the futility of making obedience to the law the basis of one's relationship to God, for no one can fulfill these commands in their entirety (Luke 10:25–28). Was this Pharisee, like Nicodemus and Joseph of Arimathea, able to break free from the suffocating traditions and to surrender to Jesus' rule? Again, there is no recorded sequel.

⇨ Read Romans 13:8–10 and once again observe how dominical tradition (the teaching of the Lord Jesus) provides the basis for Paul's approach to Christian ethics.

DAVID'S SON AND LORD

(Matthew 22:41–46; Mark 12:35–37; Luke 20:41–44)

Now Jesus takes the offensive to question his interrogators over a matter of greater substance than paying taxes to Caesar, the character of the resurrec-tion age, or legal interpretation. The Tuesday interchanges began with the source of his authority and now end with the nature of his Sonship. He asks the teachers of the law, whose son is the Messiah? Jesus wants to expose not only their faulty interpretation of the law but their deficient Christology which is at the heart of the controversy surrounding him.

They immediately reply that Messiah is universally recognized as the Son of David. Scripture abundantly attested that the Anointed One would spring from the lineage of Israel's greatest king and restore Israel's national glory (2 Sam 7:11–16; Ps 89; Isa 11:1, 10; Jer 23:5–6). Jesus asks, how is it, then, that David addresses the Messiah as his "Lord" in Psalm 110:1: "The Lord (Heb. *Yahweh*) said to my Lord (Heb. *Adonay*), Sit at my right hand, until I put your enemies under your feet"? In this opening oracle of a Psalm understood by first century rabbis as prophesying the coming of Messiah, Yahweh invites the Messiah, called by David "my Lord," to sit at his right hand, a place of honor second only to himself. The Old Testament thus testi-fies that Messiah is more than the Son of David; he is also David's Lord. Thus the answer to his question—"Whose son is he?"—is clearly the Son of God whom the Father so identified as his beloved Son at his baptism (Matt 3:17) and at the Transfiguration (Matt 17:5). Jesus Messiah is both Davidic King and suffering Servant, Son of Man and ultimately Son of God. Jesus presses his opponents to look more carefully at their own sacred text and to recognize that Messiah is more than David's Son but also his Lord.

⇨   Psalm 110:1 was to become one of the most important Old Testament prophetic texts for the early church regarding the present position of Jesus as exalted Lord (Acts 2:32–36; 5:31; 7:55–56; Rom 8:34; Eph 1:20; Col 3:1; Heb 1:3; 8:1; 10:12; 12:2; 1 Pet 3:22). In an age when Roman emperors demanded unquestioned loyalty, and at times were worshipped as universal "Lord and God" (*Dominus et Deus*), why would this ancient text have provided so much encouragement and strength to the early Christians?

WOEFUL EFFECTS OF LEGALISM

(Matthew 23:1–36; Mark 12:38–40; Luke 20:45–47)

The long day of debate in the temple court, *Tuesday* of Passion Week, ended with the religious authorities silenced but hardened in their resolve to kill Jesus (Matt 22:46; cf. Mark 11:18). The crowds had listened with delight as Jesus confounded the educated rabbis with his answers (Mark 12:37b). As his interrogators stalked out one by one, Jesus turned to his disciples and to the crowd and issued a blistering indictment of the hollow profession that filled the corridors of religious power in Israel. The censure crystallizes the essential points of difference between Jesus and the Pharisees. Here is a violent clash of worldviews, of governing values, motives and visions of the future. While the Pharisees created a faith-works synergism, Jesus stripped away every human pretension of placing God in one's debt. Even if the scribal schools originally expounded a covenantal nomism that made obedience to the law the willing response to God's gracious election, by the time of Jesus the nomistic portion had driven its covenant partner into exile.

1.   The Pharisees and legal scholars teach the law, but do not obey it (Matt 23:2–3; cf. Matt 7:1–5; Rom 2:1, 21–24). They view themselves as Moses' successors as they sit on the stone seat of the synagogue to teach.

2.   They burden down others with their exacting demands, unlike Jesus whose burden is light and who gives rest (Matt 11:28–30). They fail to

294

live up to their own standards while showing no compassion toward others who fall short (Matt 23:4).

3. The motivation behind their piety is to gain recognition: phylacteries, long fringes, places of honor at the banquets, best seats in the synagogues, salutations in the market place, and the designation of Rabbi (Matt 23:5–7; Mark 12:38–39; Luke 20:46). Jesus would remove such hierarchical designations among his followers as Rabbi, Father and Teacher. In his kingdom all are equal as brothers, all accountable to one Master (Matt 23:8–10). In the kingdom of heaven servants who humble themselves rise above self-promoting lords (Matt 23:11–12).

4. The *seven woes* (Matt 23:13–36) are not a personal attack on individuals, but the prophetic condemnation (Isa 5:8–23; Hab 2:6–20) of a system of theology that has displaced the interior life for an exterior righteousness, because it has replaced Holy Scripture with man-made traditions.

   (i)   *Obstinacy*: The Pharisees and teachers of the law take others to hell with them by refusing to surrender allegiance to the King and by persuading others to follow their course (Matt 23:13).

   (ii)   *Misguided zeal*: They are zealous to find converts who in turn exceed even their teachers in zeal for a Torah-centric way of righteousness (Matt 23:15; cf. Acts 21:20; Rom 10:2; Gal 4:17–18).

   (iii)   *Falsehood*: They create arbitrary, self-serving distinctions to mitigate their oaths, separating life into free/secular (temple, altar) and bound/sacred (gold/gift) compartments (Matt 23:16–19). For Jesus all of life is to be lived in integrity before God. Since, then, every oath is binding, he would eliminate oath-taking altogether and replace it with the unadorned word of truth (Matt 23:20–22; cf. Matt 5:33–37).

   (iv)   *Misplaced priorities*: They are meticulous in the matter of tithing even their garden spices, but neglect the weightier matters of the law: justice, mercy and faithfulness. Scrupulousness is not condemned ("without neglecting the others"), only distorted priorities. They "strain out a gnat but swallow a camel" (NIV), that is, fuss over trivialities but overlook the essential character qualities that Scripture so forcefully expounds (Matt 23:23–24).

(v) *Moral defilement*: Great attention is given to maintaining ritual purity, while the heart is left unattended. Greed is masked behind a strict adherence to ceremonial regulations such as the proper washing of cups and dishes (Matt 23:25–26; cf. Mark 7:4).

(vi) *Deceptive appearance*: In the month of Adar, just before Passover, tombs were washed with lime to alert pilgrims to steer clear and avoid ritual defilement through incidental contact with corpses (John 11:55; 18:28). The Pharisees are "whitewashed tombs . . . full of dead people's bones," that is, they give the appearance of piety due to scrupulous maintenance of ritual laws, but are inwardly full of corruption (Matt 23:27–28).

(vii) *Defiance*: They pretend to honor the prophets and saints of old by building their tombs and decorating their graves. This only heightens the guilt of those who stand in continuity with their forefathers in persecuting those who call the nation and its leaders to repent (Matt 23:29–32). They remain defiant in their opposition to God's purposes by persecuting those sent by Jesus to proclaim the kingdom (Matt 23:33–36). They will continue to add to the venerable line of martyrs that runs in the Old Testament from Abel (Gen 4:8) to Zechariah, son of Jehoiada (2 Chr 24:20–22).

To conclude, Jesus reserved the harshest language of his earthly ministry for the Pharisees and legal scholars. He called them hypocrites (23:13, 15, 23, 25, 27, 29), blind guides (23:16, 19, 24, 26), sons of hell (23:15), murderers (23:31), snakes and vipers (23:33; cf. Matt 3:7; 12:34). The seventh woe closes with a defiant, ironical imperative: "Fill up, then, the measure of (the sins of) your fathers" (Matt 23:32). Jesus denounced those in positions of influence that should have been stewards of the covenant and good shepherds of God's flock, but squandered their stewardship and led the flock astray. Jesus' catalog of the vices of legalism provides a serious admonition to new covenant leaders not to start down the path of assessing the conduct of others by extrabiblical criteria, for once one starts down that path it is almost impossible to stop.

⇨ Briefly comment how dedicated religious people, even leaders, can fall into such a perversion of priorities. How can contemporary church leaders avoid the pitfalls of hypocritical religiosity?

THIRD LAMENT OVER JERUSALEM

(Matthew 23:37–39)

The Lord's severity in the seven woes is not the fruit of a bitter spirit but the rebuke of a holy judge who longs to embrace a "disobedient and contrary people" (Rom 10:21, quot. Isa 65:21). He is conscious of his divine origin and his redemptive role as Israel's true protector, only to be rejected by "his own people" (John 1:11). Jesus repeats verbatim his sorrowful lament over the Holy City which he uttered earlier in Perea (Luke 13:34–35). He recites Jerusalem's violent history, the city symbolizing the people who inhabit her, especially the religious leaders. The city of the temple, the Davidic monarchy, sacrifices and pilgrim festivals becomes the city of the crucified Messiah. Like chicks that refuse the brooding hen's protective wings, his kinsmen reject the redemptive security he offers through his coming sacrifice (Ps 17:8; 36:7; 91:4). Because of her rejection of the Savior, the temple, city and nation will become desolate, abandoned by God to her enemies (Jer 12:7; 22:5). Even at his triumphal entry Jesus wept over a city to be destroyed by Roman armies within one generation (Luke 19:41–44). Yet Jesus looks beyond her imminent desolation to a time when Israel will cite the Hallel declaration (Ps 118:26) with true insight rather than with the hollow enthusiasm of the pilgrim crowds when he entered the city (23:39; cf. Matt 21:9).

⇨ Read 1 Thessalonians 2:14–16; Romans 9:1–5; 10:1–3; 11:25–27 and observe how Jesus' harsh denunciations, tender laments and hopeful predictions adumbrate the same themes in the writings of another lover of Israel, the Apostle Paul.

GIVING OUT OF ONE'S POVERTY

(Mark 12:41–44; Luke 21:1–4)

Toward the end of the long day of debate Jesus stood with his disciples near the temple treasury located in the court of women. They were observing the Jewish worshippers place their offerings in the thirteen trumpet-shaped receptacles. Jesus had taught his disciples to carefully guard their hearts from the allurement of material things (Matt 6:19–24). They were to trust their Heavenly Father to provide their needs (Matt 6:25–34) and to maintain a simple lifestyle and attitude of dependence on God as they engaged in kingdom ministry (Matt 10:8–10; Luke 10:3–4). They should not envy the rich person, for all the money in the world could not redeem the soul (Matt 16:26; Mark 8:36–37; Luke 9:25). His instruction about the dangers of covetousness had become a point of emphasis during the winter months leading to his final trip to Jerusalem (Luke 12:13–34; 16:1–13; 18:18–30).

Now as they watched the worshippers drop their coins in the offering boxes, Jesus called his disciples' attention to a poor widow. While the rich people threw in numerous coins "out of their abundance," this widow offered two lepta, the smallest coin in circulation in Palestine. Two lepta equaled one kodrantes which totaled 1/64 of a denarius, which was one day's wage for a laborer in the first century (Matt 20:2). Her offering was thus worth very little in terms of purchasing power. For the widow, however, this was a large sum of money: "She out of her poverty put in all she had to live on" (Luke 21:4). Whether this was her entire weekly or monthly allowance, the widow made painful personal sacrifices to support God's temple. Others offered large gifts, but had the abundance to retain much more. Jesus drove home that it is not the amount of the gift, but the degree of sacrifice represented by that amount which is central to the divine accounting. This lesson crystallized all Jesus had taught the disciples on many occasions about money. Here was a person whose heart was released from the binding control of materialism, a temptation to poor and rich alike, and was thus free to give joyfully as an expression of worship.

⇨   Are you a sacrificial giver? What are you not able to spend on yourself that otherwise you could if, like non-believers, you did not factor in regular giving into your budget? Do not congratulate yourself, but give thanks to God for the privilege of investing in matters that outlast this life.

INTER-ADVENT AGE OF TRIBULATION AND PROCLAMATION
(Matthew 24:1—25:30; Mark 13:1–37; Luke 21:5–36)

The long day of controversy, *Tuesday* of Passion Week, strained all of the mental and spiritual faculties of the disciples. They had listened intently as an assortment of religious and political alliances sought unsuccessfully to discredit their Lord. As they departed from the outer court, the disciples called attention to the magnificence of the temple complex (Matt 24:1–2). Jesus made the shocking prediction that the temple would soon be reduced to rubble. The disciples seemed to have missed the gravity of Jesus' lament over the coming desolation of Jerusalem (Matt 23:37–39). Upon their arrival at the Mount of Olives, the disciples probed him about his ominous prediction: "When will these things be, and what will be the sign of your coming and of the close of the age?" (Matt 24:3). Matthew frames the question in two parts, which suggests a distinction between the (near) event of the temple's desolation and the (far) event of the *parousia* (second advent) and the end of time. However, in the Markan (13:4) and Lukan (21:7) parallels the two events are merged, indicating that the questioners are interested in the timing and antecedent signs of a singular composite event. The extended inquiry, then, seems to indicate that the disciples envisaged the coming of the Son of Man to occur at the same time as the desolation of the temple.

Jesus answered the question in the extended *Olivet Discourse* (Matt 24:4—25:46). The most natural way of interpreting Jesus' language, in this writer's view, is to see the near event, the destruction of Jerusalem, serving as a historical anticipation of the distant event, the return of the Son of Man at the end of the age. This bifocal or bicameral approach, whereby the prophet views a distant event through the descriptive lens of a near event, is a common feature of Old Testament prophecy. The discourse expresses a preterist-futurist polarity. First, the present inter-advent age is previewed in Matthew 24:4-14. Second, the fall of Jerusalem is set forth in Matthew 24:15-28 with a double reference to the final stage of human history before the parousia. Third, the return of the Son of Man in glory to consummate his kingdom is described in Matthew 24:29-31. It must be remembered that this is a private discourse given to Jesus' closest followers to instruct them on what to expect in the days ahead as they carry out their mission to be heralds of his kingdom.

1. Antecedent signs will take place to indicate the end is near but not yet (Matt 24:4-8). These are *"the beginning of the birth pains"* (v. 8), an Old Testament expression for the period of travail or distress for God's people that precedes the arrival of the messianic kingdom (Isa 13:8; 26:17; Jer 4:31; 6:24; Mic 4:9-10). These doctrinal, political, and natural disturbances will extend through the entire inter-advent age and be accompanied by intense periods of persecution for the kingdom witnesses (Matt 24:9-14).

    (i) False Christs that deceive many (24:4-5)

    (ii) Wars and rumors of wars; conflicts between nations (24:6-7a)

(iii) Famines; earthquakes (24:7b)

(iv) Many levels of persecution and adversity: arrest, martyrdom, betrayal by apostates, deception of many by false teachers, increase of wickedness, cold orthodoxy (24:9–12). The tribulations serve to sift true believers, whose faith is evidenced by perseverance, from false professors (24:13).

(v) In the context of persecution the gospel of the kingdom is proclaimed to all the nations of the world (24:14). This redemptive mission to the Gentile nations is a recurrent theme in Matthew's Gospel (1:1; 2:1–12; 3:9; 4:15–16; 8:11–12; 10:18; 12:18, 21; 21:43; 24:14; 28:19–20).

2. Daniel's *"abomination of desolation"* (Matt 24:15; cf. Dan 8:13; 9:27; 11:31; 12:11) was initially fulfilled when Antiochus Ephiphanes in 168 BC erected an altar to Zeus Olympius in the temple courtyard in place of the brazen altar of burnt offering (1 Macc 1:45–54; 2 Macc 6:2). However, the language of Matthew 24:16–20 and especially Luke 21:20–24 seems to describe the coming destruction of Jerusalem when it will be surrounded by armies and the inhabitants put to the sword. The horror and savagery of the siege of Jerusalem is described in very similar terms in Josephus (*War of the Jews*, V: X: 1–5). A still further realization in the multi-stage fulfillment of Daniel's prophecy will take place in the *"great tribulation"* at the denouement of human history (Matt 24:21). This will be a time of unprecedented suffering for the people of God and of the deceptive work of the Antichrist (Matt 24:22–24). The *"times of the Gentiles"* (Luke 21:24) may refer to the entire period between the first and second advents of Christ in which the church fulfills her mission to proclaim the gospel to the nations. This period of proclamation will end at the return of the Son of Man.

3. After the sustained persecution of the present age, including both preliminary and final tribulations (Matt 24:9, 21, 29), the *Son of Man* will return to earth in a glorious display of salvation and judgment (Matt 24:30). Like the flashing of lightning across the sky or the gathering of vultures around a carcass (Matt 24:27–28), the event will be clearly recognizable. Cosmic disturbances will signal his return (Matt 24:29). Those who have rejected the offer of the kingdom will mourn in despair over their judgment (Matt 24:30). Angels will be sent to the four

corners of the earth to gather the elect for their places in the consummated kingdom (Matt 24:31).

4. The heralds of the kingdom, then, must carry out their mission with urgency as they strain toward the final day of accountability. Though they should be sensitive to the antecedent signs that presage the Son of Man's return and their own redemption (Luke 21:28), believers must remember that the events of the end time could unfold very rapidly (Matt 24:32–35). God the Father alone knows the exact time of the Lord's return (Matt 24:36). In the midst of the normal activities of life, which continue unabated until "*the end*" (Matt 24:6, 14), believers are to live responsibly, compassionately, courageously, and expectantly during the Lord's absence (Matt 24:37–42). The five parables that follow are a summons to vigilance and faithfulness in the intervening time of delay:

    (i)   *Absent master and entrusted servants* (Mark 13:33–37; Luke 21:34–36): Like servants who faithfully carry out their assigned tasks while the master is away, ready and not caught off guard when he returns.

    (ii) *Homeowner and thief* (Matt 24:43–44): Like the homeowner who keeps watch and thus prevents his house from being plunderd by a thief.

    (iii) *Good and wicked servants* (Mattt 24:45–51): Like the wise and faithful steward who being placed in charge of his master's household carefully carries out his duties and is entrusted with even greater stewardship at the master's return.

    (iv) *Ten virgins* (Matt 25:1–13): Like five wise bridesmaids who are prepared for delay, but also ready when the bridegroom suddenly summons them to meet and accompany him in the procession to the marriage feast.

    (v)   *Talents* (Matt 25:14–30): Like the good and faithful servants who take the talents entrusted to them and invest and multiply them for the benefit of their master.

⇨   How does this extended discourse serve as both a reality check, as well as a source of encouragement, to his disciples as they approach the end of Christ's earthly ministry? What warning is there here against

301

all attempts, so common in subsequent church history (1 Thess 5:1), to determine precisely the timing of the Lord's return?

ESCHATOLOGICAL SIFTING OF THE HUMAN RACE
(Matthew 25:31–46)

Jesus concluded the Olivet Discourse by impressing upon the disciples the gravity of the commission to be heralds of the rule of God. The authoritative proclamation of the kingdom binds for judgment or releases for salvation the listeners according to their heart response (Matt 16:19; 18:18). At the Son of Man's glorious return to establish his reign over the universe, his first act is one of judgment. All the nations of the earth are gathered before him and individuals are separated into two groups. The sheep of the flock represent his beloved children who once were lost sheep, have been found by the good shepherd, and have gone out among wolves to testify of his grace (Matt 9:36; 10:16; 18:12–14; 26:31). The goats are a symbol of those outside the redeemed community who have refused to submit to God's lordship over their lives. The King first addresses the sheep on the right, then the goats on the left. He recalls the good works of the former, who are surprised at their mention ("When did we . . . ?"). The King views the good deeds as directed toward him because of his solidarity with "these my brothers" who were visited in prison, fed, given water, and clothed. The good works of the redeemed ones, then, are evidential of their faith and loyalty to the King and also instrumental in promoting the kingdom. Those on the left, conversely, are equally surprised at their rebuke ("When did we not . . . ?"), which indicates a failure to recognize their need for repentance, the first condition for kingdom entrance. In the context of the discourse, the "least of these my brothers" (25:40, 45) must refer to Jesus' disciples who go forth to proclaim the kingdom at great personal sacrifice (Matt 12:48–50; 23:8; 28:10). In prosecuting their mission they are imprisoned, become hungry and thirsty, become ill, and are at times without warm clothing. The good deeds done to Jesus' faithful brothers show that the benefactors are equally loyal to the elder Brother. There is a final separation of the sheep from the goats. The former are invited to inherit the kingdom, while the latter are banished to eternal punishment.

⇨ Observe how the senders and the goers share together in the rewards of kingdom ministry. Where do you fit into this worldwide missionary enterprise? Assess how you are investing your time, talents, and treasures in the great mandate to disciple the nations in preparation for Jesus' return.

16

Passion Week III

Day of Consecration

Wednesday: Day of Conspiracy

THE SANHEDRIN FINDS AN ACCOMPLICE

(Matthew 26:1–5, 14–16; Mark 14:1–2, 10–11; Luke 22:1–6)

A T THE END OF the Olivet Discourse, two days before Passover which began with the slaughter of the lamb on Thursday afternoon, the Lord made the fifth direct prediction of his coming death (Matt 26:2; cf. Matt 16:21; 17:22–23; 20:18–19; Luke 17:25). *Wednesday* was a day of hidden developments, in contrast to the long day of debate and discourse on Tuesday and the activities surrounding the Passover meal on Thursday. On Sunday, Monday, Tuesday and Wednesday evenings the Lord left Jerusalem to spend the night at the home of his friends in Bethany, on the southeastern foot of the Mount of Olives, returning each morning to the temple to teach (Luke 21:37–38). Among the boisterous crowds were "people" sympathetic to Jesus (Matt 26:5), mostly pilgrims from Galilee, which prevented the religious leaders from moving against him. They were prepared to delay their plans until after the Feast of Unleavened Bread when the crowds had dispersed. The leaders had long deliberated killing Jesus since the early days of his Galilean ministry (John 5:18; 7:1, 25; 8:37, 40, 59; 10:31, 39). The resurrection of Lazarus was a catalytic event that brought the High Priest, Caiaphas, to a firm resolution that this messianic pretender had to be eliminated (John 11:53; 12:10–11). That resolve was strengthened by Jesus' renewed attack on the lucrative sale of sacrificial animals in the court of the Gentiles on Monday of Passion Week (Luke 19:47–48).

Caiaphas and the members of the Sanhedrin changed their minds and decided to act quickly against Jesus when one of Jesus' own disciples became a collaborator. Suddenly on *Wednesday* Judas Iscariot showed up in the temple chambers and offered the chief priests, supported by the officers of the temple guard, to betray Jesus for money. Much speculation has surrounded Judas' actions. The Synoptic Gospels record greed as his driving motive, which fits John's earlier record of Judas as a thief who pilfered the collections given to support Jesus' ministry (John 12:6). Judging by the deep remorse that led to his suicide, Judas was no doubt shocked that his actions would trigger Jesus' condemnation for a capital crime in a Jewish court (Matt 27:3–10). Perhaps he was seeking to force Jesus' hand and assume the kind of national messianic identity which he had envisioned all along. Whatever the reason, Judas's was a deliberate, premeditated, Satan-inspired (Luke 22:3; Jn 13:2, 27) act of betrayal for which he bears individual guilt. For the next two days he "watched for an opportunity" (NIV) to betray Jesus at a secret time and in a location away from the crowd, ultimately leading the authorities to Gethsemane where he would identify the Lord with a greeting and a kiss (Matt 27:47–49). Yet in the foreordained purposes of God an act of incalculable evil brought about the demise of one whose sacrificial death would accomplish the redemption of the world (Acts 2:23).

⇨ How is it that one so close to Jesus for over three years, observing firsthand his miracles and listening to his teaching, could continue to entertain doubts and, at the moment of crisis, hand him over to his avowed enemies? How would you distinguish Judas's act of betrayal from Peter's denials?

Thursday: Day of Consecration

PREPARATIONS FOR THE PASSOVER MEAL
(Matthew 26:17–19; Mark 14:12–16; Luke 22:7–13)

The Passover meal and subsequent seven day Feast of Unleavened Bread was the first commemorative season in the sacred calendar of Israel (the secular calendar began in the Fall). The original setting is described in Exodus 12:1–11 and its legislation in Leviticus 23:4–8. On the tenth day of the first month, Nisan, each household selected a lamb. Late afternoon of *Nisan 14*

(*Thursday*) the lamb was slaughtered by the priest in the inner temple court and its blood poured out at the foot of the altar of burnt offering on which was burned the fat of the lamb. Each household gathered after sunset, now technically *Nisan 15* (Jewish calendar reckoned dates from sunset to sunset), to eat the Passover meal consisting of roasted lamb, bitter herbs and bread made without yeast. The lamb recalled the redemption of the covenant nation from slavery in Egypt when the blood of the lamb sprinkled on the tops and sides of the doorframes protected the Israelites from the avenging angel. The bitter herbs reminded Jews of the bitter years of bondage their forefathers endured (Exod 1:14); the unleavened bread symbolized the haste with which that generation was forced to leave Egypt (Exod 12:11, 39). Jesus deliberately chose this season, "my appointed time" (Matt 26:18 [NIV]), to fulfill his saving mission which now entered its culminative stage with a meal centering on these evocative symbols. At the heart of this event is the lesson of redemption from bondage through the blood of the lamb. All of these provisional sacrifices of the Old Testament era anticipate a final, efficacious offering that delivers people from the bondage of sin through the payment of a ransom, the blood of Christ (Heb 9:22–28). John the Baptist identified Jesus as the Lamb of God who takes away the sins of the world (John 1:29, 36). Jesus interprets the death of the Son of Man as a substitutionary payment to emancipate people from sin's bondage (Matt 20:28). Paul states that "Christ, our Passover lamb, has been sacrificed" (1 Cor 5:7).

Two disciples, Peter and John, are sent ahead on Thursday morning to make arrangements for the Passover meal that evening. Fairly elaborate preparations were required: four cups of wine were served at intervals during the extended meal of lamb, vegetables cooked in bitter herbs, and unleavened bread. The disciples secured a spacious upper room in the home of a friend of their Teacher, led there providentially by a man carrying a water jar. Some hold that this was the house of John Mark, in which the upper room later served as a gathering place of the early believers (Acts 12:12). Just as with the securing of a colt for the triumphal entry (Mark 11:2–6), so with the details of the Passover setting, Jesus has made advanced preparations which unfold "just as he had told them" (Mark 14:16).

Climbing the stone steps to the second floor guest room, a visitor would notice thirteen pairs of sandals neatly arranged near the entrance, a water-pot, basin, pitcher, towel, the Passover meal on a low table, a vessel of wine and a loaf of unleavened bread. At sunset, now Nisan 15, thirteen barefooted men were reclining around the table, eating with one hand while resting on the other arm, their feet extended away from the table. Jesus was at the center of the U-shaped arrangement with John on his immediate right and Judas Iscariot on his left. Peter was evidently next to John.

COMMENCEMENT OF THE MEAL AND A SYMBOLIC ACT OF WASHING
(Matthew 26:20; Mark 14:17; Luke 22:14–16; John 13:1–20)

Jesus speaks of this final meal with his disciples as a harbinger of the messianic feast he will enjoy with them in the consummated kingdom, while directly predicting his imminent Passion for at least the sixth time (Luke 22:15–16; cf. Matt 16:21; 17:22–23; Luke 17:25; Matt 20:18–19; 26:2). He has poured out his love to his disciples over the past three years and now is moving to complete his appointed work by his redemptive death (John 17:4; 19:30). No greater love than this could he show to his friends than laying down his life for them (John 15:13). Having loved them, he would love them to the end of his earthly life and to the fullest extent (John 13:1). The Satan-inspired betrayal by Judas Iscariot was already set in motion (John 13:2). Fully aware that the fulfillment of the Father's earthly mission for him was rapidly drawing near (John 13:3), Jesus bequeathed to his closest followers one final visual lesson. Without saying a word, Jesus would inscribe indelibly on their memories the significance of all of the previous verbal lessons about servanthood (Matt 18:1–4; 19:13–14; 20:25–28). Jesus rose from supper, removed his outer tunic, wrapped himself with a towel, filled the basin with water, and began to wash his disciples' feet one by one, drying them with the towel.

Peter represented the other embarrassed disciples when he attempted to dissuade the Lord from such a menial act of cleansing his dirty feet. He once again assumed the foolish station of issuing a negative command to his Lord: "You shall never wash my feet" (John 13:8a; cf. Matt 16:22). And as before, Jesus responded to the well-intentioned but misguided words of Peter with a sound retort: "If I do not wash you, you have no share with me" (John 13:8b; cf. Matt 16:23). Jesus' explanation that followed indicates that the portion Peter would forfeit by refusing to have his feet washed was not his saving connection to Jesus, but the joy of unbroken fellowship. Peter was driven by emotion and shifted from refusal of the foot washing one moment to a request for an entire bathing of his body the next. Jesus said that those who have been bathed all over, an anticipatory reference to the forgiveness of sins through his coming death, only need to have their feet washed, symbolizing removal of defilement from contact with the world. All of the disciples, save Judas, were receiving an essential lesson for successful Christian living and leadership: when sinful thoughts and actions arise, and arise they will, regular confession would bring cleansing and restore their joyful experience of fellowship with God (John 13:9–10a; cf. 1 John 1:9—2:2).

After he completed washing the twenty-four dirty feet, the Lord returned to his place at the table and pressed the disciples for the meaning of his action. He made the application clear through a greater to lesser argument: If I have done this to you, how much more should you do this for one another (John 13:12–14). Jesus, rightly elevated as Teacher and Lord and Sender, set his disciples an example by serving them so that they, mere students and servants and messengers, might prove their identification with him by serving one another. Deliberate choices to give preference to others above themselves, followed up by menial acts of service, will demonstrate that they have submitted to the rule of the Servant-King. Pursuit of privileged positions which seal them off from the discomforts that always attend the servant's task, will place them in a role "greater" than their Lord, and disqualify them from becoming leaders enfolded by the divine benediction (John 13:16–17).

⇨ Are you in need of cleansing from defilement in thought, word or action? Draw on the promise of 1 John 1:9: humbly acknowledge your sins and receive God's cleansing from "all unrighteousness."

IDENTIFYING THE BETRAYER
(Matthew 26:21–25; Mark 14:18–21; Luke 22:21–23; John 13:21–30)

The religious leaders planned Jesus' death on Wednesday, the day of conspiracy, led by Caiaphas who was the prime agent in the plot (Matt 26:1–5). Judas had earlier feigned concern for the poor at Jesus' expensive anointing by Mary (John 12:4–6). Though restrained by the crowds in Jerusalem, many of whom were sympathetic to Jesus, the chief priests decided to move quickly when Judas offered to become their collaborator, motivated solely by greed (Matt 26:14–16). During his foot washing action, Jesus predicted Judas' betrayal in fulfillment of Psalm 41:9 (John 13:10b–11, 18–20). Luke and John detect that Satan is behind the betrayal by Judas (Luke 22:3; John 13:2, 27).

Now as the Lord returns to the table to resume the Passover meal with his disciples, he boldly predicts his imminent betrayal by "one of you." The disciples are puzzled and shocked. One after another they nervously dismiss the suggestion, "Surely (it is) not I, (is it) Lord?" (Matt 26:22 [NIV]). John, reclining closest to Jesus on his right, whispered at the insistence of Peter, "Lord, who is it?" (John 13:23–25). The Lord responded with an affirmative when Judas asks the same question as the other disciples, though addressing Jesus as Rabbi not Lord: "You have said so (and it is true)" (Matt 26:25). Judas is signaled as the betrayer when he receives from Jesus' hand a piece of bread dipped in the dish of vegetables and fruit. This identification probably took place after Jesus uttered the words from Psalm 41: 9: "He who ate my bread has lifted his heel against me" (John 13:18). Even as King David was betrayed by a trusted and honored friend who shared the delights of the royal table, so the greater Son of David was delivered over to his adversaries by one in his inner circle who shared the common dish.

Jesus ordered Judas to expedite his plans—"What you are going to do, do quickly" (John 13:27). Having received the bread and the command, Judas immediately departed the upper room. The significance of the unfolding event once again escaped the obtuse disciples and like many other developments surrounding his Passion would only be cleared up with the resurrection (John 13:28; cf. Mark 9:32; Luke 2:50; 9:45; 18:34; John 2:22; 12:16). The hour was now late, approaching midnight, since the festivities had begun in early evening (Matt 26:20; John 13:30b).

The act of betrayal is seen as a complex providential event where human responsibility intersects divine sovereignty (Acts 2:23). On the one hand, Jesus interprets Judas' action as furthering the prophetic fulfillment of the divine plan recorded in Holy Scripture, most graphically in the typology of the paschal lamb whose redemptive sacrifice is celebrated in the Passover meal (Exod 12:21–23), and/or in more direct predictions such as Isaiah 53:7–9 and Daniel 9:26. Yet Judas on his part acted with volitional intent and, opening himself up to Satan's influence, deliberately chose a course of evil for which he was culpable. Jesus pronounces special woe upon one whose action of incalculable evil invites judgment far more severe than his self-induced physical death (Matt 26:24).

⇨ How is it possible that one so close to Jesus, having witnessed firsthand his majesty and miracles over a prolonged period, could turn against

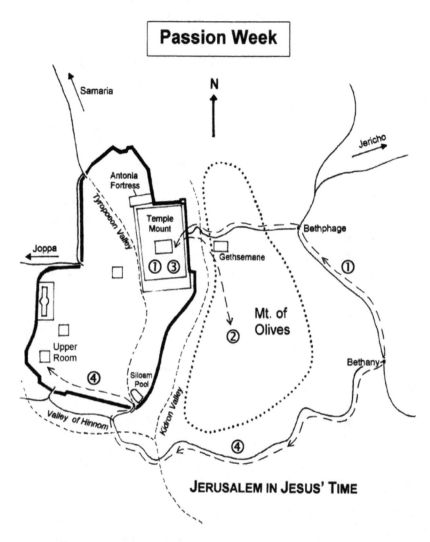

Tuesday	Debate in Temple Courts	1. **Bethany** to **Temple**
	Olivet Discourse	2. **Temple** to **Mt. of Olives**
Wednesday	Judas Iscariot's Betrayal Scheme	3. **Temple chambers**
Thursday	Lord's Supper & Upper Room Discourse	
		4. **Bethany** to **Upper Room**

him? Is there an implied warning for professing believers in the narrative of Judas' privileges, choices and destiny?

CONTRASTIVE PATTERNS OF LEADERSHIP
(Luke 22:24–30)

If one follows the order of Luke's Gospel, the argument among the disciples over who would assume the highest position in the kingdom occurred, unbelievably, after the Lord washed their feet. Luke's simple account places the dispute after the identification of the betrayer (Luke 22:21–23), which according to John took place after the foot washing and during the meal proper (John 13:18–20). It almost defies reason that the disciples could observe their Lord wash their feet and press the application to them so clearly (John 13:12–17), and then immediately engage in a fresh dispute over who would be the greatest in the coming kingdom. However, worldly ambition is not easily exorcised from the human heart and the disciples had already shown a pattern of internecine conflict over such matters (Mark 9:33; 10:13; 10:35–37, 41).

Jesus addressed the disputants by making a studied contrast ("but not so with you" [22:26]) between secular models of leadership and the posture his kingdom leaders should assume if they wish to receive the divine approbation (22:25–27).

Worldly leadership	Kingdom leadership
1. Secular rulers exercise unquestioned lordship over their subjects (22:25a; cf. Matt 8:9; Mark 10:42).	1. Kingdom leaders are willing to occupy less esteemed roles and to undertake menial tasks in order to facilitate the success of others through their service (22:26).
2. Those who exercise secular authority are given the title Benefactor, and thus bind their subjects to an obligatory relationship for favors distributed (22:25b).	2. Kingdom leadership is voluntary, free of binding obligations, and unconcerned with titles of respect. Like Jesus at the table serving the reclining disciples, the kingdom leader promotes the welfare of others over personal privilege (22:27).

The title "Benefactor" was applied throughout the Greco-Roman world to rulers and prominent persons to identify them as those whose good deeds benefit culture and contribute to the prosperity of civilization. The title brought with it respect, material prosperity, and influence over others. How antithetical this is to the designation "servant." To obey Jesus' call to servant-hood involves a radical surrender of one's natural pursuit of comfort, wealth and recognition. The leadership training program of Jesus was not to end in a specified period with graduation, credentials, and a secure vocational set-ting. The disciples were thus feeling the weight of their sacrifices (Matt 19:27). Though these aspiring leaders deserved a sound rebuke for such shocking insensitivity that they could engage in intramural disputes right after the Lord washed their dirty feet, Jesus ended by affirming their sacrifices (22:28) and promising them special roles in the coming kingdom (22:29–30). When the present rule of God assumes its universal and uncontested realm, the disciples will take their place at the table of the messianic feast (Matt 26:29; Mark 14:27; Luke 13:29; 22:18) and sit on thrones as participants in Messiah's reign over Israel and the nations (Matt 19:28; 1 Cor 6:2; 2 Tim 2:12a; Rev 20:4). The path to promotion, then, is the way of the servant both for Jesus and for his followers.

Jesus twice warned his disciples not to build their philosophy of leader-ship around the secular models of the day: "But not so with you" (22:26; cf. Mark 10:43). Secular leaders operated on the basis of unquestioned, and often arbitrary, exercise of power over their subjects, binding obligations, and titles of respect. Leadership positions were invested with power, prestige and perquisites. The New Testament vignettes of such first century leaders as Herod the Great, Antipas, Pilate, Agrippa I, Felix, Festus and Agrippa II reveal patterns of paranoia, manipulation, unjust use of power, political maneuvering, megalomania, bribery, self-aggrandizement, vanity and indul-gence (Matt 2:1–8, 16–18; 14:1–12; 27:11–26; Luke 13:31–32; 23:6–12; Acts 12:19b–23; 24:24–27; 25:23; 26:24–32). That the disciples repeatedly bick-ered over places of prominence in the coming kingdom proves they were imitating those models with which they were familiar. All aspiring kingdom leaders should pause to remember Jesus' words when they encounter the latest proposal in leadership theory: "But not so with you."

⇨ Is this a continuing problem in the church today, namely, that secular models of leadership sometimes displace biblical ones? What steps can leaders, and their congregations, do to ensure that servanthood remains the prevailing ethos of church management?

GLORY AND LOVE

(John 13:31–36)

The Son of Man is the suffering Servant who will one day be crowned King of the universe. His impending death on the cross, a vile method of executing a capital criminal, is paradoxically the glorification of the Father and the Son (13:31; cf. John 12:23, 28). Glory is manifested majesty, that is, the hidden essential character of someone displayed for all to see and embrace. The cross of Jesus reveals God to be light and love (1 John 1:5; 4:16). At the cross God's "steadfast love and faithfulness meet; righteousness and peace kiss each other" (Ps 85:10). His holiness which requires judgment of human beings who have blatantly violated his character is satisfied in the sacrifice of his Son. God is displayed as holy love. Jesus looks beyond death to his glorification when the Father will vindicate the work of his Son and restore him to the glory of communion in the blessedness of the Trinity (13:32; cf. John 7:39). Peter and the disciples cannot bear the thought of Jesus' departure, but must endure the providential delay before following Christ to his intended destination. This is the promise of paradise for those who accept his death on their behalf (13:33, 36). In the meantime Jesus' disciples are issued a "new commandment"—to love one another. Love of neighbor was the ancient governing mandate for Israel (Lev 19:18). The newness, then, must reside in the quality and paradigm of this love, captured in the comparative clause, "just as I have loved you." Jesus' self-giving, sacrificial love demonstrated on the cross is the pattern of life for the new covenant community (13:34). This cruciform life of love among believers possesses the power to arrest the attention of the world and draw them into the fellowship of the Son (13:35; cf. John 17:23).

⇨ Construct a simple definition of "love" in its biblical sense and contrast it with the way love is understood in contemporary culture.

PREDICTING PETER'S DENIALS

(Matthew 26:31–35; Mark 14:27–31; Luke 22:31–38; John 13:37–38)

The exposition of glory and love is sandwiched between predictions of betrayal and now denial. Luke and John record the first prediction given in the upper room, while Matthew and Mark record a second prediction of denial after the group's arrival on the Mount of Olives (Matt 26:30; Mark 14:26).

Before leaving the upper room Jesus addresses Peter: "Satan demanded to have you (pl.) that he might sift you (pl.) like wheat, but I have prayed for you (sg.) that your (sg.) faith may not fail. And when you (sg.) have turned again, strengthen your (sg.) brothers" (Luke 22:31–32). Satan's attempt to undermine the faith of the eleven will not succeed. Jesus' intercession will, in spite of Peter's coming setback, prevail and enable him to be the means of strengthening his faltering brothers. This promise is fulfilled when the risen Lord makes a special appearance to Peter (Luke 24:34; 1 Cor 15:5a) and later when Jesus invests Peter with a ministry of feeding his spiritual lambs (John 21:15–19). Peter's characteristic response, however, is to deny the implications of Jesus' intended meaning: "Lord, I am ready to go with you both to prison and to death" (Luke 22:33). Still stinging from the Lord's earlier rebuke (Matt 16:23), he will no longer attempt to persuade his headstrong Lord that death and Messiahship are irreconcilable concepts. Peter's thought of suffering here is one of martyrdom like the Old Testament prophets or Maccabean heroes of old, not the voluntary sacrifice in his Lord's mind. His assertion of willingness to follow Jesus even if it means death (John 13:37) is an unjustified confidence which will soon prove hollow. In Peter's heart is a mixture of sincere love that yearns to be with Jesus and not be separated even for a moment, and an ignorance that both overestimates his own grasp of the situation and underestimates his own capacity for cowardice. The Lord predicts that before the rooster crows in the early morning hour, Peter will deny him three times (John 13:38).

After the meal and a concluding hymn, the group will leave for the Mount of Olives. Later in the garden Jesus predicts the scattering of all of his disciples, in fulfillment of Zechariah 13:7, and anticipates his coming resurrection appearance to them in Galilee (Matt 26:31–32). Peter boldly reaffirms his claim of courage against Jesus' repeated statements to the contrary. He thinks he knows more than his Lord and is more steadfast than his brothers, of whom he concedes some might indeed be offended (Matt 26:33). The other disciples are not to be outdone as they also insist on their undying loyalty (Matt 26:35).

As his arrest and their subsequent dispersal draws near, Jesus issues a strange command to the disciples. First he reminds them of their previous missionary tours when he sent them without purse, bag or sandals and they lacked nothing (Luke 22:35; cf. Luke 9:1–6; 10:1–7). Then he signals a radical change in ministry context by commanding them to take not only a bag and purse but a sword as well. He supports the command by quoting Isaiah

53:12, which prediction of the suffering Servant's being "numbered with the transgressors" is on the verge of fulfillment (Luke 22:37). Clearly Jesus is not literally ordering his followers to arm themselves. Peter is in fact soundly rebuked when a few hours later he hacks off the ear of the high priest's servant with a sword at Jesus' arrest (Luke 22:49–51). When the disciples produce a pair of swords, he dismisses them with "Enough of this (kind of talk)" (Luke 22:38 [author's rendering]). The sword command signifies that those who are to be "innocent as doves" must also exercise the cautious wisdom of serpents (Matt 10:16). Their Lord's betrayal, arrest, trials and execution will now graphically prove that they are entering a period of titanic spiritual conflict in which all the weapons of spiritual warfare must be employed.

INSTITUTION OF THE LORD'S SUPPER

(Matthew 26:26–29; Mark 14:22–25; Luke 22:17–20; cf. 1 Cor 11:23–26)

The Passover meal itself concludes in the upper room with the Lord Jesus taking the two main elements, the bread and the wine, as symbols of his coming death, his body broken and his blood poured out "for you" (Luke 22:19–20). After the prayer of thanksgiving, the broken loaf of the unleavened bread is distributed. The disciples are commanded to take and eat the bread, which "is" his body. Then, after a second prayer of thanksgiving, the wine, which "is" his blood, is received. In both cases the be-verb means to signify, to recall, to validate the redemptive significance of his death on the cross for them. In the bread of life discourse Jesus used this same imagery to emphasize the necessity of personal faith in his sacrificial death as the means to receiving the gift of eternal life (John 6:53–58). Just as the Sinatic covenant was ratified by blood (Exod 24:4–8), so the "new covenant" prophesied by Jeremiah (31:31–34) is founded upon the vicarious sacrifice of Jesus, the blood signifying his life violently taken and willingly offered for others. The climactic promise of the new covenant, the forgiveness of sins, is the basis of the three other "better promises" of the "better covenant" (Heb 8:6).

The Apostle Paul draws on dominical tradition to remind the Corinthians of the proper motive for regular participation in the Lord's Supper (1 Cor 11:23–26). He recalls the Lukan account where partaking of the bread and wine is a "remembrance of me" (22:19). Just as the Day of Atonement (Yom Kipper) was the memorial service of the old covenant, signifying that sins had not yet been definitively atoned for in the ineffectual sacrifices of animals (Heb 10:1–4), so the Lord's Supper is the commemoration service of the new covenant. But in this case an effectual atonement has been made and on the basis of his Son's death God blots from his holy record and memory the transgressions of his people. In the Lord's Supper believers remember that God remembers their sins no more (Jer 31:34). There is not only this retrospective significance to the institution, but also a prospective one. Here Paul draws on Matthew and Mark which record the Lord's promise that some day he will once again drink with them the fruit of the vine in the kingdom of God (Matt 26:29; Mark 14:25). The Lord's Supper is thus commemorative, recalling the historical event upon which forgiveness is based (1 Cor 11:25), and proclamational, anticipating the Lord's return and the messianic banquet which will signal the consummation of salvation (1 Cor 11:26).

⇨ Has the observance of Communion or the Lord's Supper become a routine sacrament or is it still a fresh and much anticipated regular event in your church life? Paul instructs us in 1 Corinthians 11:17–34 what it means to partake of the Supper in a worthy manner, looking both backward and forward at the full-orbed provision of our Lord.

FAREWELL DISCOURSE

(John 14:1—16:33)

Otherwise known as the *Upper Room Discourse*, these are the carefully chosen final words of Jesus to his disciples as his earthly life draws to a close. In the middle of the discourse Jesus speaks of either his intent to leave or their actual departure from the upper room: "Rise, let us go from here" (14:31b). Probably it is a statement of intent rather than actual departure since John 18:1 relates their movement from Jerusalem across the Kidron Valley to the olive grove (Gethsemane) after the extended prayer of John 17. Three themes dominate this sermon: (i) the privilege of direct access of prayer to the Father through the Son (14:13–14; 15:7; 16:23–24); (ii) love as the mark of true discipleship, that is, believers impacting the world through their love-conditioned community (or common unity) (13:33–34; 15:9–17; 17:23); (iii) the coming of the Holy Spirit or Paraclete (Gk.), literally "the one called to be with/near/by" them as he mediates Jesus' undiminished presence to his people (14:16–17, 26; 15:26; 16:7). We will summarize the central tenets of each literary unit of the discourse, then expand on the multi-faceted ministry of the Spirit who actualizes in the experience of God's people the provisions of the new covenant (Jer 31:33a; Ezek 36:26–27).

1. *Jesus is the exclusive way to a personal relationship with God the Father because he is the wholly dependable One and the source of eternal life* (14:1–14). From somber predictions of betrayal and denial, the Servant now looks to the fruit of his imminent Passion (Isa 53:11). He reassures his puzzled disciples that he is returning to the Father to prepare for them permanent residences in the dwelling place of God. Some day he will return to the earth to usher the entire community of the redeemed to heaven. Jesus states in the most unequivocal language possible that one's eternal destiny depends on one's connection to him: "I am the way, and the truth, and the life. No one comes to the Father except through me" (14:6). To know him is to know the Father (14:9). All that he has spoken and accomplished has been an expression of his oneness in nature and mission with the Father. Now a new stage of salvation history is breaking forth as his death and resurrection inaugurates the new covenant. The efficacy of his redemptive death will be sealed by the Servant's exaltation to the right hand of the Father issuing in the gift of the Spirit and the release of God's saving power through believing prayer in Jesus' lordly name. The book of Acts records the beginning of the "greater works" (14:12) accomplished by the exalted Lord through his Spirit in answer to the prayers of believers as they proclaim the saving rule of God to the nations of the earth.

2. *The supreme gift of the new covenant era is the Paraclete, the Spirit of truth, who will take up permanent residence in the hearts of believers* (14:15–31). This is the fulfillment of Jeremiah's promised internalization of God's law (31:33a), which Ezekiel specifies as the internal presence of God's Spirit enabling a life of obedience to God's commands (36:26–27). Believers are thus not "orphans" abandoned to battle the lingering powers of the old order alone. Jesus' promise to return thus has a threefold fulfillment: in resurrection glory which is a harbinger of their own resurrection (14:19); in the person of the Spirit at Pentecost (14:18); and at the end of the age to consummate salvation (14:3, 28). The Spirit will empower a love-compelled obedience to Christ's teachings and provide a steadfast peace that drives out anxiety and fear from their hearts. The Spirit's coming will undergird their assurance that Jesus' majestic claims to perfectly represent the Father in his saving mission are true.

3. *Abiding communion with the Father and the Son alone can bring a life of fruitfulness both in terms of character transformation and in the mission of introducing others to the saving rule of God* (15:1–17). The vine is a common Old Testament metaphor for Israel, carefully planted by the Lord and intended for fruitfulness but finally proven to be faithless and barren (Ps 80:8–16; Isa 5:1–7; Hos 10:1). Now a fuller metaphor stresses the divine activity that ensures fruitfulness: the Father is the gardener who plants the vine; Jesus is the trustworthy vine that promises the gardener a rich harvest; believers are branches who abide in the vine and draw from its sustaining nutrients to produce much fruit. The Father increases the harvest by pruning the branches of all hindrances to their maximum fruitfulness. Abiding in the Father and in the Son is the absolute precondition for bearing fruit. Abiding brings with it effectual prayer and results in the revelation of God's glory. Fruitfulness signifies the transformation of one's character into God-likeness (15:8) and the extension of God's rule to the yet undiscipled peoples of the world (15:16). Sacrificial, self-giving love for others is the quintessential mark of true disciples. To love Jesus, that is to be his intimate friend, is to obey his commands which he has freely disclosed. The entire enterprise of knowing him and making him known springs from the divine initiative and enablement.

4. *The servants of the Servant are called to represent Father and Son in a context of determined opposition from a world that rejects God's demand for repentance* (15:18—16:4). Here is a sharp distinction between the community who bears allegiance to Jesus and "the world" which hates Father and Son and those who represent them. Hatred, that is, implacable hostility toward the majestic claims of Jesus, is the posture of the system of thought and values that dominates the minds of fallen human beings (15:18, 19, 23, 24, 25). The Lord's searching light exposes the darkness of hearts, pinpointing guilt and removing all excuses. As disciples go forth to proclaim the rule of God through Jesus Messiah with its demand for repentance and faith, they will encounter fierce persecution, even martyrdom, supported by religious justification. The treatment accorded their Master, prophesied in the law (Ps 35:19b), will transfer to the servants.

5. *The Holy Spirit effectualizes the post-Easter mission of the church by his convicting work toward the world and revelatory ministry to the apostles*

(16:5–15). In spite of intense opposition, the great missionary enterprise is not a hopeless one. The Spirit who comes from the Father convicts the world of its sin, its need for righteousness, and its certain judgment along with the condemnation of its ruling prince, the devil. The triune Godhead works in perfect solidarity to ensure the fruitfulness of the emissaries: the redemptive drama that the Father plans and superintends, the Son carries out and the Spirit applies. The truth is sourced in the Father, incarnated through the Son, and communicated without flaw to believers by the Spirit.

6. *Sorrow will overcome the disciples at the events surrounding their Lord's violent death, but such grief will turn to joy at his resurrection from the dead* (16:16–22). The disciples are puzzled when Jesus speaks paradoxically—"A little while, and you will see me no longer; and again a little while, and you will see me" (16:16). His arrest, trial and death are about to submerge them into deep sorrow, but on Sunday their grief will turn to incalculable joy as the risen Lord appears to them. Like a woman whose birth pangs are soon forgotten in the fruit of her travail, a healthy child, so their sorrow will turn to lasting joy when his resurrection validates the eternal benefits of that terrible sacrifice.

7. *Prayer to the Father in the name of the Son is to be the constant recourse of disciples in a troubling world* (16:23–33). More than a subjective exercise that transforms those who pray, Jesus' language points toward an objective transaction—"whatever you ask"—whereby God pledges to act in response to the prayers of his people. Of course, there are holy conditions behind authentic prayer: no unconfessed sin (Ps 66:18) or strained relations which demand forgiveness and reconciliation (Matt 5:23–24; 6:12; 1 Pet 3:7); pure motives that seek God's glory, not self-aggrandizement (Jas 4:3). Further, God is a loving Father who grants his children "good things" when their exact requests might be harmful to themselves and counterproductive to his saving mission (Matt 7:9–11). Nevertheless, with pure hearts attuned to enhancing God's reputation, disciples are encouraged to pray with importunity and specificity and to expect in faith the Father's gracious provision of those very needs. Jesus' return to his Father brings great assurance to believers whose prayers are in the name of his beloved and exalted Son.

⇨ Is your life governed by the priorities expounded by the Lord in his farewell message to his disciples: steadfast confidence in the exclusivity of his person and work; a heart that welcomes not obstructs the indwelling presence of the Spirit; intimate communion with Father and Son as the basis of fruit-bearing; courageous witness even when facing rejection; reliance on the Spirit's work of conviction of those who need Christ; joyful hope in the risen Lord; an engaged life of prayerful dependence?

ANOTHER PARACLETE

(John 14:16, 26; 15:26; 16:7)

Jesus sought to strip away the layers of scribal tradition and to restore the functional authority of Holy Scripture over those in training to be kingdom leaders. He showed little regard for the rabbis' scrupulous adherence to oral traditions that surrounded such practices as fasting, ritual washing, tithing, and keeping the Sabbath. Jesus' concern was that the disciples give first priority to the interior life out of which would then flow the willing obedience of a thankful heart. In this sense Jesus' ethical demands, encapsulated preeminently in the Sermon on the Mount, were far more penetrating than the most exacting standards of the rabbis, for they searched the motives, thoughts and intents of the heart behind the acts of service. Herein resides the dilemma of authentic kingdom living. How can the disciples fulfill such absolute ethics, for example, as freedom from lustful desires and love for one's sworn enemy (Matt 5:28, 44)?

In the *Upper Room Discourse*, the Lord promised his disciples an unparalleled resource that would provide such enabling grace to fulfill, provisionally if not perfectly, his searching demands. His distinctive term for the Holy Spirit was Paraclete, literally, "the one called to be beside (them)" (John 14:16, 26; 15:26; 16:7; cf. 1 John 2:1 where it is used in its historical sense of a legal advocate or defense lawyer). All of the attempts to find a dynamic equivalent of this Greek term in the English translations (Comforter, Helper, Counselor, Advocate) have failed because of its deliberately ambiguous and thus comprehensive meaning. It is best to simply transliterate the term and then pour into it the semantic content derived from each context. This is the person, the third person of the triune Godhead (Matt 28:19), who will provide every resource needed for the disciples to attain the kingdom quality of heart righteousness and to gather in the kingdom harvest of souls. He will be their counselor, comforter, strengthener, helper, teacher, and everything else that Jesus has been to them in his earthly ministry. The Spirit is "another Paraclete" to replace the one who has until now fulfilled that role (John 14:16). In fact, he will provide even more for them than Jesus has during his earthly state of humiliation, because he will mediate the presence of the now risen and exalted Lord (John 14:12–14; 16:7). It is instructive at this point to summarize Jesus' doctrine of the Spirit recorded in the Gospels.

1. *Regeneration*: Jesus told the Pharisee Nicodemus that a new birth was required to enter the kingdom of God. Nicodemus could only think of physical procreation, but Jesus spoke of being reborn of the Spirit (John 3:5, 6, 8). To be born "of water and the Spirit" (John 3:5) is a composite phrase drawn from Ezekiel 36:25–26 and means the cleansing, regenerative work accomplished by the Spirit of God in the heart of one who believes and repents (Ezek 39:29; Joel 2:28). The flesh, that is, natural human life with its limitations and transience, contains no potential for generating spiritual life, which is the precondition for entrance to God's rule. The words of Jesus offer life in the spiritual realm to those who personally appropriate them (John 6:63). The Spirit of God creates new redemptive life and becomes like "rivers of living water" that flow from within to satisfy the heart with deep assurance of forgiveness and a restored relationship with the Father (John 7:37–38; cf. 4:13–14).

2. *Baptism with the Spirit*: The settled residence of the Spirit in the hearts of believers would become a reality at the Pentecostal outpouring (John 7:39). This event is anticipated in the acted parable where Jesus breathed on the disciples and commanded them to receive the Spirit (John 20:22). John the Baptist spoke of the one who will come after him and baptize people "with the Holy Spirit and with fire" (Matt 3:11). The immediate context points toward two separate baptisms, one of regeneration for believers and one of judgment for unbelievers (Matt 3:12). The baptism of the Spirit, predicted by John, took place at Pentecost and not only brought regeneration to individual believers, but incorporated them into the new covenant community (Acts 1:4–5). Since that time when individuals or groups of individuals believe, they are baptized with the Spirit of God and incorporated into the body of Christ (Acts 11:15–16; 1 Cor 12:13). God the Father or the Lord Jesus is the baptizer and the Holy Spirit is the (personal) element in or with whom believers are baptized.

3. *Help in verbal witness*: One of the ministries of the Holy Spirit, Jesus promised, will be to provide wisdom and courage for witness in times of persecution (Matt 10:20; Mark 13:11; Luke 12:12). Jesus anticipated for his disciples, and succeeding generations of disciples, a worldwide witness to the nations that transcends the present evangelistic tours within Israel (Matt 10:23; Mark 13:10). Witness elicits persecution that will in turn provide further opportunity for witness. They need not be anxious in such circumstances, for the Holy Spirit is to be their Paraclete, "the one beside them," to guide and strengthen their witness to the person and work of Jesus (John 15:26–27).

4. *Mediation of the divine presence*: The Spirit of God had certainly been present in special times during the old covenant era to provide enabling for God's servants to fulfill their divine calling (Exod 31:3; Num 11:29; Judg 3:10; 15:14; 1 Sam 10:6; 16:13; 1 Kgs 18:12; 2 Kgs 2:16; Neh 9:30; Ps 51:11; Isa 48:16; Ezek 2:2; 3:14). During Jesus' earthly ministry the Spirit was "with" the disciples as they toured Israel and heralded God's rule. But now, in the new era to be formally inaugurated by his death and resurrection, Jesus promises the Paraclete will be "in" them (John 14:17). The promise of the indwelling presence of God's Spirit in the hearts of believers is one of the foundational realities of the new covenant prophesied by Ezekiel (Ezek 11:19; 18:31; 36:26–27) and Jeremiah (Jer 24:7; 31:33). As an ever-present companion, the Spirit will represent Jesus who is ascending to the right hand of the Father. This is the sense of Jesus' promise: "I will not leave you as orphans; I will come to you (in the person of the Spirit)" (John 14:18). The Spirit will assure them of the abiding love of the Father and the Son (John 14:19–20). He will enable them to reciprocate that love by obeying his commands (John 14:15, 21).

5. *Revelation of authoritative truth*: After his departure the "Spirit of truth" (John 14:17; 16:13), that is, the Spirit who is himself truthful and communicates truth, will perform a critical ministry for the character of the new community. He will reveal authoritative truth that becomes the doctrinal foundation for the faith and life of those under God's rule. Jesus predicts several components of the Spirit's task. First, he will help the apostles remember the words that Jesus spoke when he was with them (14:26b). This was imperative since they possessed the common tendency to selective hearing (John 2:22). Second, the Spirit will enable

them to understand and interpret the meaning of those words (14:26a), something they often lacked during his earthly ministry (John 12:16). Third, there are "many things" the apostles still needed to learn, but were at present unable to grasp (John 16:12). The Spirit of truth will guide them into new and deeper stages of truth about Jesus' person and work (John 16:13). It is the things that relate to Jesus, both present and future, that will be the essence of the revelatory corpus (John 16:14–15). There is perfect harmony in the process of the self-revelation of the triune Godhead: Father, Son, and Spirit share an exclusive body of knowledge and cooperate in communicating the portions essential to kingdom life to the apostles. This ensures the reliable transmission of the charter for faith and mission to the kingdom community.

6. *Conviction of the world*: As the apostles and succeeding generations of kingdom heralds fulfill their mission of discipling the nations, the Spirit will attend their verbal proclamation with the work of conviction. The Spirit will identify, like a prosecuting attorney, three areas of guilt people must face and repent of. First, he convicts people of their sin because they have rejected Christ whose death is the sole means of removing that guilt (John 16:9). Second, he convicts people of their need for righteousness because Jesus has ascended to the Father and from his position as exalted Lord will justify all who believe (John 16:10). Third, the Spirit convicts people of the certainty of eschatological judgment because the prince of the world, Satan, and the entire world order were condemned at the cross. Therefore, final condemnation is certain and can be averted only by embracing Jesus' death and resurrection (John 16:11).

⇨ The *Sermon on the Mount* and the *Upper Room Discourse* together expound the full-orbed character of new covenant life. The former sets forth the standard of God's perfect righteousness toward which believers must strain and the latter details the resource by which this standard can be provisionally attained. The Word of God and the Spirit of God are the two complementary resources for authentic Christian living. Is your daily walk characterized by conscious reliance upon these two provisions?

INTERCESSION FOR DISCIPLES PRESENT AND FUTURE

(John 17:1–26)

Jesus consecrated himself to the completion of the Father's appointed mission with a high priestly intercession that is the true 'Lord's prayer.' What John records here is the prelude to the Lord's final season of prayer in Gethsemane described in the Synoptic accounts. The theme of both of these intercessory moments is Jesus' determination to fulfill the Father's purpose to draw a people to himself both now and in successive generations through his death and resurrection.

1. *Prayer for his own glorification* (17:1–5)

    The determined "hour" (John 2:4; 12:23, 27; 13:1; 16:32) has now arrived for God's glory to be revealed through the cross-work of the Son. In Jesus' death God is shown to be holy love and in Jesus' resurrection glory that death is vindicated in terms of its saving efficacy (John 12:23, 28; 13:31–32). Jesus anticipates as the faithful Servant of the Lord the justification of many sinners; he foresees restoration to his preincarnate glory accompanied by a redeemed people (Isa 53:10–12). By completing the Father's assigned work he provides the basis for the forgiveness of sins and the gift of eternal life, defined as true knowledge of Father and Son. Jesus' self-consecration precedes his prayer for present and future disciples because the cross provides the basis of his authority to bestow eternal life to the people chosen by the Father.

2. *Prayer for the sanctification of present disciples* (17:6–19)

    The embryonic community of the kingdom centered on a tiny band of eleven Galileans (the one Judean member, Judas Iscariot, had already parted to carry out the betrayal) whose loyalty was about to be severely tested. Three years of hard labor had produced what seemed a very poor harvest. Yet Jesus is confident in God's saving purposes in and through these men who received, knew and believed that he was truly the Messiah sent from the Father. He rests his legacy in God's faithful preservation of these vessels who will proclaim after his departure the promise of the forgiveness of sins to the nations. Their relationship with the godless "world" system in which they reside is his special concern: the disciples are to be "in the world" (17:11) while "not of the world"

323

(17:14, 16); he will not take them "out of the world" (17:15) but send them "into the world" (17:18).

The disciples must maintain their distinctive moral compass and spiritual bearings if they are to impact people who live under the binding authority of the world system, one ruled over by its prince, the devil (John 12:31; 14:30; 16:11). His prayer is for their protection (17:11, 15) and their sanctification (17:17–18). Jesus prays for their protection from the frontal assaults and insidious temptations of the evil one, undergirding the very prayer he instructed them to pray for themselves (Matt 6:13). The "name" of God, that is, his character as holy and loving Father, and the name bestowed on Jesus in the aftermath of his resurrection, exalted Lord, will be the recourse for tested and tempted disciples to live triumphantly in the world. Their personal holiness in a corrupt environment will depend upon their divinely enabled application of God's truthful word of promise and admonition that he has and will impart to them under the Spirit's inspiration. Thus it is as empowered and sanctified vessels that the disciples are commissioned to kingdom proclamation (17:15–18). The self-consecration of the Son in his death accomplishes the defeat of Satan (John 12:31), the overcoming of the world (John 16:33), and the consecration and commissioning of the kingdom emissaries (17:19).

3. *Prayer for the unity of present and future believers* (17:20–26)

Jesus then extends his horizon to future generations of disciples brought to faith through the proclamation of the gospel beginning with that first generation. He prays that the perfect fellowship of Father and Son will reflect itself in the relational unity of believers. This is not an artificial ecumenical unity that disregards doctrinal purity, for this request follows the prayer that believers will be consecrated by the word of truth (17:17). The love of the Father and the Son indwells the fellowship of believers who then walk in unity with one another (17:23, 26). Such love-enabled unity alone possesses the power to arrest the attention of an unbelieving world (John 13:34–35) which looks with longing to be a part of this much-loved community.

⇨ Why does the love of believers expressed one toward another attract the attention of a cynical and jaded world? Conversely, how is the impact of the church weakened by the relational discord among professed followers of Christ?

17

Passion Week IV

Day of Consummation

Friday: Day of Consummation

ANGUISH IN GETHSEMANE

(Matt 26:30–46; Mark 14:26–42; Luke 22:39–46; John 18:1)

JESUS SPENT THE EARLY hours of *Friday*, approximately *12:00–3:00 a.m.*, in a garden situated in an olive grove on the western slope of the Mount of Olives where he and his disciples had often retreated for prayer (John 18:1-2). Gethsemane, which means "olive press," now becomes a scene of conflict. The God-man faces death in order to redeem people by bearing their sin upon himself. As he enters the garden Jesus leaves eight disciples at the entrance, but invites the inner circle of Peter, James and John to observe his torment. Several terms are used to describe Jesus' emotional state, all of which fulfill Isaiah's prophecy of a "man of sorrows" (53:3): sorrowful, troubled, deeply distressed, overwhelmed with sorrow even to the point of death. The three disciples are enjoined to stay alert and remain in prayer as he retreats a short distance to be alone with his Father. In his initial prayer Jesus asks that "if it be possible," the cup, signifying his appointed destiny of bearing the Father's wrath against sin, the common meaning of the metaphor in the Old Testament (Ps 75:8; Jer 25:15–17; Hab 2:16; cf. Rev 14:10; 16:19), might be removed from him. He uses the Aramaic term for familial intimacy, Abba, in approaching the Father in his hour of desperation (Mark 14:36). Here is the perfect humanity and true deity of Jesus shrinking from the horror of separation from his Father as he bears in his body the sins of the world (1 Pet 2:24). His prayer anticipates the cry of forsakenness on the cross

(Mark 15:34). Luke adds material from an ancient source which refers to an angel ministering to the Lord whose spiritual agony produced heavy beads of sweat falling like drops of blood on the ground (22:43–44). Returning to the three disciples, he found them asleep, "exhausted from sorrow" (Luke 22:45 [NIV]). They remain unaware of the redemptive drama unfolding before them and quickly fall asleep again each time the Lord retreats. The Lord warns them that their spiritual dullness will render them vulnerable to fall into the "temptation" to forsake him at his impending arrest.

There is clear progression from the first to the second prayer. God can only act in accordance with his will. Thus Jesus commits himself irrevocably to carrying out the Father's purpose knowing the full consequences of that decision. "Since it is *not* possible for this cup to be taken away . . . may your will be done" (Matt 26:42 [author's rendering]). The third prayer is one final confirmation of his complete surrender to his Father's will. 'Not my will but yours' is the reversal of the first Adam's stance in the garden of Eden whose act of defiance plunged his descendants into death, which is eternal separation from God. Now the second Adam through his vicarious death will bring eternal life to those who believe (Rom 5:18–19; 1 Cor 15:22). On his third return he awakens the sleeping disciples with the shocking announcement of his imminent arrest as the company of soldiers led by Judas draws near. Now is the call for vigilance not rest, for the Son of Man has reached his appointed "hour" as the suffering Servant. How will the disciples fare in this critical moment of testing?

⇨ How is Jesus' prayer—"your will be done"—both like and unlike the disciples' prayer to the same effect (Matt 6:10)? To what degree can we see into the future and calculate the consequences of our commitment to God's will compared to that of the Lord Jesus?

ARREST IN THE GARDEN

(Matt 26:47–56; Mark 14:43–52; Luke 22:47–53; John 18:2–12)

The darkness and solace of the garden is pierced by an approaching mob holding torches and lanterns. They are led by their paid informant, Judas Iscariot, who reappears a few hours after his hasty departure from the upper room. The seizure is organized by certain members of the Sanhedrin accompanied by temple police under their jurisdiction, and a detachment of Roman soldiers under the command of the chilarch (certainly not an entire unit of 600). Both groups were heavily armed with swords and clubs. Judas signals which one Jesus is by the familiar greeting, "Rabbi," and the oriental kiss on the cheek. Jesus' questions to Judas express ironical surprise mixed with resignation to fulfill his designated role as the Son of Man (Matt 26:50; Luke 22:48).

John makes no mention of the spiritual struggle in Gethsemane; his account focuses on Jesus' mastery of the encounter, a conflict moving forward in accordance with the divine plan. Jesus takes the initiative to manifest himself to the crowd with the authoritative pronouncement, "I am he" (John 18:5, 8), while at the same time requesting that his disciples be left alone. Such protective care fulfills the Lord's earlier promises that none of those given to him by the Father would, in spite of their initially failing the test, permanently fall away (John 18:9; cf. John 6:39; 17:12). Peter once again proved the reactionary and, wielding his sword at the unknown assailants, hacked off the ear of the servant of the high priest, one named Malchus. The Lord's stinging rebuke of such misguided zeal underscores the burden of the narrative to show that Jesus had nothing in common with the political zealots of his day. His mission is universal redemption not national liberation. He affirms his commitment, validated earlier in the garden, to drink the cup of God's wrath against sin to the full (John 18:11). His suffering as the Son of Man prophesied in Scripture must be fulfilled even though he possesses the authority to marshal twelve legions of angels to destroy his enemies (Matt 26:53-54). He touches and heals the ear of the injured servant, his final recorded miracle of healing (Luke 22:51). The Lord reminds the crowd that such violent seizure is unnecessary since he could have been apprehended while teaching openly in the temple courts each of the past five days.

All is unfolding as scripted by God in accordance with prophetic Scripture. The impending death of the Son is on one level the revelation of God's glory, but on another the reign of darkness (Luke 22:53b; cf. John 13:31). Using the cloak of darkness to shield their actions from the more sympathetic pilgrims gathered for Passover in Jerusalem renders the action of the Sanhedrin even more insidious. The overwhelming force of the mob frightens the disciples who flee into the darkness. Their earlier boasts of death-defying courage have proven to be a sham (Mark 14:31). The mass desertion underscores their faulty faith and anticipates the more dramatic denials of the chief apostle, Peter. Mark refers to a young man who, wearing only the outer garment (without the undergarment or tunic probably due to having dressed in haste), was forced to flee naked when he was also seized (14:51–52). It seems to be his way of saying, "I was there."

⇨ Why did Peter respond in the way he did? What does it reveal about his level of understanding of Jesus' identity and mission even at this late date?

JEWISH TRIAL OF JESUS

The trial of Jesus begins with the Jewish deliberations before the high priest and his associates who conspire to establish the charge of blasphemy (3:00–6:00 a.m.). The scene then moves to the court of Pilate, governor of Judea, who alone possesses the right to prosecute and punish capital crimes (6:00–9:00 a.m.). The charge of contravening Jewish law would never stand in a Roman court (Acts 18:12–17), so the charge shifts to treason and sedition, both capital offenses punishable by death. Both religious and secular trials move forward in three phases.

PHASE ONE: PRELIMINARY HEARING BEFORE ANNAS
(John 18:13–14, 19–23)

The soldiers bound the hands of Jesus and brought him to the private home of Annas, near Gethsemane on the Mount of Olives. Alternatively, Annas conducted the hearing at the home of Caiaphas, located in the upper city of Jerusalem. Annas, formerly high priest (AD 6–15), was the father-in-law of Caiaphas, the official high priest (AD 18–36). Annas had been deposed by the Roman governor Valerius Gratus (AD 15–26) but continued to exert singular influence on Jewish religious affairs and, in fact, was recognized by many as the rightful high priest. The purpose of this initial interrogation was to gather further information about Jesus' doctrine and the extent of his following so the council might know how to proceed in prosecuting Jesus. This seasoned participant in Jewish-Roman relations could help the Sanhedrin gage the reaction of the Passover crowd and assess the governor's strength should they meet resistance.

Annas violated Jewish legal protocol by attempting to entice Jesus into self-recrimination. Jesus protested this line of inquiry. His teaching had been openly declared in the synagogues, public gatherings, and most recently in the temple courts (Mark 14:49). His ministry was no secretive indoctrination

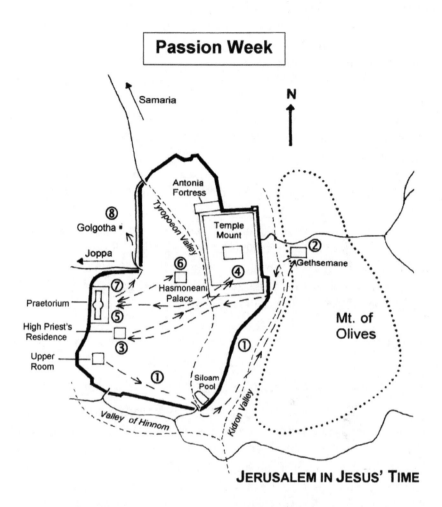

Passion Week

Samaria

N

Antonia
Fortress

⑧
Golgotha

Tyropoeon Valley

Temple
Mount

Joppa

②
Gethsemane

⑥

④

⑦

Hasmonean
Palace

Praetorium

⑤

High Priest's
Residence

③

Mt. of
Olives

Upper
Room

①

Siloam
Pool

①

Kidron Valley

Valley of Hinnom

JERUSALEM IN JESUS' TIME

Friday	1. To **Gethsemane** (12 am ~ 3 am)
Arrest	2. **Gethsemane**
Jewish Trials: (3 am ~ 6 am)	
Before Annas & Caiaphas	3. **High Priest's Residence**
Before Sanhedrin	4. **Temple Chambers**
Roman Trials: (6 am ~ 9 am)	
Before Pilate	5. **Praetorium**
Before Antipas	6. **Hasmonean Palace**
Before Pilate	7. **Praetorium**
Crucifixion	8. **Golgotha**

of a band of revolutionaries. Let Annas provide answers to his own questions by summoning credible witnesses who have heard him teach. If and until such evidence is gathered and prepared, the (de facto) high priest has no right to examine him, much less bind him for trial. Jesus keeps the attention on himself ("I ... I ... I ... me ... me ... I") in order to protect his disciples from guilt by association.

For his bold rejoinder one of the temple guards standing there struck Jesus in the face, then rebuked him for disrespecting the high priest. The trial, both Jewish and Roman, assumes more of the character of a torture session than a legal proceeding. Jesus repeated his challenge to desist from intimidation and make truth their standard of judgment. But his challenge will go unheeded as the trial moves to the villa of Caiaphas, the one who earlier issued the cold calculation that taking the life of one man, even an innocent one, would be preferable to allowing the nation to be disturbed and their vested interests threatened (John 11:49–50). It is no wonder, then, that the trial proceeds toward a guilty verdict predetermined by a cynical, calculating politician bent on silencing Jesus.

PHASE TWO: INTERROGATION BEFORE CAIAPHAS AND SOME COUNCIL MEMBERS

(Matthew 26:57–68; Mark 14:53–65; Luke 22:54–65; John 18:24)

Caiaphas' gated villa with the large courtyard is the early morning setting for a hastily assembled meeting of the high priest with representative members of the Sanhedrin, probably less than the twenty-three (of seventy total) necessary to establish a quorum for official action. All three factions of the ruling council were present: teachers of the law, largely belonging to the Pharisees; elders or venerated heads of aristocratic families; priests presiding over the temple activities, almost exclusively Sadducees. The trial of Jesus continued to be a charade. False witnesses were brought forward whose testimony conflicted. The law stipulated that the non-contradictory testimony of two or three witnesses was required to establish a verdict in a Jewish court (Deut 17:6; 19:15). A malicious witness whose testimony was proven false was to be punished with death (Deut 19:16–21). Some charged Jesus with speaking against the temple of God, which was a distortion of his metaphorical saying where he referred to the dissolution, then resurrection, of the temple of his body (John 2:19–21). Indeed Jesus did predict the destruction of the temple privately to his disciples, but never in the sense of a personal assault on the Jewish holy place (Matt 24:2). In the face of malicious slander, false testimony, and intentional distortion of his words, Jesus remained, as the Isaianic servant (53:7), silent.

Then Caiaphas challenged Jesus directly to affirm or deny whether he was making the claim to be the Messiah, the Son of God, the Son of the Blessed One. Jesus weighed his response carefully because these messianic designations were laden with socio-political connotations. Most likely Matthew's record of Jesus' reply preserves his actual words, literally, "you have said so" (26:64), while the parallel in Mark is most likely the interpretive equivalent, "I am" (14:62). Taken together, it appears that Jesus issued a qualified affirmative to the question, captured accurately in the NIV: "Yes, it is as you say (but not as you mean)" (Matt 26:64). Indeed he is the Messiah of prophetic hope and the God-man uniquely qualified to provide an efficacious sacrifice for sin. But he is no claimant to a temporal, earthly kingship centered on empirical Israel and the nationalistic hopes of her priests and scribes.

Then Jesus spoke with audacious boldness. If Caiaphas wants a straight answer to establish the charge of blasphemy, Jesus will provide it with a self-attestation that demands a verdict. He employs his favorite self-designation, Son of Man, but this time draws on Psalm 110:1 and Daniel 7:13 to predict his return in glory. Having completed the work of redemption and vindicated at the Father's right hand, he will one day descend to earth through the clouds of heaven for his coronation as universal Ruler and Judge. Jesus leaves no middle way; he is lunatic, liar or Lord. He prefers Son of Man to the titles Messiah and Son of God because the former does not possess the politicized force of the latter. The suffering Son of Man (Mark 10:45) will become the exalted Son of Man (Mark 14:62).

With this the high priest and assembled leaders pronounce that he is deserving of death as a blasphemer (Lev 24:16). Caiaphas tore his robes as a visual sign of horror at such an affront to God's character (Gen 37:29; 2 Kgs 19:1). A purported trial with the right of due process deteriorates into abusive mockery of the defendant unrestrained by the presiding authority. The one who moments earlier claimed to have authority to vanquish his foes is spat upon, struck with fists, then blindfolded and commanded to prophesy who hit him, slapped, insulted and mocked by members of the council, as well as by the temple guards holding him in custody. Though he had predicted such treatment multiple times, how absurd his authoritative claims must have appeared not only to his enemies, but also to many superficial sympathizers and even to his inner circle of disciples. Meanwhile, Peter and an unnamed disciple, almost certainly John, gathered enough courage to stumble out of the darkness into which they had fled (Mark 14:50). They quietly made their way to the upper city of Jerusalem toward the house of Caiaphas where the trial of Jesus was taking place.

DENIALS OF PETER

(Matthew 26:69–75; Mark 14:66–72; Luke 22:55–62;
John 18:15–18, 25–27)

John, by virtue of some level of relationship with the high priest or his household, helped secure access for Peter to the courtyard of the villa as the second phase of the Jewish trial proceeded in the chambers inside (John 18:15–16). First, a girl on duty at the gate, at John's request, allows Peter entrance to the central courtyard. As Peter begins warming himself in the light of the fire, she identifies him as one who was with the infamous Galilean. She and others call Peter "one of this man's disciples." Peter responds: "I am not" (Matt 26:69–70; John 18:17–18, 25). Next, another servant girl at the entryway to where Peter has withdrawn identifies him as "one of them" who was with the Nazarene. Peter denies it with an oath: "I do no know the man" (Matt 26:71–72). Finally, still in the courtyard about one hour later, a bystander identifies Peter as one of Jesus' Galilean followers, betrayed by his accent. This man is a relative of Malchus and claims he saw Peter in the olive grove at the time of arrest (John 18:26). Peter spews out curses and swears, "I do not know the man" (Matt 26:74). The denials are forceful and with increasing vehemence. At the third denial the rooster crowed and Peter recalled the prediction of the Lord, left the courtyard, and wept bitterly (Matt 26:75; cf. Matt 26:34). Luke adds that between Peter's third denial and his departure "the Lord turned and looked straight at Peter" (Luke 22:61 [NIV]), probably as Jesus was being led across the courtyard bound for the formal trial of the Sanhedrin in the temple courts.

Here is the darkest moment of Peter's life. His boisterous claims of loyalty have proven hollow (Matt 26:35). His exalted confession of Jesus' Sonship appears as a sham (Matt 16:16). He has disappointed himself, failed in his leadership role in the team, and, above all, dishonored the one who meant more to him than life itself. In Mark's Gospel, drawn from Peter's sermons to the church in Rome, the chief apostle is never mentioned again. It is left to John, who alone witnessed the denials of his fellow apostle, to record the sequel of hope (John 21:15–23).

⇨ How could one so bold as to attack Jesus' opponents with the sword turn into a coward when pressed to admit his connection to the Lord? What contributes to Peter being paralyzed by the "fear of man" (Prov 29:25)?

PHASE THREE: FORMAL HEARING OF THE SANHEDRIN
(Matthew 27:1; Mark 15:1a; Luke 22:66–71)

The third and final phase of the Jewish trial was a formal meeting of the Sanhedrin at daybreak (shortly before 6:00 a.m.). It took place almost certainly in the official council chamber in the temple precincts. This final deliberation was intended, first, to establish before a full quorum of council members that Jesus was guilty of blasphemy. Once again the high priest demands that Jesus give a forthright answer to the question of his messianic identity. Jesus affirms for the second time that he is the greater Son of David, in fact David's Lord, who will be exalted at the right hand of God in fulfillment of Psalm 110:1. To the further question, "Are you the Son of God, then?," Jesus again slightly qualifies his affirmation—"You yourself are stating it (rightly)" (author's rendering)—because he does not want his Sonship to be interpreted in an earthly, nationalistic manner (Luke 22:70). No further evidence was needed. The council, despite a few dissenting voices, determined to seek the death penalty from the Roman authority. Knowing, however, that the religious charge of blasphemy would be dismissed in a Roman court of law, the Sanhedrin deliberated how they would press their case to Pilate. As Jesus is transferred to the secular court the charge will shift from blasphemy, the real reason for his condemnation, to treason (Luke 23:2). Annas and Caiaphas are well-versed in the power politics of the day and counsel the Sanhedrin to proceed along lines that will apply the greatest pressure on the governor to accede to their demands.

SUICIDE OF JUDAS ISCARIOT
(Matt 27:3–10; cf. Acts 1:18–19)

Matthew inserts in his narrative an account of Judas's subsequent fate in order to once again show how all of the developing events of Passion Week fulfill the detailed prophecies of the Old Testament. Everything is moving forward in accordance with the divine plan. Judas had yielded to satanic influence in his calculated act of betrayal of one whose company he had enjoyed for three years, climaxed by one final meal together (Luke 22:3; John 13:26–30). Like the other apostles, he had been chosen in answer to prayer (Luke 6:13) and even been entrusted with managing the funds for the ministry (John 12:6). The Gospels indicate that greed was the force that pulled his heart away from Jesus (Luke 22:5–6; John 12:6). As the trial moved from the Jewish to the Roman court and a death sentence was gaining momentum, Judas felt remorse for betraying one who he knew was innocent of the charge of blasphemy. His admission of guilt and attempt to return the payment of thirty silver coins to the chief priests was treated with scorn. Judas' remorse at least reveals some level of human decency remaining, unlike the priests who callously proceeded to condemn an innocent man.

But remorse for the consequences of one's action does not necessarily produce heartfelt repentance over the underlying faithlessness and greed that produced the action (2 Cor 7:9–11). In Judas' case his sorrow moved inward and downward, leading to his suicide. Apparently he hung himself from the branch of a tree on a promontory. When the tree or rope broke his body fell to the valley below causing his bowels to spill out (Acts 1:18–19). The chief priests were in a quandary over what to do with the money that Judas threw down in the temple. Their hypocrisy is shocking: having paid an informant, probably with money from the temple treasury, they now show scruples over returning to the treasury "blood money." Sequestering false witnesses (Matt 26:59) was not nearly as serious a matter in their eyes as contacting ritual impurity from tainted silver coins. So they used the money to purchase a potter's field as a burial place for foreigners, one that assumed the infamous label "field of blood," further defiled by dead peoples' bones. This fulfilled the typological (i.e. anticipatory) actions of Zechariah (Zech 11:12–13) and Jeremiah (Jer 19:1–13). Zechariah was paid thirty pieces of silver for severing his relationship with the flock, the people of God, which rejected his attempt to faithfully shepherd them (Zech 11:7–10). He then cast the money down in the temple, which was taken up by potters engaged in fashioning silver idols for the syncretistic worship. Jesus, like Zechariah, is the faithful shepherd who is sold for the price of a slave (Exod 21:32) and whose purchase price is cast down in the temple and used for profane purposes. Jeremiah was commanded to purchase a clay jar from the potter and, after pronouncing judgment on idolatrous Judah, to smash the jar in the defiled Valley of Hinnom, soon to become the Valley of Slaughter, to symbolize the smashing of the covenant nation beyond repair. Jesus, like Jeremiah, is the defamed prophet associated with a potter and a polluted piece of land whose rejection seals the ruin of the entire temple system (Matt 24:2, 15–22). Both prophetic pictures presage the Passion of the Servant.

⇨ Embedded in the account of the trials of Jesus is the record of Peter's denials and Judas' betrayal and suicide. Are the Gospel writers making a studied distinction between these two apostles and their failures? If so, how do they differ and what are the possible theological implications?

ROMAN TRIAL OF JESUS

Between two interrogations of Jesus by the Roman governor, Pontius Pilate (AD 26–36), is sandwiched a brief hearing before Herod Antipas, tetrarch of Galilee (4 BC—AD 39), under whose jurisdiction Jesus had carried out most of his activities. Pilate hoped to escape the responsibility of sentencing an innocent man guilty of a capital crime so he will shift the burden to another. His hopes proved fruitless, however, as Antipas acts solely to satisfy his curiosity, not to relieve Pilate of his dilemma. Pilate is, in one sense, the tragic figure here, caught between his Roman duty to preserve justice and the desperate need to preserve workable relations with the recalcitrant leaders of Israel. In the end political pressures trump the voice of conscience and Jesus is sentenced to die. The Roman trial takes place 6:00–9:00 a.m.

FIRST PHASE: INTERROGATION BY THE ROMAN GOVERNOR, PONTIUS PILATE

(Matthew 27:2, 11–14; Mark 15:1b–5; Luke 23:1–5; John 18:28–38)

Pilate convenes the trial at his official residence, the Praetorium (John 18:28, 33; 19:9), which is normally identified with Herod's palace on the west side of Jerusalem near the Jaffa Gate, though some understand it as the judicial chamber inside the Antonia Fortress on the northwest corner of the temple. The governor's permanent residence was in Caesarea (Acts 23:35). His Jewish accusers are reticent about entering the Gentile court because they would thereby contract ritual defilement and be prevented from eating the Passover (John 18:28). This seems to contradict the Synoptic accounts where Jesus has already enjoyed the Passover meal with his disciples on Thursday evening (Matt 26:18; Mark 14:14; Luke 22:11). Some see the solution as a calendrical one: the Synoptics follow the reckoning of the Pharisees, while

John follows a calendar used by the Sadducees in Judea. More plausible is the view that "Passover" in John 18:28; 19:14 means the entire Passover festival, which included the initial Passover meal (day 14; Synoptics) as well as the subsequent Feast of Unleavened Bread (days 15–21). The Jewish leaders did not want to be kept, due to ritual impurity, from eating the unleavened bread specified for the seven days of the festival (Deut 16:3). What is striking here is that once again Jesus' opponents are much less concerned about sequestering false witnesses, deliberately distorting his words and pursuing illegal judicial proceedings than they are about violating the ceremonial requirements of the law. Pilate is forced to repeatedly move back and forth between the judicial chamber inside, where Jesus is being held, and the prosecuting party waiting anxiously outside the Praetorium working the crowds.

The Sanhedrin's purpose in prosecuting Jesus at the highest level is to pressure the governor to issue the death sentence for a capital crime, a prerogative not granted the Jews in their limited self-governance (John 18:31b). Pilate first asks for the formal accusation from the Sanhedrin. They charge Jesus with treason supported by two pieces of evidence, first, that he forbids tribute to Caesar and, second, that he is making a claim to kingship. The first claim is a blatant lie, since Jesus affirmed the duty of Roman subjects to pay their taxes and to obey civil law unless it directly contravenes the will of God (Matt 22:18–21). The second is a distortion of the intended meaning of his words regarding the kingdom of God, as he will clarify in his interchange with the governor (John 18:36–37). Pilate already recognizes, based on some preliminary investigative work, that Jesus is no criminal, and so tries to dismiss the case. But the Jews are intent on the death sentence, not the temporal punishments permitted to them for proven religious offenders. John interprets their actions as the fulfillment of Jesus' earlier prophecy regarding his own manner of death (John 18:32; cf. John 3:14; 8:28; 12:32–34).

Pilate returns to the chamber to engage Jesus over the serious charge that he is challenging Caesar as a rival king. Pilate's question is direct: "Are you the King of the Jews?" (John 18:33). Jesus knows that Caiaphas is behind the question, one for whom king signified a national liberator who would rally Israel to throw off her Gentile oppressors much like the Maccabean rulers had done two centuries before. If such is the case, Jesus is challenging Caesar's rule over this volatile Roman province. For the third time Jesus answers a direct question affirmatively, but with qualification (Matt 26:64; Luke 22:70). The brief response in the Synoptics—"You yourself are saying (I am a king)" (Matt 27:11 [author's rendering])—is amplified in John's Gospel

(18:34–37). Jesus affirms that he is a king but that his reign is "not of this world." Rather, he is establishing a sovereign rule over the hearts of those who submit to his soul-accosting claims. He has no interest in mobilizing his followers into a military force. At the outset he resisted Satan's attempt to lure him after earthly kingdoms (Matt 4:8–10) and since then has repeatedly withdrawn from all attempts to co-opt him to a socio-political role (John 6:15). His kingdom is of a wholly different nature than Caesar's. The mission of his earthly life is to bring the truth of God's sovereign authority to bear upon individuals and communities, providing redemption through faith in his coming death wholly apart from a tradition-centered righteousness. He is the servant-king whose humiliation must precede his exaltation.

Pilate offers a cynical retort: "What is truth?" Before Jesus can answer—probably in the terms of his earlier self-attestation (John 14:6)—Pilate exits the Praetorium and announces to his accusers that he finds Jesus not guilty of treason. The first phase of the trial has confirmed his preliminary assessment of innocence (John 18:31). But the chief priests' accusations only grow stronger and louder, this time adding sedition to the initial charge. They accuse Jesus of inciting anti-Roman sentiment all over Judea, beginning from Galilee (Luke 23:5). Pilate marvels when Jesus remains silent before his accusers, but discovers in the reference to Galilee a propitious moment. Antipas is visiting Jerusalem for the Passover festival and may be willing to undertake the responsibility of issuing a verdict toward one whose activities have been carried out largely in his jurisdiction

SECOND PHASE: TRANSFER TO HEROD ANTIPAS, TETRARCH OF GALILEE

(Luke 23:6–12)

Antipas held court in the Hasmonean palace in central Jerusalem, not far from Herod's palace, the probable location of the first phase of the Roman trial. Pilate is seeking to evade the inevitable by shifting the responsibility of sentencing to another. Luke alone records this second phase before Antipas, tetrarch of Galilee and Perea (4 BC—AD 39), whose unlawful relationship with Herodias, estranged wife of his half brother Philip I, elicited John the Baptist's condemnation and led to the prophet's death (Luke 3:1; 9:7–9; 13:31). Herod has long wished to see Jesus perform one of his patented miracles of which he has heard but never witnessed. He is also curious about his teaching and so plies him with many questions. But as Jesus remained silent before Caiaphas when false witnesses distorted his words (Matt 26:63), and before Pilate when the chief priests verbally attacked him (Matt 27:12-14), so he refuses to open his mouth to Antipas. Whether articulate or silent, Jesus directs the proceedings. Though he will answer the high priest and the governor when they press him to reveal his true identity, Jesus refuses to defend himself against malicious attacks or accede to demands for miracles. He is the lamb silent before its shearers as it is led to slaughter (Isa 53:7). The hearing ends with Jesus dressed in royal apparel and paraded before ruler and soldiers as a powerless king, a mockery to be repeated just prior to the crucifixion (Mark 15:16-19). The transfer back to the governor's court in the Praetorium without a formal verdict signals to Pilate that Antipas shares his perspective that Jesus is no threat to Rome, an agreement which he later cites to the chief priests (Luke 23:15) and which brought a measure of reconciliation between these two former adversaries (23:12).

THIRD PHASE: RETURN TO PILATE AND FINAL SENTENCING

(Matthew 27:15-30; Mark 15:6-19; Luke 23:13-25; John 18:39—19:16a)

This final stage of the trial is dominated by Pilate's desperate maneuvering to find an alternative to sentencing an innocent man to death. For the third time (initial appraisal [John 18:31]; after the first phase [John 18:38]) Pilate issues a declaration of Jesus' innocence, this time of being a seditionist (Luke 23:14). Fearing Jesus' imminent release, the chief priests, with the crowd under their spell, recall the custom of paschal clemency where annually at Passover the governor would release one incarcerated criminal that the people requested, a custom referred to in the Mishnah (m. Pesahim 8:6). Pilate offers to the crowd a choice between Jesus and the notorious prisoner Barabbas, a robber and murderer who had taken part in an armed insurrection against the Roman authorities (and probably their Sadducean collaborators). Surely they will prefer Jesus, in spite of their envy at his popularity among the Passover pilgrims who hailed his advent in Jerusalem just five days before, over one who has violently challenged Roman rule and the temple hierarchy that supports it. But this was a tactical blunder. Pilate has grossly underestimated both the deep level of hatred the religious leaders have for this messianic pretender and their ability to gather the crowd to their side. Peter will later recall the fateful decision of the leading men of Israel who disowned the Holy and Righteous One, the one who came to offer them life, pressuring the governor instead to release a murderer (Acts 3:13–14). Pilate was further troubled by an admonition from his wife to "have nothing to do with that righteous man" due to a frightful dream she had (Matt 27:19).

So Pilate decides to chastise Jesus, which he hopes will be punishment enough to satisfy his accusers, and then to release him (Luke 23:16, 22). This flogging with wooden rods (John 19:1–5) is not the terrible scourging with the flagellum that later precedes the crucifixion. Nevertheless, it was a severe beating with an unspecified number of strokes (distinct from the Jewish synagogue whipping of thirty-nine strokes) designed to elicit pity on the victim. Pilate brings Jesus forth and commands his accusers to look closely at "the man," bruised and bloodied, arrayed in a purple robe, pressed with a crown of thorns. Surely they will acquiesce to his fourth declaration of Jesus' innocence (John 19:4), a pathetic figure who could not seriously be considered a king, much less a threat to Rome. None of his maneuvers elicits even an ounce of pity; rather, weakness invites deeper disdain. The manipulated crowds shout out their demands that he be crucified, the type of death that signified under the Mosaic law the divine curse upon a blasphemer (Deut 21:23). His accusers tacitly admit that the secular charges of treason and sedition have only been a cover for the fundamental religious charge when they insist Jesus must die for claiming to be the Son of God (John 19:7).

Declaring Jesus innocent for the fifth time (John 19:6), Pilate's superstitious fears elicit a final interrogation. He is stunned when his question— "Where are you from?—meets with no response. Pilate warns him that he holds in his hands the power of life and death. But Jesus is unimpressed, relegating ultimate command of his destiny to the sovereign God, while underscoring the severe guilt of Caiaphas and the Sanhedrin who have delivered him over to be executed (John 19:11). This singular verse sets forth the mysterious complement of divine purpose and human culpability: the death of Jesus is both the foreordained plan of a loving God, as well as an act of incalculable human evil, not just of priests, governor, soldiers and crowds, but of the entire sinful world for whose redemption it is offered (Acts 2:23–39). Pilate's final attempt to set Jesus free meets with the Jews shouting out threats to lodge a complaint against him in Rome for failure to prosecute one claiming to be a king, a return to their original charge (John 19:12; cf. Luke 23:2). If he releases Jesus he is "not Caesar's friend," they shout, as if their demand for the release of a convicted insurrectionist, Barabbas, proves their loyalty to the Emperor.

This is at least the fourth time that the frenetic Pilate has paced back and forth between the judicial chamber in the Praetorium to the leaders and crowds in the courtyard (John 18:31, 38; 19:4, 12). He now collapses under the pressure and derisively calls Jesus "your King" as he delivers him over to be crucified. Ironically, the chosen nation declares its preference for a pagan ruler to the one sent to be their Redeemer-King (John 1:11). The sentence is formally pronounced from the judgment seat known as Stone Pavement prior to 9:00 a.m. ("third hour" in Jewish reckoning) when the crucifixion takes place (Mark 15:25). John's reference to the "sixth hour," or 6:00 a.m. in Roman reckoning (19:14), seems to refer to the beginning point for the entire Roman phase of the trial which now reaches its culmination three hours later. Though tormented by a guilty conscience—knowing Jesus' innocence (declared five times) and the envy of the Jews (Matt 27:18)—and buffeted by suspicious fears—his wife's admonitory dream (Matt 27:19) and Jesus' bold claims to truth, kingship and authority (John 18:36–37; 19:11)—, Pilate washes his hands as a symbolic act to divest himself of responsibility and transfer his guilt to the Jewish crowds (Matt 27:24). Pilate is not exonerated by that act nor are the Jews under a multi-generational curse for embracing full culpability for the decision—"his blood be on us and on our children" (Matt 27:25). While the historical causes are recorded, the New Testament interprets the death of Jesus as a "ransom for many" (Mark 10:45), as the shedding of blood "for many for the forgiveness of sins" (Matt 26:28). In the Passion narrative all sinners, Jew and Gentile, can see themselves reflected in the faces of the chief priests, soldiers, Pilate and even Judas Iscariot.

Jesus was handed over to the soldiers for the scourging with the flagellum, a leather whip embedded with pieces of bone and metal which brutally tore the flesh of the victim. This was the Roman torture known as *verberatio*, with the number of strokes not prescribed, which prepared the capital criminal for crucifixion, but which often brought about his death. Inside the Praetorium the final act before leading him to crucifixion was the mockery of Jesus' claims to kingship by the Roman soldiers. Similar treatment had taken place after the hearing before Antipas (Luke 23:11) and after the initial flogging by Pilate (John 19:2–3), but now reached a new level of intensity. He is stripped, clothed with a scarlet robe, pressed with a crown of thorns, made to hold a reed in his right hand, subjected to false homage—"Hail, king of the Jews"—, spat upon and repeatedly struck on the head with the reed. All of this fulfilled Jesus' detailed predictions of his suffering (Matt 20:17–19). Such gratuitous violence was more than a travesty of Roman justice, even for the condemned, but was detailed by the Gospel writers to unmask the depravity of human beings for whose redemption the most terrible price is about to be exacted.

⇨ Why does John's extended record of Pilate's interaction with Jesus center on the theme of kingship? How does Pilate's understanding of royal authority differ from that of Jesus? Does this interchange validate or contradict our earlier definition of "kingdom?"

PROCESSION TO GOLGOTHA

(Matthew 27:31–34; Mark 15:20–23; Luke 23:26–33a; John 19:16b–17)

The mock royal apparel was removed and Jesus was dressed again in his own clothes. He was led to be crucified by an execution squad of four soldiers, he himself dragging the horizontal crosspiece to which his hands would be nailed. Often the stump of a tree served as the vertical member to which the overlapping ankles were fastened. The upright beam was already in place and was used on repeated occasions. A small crossbar served as a seat on which the victim could pull himself up for a measure of relief. The way to the cross, the *via dolorosa*, ran from Herod's palace eastward, then northward, through the upper city to the city gates, then due north to a place called Golgotha, Aramaic for skull, called Calvary for the equivalent term in Latin (*calvaria*). Golgotha was near the northern wall of the city and adjacent to roads that led west to the Mediterranean coastal highway and north through the Samaritan heartland. That Jesus was crucified outside the city gate signified his total rejection by the nation of Israel as a blasphemer (Lev 24:14) and the identification of Jesus' sacrifice in Christian typology with the Old Testament sin offerings stipulated to be consumed "outside the camp" (Heb 13:11–13; cf. Lev 4:12; 9:11; 16:27).

Due to lack of sleep and the loss of blood from the initial flogging and the final scourging, Jesus was severely weakened and stumbled under the weight of the beam. One Simon, probably a Jewish worshipper from Cyrene in North Africa, was conscripted to bear the crosspiece from the city gates to the place of execution. If, as is plausible, the Rufus of Mark 15:21 is the same person by that name in Romans 16:13, then Simon's son and wife (whom Paul figuratively says "has been a mother to me as well") later became Christians and prominent members of the church in Rome for which Mark's Gospel and Paul's Epistle were written. Jesus was followed by a large crowd and expressed special concern for the many women who were weeping at the tragic development. For at least the fourth time the Lord predicted the holy city's desolation and the slaughter of its inhabitants, citing the words of Hosea 10:8b (Luke 13:34–35; 19:41–44; 21:20–24; 23:28–31). This catastrophic judgment would occur within one generation (AD 70) and exterminate the aristocratic ruling class and its zealously guarded temple system. Upon his arrival at Golgotha and just before the excruciating agony of the crucifixion, Jesus was offered wine mixed with myrrh (Mark 15:23), which made the concoction bitter like gall (Matt 27:34). Though it may have been offered in sympathy as a narcotic, perhaps by the women, more likely the Gospel writers see Jesus once again fulfilling Old Testament Scripture, this time Psalm 69:21, so that Jesus, like David, was offered (probably by the soldiers) a bitter mixture to increase his torment. Rejection and disdain mark the Passion of the Servant at every turn (Isa 49:4, 7; 50:6; 52:14; 53:3, 7).

FIRST THREE HOURS AND THE FIRST THREE WORDS FROM THE CROSS

(Matthew 27:35–44; Mark 15:24–32; Luke 23:33b–43; John 19:18–27)

At approximately 9:00 a.m. (the Jewish "third hour" [Mark 15:25]) on *Friday*, Nisan 15, AD 30 Jesus Christ was crucified at a place called Golgotha just north of the old city of Jerusalem. All four Gospels record the brief historical fact without elaboration: "they crucified him" (only two words in the Greek text). There is no fascination with detailing the horrific nature of this ancient method of execution practiced for centuries by Assyrians, Persians, Greeks and now Romans. Crucifixion displayed the offender in a prolonged state of public exposure, designed to shame and degrade one guilty of the most heinous crimes. Eventually the victim would die from heart failure or asphyxiation. In Hebrew law (Deut 21:23) crucifixion or, literally, impaling a person on a pole, signified God's curse upon a capital offender. Two thieves, likely accomplices with Barabbas in the armed insurrection (Mark 15:7), were also crucified, one on each side of Jesus. As the Isaianic Servant, Jesus was "numbered with the transgressors" (Isa 53:12; cf. Luke 22:37). Four parts of his clothing—head covering, outer garment normally made of wool, sandals, and leather belt—were divided one part each among the four soldiers, fulfilling another piece of the depiction of the godly sufferer in Psalm 22 (v. 18). They decided not to tear the seamless undergarment or tunic because of its finely woven fabric and cast lots to determine who would receive it. At the top of the vertical beam of the crucifix was attached a white tablet with the charge written in visible red or black letters in Aramaic, Latin and Greek. The inscription in its full form read: "This is Jesus of Nazareth, the King of the Jews." The chief priests protested that the criminal act was framed as a declarative statement and requested Pilate to change the inscription to read: "This is Jesus of Nazareth, who falsely claimed to be the King of the Jews." But Pilate refused to amend it. The unchanged indictment published in the major languages of the pilgrims assembled in Jerusalem for Passover underscores that God's saving rule is inaugurated through the death of the Servant-King, one placarded before and sacrificed for all peoples—Jews (Aramaic), Romans (Latin) and Greeks (Greek).

Then came the *first word* of Jesus from the cross: "Father, forgive them, for they know not what they do" (Luke 23:34). This is, first, a plea of divine mercy for the chosen nation that has unwittingly failed to recognize her Messiah when he visited her (Luke 19:44). Both Jesus and Paul anticipate a day when the preponderance of the Jewish people will repent and receive from Jesus Messiah the gift of the forgiveness of sins (Matt 23:39; Rom 11:25–29). But this prayer, secondly, enfolds all people whose depravity is represented by the original historical agents of Jesus' death—Judas, Caiaphas, chief priests, Roman soldiers, crowds. The condition of all sinners is reflected in the faces of those first century participants in this momentous event. Forgiveness of sins is the climactic promise of the new covenant (Jer 31:34), the centerpiece of the apostolic proclamation, a free gift offered to all who readily admit their guilt and turn to Jesus Christ as their sin-bearer (Luke 24:47; Acts 10:43; 13:38; Rom 3:23–26; Eph 1:7; Col 1:14; Heb 9:22–28; 1 Pet 2:24). Finally, Jesus' prayer embodies like no other the posture of forgiveness that is to characterize his followers in their relationships with one another and even toward their enemies—to forgive because they have been so abundantly forgiven (Matt 5:43–47; 6:12, 14–15; 18:21–35).

Westcott offers the perceptive comment that "all those who were present at the scene acted according to their true natures." First, those who were passing by, either Gentiles for commercial pursuits or Jewish Passover pilgrims returning to their homes, derided his claims to be the Son of God (Matt 27:39–40). Ironically, it was because he was the Son of God that Jesus would not save himself. God would vindicate him by raising him from the dead on the third day, the true sense of the temple saying that they had failed to grasp (John 2:19). The crowds elevated the assertion of raw power; the divine economy chose humiliation as the prelude to exaltation. Second, the vain priests who had demanded that Pilate reword the embarrassing inscription now ridiculed his claims to be the King of Israel and the Son of God (Matt 27:41–43). Again, their taunts—"he saved others; he cannot save himself"—are full of paradox: he will save others from their sins (Matt 1:21) by not saving himself from the cross. The derision of crowds and priests is adumbrated in the godly sufferer of Psalm 22:7–8 who endures sustained attacks without cause from his enemies. Third, the soldiers continued their pattern of mockery and offered him vinegar to increase his torment (Luke 23:36–37; cf. Ps 69:21). To all these groups—crowds, priests, soldiers—the cross was the ultimate proof that Jesus could not be the messianic King he claimed to be. The wisdom of God was and is foolishness to people (1 Cor 1:18–25). Fourth, the two thieves crucified with Jesus hurled insults at him (Matt 27:44). Later, however, one criminal distinguished his own just punishment from the undeserved suffering of Jesus and pleaded for mercy (Luke 23:40–43). Surely it was the way that Jesus, suspended on the cross, responded to his accusers—without retaliation or threats even when reviled, but entrusting himself to the Father's vindication (1 Pet 2:22–23, quot. Isa 53:9)—that brought him to recognize the truth of his royal claims and to plead "remember me when you come into your kingdom." To this earnest plea Jesus issued a *second word* from the cross, namely, the promise of paradise (Luke 23:42–43), the restored Edenic garden of beauty and delight that the consummated kingdom is compared to (Isa 51:3; Rev 2:7; 22:2). This man is the preeminent example of the truth that salvation is a gift of divine grace wholly apart from human merit. A human being with a dark past, a non-existent future, and absolutely nothing to offer is granted the gift of eternal life (Eph 2:8–9).

Finally, there is the tiny band of loyal followers who remained with him to the end (John 19:25–27; cf. Matt 27:56, 61; Mark 15:40, 47). Five mourners, among many others (Matt 27:55), are singled out: Mary the mother of Jesus (the mother of James and Joses); Mary's sister, Salome (the mother of Zebedee's sons); Mary the wife of Clopas; Mary Magdalene; and John, "the disciple whom he loved." John was the only one of the original twelve who was with Jesus in his final hours. Devastated but faithful, he stood before the cross and must have pondered what all this could mean. The other apostles had fled into the darkness at Jesus' arrest. One had openly betrayed the Lord and another, his closest friend, had repeatedly denied any connections to the Nazarene. As Jesus hung on a Roman gibbet, condemned as a common criminal and cursed by God (Deut 21:23), John surely agonized over how a faith adventure that began so gloriously could end so tragically. Yet he was there to carry out Jesus' testamentary charge, his *third word*: "Behold your mother" (John 19:26–27). Jesus committed the care of his mother into the hands of his beloved disciple rather than to the sons of Mary, his half-brothers, who at this time did not believe in him (John 7:5). In obedience John would bring Mary into his home and provide for her as his own mother.

⇨ What was it about the death of Jesus that produced such contrasting effects on its eyewitnesses? How is it that the cross has the power to unmask human character for what it is, as well as the power to transform those who gaze intently at the Man hanging there?

LAST THREE HOURS AND THE FINAL FOUR WORDS FROM THE CROSS

(Matthew 27:45–56; Mark 15:33–41; Luke 23:44–49; John 19:28–30)

For the final three hours of the crucifixion of Jesus (12:00–3:00 p.m.) the entire land of Israel was shrouded in darkness. In biblical imagery darkness is a sign of judgment, for example, upon Egypt for oppressing Israel (Exod 10:21–22) or upon the covenant nation for her idolatrous practices (Amos 5:18, 20; 8:9–10). Most applicable to the present context is Jesus' usage of darkness as a designation of hell itself, the place where God is not (Matt 8:12; 22:13; 25:30). The darkness represents divine judgment on a nation that has rejected her morning star (Num 24:17; Rev 22:16) and on the human race that has chosen to recede into darkness away from the light of the world (John 3:19; 8:12; 12:46). With darkness enveloping the scene and death drawing near, Jesus cried out in Aramaic the words of Psalm 22:1: "My God, my God, why have you forsaken me?" His *fourth word* is a cry of despair that plumbs far greater depths of pain than that experienced by David under the sustained and undeserved attacks of his enemies. This is the cry of abandonment of one whose preeminent joy has been unbroken communion with his Father. The separation from the Father that he dreaded in Gethsemane (Matt 26:38–39) now reaches full force as the sins of mankind descend upon him, driving him away from the presence of the Holy One. The apostles employ the term *propitiation* to unlock the meaning of the cross: God's holy wrath against sin is satisfied by being poured out on a substitute, the sinless God-Man, so that for a mysterious and imponderable moment of time the first and second persons of the Trinity, Father and Son, are alienated from one another (Rom 3:25–26; 1 John 2:2; 4:10). Christ bears upon himself the penalty of sin deserved by all people, namely, physical death—separation of body and soul—and spiritual death—the banishment of the soul from God's presence. By being nailed to the cross Jesus bears the divine curse upon law-breakers in their stead (Gal 3:13, quot. Deut 21:23). Through faith in the Substitute comes the gift of the forgiveness of sins, wholly established in the merits of another. This penal substitution is not a cold commercial transaction but the gracious act born of the Father's love and the Son's obedience. The salvation of people is the passion of the Servant (Isa 53:10–12).

The Aramaic term for "my God," *eloi*, sounded like Elijah, and was misunderstood as a cry of help for the famous prophet of old. Jewish tradition held that Elijah, who was translated to heaven without seeing death (2 Kgs 2:12) and who will one day come to prepare the people before the Lord's return (Mal 4:5), ministers during the interim period as a source of consolation, strength and healing for God's righteous ones. Jesus was hoping in vain for Elijah's rescue, they reasoned. The final four words of Jesus from the cross were spoken in rapid succession at the very end. He next uttered his *fifth word*, "I thirst" (John 19:28). This brought to fulfillment Psalm 69:21 when some witnesses soaked a sponge in wine vinegar, placed it on the long stalk of a hyssop plant, and lifted it to Jesus' lips. This time (unlike the first two, once before [Matt 27:34] and once during [Luke 23:36–37] the crucifixion) the drink was offered, not to torment him, but in sympathy at his request and he received it. In the fourth Gospel "thirst" denotes more than the physical need for water but the parched condition of the heart that can only be quenched by a relationship with Jesus and his bestowal of the life-giving Spirit (John 4:13–15; 6:35; 7:37; cf. Rev 21:6; 22:17). He endures a vicarious death for those perishing in the desert of sin—he thirsted, in separation from the Father, so that our spiritual thirst may be permanently satisfied.

The *sixth word* is, literally, one word in the Greek: "It is finished" (John 19:30). Here is the completion of his mission as the suffering Servant. To bring glory to the Father by finishing his assigned work was his very food (John 4:34; 5:36; 17:4). His cry of despair now becomes a shout of victory. A perfect life concludes with this crowning act of obedience—a fully accomplished substitutionary sacrifice for the sins of the world. His *seventh and final word*, presaged by the Psalmist (31:5),—"Father, into your hands I commit my spirit" (Luke 23:46)—signifies that Jesus' death is a voluntary act of release, not a tragic ending (John 10:17–18). Moments earlier forsaken by God, Jesus now voiced his resolute confidence in the one who designed this very moment. Bowing his head, he reposed his spirit in the bosom of the Father (John 1:18).

At the moment of Jesus' death the curtain in the temple that separated the Holy Place from the Holy of Holies (Exod 26:31–35) was torn in two from top to bottom. This heavy curtain (recorded in ancient sources to be sixty feet long with the thickness of the palm of the hand) shielded priests performing their ordinary duties in the outer compartment from God's presence above the ark of the covenant in the Holy of Holies, accessible only to the high priest once a year on the Day of Atonement (Lev 16). Jesus' body was torn, like the curtain, to provide open and direct access into the presence of God at any time and place (Heb 4:16; 6:19–20; 10:19–22). An earthquake, symbolizing God's powerful intervention and majestic rule over the created world (Isa 29:6; Jer 10:10; Hag 2:6), shook the land at both the death (Matt 27:51b) and the resurrection (Matt 28:2) of Jesus. These cataclysmic events in the drama of redemption caused the natural world to convulse. Just as the giving of the law at Sinai was accompanied by a terrifying earthquake (Exod 19:18), so the inauguration of the new covenant, signifying the obsolescence of the temple and the law, is signaled by the shaking of the earth.

The earthquake caused many tombs in Jerusalem to break open (Matt 27:52a). Then, on the third day, after the resurrection of Jesus, many holy people were raised to life, came forth in their resurrection bodies, and appeared to many people in the holy city (Matt 27:52b–53). These were probably a representative number of Old Testament saints whose early resurrection is recorded here by Matthew as an anticipatory bridge between the narrative of Jesus' death and the narrative of his resurrection that follows his burial. The theological significance of this mysterious entry seems to be that the death of Jesus not only propitiates God's wrath and opens access to God's presence, but also, by virtue of his own resurrection, guarantees the resurrection of all saints including those who died before his coming. One concluding act in the Passion drama remains: now the Father will vindicate Jesus' claims to Sonship and validate the efficacy of his death by raising him from the dead (Rom 1:3–4).

The cruel mockery of passers by, chief priests and scribes, robbers crucified next to him, and Roman soldiers was not the whole story. The death of Jesus had a transforming effect upon some who looked and pondered more deeply. The Roman centurion along with some of the soldiers stationed at the scene, both terrified at the earthquake and moved by the manner of his death, confessed he was surely the Son of God. The centurion's understanding of Sonship was elementary (Luke records the less elevated confession, "surely this was a righteous man" [23:47, NIV]), but it is a reversal of the earlier taunts (Matt 27:40, 43). Many observers, including some who had earlier participated in the mockery, returned to their homes in contrite mourning (Luke 23:48). And the faithful Galilean women who had supported the ministry (Luke 8:2–3) and followed him to Jerusalem remained to the very end in the shadow of the cross.

⇨ Review and list the seven words spoken by Jesus on the cross. How do these words, taken as a whole, validate our understanding of the Gospels as "*Passion narratives with extended introductions*"?

CERTIFICATION OF DEATH AND INTERMENT OF THE BODY
(Matthew 27:57–66; Mark 15:42–47; Luke 23:50–56; John 19:31–42)

Friday was the day of Preparation for the Sabbath day to follow. While the Romans would leave bodies on their crosses to decompose for days, Jewish law stipulated that the body of an impaled victim must not be left overnight but taken down and buried that same day lest the land be defiled with the prolonged visible decay of the body of one under the divine curse (Deut 21:22–23). Crucified victims would attempt to push themselves up by their legs to keep their chest cavity open in order to breathe. The Roman soldiers complied with the Jews' request that the victims' legs be shattered with a heavy iron mallet so that they could not delay their inevitable death by suffocation or heart failure. After breaking the legs of the two thieves, they came to Jesus but found him already expired, making it unnecessary to break his legs. Severely weakened by the chastisement and scourging, Jesus died relatively quickly (six hours). One of the soldiers pierced Jesus' side with a spear causing a flow of blood and water to spill on the ground, certifying his death. John underscores the truthfulness of his eyewitness testimony. The details surrounding his death bring to fulfillment two prophetic lines of witness from the Old Testament: first, Jesus is the Passover lamb sacrificed for sin (Exod 12:46) and the righteous sufferer ultimately delivered by the Lord (Ps 34:19–20), both of whose bones are not broken; second, he is the one pierced for transgressions whom Israel and the nations will one day receive as their Savior in mournful repentance (Isa 53:5; Zech 12:10; Rev 1:7).

With evening approaching and the commencement of the Sabbath (*Saturday*), one Joseph from the Judean village of Arimathea courageously stepped forward and requested from Pilate the body of Jesus in order to give him a proper Jewish burial. Joseph is variously described as a rich man (Matt), a respected member of the Sanhedrin (Mark), a good and righteous man who did not consent to the decision of the council to condemn Jesus (Luke), one who was waiting in faith for God's promised kingdom (Mark/Luke), and a secret disciple of Jesus (Matt/John). After confirming from the centurion that Jesus was dead, Pilate granted Joseph's request because he knew that Jesus was the innocent victim of religious envy rather than, like the two thieves, guilty of a capital crime. Joseph took the body down from the cross and moved it to his own freshly hewn burial tomb, located in a garden near Golgotha. He was assisted by his fellow council member, Nicodemus, earlier introduced in John's Gospel for his interview of Jesus at night (3:1–9) and his protest at the unjust treatment of Jesus by his fellow Pharisees (7:50–51). The two men carefully prepared Jesus' body for burial in accordance with Jewish custom, placing an abundant mixture (about 100 litrai or sixty-five pounds) of the spices of myrrh and aloes in the linen wrappings to retard the odor of the decomposing corpse. The linen strips were then wound around the body and a one-piece shroud wrapped around Jesus' head (John 20:5–7). Jesus was laid in the tomb which was sealed by a large disk-shaped stone that fitted into a slot on a steep incline, protecting the contents from wild animals or grave robbers. The bold and pious actions of these secret disciples are in stark contrast with those of Jesus' open disciples who at the moment of crisis had betrayed him (Judas), fled into the darkness, denied any association with him (Peter), or stood demoralized before the cross (John).

The Galilean women followed Joseph to the garden and watched as the two men carried Jesus' body and placed it in the tomb. Mary Magdalene and Jesus' mother, Mary (assuming her to be the "other Mary" [Matt 27:61], the mother of Joses [Mark 15:47]), waited for a while opposite the tomb. They returned to their homes before Sabbath began at sunset and prepared spices and perfumes (Luke 23:56) which they would bring with them early Sunday morning with the intent of anointing Jesus' body (Mark 16:1). These devout women then rested on the Sabbath day. Whether or not they were aware of the preparation of the body by Joseph and Nicodemus, they desired to pour aromatic oils over Jesus' head as one final act of personal love and devotion, even as Mary of Bethany had anointed Jesus' head for burial nine days before (John 12:1–8).

No one among these followers entertained hopes of resurrection. Ironically, it was leading members of the Sanhedrin, chief priests and

Pharisees, that recalled Jesus' predictions of rising again on the third day (Matt 16:21; 17:9; 20:19), perhaps cynically related to them by Judas Iscariot on Wednesday when he initiated the betrayal (Matt 26:14–16). So the Jewish authorities requested that Pilate secure the tomb through Sunday in order to prevent Jesus' disciples from stealing the body and perpetuating a fraud of resurrection in fulfillment of Jesus' predictions. Pilate would not dispatch his own soldiers but granted the Sanhedrin authority to post some of their own temple police to guard the tomb (Matt 27:65–66). The stone which fortified the entrance was further sealed with an official wax seal after the guard confirmed that the body of Jesus was inside. Thus the location of the garden tomb where Jesus' dead body lay was verified by multiple witnesses: by Joseph and Nicodemus, by the Galilean women, and by the temple authorities and their guard. Strangely, these same religious leaders would end up circulating the stolen body theory when their attempts to prevent an empty tomb proved futile (Matt 28:11–15).

⇨ Why is Jesus' burial an important part of the basic content of the gospel as proclaimed by the apostles (1 Cor 15:3–5)? What does the burial symbolize with respect to salvation in Christ (Rom 6:4)?

18

Passion Week V

Day of Conquest

THE APPEARANCES OF THE RISEN LORD

JESUS WAS DEAD AND with his interment the hopes and aspirations of his closest followers seemed to be buried with him. In spite of his clear promise to be reunited with them (John 16:19–22), the apostles seemed to entertain little or no hope in his resurrection. Yet within a few weeks the demoralized band of mourners was transformed into witnesses who boldly proclaimed that the Lord Jesus was risen from the dead (Acts 1:22; 3:14–15; 4:1–2, 10–12, 33; 5:31–32; 10:39–41). To the apostles the resurrection of Jesus Christ was the mighty intervention of God the Father acting to vindicate his Son's majestic claims and validate the efficacy of his cross-work for the redemption of the world (Rom 1:3–4; 4:25; 10:9; 1 Cor 15:20–24). Many speculative theories have been offered to explain the purported 'myth' of Jesus' resurrection: the body was stolen and a fraud was perpetuated; Jesus lost consciousness or 'swooned,' but did not actually die and later revived; Mary went to the wrong tomb and convinced the others of her imaginary meeting with the Lord; the disciples, fueled by deep longings for reunion with Jesus, experienced subjective visions out of which emerged the Easter event. The uniform testimony of the four Gospels is that one reality alone had the power to convince the skeptical and despairing followers of Jesus that he had indeed risen from the dead—a series of space-time appearances of the living Lord over forty days, first in Jerusalem and later in Galilee (Acts 1:3).

Harmonizing the resurrection narratives of the four Gospels is a thorny problem. The chart below lists the twelve appearances of the risen Lord, nine from the Gospels and three more added by Paul at the beginning of the great resurrection chapter, 1 Corinthians 15.

Event	Date	NT Passage
1. At the empty tomb outside Jerusalem to three women	Early Sunday morning	Matt 28:1–10; Mark 16:1–8; Luke 24:1–12; John 20:1–9
2. To Mary Magdalene at the tomb after Peter and John leave	Early Sunday morning	John 20:11–18; [Mark 16:9–11]
3. To two travelers on the road to Emmaus, seven miles from Jerusalem	Sunday at midday	Luke 24:13–32; [Mark 16:12–13]
4. A personal appearance to Peter in Jerusalem	Sunday afternoon	Luke 24:34; 1 Cor 15:5a
5. To the ten disciples (minus Thomas) in the upper room in Jerusalem	Sunday evening	Luke 24:36–43; John 20:19–25; [Mark 16:14]
6. To the eleven disciples in the upper room in Jerusalem	"eight days later" (John 20:26), that is, Sunday evening one week later	John 20:26–31; 1Cor 15:5b
7. To seven disciples fishing on the Sea of Tiberius (Galilee)	"afterward" (John 21:1), that is, one day at daybreak	John 21:1–23
8. To the eleven disciples on a mountain in Galilee	some time later	Matt 28:16–20; [Mark 16:15–18]
9. To more than five hundred brothers at the same time	unknown	1 Cor 15:6
10. To James, half-brother of the Lord	unknown	1 Cor 15:7a
11. At the ascension on the Mount of Olives	forty days after the resurrection (Acts 1:3)	Luke 24:44–53; Acts 1:3–11; [Mark 16:19–20]; 1 Cor 15:7b
12. last of all to Paul, "as to one untimely born"	near Damascus, approx. two years later	1 Cor 15:8 (cf. Acts 9:1–8; 1 Cor 9:1)

Matthew records two appearances, one in Jerusalem and one in Galilee; Mark records the first Jerusalem appearance (five more are added in the long ending of 16:9–20); Luke contains five appearances, all in or near Jerusalem; John also has four Jerusalem appearances, as well as the exclusive account of Jesus' visit to seven disciples at the Sea of Tiberius. Various attempts have been made to reconstruct the order of events on that first Easter Sunday. The following is one plausible sequence of the appearances that commends itself to the present author, though, like all proposals, it is not without its difficulties. The primary texts for each stage of the reconstruction are in *italics*.

1. Before sunrise on *Sunday*, the first day of the week, a number of the believing women from Galilee come to the tomb in order to anoint Jesus' body with the spices and perfumes they had purchased and prepared late Friday. Four are named: Mary Magdalene; Jesus' mother, Mary, also called the mother of James (or "the other Mary" [Matt 28:1]); Salome, the mother of John; and Joanna. They were probably unaware of the extent that Jesus' body had already been prepared for burial by Joseph and Nicodemus (John 19:39–40). They wondered on the way whether someone might be found to help them move the heavy stone from the entrance. (*Matt 28:1; Mark 16:1–3; Luke 24:1, 10; John 20:1*)

2. When they arrive the stone has already been rolled away and the tomb is empty. The barrier was removed not to let Jesus out but to let the disciples in. Another earthquake has signaled a momentous redemptive event (Matt 28:2; cf. Matt 27:51b, 54). The stone was rolled back by an angel of the Lord, evidenced by the lightning-like appearance and pure white raiment as he sat on the stone. The temple guards were, like the earth, shaken and became frozen in fear. (*Matt 28:2–4*)

3. Mary Magdalene rushes off to tell Peter and John that the body of Jesus has been stolen. Matthew may be compressing the events of that pre-dawn earthquake and angelic appearance (28:2–4). When the women first arrived, it seems they discovered an open and empty tomb with the guards nowhere to be found. It seems likely that the angel's visible appearance and communication takes place after Mary's hasty departure. (*John 20:2*)

4. Suddenly the women who remain encounter two angels in dazzling appearance. Matthew focuses on the angel of the Lord who rolled the stone away and is the primary spokesman; Mark refers to a young

man dressed in a white robe sitting on the right side of the tomb; Luke records there were two men in gleaming apparel; John interprets the phenomenological record of the Synoptics by recording that there were two angels dressed in white (John 20:12). Angels at times assume human appearance when they visit the earth (Gen 18:2; 19:1; Judg 6:11–13; 13:6, 21; Heb 13:2). The central affirmation of the angels to the women who are seeking Jesus is: "He is not here, for he has risen, as he said" (Matt 28:6). They are told not to fear and are invited to enter and see the place where Jesus' body was interred. They are reminded of their Lord's predictions of suffering and death, as well as his promise of resurrection (Matt 16:21; 17:22–23; 20:18–19; 26:31–32). They must relate to Peter and the others that Jesus will appear to them in Galilee, just as he promised (Matt 26:32). (*Matt 28:5–7; Mark 16:4–7; Luke 24:2–8*)

5. The women flee from the tomb, filled with fear and joyful amazement at what they have seen and heard, speaking to no one about their encounter (*Matt 28:8; Mark 16:8*). Mark's Gospel ends on this note of mystery and expectation. A little later in the day Jesus greets the women (not necessarily in the garden) who have fled the tomb. They fall prostrate, grasping his feet and worshipping him. This is the *first appearance* of the risen Lord. He tells them to inform his disciples ("my brothers") that he has risen and will appear to them in Galilee, just as predicted earlier by the angel (Matt 28:7). The disciples are still scattered at this time (Matt 26:56b). (*Matt 28:9–10*)

6. Meanwhile, Peter and John, having been informed by Mary Magdalene of the missing body, run to the tomb after the other women have left. Though John arrives at the entrance first and peers in, Peter bolts into the tomb and finds the linen strips lying on the ground and the head wrapping folded separately. It is an orderly scene, not one disturbed in haste by friends or foes. Did Jesus' resurrection body pass through the linen strips without moving them so that he was then free to carefully unwrap and fold the head piece before departing? It is unclear. John then followed Peter into the tomb and, probably recalling the Lord's predictions, believed in his resurrection though he failed to fasten this event to its prophetic mooring in the Old Testament (Ps 16:9–11; 110:1; Isa 53:11). The resurrection event itself created faith in the risen Lord and then stimulated the apostles to search the Old Testament for its

significance in the plan of redemption. Peter and John then returned to their residences in Jerusalem (*John 20:3–10; Luke 24:12*).

7. Mary Magdalene returns to the tomb after Peter and John have left. They had run to the tomb leaving Mary behind (John 20:4). When she peers into the chamber she sees the two angels sitting where the body of Jesus had been. She laments over the Lord's body having been stolen, unaware of the experience of the women she left earlier in the garden. The empty tomb by itself does not produce faith but despair. Jesus then appears to Mary Magdalene whom she recognizes when he calls her "Mary." She begins to embrace the Lord but is told to stop, "for I have not yet ascended to the Father." The Lord's time of being physically present with his disciples is soon to be replaced by a new order in which his exalted presence, at the Father's right hand, will be mediated by the Holy Spirit. Jesus commands Mary, like the other women at his earlier appearance (Matt 28:10), to tell "my brothers" that he is alive and will soon return to his Father. Disciples will now enjoy direct access to "your Father" and "your God" through his death, resurrection and exaltation. This is the *second appearance* of the risen Jesus (*John 20:11–17*).

8. Some of the disciples, including Peter and John, have now gathered together and hear the report of the Galilean women who break their silence about their encounter with the two angels. The words seemed like nonsense to the listeners (*Luke 24:9–11*). Then suddenly Mary Magdalene comes in and claims that Jesus appeared to her in the garden (*John 20:18*; cf. Mk 16:9–11).

9. Temple guards under the authority of the high priest had been posted at the tomb, with Pilate's permission, to prevent Jesus' disciples from stealing the body and perpetuating the fraud of a resurrection (Matt 27:62–66). Early on Sunday morning these guards were paralyzed in fear at the earthquake, removal of the stone and appearance of the angel of the Lord (Matt 28:2–4). The guards then left the tomb and reported to leading priests of the Sanhedrin all that had happened along with the disappearance of the body. The priests conferred with some of the elders on the council and devised a plan: the guards are to report that Jesus' disciples stole the body in the middle of the night while they were sleeping. The guards agree to circulate this story for payment of a substantial bribe and for promises that they will not be punished by the Roman governor for their failure to secure the tomb. For Roman soldiers such

dereliction of duty was punishable by death (Acts 12:19; 16:27; 27:42), but that may not have applied to temple police. The stolen body rumor was still circulating at the time of the composition of Matthew's Gospel approximately thirty years later and was, in fact, alive and well in the days of Justin Martyr over a century later. (*Matt 28:11–15*)

10. Sunday afternoon Jesus appears to two disciples, one named Cleopas, who are en route to the village of Emmaus sixty stadia or about seven miles northwest of Jerusalem. This is the *third appearance* of the risen Lord (*Luke 24:13–35*; cf. Mk 16:12–13). While walking along the way, the two men are discussing the events surrounding Jesus' death and the emerging reports of his resurrection. Suddenly a stranger joins in the walk and inquires about their conversation, feigning ignorance of the events of recent days. Has the stranger not heard of the momentous happenings in Jerusalem—the death of Jesus of Nazareth, a mighty prophet, powerful teacher and miraculous healer, the one "we had hoped . . . was the one to redeem Israel"? The disciples are still clinging to nationalistic notions of Messiahship. Their downcast looks prove that the reports of the women who claimed an encounter with angels who announced that Jesus was alive and the confirmation of an empty tomb by Peter and John have done little to revive their hopes. Without warning, their unknown companion issues a stern rebuke for their failure to grasp what is clearly set forth in their own prophetic writings—the humiliation and subsequent exaltation of the Messiah. Rebuke is followed by exposition as Jesus unlocks text after text from Moses to the prophets that point to himself as the suffering Servant and exalted King. Jesus spends part of the evening in Emmaus with the two disciples and is finally recognized when they break bread together. Suddenly he disappears from their sight, leaving the two to reflect on the power of the Lord's biblical exposition of suffering and glory as they walked along the road. They return to Jerusalem to announce their startling discovery.

11. Sometime Sunday afternoon the Lord makes a special appearance to Peter, the *fourth visible demonstration* of his resurrected life to his disciples (*Luke 24:34*; cf. 1 Cor 15:5a). The reader of the narrative longs to know what words, if any, were exchanged between the Lord, whom Peter had last seen as Jesus glanced in his direction in the courtyard following his denials (Luke 22:61), and the apostle he promised to restore

(Luke 22:31–32). Alas, Luke's record is silent. A series of independent confirmations is emerging as the assembled disciples hear the reports, not only of an empty tomb but of a living Lord—from the Galilean women (#5), Mary Magdalene (#7), the two Emmaus disciples (#10) and now Peter.

12. On Sunday evening Jesus suddenly appears to ten apostles (minus Thomas), among many others (Luke 24:33), gathered in a locked room due to fear of the Jewish authorities. The disciples had been scattered but the testimony of the three women (Matt 28:8; Luke 24:9–11), of Peter and John (John 20:10; Luke 24:34), then of Mary Magdalene (John 20:18), and finally of the two Emmaus disciples (Luke 24:33–35) served to bring them together. This is the *fifth appearance* of the risen Jesus, a reunion he promised would turn their grief to joy (John 16:19–22). His characteristic Jewish greeting of *Shalom* frightens them. When Jesus invites them to look carefully and to touch his hands and feet there is joyful disbelief and wonder. He eats a piece of broiled fish before them. Jesus' resurrection body is tangible and real: his wounds are visible; he speaks, can be seen and touched; he receives food; he breathes upon them. Yet his new bodily existence is one with supernatural properties: he can suddenly appear, disappear and pass through material barriers such as walls or a locked door. In an acted parable—"he breathed on them"—Jesus anticipates the definitive event of Pentecost by commissioning them to go and preach forgiveness and judgment in the power of the Spirit as his ambassadors (John 20:21–23). When Thomas is later told by his excited colleagues of the Lord's appearance, he demands proof and asserts in no uncertain terms that he must have a firsthand faith based on visible evidence: "Unless I see in his hands the mark of the nails, and place my finger into the mark of the nails, and place my hand into his side, I will never believe" (John 20:25). His language is the most emphatic negative expression possible in the Greek language. Far from being psychologically fragile men poised on the precipice of belief, needing only a subjective vision to push them toward an Easter faith (as historical critics often portray them), the Gospels uniformly describe the apostles as inclined to doubt and disbelief, needing multiple appearances to really convince them that Jesus rose from the dead (Luke 24:38, 41; John 20:25, 27; Matt 28:17; cf. Mark 16:14). (*Luke 24:36–43; John 20:19–25*; cf. Mark 16:14).

13. Eight days later (both Easter Sunday and the following Sunday factored in the inclusive reckoning [John 20:26]), that is, on Sunday evening the week following Easter, the Lord appears to the eleven apostles. Once again he passes through the locked doors of the house and offers a benediction of peace. He particularly accommodates Thomas who has made the noble demand for objective evidence to substantiate the verbal claims of his friends. Even without touching the Lord, his earlier precondition for believing, doubting Thomas becomes worshipping Thomas, confessing the living Jesus as "my Lord and my God." The sight of the wounds banishes Thomas' doubts and leads to the most exalted confession of Jesus' lordship and deity on the lips of a human being during the entire earthly ministry. While Thomas is commended for believing, Jesus pronounces a greater blessing upon those "who have not seen and yet have believed" (John 20:29), the future generations of believers he prayed for in his priestly intercession (John 17:20). Faith is heartfelt confidence in the person and work of the Lord Jesus Christ based upon the truthful eyewitness testimony of the apostles. John reveals the purpose behind his writing of the fourth Gospel: it is a selective account of the miraculous works (and interpretive words) of Jesus intended to lead the reader to acknowledge that Jesus is the Jewish Messiah and the divine Son of God through which believing one might receive the gift of eternal life. This is the *sixth appearance* of the risen Jesus (*John 20:26–31*; cf. 1 Cor 15:5b).

14. Jesus promised before his death (Matt 26:32) and in his appearance to the Galilean women (Matt 28:7, 10) that he would meet his disciples in Galilee. Seven disciples, including Peter and the sons of Zebedee, have returned to Galilee and are fishing together on the Sea of Tiberius. At dawn Jesus appears on the shore, though unrecognized, and instructs them to cast the net on the right side of the boat. Peter, James and John must have recalled a similar incident three years before (Luke 5:1–11). Now, as then, they have toiled all night without success, but at a stranger's command they make a catch so large they cannot haul it in. John recognizes it is the Lord. Peter reacts by wrapping up with his outer garment and jumping into the water. Is he so eager to greet the Lord that he cannot wait and must quickly swim ashore? Does the garment, even drenched, prepare him to greet the Lord more acceptably? However

one interprets Peter's impulsive response, the sequel is a breakfast of bread and roasted fish with his favorite companion.

After they finish eating, Jesus and Peter enter into an emotional interchange (John 21:15–23). Three times Jesus directs the same question to his disciple: "Do you love me (more than these)?" The basis of the comparison "than these" in the first question, and assumed in the following two, is unclear to the reader; Peter does not take it up and Jesus never interprets it. If the demonstrative pronoun is masculine, Jesus is inviting comparison between Peter's devotion to that of the other disciples: "Do you love me more than these other disciples do?" However, it is doubtful that Jesus would seek such a comparative assessment, especially in light of the rivalry among the disciples that earned his rebuke (Mark 10:41–43), as well as Peter's past tendencies toward overconfidence (Matt 26:33; John 13:37). Further, in the follow-up conversation Jesus mildly reproves Peter for being distracted with John's destiny (John 21:20–23). If the pronoun is neuter, the rendering is, "Do you love me more than these things?" The Lord would be pointing to Peter's fishing gear, which represents his previous career with its material provisions and security. Jesus is, then, calling Peter to reaffirm his commitment, made over three years before on this same shore of Lake Galilee, to fish for (and to feed) people rather than to catch fish (Matt 4:18–20).

With each affirmative answer comes the same question, which grieves Peter (John 21:17). The Lord knows his heart and cannot be questioning his sincere love, in spite of all the foolish chatter, impulsive actions, bombastic claims, and bitter setbacks of the past. What Jesus underscores with such sanctified redundancy is that if, as is true, Peter loves him, then that love must be translated into the ministry of caring for his spiritual lambs (John 21:15, 16, 17). At the outset of his pilgrimage Peter is called to fish for people (Matt 4:19); at the conclusion he is commissioned to shepherd the lambs. The two metaphors for evangelistic and pastoral roles respectively will be Peter's life work as the foundational "rock" of the church (Matt 16:18). Jesus' reinstatement of Peter involves more than forgiveness of the past; it dignifies his future with a role of supreme importance. This is the fullest measure of restoration there could be. Peter's tendency to get distracted emerges again when Jesus speaks in cryptic terms about his disciple's coming violent death (John 21:18–19). Peter turns to John and asks the Lord,

"What about this man?" John's record of this conversation is, in part, to dispel the rumor that he would be spared death. The Lord made no such promise, only reminding Peter that his responsibility was to follow Jesus wherever his ordained path might lead and to leave John and the future in his capable hands. Years later as his life draws to a close, Peter, the rock, recalls the Lord's words and will make his "exodus" (literally, departure in death) with perfect composure (2 Pet 1:13–15), an exodus that will be an "entrance" into the eternal kingdom of the Lord Jesus Christ (2 Pet 1:11). This is the *seventh appearance* of the risen Jesus (*John 21:1–23*), the third time he appeared to his disciples as an assembled group (21:14; cf. John 20:19–25; 20:26–31).

15. The eleven apostles went to a designated mountain in Galilee as Jesus had instructed them (Matt 28:16). When Jesus appeared they worshipped him, "but some doubted" (Matt 28:17). The doubters were most likely some of "my brothers" (28:10), that is, a wider group of disciples beyond the eleven who until now had not had a firsthand encounter with the risen Lord and who hesitated when he appeared to them. The Lord issues his *Great Commission* (for details see below). His followers are to go out in his authority, disciple all the nations by baptizing those who believe and teaching the new believers to obey all of his commands. They are promised the Lord's presence each and every day until the end of the present age. This is the *eighth appearance* of the risen Lord (*Matt 28:16–20*; cf. Mark 16:15–18).

16. The forty days of appearances (Acts 1:3) conclude with Jesus' visible ascension to heaven from the Mount of Olives. Before his departure the Lord expounds the details of his life, death, resurrection and worldwide redemptive proclamation in light of the anticipatory record in the Old Testament. All that has taken place in his incarnation is the fulfillment of the divine plan recorded in Holy Scripture. The Lord reminds his disciples that they should not be overly taken up with the details and timing of future prophetic events, but to dedicate their energies to being his witnesses to the ends of the earth. As he is taken up into heaven, with the promise that he will one day return in like manner, the disciples worshipped Jesus and returned with great joy to Jerusalem to wait for the promised baptism of the Holy Spirit. This is the *eleventh appearance* of the risen Jesus (*Luke 24:44–53; Acts 1:3–11*; cf. Mark 16:19–20; 1 Cor 15:7b). Paul adds three further appearances, which we number

the *ninth, tenth and twelfth appearances* respectively: to more than 500 brothers at the same time (1 Cor 15:6); to James, the half-brother of the Lord (1 Cor 15:7a); and last of all (approximately two years later) to Paul himself, "as to one untimely born" (1 Cor 15:8).

TESTAMENTARY COMMISSION

(Matthew 28:18–20; Luke 24:44–49; John 20:21–23; Acts 1:6–8)

Three of the four canonical Gospels conclude with the testamentary charge that Jesus delivered to his disciples. This *'Great Commission'* as it is often called, was spoken at three separate appearances of the risen Lord. Coming as it does in the aftermath of the Easter event, the message of the kingdom now takes on its full-orbed character, that is, the gospel of the crucified and risen Lord Jesus Christ (1 Cor 15:3–4). John's Gospel records the charge given after Jesus' appearance to the ten disciples in the upper room (John 20:19–25). Matthew's account relates the commission of the disciples on a mountain in Galilee (Matt 28:16–20). Luke-Acts contains the final words of Jesus before his ascension from the Mount of Olives (Luke 24:44–53; Acts 1:3–11). There is a solemn character to the redundancy. The risen Lord rests his legacy on the Spirit-energized obedience of the disciples to his final command. The provisions and parameters for its fulfillment are carefully detailed.

1. *Missional continuity*: The program of redemption was planned by the Father and carried out by his Son. The work of redemption accomplished by the Son is entrusted to the disciples to proclaim to the nations. The Son is the great missionary of the Father and disciples are in turn his 'sent ones' (John 20:21). The preparation, execution and proclamation stages of the redemptive program are in perfect solidarity, bound together by a driving passion to enter the world of lost humanity.

2. *Internal empowerment*: In his appearance to the ten disciples Jesus breathed on them and pronounced the reception of the Holy Spirit (John 20:22). This was an acted parable anticipatory of Pentecost when the Spirit would descend upon the Jerusalem believers (Luke 24:49; Acts 2:1–4). God the Father created the universal church through his baptizing work with the Spirit (Acts 1:4–5; 11:15–17). The Spirit in turn empowers the church for its universal witness to the person and work of Christ (Acts 1:8).

3. *Royal authorization*: The resurrection of Christ was the prequel to his exaltation to the right hand of the Father and his investiture as Lord and King (Acts 2:32–36; Phil 2:9–11). The exercise of universal authority both for salvation and judgment has been committed by the Father to the Son (Matt 28:18). The inferential conjunction "therefore" (Matt 28:19a) establishes the accomplishment of the mission as the logical and necessary consequence of Christ's investiture with universal authority. The authorized ambassadors of the King go forth and proclaim forgiveness or retention of sins based on the response of the listeners (John 21:23).

4. *Comprehensive task*: The central mandate is to disciple the nations, which incorporates both evangelism and teaching (Matt 28:19–20a). Water baptism is the public verification of the personal response of faith to the gospel and incorporation into the community of faith subject to the lordship of the Triune God. Teaching new believers all the commands of Christ with a view to obedience is the task of each generation of disciple-makers. The mandate, then, aims to bring new believers to submit every dimension of their lives to the lordship of Christ. Because the Lord Jesus Christ is invested with universal authority as Savior and Judge, his teachings form the binding constitution for the transformed character and behavioral standards for the new covenant community.

5. *Universal scope*: All the peoples of the earth are viewed as potential disciples of the King. Jesus' constant concern for the non-Jewish peoples (Matt 4:15–16; 8:5–13; 10:18; 13:38; 24:14) now issues in a centrifugal mission to go, seek, find, and proclaim to "all nations" that the suffering Servant is the exalted King (Matt 28:19; Luke 24:47–49; John 20:21; Acts 1:8).

6. *Benedictory presence*: In the intervening period while he is physically absent, the Lord promises to mediate his presence to his disciples through the Holy Spirit (John 14:16–18; 16:12–16). His abiding presence with the disciples encompasses, literally, "all the days until the consummation of the age" (Matt 28:20b). "Day by day and with each passing moment," in the words of the familiar hymn, the kingdom witnesses draw strength from their constant Companion until time recedes into eternity and a tiny mustard seed becomes a mighty tree (Matt 13:31–32).

7. *Anticipatory hope*: Just before his ascension the apostles inquire if now, at last, Jesus will usher the nation of Israel into her kingdom glory (Acts 1:6). The Lord neither corrects nor affirms the implications of the question regarding Israel's destiny. They must, he counters, resist the temptation to speculate on the finer points of eschatology and leave the "times or seasons" to his sovereign disposition (Acts 1:7). Their task is to engage in ever-expanding concentric circles of witness from their present neighborhood to "the end of the earth" (Acts 1:8). The promise of his personal and visible return to earth comprised the angels' culminative words that rang in the apostles' ears as Jesus disappeared from their sight (Acts 1:11).

⇨ On what level are you an active participant in the great missionary enterprise which the risen Lord entrusted to that first generation of apostles and to all subsequent generations of disciples "to the end of the age" (Matt 28:20b)? This enterprise requires both goers and senders, the latter comprised of those who pray, give and actively encourage the front-line 'sent ones.' Identify one level on which you can deepen your commitment to the mission of the church, such as joining the missions committee at your local church (or helping to form one if it does not yet exist).

Chronology of the Life of Christ

Date	Event	Text
5–4 BC	Birth of Jesus in Bethlehem (before death of Herod in 4 BC)	Luke 2:1–7
AD 26	Commencement of John the Baptist's ministry in the Jordan valley situated in secular history	Luke 3:1–3
Spring/Summer AD 26	Jesus' baptism around age 30 (Luke 3:23)	Matt 3:13–17
Summer AD 26–Spring 27	Opening events of Jesus' public ministry: baptism; temptation (40 days); Cana wedding feast; to Capernaum	John 1:19—2:12
April AD 27	First cleansing of the temple at Passover	John 2:13
Spring–Fall AD 27	Early Judean Ministry	John 2:13—4:42
Winter–Fall AD 28	Early Galilean Ministry: arrival in Galilee until the choosing of the Twelve and Sermon on the Mount	Mark 1:14—3:19 Matt 5:1—7:29

September AD 28	To Jerusalem for the Feast of Tabernacles	John 5:1
Late Fall AD 28– Early Summer 29	Middle Galilean Ministry: from the close of the Sermon until, but not including, the northern withdrawal	Mark 3:20—7:23
Summer–Fall AD 29	Later Galilean Ministry: northern withdrawal to the trip to Jerusalem for Tabernacles	Mark 7:24—9:50
Fall AD 29	Later Judean Ministry: Feast of Tabernacles to the Feast of Dedication	Luke 9:51—13:21 John 7:2—10:39
January – Mid-February AD 30	Early Perean Ministry	Luke 13:22—17:10 John 10:40—11:53
Mid-February – late March AD 30	Later Perean Ministry	Luke 17:11—19:28 Mark 10:1–52
Spring AD 30	Passion Week	
Friday, Nisan 15, AD 30	Crucifixion	

Bibliography

Barclay, William. *Introduction to the First Three Gospels*. Rev. ed. Philadelphia: Westminster, 1975.

Beale, G. K. and D. A. Carson, eds. *Commentary on the New Testament Use of the Old Testament*. Grand Rapids: Baker, 2007.

Bruce, A. B. *The Training of the Twelve*. Reprint ed. Grand Rapids: Kregel, 1971 (1894).

Bruce, F. F. *The Hard Sayings of Jesus*. Downers Grove, IL: InterVarsity, 1983.

Danby, Herbert. *The Mishnah*. Oxford University Press, 1933.

Edersheim, Alfred. *The Life and Times of Jesus the Messiah*. One vol. ed. Grand Rapids: Eerdmans, 1971.

France, R. T. *Matthew: Evangelist and Teacher*. Grand Rapids: Zondervan, 1989.

Green, Joel B. and Scot McKnight, ed. *Dictionary of Jesus and the Gospels*. Downers Grove, IL: InterVarsity, 1992.

Hoehner, Harold W. *Herod Antipas*. Cambridge: At the University Press, 1972.

———. *Chronological Aspects of the Life of Christ*. Grand Rapids: Zondervan, 1977.

Howell, Don N. Jr. *Servants of the Servant. A Biblical Theology of Leadership*. Eugene, OR: Wipf & Stock, 2003.

Jeffers, James S. *The Greco-Roman World of the New Testament Era*. Downers Grove, IL: InterVarsity, 1999.

Jeremias, Joachim. *Jerusalem in the Time of Jesus*. Philadelphia: Fortress, 1969.

Keener, Craig S. *The IVP Bible Background Commentary*. Downers Grove, IL: InterVarsity, 1993.

Kingsbury, Jack Dean. *Matthew as Story*. 2nd ed. Philadelphia: Fortress, 1988.

———. *Conflict in Mark*. Minneapolis: Fortress, 1989.

———. *Conflict in Luke*. Minneapolis: Fortress, 1991.

Ladd, George Eldon. *A Theology of the New Testament*. Rev. ed. Edited by Donald A. Hagner. Grand Rapids: Eerdmans, 1993.

———. *I Believe in the Resurrection of Jesus*. Grand Rapids: Eermans, 1973.

Martin, Ralph P. *Mark: Evangelist and Theologian*. Grand Rapids: Zondervan, 1973.

Marshall, I. Howard. *Luke: Historian and Theologian*. Grand Rapids: Zondervan, 1970.

Neusner, Jacob and William Scott Green, eds. *Dictionary of Judaism in the Biblical Period*. Peabody, MA: Hendrickson, 1999.

Reicke, Bo. *The New Testament Era*. Philadelphia: Fortress, 1968.

Ryken, Leland, James C. Wilhoit and Tremper Longman III, eds. *Dictionary of Biblical Imagery*. Downers Grove, IL: InterVarsity, 1998.

Scroggie, W. Graham. *A Guide to the Gospels*. Old Tappan, NJ: Revell, 1948.

Shepherd, J. W. *The Christ of the Gospels. An Exegetical Study*. Grand Rapids: Eerdmans, 1939.

Tenney, Merrill C., ed. *The Zondervan Pictorial Encyclopedia of the Bible*. 5 vols. Grand Rapids: Zondervan, 1975–76.

Scripture Index

---

* Texts in bold type indicate major passages in the Gospels given detailed treatment in the sections with page numbers listed in bold type.

1 Peter (cont.)

5:6	258
5:7	111

2 Peter

1:11	360
1:13–15	360
1:16–18	191
1:20–21	250
2:4	63
3:8–14	256

1 John

1:3	50, 282
1:5	312
1:7	282
1:8—2:2	108
1:9	107, 307
1:9—2:2	307
2:1	319
2:2	346
2:15	96
2:16	34, 109
4:1	113
4:10	282, 346
4:16	312
5:2	99
5:3	128
5:4–5	281
5:14–15	223
5:19	33

3 John

5–8	238

Jude

6	63

Revelation

1:7	190, 348
1:9	264
1:10	84
1:13–18	190
2:7	134, 344
3:7	185, 226
4:1—5:14	106

11:3–6	191
14:10	263, 325
16:19	263, 325
19:9	118, 168, 238
19:11	275
20:4	311
20:7–10	224, 281
20:12	218
20:15	218
21:1–9	93
21:3	106
21:4	65
21:6	346
21:7	106, 134
21:14	185
21:22	42
21:22–26	93
21:27	218
22:1–5	65, 93
22:2	344
22:16	345
22:17	210, 346
22:20	106